"People the world over are flocking to the Internet, and covering the Church of Jesus Christ of Latter-day Sain tured the essence of each and has melded them together *in this book. I* recommend it as *must reading for anyone interested in religion and/or the Internet."*

—Arthur Wilde, LDS Section Leader, the CompuServe Religion Forum

"I thought I was pretty knowledgeable about LDS web sites, but Mormons on the Internet *has opened my eyes to a vast universe of LDS resources and online communities. This book has now created a problem for me: to express it in bumper sticker vernacular,* So many LDS web sites, so little time!"

—Robert D. Starling, LDS Film/TV Producer, Founder, Associated Latter-day Media Artists (ALMA)

"At last, someone has done it all and done it right! Moses was enabled to see everything in the universe; when it comes to the universe of the World Wide Web, this book does the same."

—Chris Conkling, Author of *A Joseph Smith Chronology, Lord of the Rings* (United Artists screenplay)

"This book will become an incredibly valuable resource for all Latter-day Saints who have found the helpful wonders of the Internet."

—Robert J. Allen, M.D

"Mormons on the Internet *is a great way for members of our worldwide church to stay linked. LauraMaery's book is not only a font of information, it's a lot of fun. This is a* must have *book for anyone hooked up to the Internet."*

—Michael Rutter, Author of *Run of the Arrow* and *The Corporate Edge*

"This is the resource you've been looking for—a friendly, step-by-step guide to all things Mormon on the Internet. LauraMaery Gold is irresistible, combining a strong business and Internet background, a wonderful writing style, and a lifetime of service as an active Latter-day Saint."

—Cathy Gileadi, Author of *Homeschool Genesis* and *Everywoman's Herbal*

MORMONS
ON THE INTERNET

LAURAMAERY
GOLD

PRIMA PUBLISHING

Prima Publishing and colophon are registered trademarks of Prima Communications, Inc.

The Internet is a new frontier. Places come, place go. This text is the best representation of the state of the LDS Internet when we went to press.

Library of Congress Cataloging-in-Publication Data

Gold, LauraMaery.
   Mormons on the Internet / LauraMaery Gold.
     p.   cm.
   Includes index.
   ISBN 0-7615-1148-2
   1. Mormons—Computer network resources—Handbooks, manuals, etc. 2. Church of Jesus Christ of Latter-day Saints—Computer network resources—Handbooks, manuals, etc. 3. Internet (Computer network)—Handbooks, manuals, etc. 4. World Wide Web (Information retrieval system) I. Title.
BX8638.G65 1997
004.67'8'088283—dc21   97-39987
                                                  CIP

97 98 99 00 96 DD 10 9 8 7 6 5 4 3 2 1

Printed in the United States of America

HOW TO ORDER

Single copies may be ordered from Prima Publishing, P.O. Box 1260BK, Rocklin, CA 95677; telephone (916) 632-4400. Quantity discounts are also available. On your letterhead, include information concerning the intended use of the books and the number of books you wish to purchase.

Visit us online at http://www.primapublishing.com

CONTENTS

PART ONE
BUILDING A COMMUNITY

1   LATTER-DAY SAINTS ONLINE   3

PART THREE
LIVING A LATTER-DAY SAINT LIFE

11 PURSUIT OF EXCELLENCE   241

12 THE GLORY OF GOD IS INTELLIGENCE   275

13 WHAT'S MISSING   319

Foreword

By Keith Irwin

About 12 years ago I stumbled across a group of Latter-day Saints talking to one another on CompuServe, at that time a relatively new computer network. Living in the rather lonely world of the frequent business traveler, I was intrigued that, on a daily basis, I could post messages that would be read and replied to by Latter-day Saints not only from different parts of the United States, but from around the world.

I thought I was a pretty typical Latter-day Saint. I grew up in the Church and have served in bishoprics and on several high councils. But these were people whose experience was different from my own. One member lived near the Arctic Circle. Another had left the Church years earlier over his inability to reconcile some doctrinal issues. Still another was a bishop in Utah Valley. Yet another lived in an inner-city ward in the Midwest. Still another was actively RLDS. Several had struggled with substance abuse and marital problems. A disproportionate number were proficient musicians. Many had lived outside the United States. These differences made for wonderful, nearly addictive conversation. I found myself hurrying through my work each day so I could log on and see what my newfound cyberfriends had to say.

Today, technology has enabled nearly anyone to connect to the Internet and join in the global conversation. The growth rate of Internet users has been astronomical, and it is likely that the number of users interested in discussing the Mormon experience is likewise growing dramatically. This creates great opportunity for Latter-day Saints, but it is not without some serious challenges.

The hazards of the Internet have been well publicized. All the vices are there: gambling, pornography, scams—even stalkers and child molesters. I often tell inquiring friends that the Internet is a reflection of the world. Anything you can find in the world, regardless of its merit, can be found somewhere on the Net. I pass on a maxim of a former mentor, Bonner Ritchie, "You can't make the world safe for people; you have to make people safe for the world." Indeed, I doubt if it is even possible to control the content of the Net, given its global configuration. But by taking the same precautionary measures you would take when you leave your home, your trips into cyberspace will likely be as safe as your walks down the street. You wouldn't walk into an "adult" bookshop. Neither should you wander into an adult Web site (most of which are well marked). You wouldn't give your address to a stranger. Neither should you give your phone number or street address over the Internet to someone you don't know. You wouldn't let your children wander around without knowing where they are. Neither should you let your kids wander around the Net without knowing what they are doing.

The most "hyped" feature of the Internet is the World Wide Web. A search using services such as Yahoo *<http://www.yahoo.com>*[1] or AltaVista *<http://www.altavista.digital.com>* will turn up hundreds of sites that deal with Mormonism. Many are simply lists of other Web sites. Others are adversarial. But some are truly extraordinary. Take a look at Arden Eby's resources on early Christianity *<http://www.teleport.com/~arden>* or Dave Crockett's pages on Mormon History *<http://www.indirect.com/www/crockett/history.html>*. There is enough information on these pages to bring new life to any Gospel Doctrine lesson.

The commercial use of the World Wide Web has not been overlooked by Mormon businesses. Interestingly and fortunately, their marketing approach seems to focus on creating a significant set of resource pages for Latter-day Saints, only part of which is promotion of their products. Zarahemla Book Shoppe *<http://www.zarahemla.com>* created one of the first commercial Web sites. It established pages for each of the auxiliaries as well as for other typical LDS interests such as genealogy. Infobases has an enormous Web site with pages for all aspects of Mormonism. Deseret Book *<http://www.deseretbook.com>* is a late entrant with an apparently similar strategy. In each case, Latter-day Saints come out with terrific databases of information.

---

[1] Editor's note: Internet sites described in this book are listed along with their addresses, or "URLs." URLs appear in angle brackets (<>) throughout this text, as do e-mail addresses. If you're new to the Internet, see page 43 for information on using the addresses.

I've often lamented the inefficiency that takes place when Latter-day Saints exert tremendous time and energy preparing the same lessons. The computer connection to Latter-day Saints around the world is changing that. Think of the possibilities for a seminary teacher, for example. Each day a thousand or more seminary teachers struggle to find new and interesting ways to present the same lessons. Now, though, when a new idea is conceived, it can be instantly shared with others via the seminary mail list or on Web sites with pages devoted to seminary. Similarly, seminary teachers can discuss the challenges of their callings as well as rejoice in their successes with others sharing the same experience. With similar lists for Primary, Sunday School, and Young Men/Young Women, no teacher in the Church ever needs to feel that he or she is without support.

The global connection of Latter-day Saints creates new challenges as well. In pre-Internet days, the Mormon rumor mill may have extended only from Logan to St. George, with occasional telephone forays into the rest of the country. Now a juicy tidbit that has some face validity can spread from to Alberta to Auckland in a matter of minutes. Recently a general authority attending a stake conference in the Midwest mentioned a significant change in curriculum for the Relief Society and Melchizedek Priesthood. A member who heard the news immediately posted it to the Internet, where it became the subject of discussion by members around the world. Another member saw the report and decided to check it with the Church Curriculum Committee in Salt Lake. An astonished Church employee replied that this information was not officially released. When told that it was already on the Internet, he was speechless.

The ability to manipulate the online community is best illustrated by the "Great April Fools Prank" played out in the early days of the Internet on LDS-NET, the very first LDS mailing list. Freewheeling discussions featuring many unorthodox positions were a frequent staple of LDS-NET. Early on April first, one of the members posted that he had been at a social where Church employees mentioned that the General Authorities were monitoring the LDS Internet mailing list discussions. Several replies reflected astonishment and mild paranoia. Then a coconspirator in the prank posted that his stake president was calling in people who were participating in Internet discussion groups. This report generated a furor in which people asked if they could edit their prior posts out of the archives. Others blasted the General Authorities for "spying." Still others took themselves off the list. This cacophony of anxiety and anger was not put to rest until nearly midnight, when the originator of the discussion posted "April Fool."

More recently a bogus news story about a Brigham City, Utah, school board received such wide circulation that it made the national news. Another equally fraudulent story about BYU archeologists working at Adam-Ondi-Ahman and a concurrent Mormon land rush in Missouri is just beginning to make the rounds. We'll see how far this one circulates before being debunked. Sorting information, misinformation, and disinformation may be one of the greatest challenges any Internet user confronts.

The most valuable feature of the Internet is not the plethora of information in the Web sites, but the interactive features such as mailing lists and newsgroups. These features allow the creation of communities where ideas and experiences can be exchanged and great learning can take place. When CompuServe asked me to lead the LDS group several years ago, I felt it important to set parameters on discussions so the group would have a focus. Messages, for example, should obviously have something to do with Mormonism. But what other guidelines should there be?

Some LDS groups had set pretty strong rules ensuring orthodoxy among their members. Others with no parameters degenerated into slug-fests between LDS and Evangelical Christians.

Seeking to create something different, I pondered what it might be like in my ward if all the people we say we want to come to Church—nonmembers, former members, less actives, and others—actually showed up and participated. The thought was a hilarious mental feast. I could see raucous debate where orthodoxy was up for grabs and anarchy reigned.

Then I thought of some simple guidelines for engagement. What if people were required to treat each other with civility? What if inquiry was as valued as advocacy? What if respect for others' beliefs was required behavior? These became the parameters of our community. The gates were open wide. We welcomed anyone interested in discussing Mormonism, be they active, inactive, former, liberal, conservative, straight, gay, LDS, RLDS, polygamist, or monogamist—but the content and tone of all posts had to be respectful of people and their beliefs. I also set discussions of the specifics of temple ordinances off limits—but any other topic was fair game.

The result was the most savory mix of conversations I have yet experienced in cyberspace. People not only talked about their agreements and differences rationally, but after some time, discussions began to demonstrate that people genuinely cared about each other. Soon conversation about our personal lives became as common as esoteric theological debate. While there were a few who could not tolerate the presence of "the unfaithful," most found it a unique and valuable community. I know of no one who became estranged from the Church as a result of interaction with this diverse group, but I do know of several baptisms and many reactivations that came, at least in part, from our association.

I once related this experience in a talk in stake conference. After the conference, the visiting member of the Quorum of the Twelve, L. Tom Perry, challenged me to "Keep that group going." As a result, I sometimes refer (tongue in cheek) to the LDS group on CompuServe as the only one with an apostolic mandate.

Unfortunately, there are too few broad-based LDS discussion groups where civility is the rule. The lack of civility, in my opinion, has led to a specialization of discussion groups. ZION is decidedly conservative. MORMON-L has a reputation of being a liberal free-for-all. JOSEPH is a moderate and quite orthodox list that avoids discussion of political or social issues. LDS-NET still exists as the lone general-purpose mail list with a broad spectrum of membership, though it is currently home to a fairly small group of people. I'm hopeful that other "general purpose" mailing lists will develop and communities evolve where inquiry is more valued than advocacy and where genuine dialogue about differences can take place. Orson Scott Card's new Nauvoo Web site *<http://www.nauvoo.com>* has an interactive feature that seems to be in this tradition. And the new newsgroup *soc.rel.mormon* has a similar aim.

There are many other terrific lists that specialize by interest rather than by philosophical outlook. AML-LIST is a very active group focusing on Mormon literature. EYRING-L focuses on science and religion. My own list, LDS-BOOKSHELF, is devoted to collectable Mormon books. I'm certain that a trip through this book will turn up a list devoted to your interests. But if it doesn't, it's easy to start one of your own.

For Latter-day Saints, the possibilities of the Internet are in their infancy. Distance learning technology using the Internet could easily be translated into virtual wards in remote areas of the world. General Conference can be brought into every home and possibly even made interactive! One can only begin to ponder the changes that might come from instant two-way communication between the Church and its membership. I don't know for certain how this technology is going to change our lives, but I do know for certain that it will.

Keith Irwin
San Jose, California
<kirwin@wenet.net>

ACKNOWLEDGMENTS

There are so many Latter-day Saints who helped with this project that I couldn't even begin to name them all. Well, OK, I could begin. There's Jamie Miller, my editor and new Best Friend, who spearheaded this entire project. Thank you, Jamie, for your enthusiasm and your confidence. And my thanks also to Andi Reese Brady, for jumping in to help with the editing process. You're a joy to work with.

There's the irresistible Keith Irwin, who made my first foray onto the Mormon online community so delightful. Several years ago, when I was going through a rough patch in life, Keith appointed himself my electronic home teacher and saw me through. Keith's perspectives on the power of online communication have been invaluable in informing my own thoughts on the matter. Thanks, Ellen, for letting him loose.

My thanks go to Elder Jeffrey R. Holland, who took the time from his packed schedule to talk with me about the future of the Internet as a missionary tool. Thank you, Elder Holland, for that and for many years of your inspired and inspiring counsel. I'm only a face in the bleachers, but the Lord has spoken to me many times through your words.

To all the Mormon Internetters who responded to my questions and were generous with their time and their insight: I appreciate your kindness in taking the time to share.

To the "five horsemen" of the Internet: Clark Goble <cgoble@fiber.net>, Kent S. Larsen II <klarsen@panix.com>, John Walsh <mormon@mormons.org>, Dave Crockett <crockett@goodnet.com>, and David Kenison <dkenison@xmission.com>, who have among them thoroughly indexed the Mormon Internet. More than that. They have, in large measure, created and defined the entire LDS online experience. They are only the brightest lights among the hundreds of Latter-day Saints who have built and maintained a Web of faithful Internet sites. I am indebted to them all.

My appreciation to Infobases, creator of the delightful LDS Collectors Library, and the source of many of the quotes found in this text. If you don't have your own copy of Collectors Library, you're missing out. Stop by the Infobases Web site <http://www.infobases.com> to place your order.

To Carol James, my visiting teaching companion, who patiently picks up the slack for me month after month: Thank you. Thank you very much.

To my grandpa and grandma, Stan and Vera Zielinski, who gave me the foundation to be whatever good thing I am today, I love you and miss you.

And then there are saints of an entirely different stripe: To Andrew Zack, my Jewish agent who had the chutzpah to laugh when I described him as a Gentile. Thanks, Andy, for negotiating the hard part of the work.

To all the rest of the editorial staff at Prima, my gratitude for working through tight deadlines, bizarre technological glitches, and a manuscript full of unfamiliar ideas.

And most of all, to my wonderful husband—the best man in the world—who watches over me, takes care of me, and raises our babies when I'm glued to a keyboard. Danny, I love you more every day.

INTRODUCTION

A Community of Mormons

It was in the early '70s, at a youth conference in the Seattle area, that I first caught the vision of technology's role in the future of the Church of Jesus Christ of Latter-day Saints. A large group of young people gathered in the stake center to hear our Stake Patriarch talk to us about the growth of the Church, and about our role in that growth.

In awe I listened to this venerable, inspired man describe a Church growing so fast that we'd one day have temples in operation in every corner of the globe, general conferences broadcast to the world via satellites, a missionary effort that would go not to dozens of people, but to thousands of people at one time. As we come ever closer to the time of Christ's return, he told us, the work of the Lord will proceed at an ever more rapid pace, and God will give us the knowledge we need to make that work go forward.

It all seemed too fantastic to a young girl whose entire exposure to computers had been the panels of blinking lights on *Star Trek* reruns. But for the past quarter of a century, I've kept the memory of that prophetic declaration in the back of my mind, looking forward to a day—perhaps near the end of my life—when I would live to see those words fulfilled.

I grew up in the middle of a communications revolution, oblivious to what I was experiencing. In 1978, as a young journalist at the *Daily Herald* in Provo, Utah, I watched stories spool out of the wire-service machines on machine-readable punched strips of yellow tape. The decoding process was so complex, though, that the miracle of the transmission itself was obscured.

I first went online in 1982, when, as a student at BYU, I got access over a 300-baud modem from my home computer to a gigantic mainframe computer on campus. I used the connection to print school papers on a room-sized laser printer. Over the years I used online connections to send stories from my home in Taipei to my editors in Hong Kong, and later to build an electronic bulletin board for readers of the computer magazines I edited in Singapore, Malaysia, and Hong Kong. Still, I couldn't envision the complicated BBS technology evolving into anything bigger.

Imagine my delight when, in mid-1994, I discovered a thing called the World Wide Web, the part of the Internet that allows anyone to publish anything they want to say and make it available to readers anyplace in the world. Within a year the Web software and Internet connections had evolved to the point where it became practical for Just Plain Folks to get online. Within days of an Internet service provider setting up shop in my calling area, I was on the Internet, and building my own Web page. In honor of my Patriarch, I began collecting testimonies, conversion stories, temple experiences, and missionary experiences for publication on the Internet—my own missionary effort being broadcast to the world, as in the vision of that Patriarch, via satellites.

We Mormons have an awesome world view. We see God's hand in every good thing. From the Reformation to Columbus to the United States Constitution, we see a world directed by a God who wants us back. And at the same time, we see the malevolent work of an anti-Christ, a Satan who can use those same tools to bring about the destruction of mankind if we're not vigilant.

I see God's hand in the technology revolution taking place in the world today. I see communities of like-minded Latter-day Saints coming together from their homes and offices in every little village in the world to inspire one another, to support one another, to work out the programs of the Church in their own ways. I see Scouting Saints working together to share ideas. I see single Saints extending the hand of fellowship and support to one another. I see conservative Saints discussing politics, and liberal Saints discussing conservative Saints. I see Latter-day Saints struggling with same-sex attraction acting as support and help for one another. I've seen Saints struggle with every kind of trial, and receive kind words, loving advice, and cyber-pats on the back as they worked through their difficulties. I have seen miracles take place in the lives of members—and nonmembers—of the Church through the friendships they've found in online LDS communities.

I've also seen the opposite of every one of these good things. There are places on the Internet rife with contention, filled with slurs against everything Latter-day Saints hold true and sacred. I've seen true hatred, vicious lies, half-truths, and unwarranted attacks. I've seen sacred things held up for public ridicule. I've seen slanted points of view, the expression of fringe opinion, and cloaked requests for "information" that turned out to be nothing more than bait for later attacks.

In the words of my cyber-hero, Keith Irwin, who for many years moderated the LDS section on the CompuServe Religion Forum, "You can find anything in Cyberspace that you'd find in real life." It's just easier to find it on the Internet.

Isn't it comforting to know, when you do find things that send you to the stacks for further research, that there's also a community out there of intelligent, thoughtful, well-educated Latter-day Saints who are eager to discuss them with you?

This, then, is the Mormon Internet: An eclectic collection of Web sites, chat rooms, e-mail lists, discussion forums, and newsgroups operated and populated by people who love the Church and the gospel, and who want to share their joy with anyone willing to participate.

And as an enthusiastic cheerleader for all who share the vision of a worldwide community of Latter-day Saints, I stand at the gates of a New Jerusalem, and bid you enter.

LauraMaery Gold
Glassboro, New Jersey
<MormonNet@aol.com>

PART ONE

BUILDING A COMMUNITY

1

LATTER-DAY SAINTS ONLINE

Welcome to the world of the Mormon Internet, a vast community of Latter-day Saints, our e-mail lists, our discussion groups, our Web pages, our chat areas, and our community.

The LDS online community includes people of every description—active members, less-active members, even nonmembers. It takes in members from the Pacific Rim, Europe, and South America.

It includes the devout, the skeptical, the missionary-minded, the disenfranchised, the young, the old, the married, the single. It includes the brilliant, the clever, and the distressed.

Members of the community participate at every level: from those who should be in a 12-step program for their hourly involvement in chat areas and newsgroups, to people who barely have time to check their e-mail every couple of weeks.

What they all have in common is this: access to an online connection, and a fascination with the Church of Jesus Christ of Latter-day Saints.

WHAT YOU'LL FIND IN THIS BOOK

This book does more than tell you how to get online. And it's more than a directory of LDS sites on the World Wide Web. Here you'll also find reviews of many of those Web sites, along with ratings that will help you find your way around with a minimum of wasted effort. Compiled here, for the first time, is the fascinating story of the development of the Mormon Internet—perhaps the major LDS pioneering effort of the twentieth century. The book also features interviews with the people who have contributed to the LDS online community. They explain, in their own words, their vision for a world in which Latter-day Saints in every condition—in sickness, in health, in poverty's vale, or abounding in wealth—ahem, in every circumstance can find joy in one another's fellowship.

HOW THIS BOOK IS ARRANGED

This book is arranged in three parts: Building a Community, The Mission of the Church, and Living a Latter-day Saint Life.

Part 1 describes the Mormon online community, the Church's Web site, the process of getting online, and the first steps in getting around the Internet.

Part 2 addresses the threefold mission of the Church, showing how Latter-day Saints are using the resources of the Internet to Proclaim the Gospel, Perfect the Saints, and Redeem the Dead.

In Part 3, Living a Latter-day Saint Life, you'll find a guided tour of Internet sites related to the following areas:

- **The Living Church.** International sites, events and activities, news and LDS publications, units of the Church, and a multitude of broadly focused discussion areas.
- **Auxiliaries.** Priesthood, Primary, Relief Society, Seminary, Single Adults, Sunday School, and Young Men and Young Women.
- **Interest Groups.** Youth, dating and courtship, fulfilling callings, women, professional groups, home schooling, health resources, Saints dealing with same-sex attraction, and commercial sites.
- **Pursuit of Excellence.** Personal scripture study, Mormon arts and letters, humor, and emergency preparedness.
- **The Glory of God Is Intelligence.** Resources on Church history, research groups, science and religion, the Church in society, doctrinal issues, and comparative theology.

Finally, you will find an overview of the top twenty LDS sites on the Internet, along with suggestions for getting involved in building a meaningful contribution of your own.

WHAT YOU'LL FIND IN THIS CHAPTER

This chapter provides an overview of the power of the Internet in the LDS community. You'll first meet a member, a former Baptist minister, who joined the Church because of his online experience. You'll be introduced to some of the pioneers of the Mormon Internet, and will learn what motivated their decisions to contribute their resources to the community.

After that, you'll find a section on how Latter-day Saints use the internet, in which a large number of Latter-day Saints who frequent the online communities of the Internet talk about why they're there. These members explain for themselves what they find on the Internet that helps them in their families, their work in the Church, and their daily lives.

At the end of the chapter, you'll find a description of the system used throughout this text to rate Internet resources. You'll want to keep a finger in that final page.

THE POWER OF THE INTERNET

There's no question but that the Internet is a powerful force. How powerful? It's a forum for discussion. A repository of information. A facilitator of friendships. But it's even more than that. It is, in fact, a whole new paradigm for spreading the gospel. There are already countless new members of the Church who credit their Internet experience as a significant factor in their decision to be baptized. Some investigators encounter the Church as a result of friendships they develop over the Internet. Others use the resources of the Internet to research the Church and its teachings, and only later make friends with Latter-day Saints.

Over the past few years, I have run across a number of Latter-day Saints who affirm that the Internet played a role in their conversion. A member of my own ward was introduced to the Church through an online acquaintance. Pam was baptized last summer, and though she's moved to another town to finish school, she keeps in contact via e-mail.

Another friend, whom I know only through years of online discussions, worked through some doctrinal issues in online conversations with loving Latter-day Saints and rejoined the Church years after he'd asked to have his name removed. He's since seen other members of his family come back to the Church they'd once left behind.

Another Latter-day Saint says his Internet discussions have made the difference in his ability to remain in the Church, despite the loneliness he sometimes feels in his own ward.

Other Latter-day Saints tell of inactive or former members that came back to full membership because of encouragement they'd received from online friendships.

Ronald Conrad Schoedel III, a Latter-day Saint living in Ontonagon, Michigan, credits the Internet as the single most significant factor in his conversion. Brother Schoedel *<schoedel@up.net>* had a Baptist upbringing, and was ordained a Baptist preacher and practiced in the ministry for about three years. "As you may know, members of that faith are responsible for some of the more ludicrous anti-Mormon literature and propaganda," he writes, "so for most of my Baptist life, those falsehood-filled books shaped my opinion of the Church."

Ironically, though, Brother Schoedel believed and taught for a number of years that Christ visited the Americas, that prophecies in the Bible pointed to a gathering of His people in the Western hemisphere, and that Christ would return to the Americas.

After leaving the Baptist church over some differences of doctrine, he remembered hearing that the Book of Mormon addressed some of those same issues. He located a copy of the Book of Mormon, and read it carefully. He says he "was convinced more or less right away that it was the Word of God. Of that I had no doubt; but still, with all the anti-Mormon propaganda I had been exposed to for so long, I had a hard time thinking that the Church could be God's true Church."

He went to the Internet to try to "objectively" find the Truth.

I searched everything. All the anti-works one could find on the Net (of which there are plenty!) as well as all the sites put together by faithful Mormons, which detailed information about their faith and their Church. I began comparing the materials on each side, and saw many, many falsehoods in the anti-LDS literature and Web sites. About the time that I had come to the conclusion that *maybe* the Church could be correct, I contacted the Church and had some discussions with the missionaries. But still I focused most of my time and efforts on independent and individual study, to arrive at the conclusions I arrived at . . . which led me to be baptized and join the Church.

The Internet played a *huge* role in my finding true LDS doctrine, which I found basically in agreement with what I had believed and taught for years. But had it not been for the Internet, I don't believe I would have bothered to research the issues as intently as I did. I give much credit to those faithful Saints who have gone through the effort and time to set up Web sites sharing their faith, for those sites were instrumental in me gaining a true and correct picture of what the Church actually believes and teaches. By allowing individual Saints to publish their articles online, the Internet cut through the lies and deceit that big-money publishers have put out against the Church. The Internet allows all Saints to share their faith in a manner that can effectively combat the lies that abound. The Internet did it for me, by allowing me to find the Truth. Of course, all credit goes to Heavenly Father for allowing this.

A community has power—the power to draw together, to support one another, to respond to questions, and to help in times of trouble. The Internet community also provides fellowship unavailable in any other forum.

With that power comes responsibility. A responsible member of the LDS community behaves while on the Internet at least as well as he would IRL—e-mail shorthand for "in real life"—with the knowledge that his words, which seem ethereal in their electronic form, are being recorded not only in electronic archives, but in the hearts and minds of readers who may be searching for strength.

The following letter by author Craig J. Patchell of Orange County, California, appeared on AML-List, a literary e-mail list distributed by the Association of Mormon Letters. In his message, Brother Patchell <patchellcj@aol.com> describes the elements that create a community. While he speaks to writers of LDS fiction, his thoughts on building a community apply equally to Latter-day Saint writers who publish their thoughts in other forums—notably on the Internet. (Excerpts from this letter are reprinted with the author's permission.)

> ON HAVING THE POWER TO DRAW PEOPLE TOGETHER
>
> I feel that the Internet is awesome. I marvel that so many people from all over the world can chat in a room together and meet whenever they have the time. The Internet has brought many people to my home whom I would have never met otherwise. I am fascinated, totally fascinated.
>
> Julie A Siler, Inkom, Idaho

. . . One of the prime purposes of literature, which is the modern day successor to the bardic storytelling tradition, is to build community. One of the most direct devices for doing that, especially among a geographically and culturally diverse people, is to invoke the commonality of shared experiences. Our lives are intensely personal experiences, and, in a day when we have to a large extent lost the close-knit communities and inter-connectedness that was the rule only two generations ago, we often suffer from perceived isolation.

The writer . . . can bond hundreds and thousands of people into a kind of meta-community, unhindered by geographic dislocation.

Mormons are a meta-community in and of themselves through their religious experience, but what happens to us beyond the chapel walls is the compelling and defining experience. . . .

It's a heady feeling of power, knowing that what you say can be heard not only by your small family, or even your large ward, but by hundreds, thousands, even millions of readers, at every level of faith, everywhere in the world.

The Internet makes everyone a publisher. "The Internet pulls down the walls or glass ceilings so that anyone may publish words, music, video, or art, and have anyone get access to their material," says Grant Johnson, a Latter-day Saint from Fair Oaks, California. "Wrong or right, that is what the Internet does. Personally, I think it is right. How *many* good ideas and products never see the light of day because some person in power rejected the idea for any number of reasons (personal, religious, political, or economical)."

What the Net allows, says Brother Johnson, is the ability to bypass the traditional roadblocks. Brother Johnson *<webmaster@new-jerusalem.com>*, Webmaster at the New Jerusalem Web site, calls the Internet "a champion of the 'little guy.'"

For the Internet to have any real power over the lives of the Latter-day Saints, however, will require taming that urge to use words as weapons. It requires abiding by the counsel of the Lord that "the powers of heaven cannot be controlled nor handled [except] upon the principles of righteousness. . . . We have learned by sad experience that it is the nature and disposition of almost all men, as soon as they get a little authority, as they suppose, they will immediately begin to exercise unrighteous dominion" (D&C 121:36–39).

In abiding by correct principles, members of the Church leave open the door for the Lord to work miracles in the lives of people they meet in every part of the world.

Brian Phelps, a Saint from Livermore, California, sees the Net as more than a missionary tool. He believes the resources of the Internet can be useful within the Church itself. Brother Phelps *<btphelps@netwizards.net>* says the Internet has the potential to positively influence the Mormon community worldwide, making Gospel-centered information more readily available. Brother Phelps runs the LDS Internet Resources FAQ Web site at *<http://www.netwizards.net/~btphelps/mormon>*. He anticipates a time when the Net will be an integral part of the administration of the Church. "Ten years down the road, I'd bet every meeting house will be plugged in, and Conference will be broadcast via the Internet instead of TV satellite."

Latter-day Saint Mark Cheney from Prescott, Arizona, has a similar vision. He foresees a time when the Internet will be used for e-mailing church reports of all types. "We already use computer modems to communicate between the wards and Salt Lake. But member locating service applications could be taken over the Internet. And much genealogical research is already being done and shared over the Net."

Another Internet user, Ken Burton from Murray, Utah, thinks that day is close at hand. Brother Burton says he gets the sense that leaders of the Church know that this communication medium will have a profound effect on the Church and the world. He sees both apprehension (as seen in the church's slowness to take advantage of the technology and the occasional warnings from general authorities) and excitement. "Those who have a true understanding of the mission of the Church are willing to embrace any technology that can be used to further that mission," says Brother Burton. "Caution is warranted, but eventually the distribution of Church information will be instantaneous throughout the world—much like conference reports and the LDS-GEMS [a widely distributed e-mail list of Church news and other information] mailings."

HOW THE INTERNET PROVIDES A NEW MEANS OF SPREADING THE GOSPEL

The Internet provides a whole new way of reaching our brothers and sisters. Not only does it open the possibility of talking with people who are geographically diverse; it also clears the way to people who are reluctant to talk with members in all the traditional settings. If you find yourself uncomfortable approaching coworkers, neighbors, and your seatmate on the airplane about the gospel, you'll find that your inhibitions quickly disappear in the anonymity of the Internet.

In the same way, people who are resistant to speaking with missionaries on their doorstep or in public grocery stores have no such hesitation when it comes to speaking to member missionaries in the nonthreatening environment of the Internet.

Craig S. Matteson, a computer professional from Ann Arbor, Michigan, acknowledges that the technology permits anonymity and the possibility of falsifying identities, but says his experience there has been one where he's found "a real opportunity for emotional intimacy and openness." Because the contacts are not face-to-face, but person-to-person, he says, the friendships are real and lasting. He's right. I met Brother Matteson about five years ago in an online discussion forum, and we continue to keep in touch, though we've never met in person.

The Internet creates opportunities for learning and understanding that would never occur in any other setting. I met Jeffrey B. Winship, a member of the Reorganized Church of Jesus Christ of Latter Day Saints who lives in Independence, Missouri, through an online discussion group. When I moved to Missouri the following year, Brother Winship and another participant in that group who lived in

> **ON HARVESTS**
> Computers can be used to do much good. In fact, the electronic medium offers an untapped potential to spread the good news of the gospel to those who are ready to receive it. As church members, we are often told that "the field is white and ready to harvest" (D&C 4:4). I am convinced that this scripture applies to the new "field" of electronic communities, and that great and marvelous works will be accomplished by virtue of this new technology.
>
> Kathryn H. and Clark L. Kidd, Algonkian Ward, Warrenton-Virginia Stake

Missouri were instrumental in helping me get acclimated. Later we had a chance to sit down together and discuss our differing views of the restoration and the gospel, a discussion that forever changed the way I see the world and live my life. Brother Winship's Christ-like example often set the tone for tolerance in that discussion group, so his thoughts on communicating in an electronic medium are worth reading. "People are more open to sharing their real feelings and understanding of principles, knowing that in few cases will they ever meet those with whom they are interacting," he writes. "They can be honest without being confrontational." Most significantly, he says, "the form of communication gives people the opportunity to think before they speak—very important when sharing testimonies with other people."

HOW LATTER-DAY SAINTS USE THE INTERNET

There are hundreds of reasons Latter-day Saints use the Internet. They find it helpful in building their families, finding solutions to problems, keeping up to date on the news of the Church, fulfilling their callings, and learning Church history.

Interviews with dozens of LDS Internet users about their online experience generated responses that form a pretty accurate picture of the best ways members of the Church make the Mormon Internet a part of their learning and growth. In this section, LDS Internet users describe how they use the Internet.

To Participate in a Community

Internet users say the online experience gives them a sense of community, a feeling of belonging even when they're far away.

Jim Picht lives in Kyrgyzstan, on the Western border of China. He says that for the past six months, the Internet has been his only link to the Church. "My mom's home teachers have been in touch with me by e-mail, as have friends from her home ward. I have no formal contact with even the international mission, but the AML-L and EYRING-L mailing lists have provided me with some interesting conversation with members, which has been very helpful to me." (See chapter 8 for more on mailing lists.)

Brother Picht occasionally spends Sunday mornings browsing the LDS-oriented Web sites—which passes sometimes as his Church activity for the day—and reading resource materials for Sunday School teachers and articles on scripture topics. "The Internet provides me a sense of LDS community, the only one I have," he says, "and if it hasn't made my testimony grow, it's probably kept me thinking about it more than I would have otherwise."

Ardis Parshall, a Saint living in Orem, Utah, doesn't suffer from geographic isolation, but says the idealogical isolation can be just as difficult. "Oh, all right," he says, "I'll finally admit that I've been completely inactive for several years, for social rather than doctrinal reasons. My contacts with Church members on the Net over the past year have been overwhelmingly positive, and I finally feel like I fit into the community somewhere." Although the Internet is not an "official" resource, he finally has met some people he can actually talk to as friends about gospel topics.

Thom Duncan, who also lives in Orem, is much more blunt. "The LDS online community is the only community in which I feel comfortable," he says.

There are other kinds of isolation that the Internet community helps resolve. Author Benson Parkinson, from Ogden, Utah, works at home, "with preschoolers for company." Brother Parkinson says the Internet has made a "huge" difference in his life. "My e-mail box is like the church foyer and a faculty room rolled into one." Brother Parkinson operates AML-List, an e-mail discussion group for writers and fans of Mormon Literature. "My particular interests are relatively rare, even in the Church, and that's even more the case for people outside Utah. Fans of Mormon literature are one to an office and two to a city. Our discussion group gathers about 200 readers and writers of Mormon literature from around the country and world, many of whom have never had anyone to talk to their interests about outside their families."

That sense of community is shared by AML-List participant Scott Parkin, from Pleasant Grove, Utah. "The AML-List has been especially important to me in developing a sense of community. Because of AML-List, I have become quite interested in Mormon literature as one face of our faith, and that interest has led me to a more thorough investigation of Mormon literature, history, critical thought, and simple storytelling. The more I think about it, the more I become convinced of the reality and importance of the restoration and the modern Church."

People further away from the main body of Latter-day Saints say they find support in the discussion groups they find online. Craig Anderson, who lives in Seattle, has been an active participant in online discussion groups for many years. "On CompuServe it felt like a family," he says. But the Internet is different. "On the Internet, there's a bit of 'It's us against them, boys' sort of feel. Kind of like circling

> ON COMMUNITY
>
> There is a definite sense of community on the Internet. . . . I count some of the people I have met on the Internet among my dearest friends, even though we have never met face-to-face. Last year when our son died, some of the people I met online were the first to call me on the phone to express their sorrow at our loss. This was literally the first time I had ever spoken with most of them on the phone, but they were as sympathetic to my loss as many who had been my friends for years and years.
>
> Lynne Pike, Nashville, Tennessee

the wagons for mutual protection." But there's an up side. "Whenever I've encountered a situation where I had something in common with another Latter-day Saint, it's been nice to reminisce. For instance, I encountered on the Net a fellow I had met briefly in the Germany South mission."

The sense of community on the Internet is very strong. Dean Macy, from Peterborough, New Hampshire, wonders, in fact, if the LDS community isn't the mainstay of the entire online community. "Since I deal with LDS businesses, I have sometimes wondered if the LDS links take up most of the Web," he writes. "I feel a strong community presence."

To Strengthen Testimonies

Net users say their experience has had an overall positive effect on their testimonies of the gospel, helping them find answers to questions and draw strength from the insight of other members.

Sometimes that positive influence comes from unexpected sources. Brother Anderson from Seattle gives credit to his Internet contacts for helping to strengthen his testimony, "though I must admit that often it was spurred by the anti-Mormons who have pushed me to research our history and understand it better than I did before. In each case, I've come away stronger than before."

He offers advice to people just getting their toes wet in discussion groups. "For those who take things at face value and are offended or easily put off, I would say that the Net is a land mine waiting to annihilate you. For those who are strong to begin with, and patient enough to gather all the evidence and truth, the Net can be a fortifier of your testimony."

Oremite Thom Duncan says he found strength in meeting Saints who shared his "liberal" bent. "The Internet has had a positive effect on my testimony—and I mean this literally. When I first got on the Internet, my testimony was very shaky. It wasn't long before I found I was not the only Mormon liberal in the world and that many others had found a way to make their liberalism and their Mormonism work for them. I have learned from them and have actually implemented some of their suggestions. So I am still active today, possessed with an intellectual and a cultural testimony, but at least my temple recommend is current."

Robb Cundick, a Latter-day Saint living in Salt Lake City, has been strengthened by the "wonderful spiritual feelings" he's had while reading the personal experiences and testimonies he found on various Web pages and mailing lists, in particular a list called LDS-GEMS. "The LDS-GEMS mailing list has been tremendous! The stories of sacrifices made by early members of the Church have given me renewed motivation to emulate their example in facing life's challenges. I feel they've also blessed me with a stronger resolve to remain true to the faith."

To Expand Their Understanding of Gospel Topics

Another way Latter-day Saints use the resources of the World Wide Web is to study the gospel and expand their understanding.

When list discussions take an occasional turn toward the religious/philosophical side of things, says Brother Picht in Kyrgyzstan, they help him think about Gospel topics he'd given "short shrift" before. He says some of the ancient studies/ ancient scripture sites he's run across have been extremely interesting and thought-provoking.

Brother Matteson, in Ann Arbor, has a fondness for historical sites, saying they give him access to information that's normally available only to Saints who live in Utah.

To Share the Gospel

Missionary work is a major motivation for Internet users who build Web pages, moderate newsgroups, and participate in various e-mail lists.

Latter-day Saints Kathryn and Clark Kidd, from the Warrenton-Virgina Stake, say the anonymity of the Internet lends courage to Saints who feel awkward approaching friends or strangers with the message of the Gospel. "Although some people feel comfortable about walking right up to a stranger and asking the 'golden questions,' that approach doesn't work for everyone," say Brother and Sister Kidd. "Computers appeal to the kind of person who would never think of striking up a Gospel conversation on an airplane, or in a grocery store. Even the most cowardly person can talk about the Gospel (or just about any subject) through the written word. Because the computer user can neither see nor hear the person on the other end of the modem, the online missionary will never have to worry about having a door closed in his face."

Arthur L. Wilde of Baytown, Texas, operates the LDS discussion forum on CompuServe. He says the online community was "instrumental" in bringing a Brother back into the Church who had been absent 26 years. "We'd never have had the opportunity to meet otherwise, as I was in Texas, he in Los Angeles."

Brother Parshall from Orem says he's had many opportunities to discuss the Gospel with people he's met online. "In two cases, I have answered questions about touchy-churchy things (polygamy, Mountain Meadows); as part of that, I have offered my contacts a history of the Church to explain more. They have both accepted, so in addition to the textbook (the institute manual), I have sent copies of the Book of Mormon and *A Marvelous Work and a Wonder*." He's uncertain about the effect of his sharing. "It's too soon to know of any results from that, other than return messages that have been very favorable to the Church, our (my) candor about the touchy things, and a generally positive reaction. While I set out to be a helpful friend first, and a missionary second, these contacts would only have been possible through the Internet."

A member from Columbia, Missouri, Cindy Kilpack Potts, recalls a discussion where she spoke with a Muslim woman and a Catholic woman at the same time. "They more or less just asked questions about the godhead, and what doctrine supported our belief," she says.

> ## ON BEING AN ONLINE MISSIONARY
> Discussing the gospel with nonmembers, whether in person or online, always enlivens my testimony and makes me even more excited about the gospel. And the conversations I have had with members who are having some difficulties are always moving.
>
> Craig S. Matteson, Ann Arbor, Michigan

Cathy Gileadi from Salem, Utah, approaches discussions in a different way. "I always mention BYU and Utah in context when I can, but it's pretty sideways missionary work."

Brother Cundick from Salt Lake City sees the missionary work being done on the Internet in more general terms. While not using the Internet for the specific purpose of proselytizing, he says, he has viewed it as a wonderful resource for spreading goodwill and a positive image of what members of the Church are really like. Because he's a member of the Tabernacle Choir, he's had even more opportunity to discuss "areas of common interest," he says.

Mike Downey, a Latter-day Saint living in Mesa, Arizona, writes that several years ago he had the unusual experience of participating in the conversion of an "anti-Mormon."

Brother Duncan says he's done his own brand of missionary work. "I helped reactivate a man through my participation on CompuServe. He found my liberal leanings quite refreshing and decided that not all Mormons were right-wing, anti-gay conservatives."

As a Resource for Work

When it comes to supporting a family, the Internet can be a valuable resource.

Chris Bigelow, a writer and editor in West Valley, Utah, invites members of his ward to submit material by e-mail for the ward newsletter he edits. As a Church employee at the *Ensign* magazine, he uses e-mail extensively to communicate with authors, Church leaders, and members worldwide.

Brother Downey from Mesa teaches Seminary, and finds useful material for his classes over the Internet. He corresponds with students by e-mail, as well. "I have been able to answer questions for students who didn't want to ask in class, as well as have makeup work sent to me," he says.

Another teacher, Thomas R. Valletta from central Utah, makes "extensive" use of the Net to aid his teaching. "I am constantly following specialty news and resource pages on the World Wide Web (e.g., *Jerusalem Post*, *Virtual Jerusalem*). The Web is now considered a basic aspect of my research methodology in preparing lessons and papers."

Writer Scott Parkin from Pleasant Grove says he has found e-mail discussion lists to be "absolutely wonderful" as a tool for interviewing people and getting a better sense of what they think and believe.

Another writer, Mark Cheney from Prescott, Arizona, is writing an LDS novel about ancient America, and does his research online.

To Increase Knowledge

Many members report that the Internet has opened a whole new universe of information on Church history, scripture commentary, and other resources never before available to them.

Kevin Cundick, a Latter-day Saint from Ogden, Utah, says that because of his Internet experience, his knowledge of Jesus Christ has grown leaps and bounds. "Through the articles I have set up on my LDS site, I have learned much of Christ, and my love for Him has grown because of it."

Another Latter-day Saint, Jacob Proffitt from Vancouver, Washington, says that the Internet exposure has put his ideals to the test "in an arena where broad consideration and criticism are applied." As a result of the intellectual exercise, he has strengthened his own views, arguments, and historical knowledge "in order to stand up to the careful scrutiny occasionally applied."

Joe Laflin, a Bradenton, Florida Saint, expresses amazement at how little he knows about the Church when he encounters the words and knowledge of other Netizens. "My strength and focus has always been on the spiritual part of the Church," he says. "The Net allows me to see a whole other side or view. I appreciate that."

Lynne Pike, from Nashville, Tennessee, appreciates the doctrinal material available online. "There are a couple of scripture lists that I have found particularly beneficial: scripture-l and Kurt Neumiller's Isaiah Commentaries and LDS Seminar. I've also learned so much from a number of Web sites: an online scripture search utility, the various archives of different lists, the reference to the Davidic

Chiasmus, and several other scripture sources from various religious organizations. Without the information I gleaned from those sources, my studies and understanding of the scriptures would be much more shallow than it is (not that I'm a "scholar" in any sense of the word). I have been enriched, enlightened, and edified by these resources."

Brother Anderson from Seattle says he's found a wealth of information on the Internet, things he'd never seen before he went online. "Through the Internet, I've learned tons of stuff about Church history that I had no inkling of before," he says. "Additionally, it has been wonderful to learn of archaeological evidence, linguistic evidence, etc., that favors the Book of Mormon and scriptures of the Church. Also, I've learned that for every situation in which there appeared to be something suspicious about a quote or criticism, there has always been a reasonable explanation, often exposing the critical stuff as being out of context, contrived, misrepresented, etc."

But it's more than just increasing the level of exposure to research materials. Robb Cundick from Salt Lake City also appreciates the opportunity the Internet gives him for learning from the experiences of other people.

According to Matt Grant from Walnut, California, the Net is a primary source for learning what other Saints think and believe. "It is interesting to hear different people's points of view, and see what others are thinking. Some things that I have read have made me curious and have prompted me to do some research, so I would say it has helped." He worries, though, that some users will falter at their first exposure to difficult issues or unfamiliar doctrine. He warns: "Do not change your opinion because of something you read on the Net without properly researching it first."

> ON THINKING THINGS THROUGH
>
> Participating in e-mail discussion groups has definitely exposed me to ideas and material I probably wouldn't have otherwise encountered. Sometimes the Internet seems to contract as well expand my gospel understanding, such as when someone's opinion or expression confuses my own gospel outlook or tempts me into worldly or secular thinking.
>
> Chris Bigelow, West Valley, Utah

To Keep Up to Date

With quick electronic access to Utah newspapers, LDS Radio, the *Church News*, e-mail news lists, newsgroups, and virtually every LDS-oriented publication, members find themselves at the heart of every event.

Quint Randle, from East Lansing, Michigan, enjoys using the Internet to log into the *Deseret News* site. There he not only gets to read the news, but also can get the talks from Conference right away, rather than waiting for the *Ensign* to come out.

A Latter-day Saint from Ipswich, England, Hilary A. Croughton, finds the official LDS Web site particularly useful in keeping up to date. "The Church's Web site gives me a reference place for those who wish information about the Church, and at General Conference time provides me with the news, talks, etc. weeks before I would find out about them otherwise."

To Correct Misperceptions

Over and over, calm reasoned discussions and explanations are changing the hearts of even the most bitter critics of the Church.

The Kidds in Warrenton, Virginia, say they're heartened to see how much good one person can do by influencing just one other individual. "At one point, I was contacted by a stranger who had questions about the Church," says Brother Kidd. "It turned out that he was a student in a Protestant seminary, studying for the ministry. By the time we finished corresponding, he told me that he was going to use his pulpit to correct the misunderstandings that people of his denomination have about the LDS Church. He also wrote that he had shared our correspondence with other students at his seminary, and that every one of these future ministers had a new respect for Mormonism as a religion and for Latter-day Saints as followers of Christ."

To Conduct Ward Business

More and more, wards and branches of the Church are turning to the Internet to keep members updated, and to conduct the administrative work of the Church.

In Poway, California, says Internet user Toni Thomas, the local ward actually has a ward e-mail list that serves as a bulletin board for announcements—people looking for houses, jobs, and Elders Quorum service project pleas for able bodies. "I also use e-mail for my stake calling (Media Specialist, Public Affairs Committee) to obtain approval from the high councilman and then to send articles to the media. And I use the Net to research lessons and other Church-related presentations."

Shelly Johnson-Choong, a Latter-day Saint living in Western Washington, has used the Internet to send e-mail to the Young Women's president, who uses the Internet to get ideas and see what others in her position are doing.

Brother Randle says that in his ward in the Michigan State University area, the Elders Quorum secretary keeps in touch and follows up on home teaching via the Internet. Brother Randle's wife, who is the Relief Society president, keeps in touch with the bishop via e-mail.

To Conduct Genealogical Research

While genealogical resources can't yet give you an automated printout of your pedigree chart, the Internet is opening the way to vastly improved research. Sharing resources over the Internet is becoming a way of life for family history researchers.

My aunt, Internet user Judith Sullivan in Tacoma, Washington, says she has a very real sense of an Internet community, especially in the genealogical area.

Orem's Ardis Parshall has had some interesting experiences with genealogy and the Internet recently. "In the last few weeks, I have come into contact with three nonmembers who have just discovered that they have Mormon pioneer ancestry. Since genealogical and historical research is my 'thing,' I have helped find material on their families, visited and photographed family graves, and put them in touch with LDS cousins."

Brother Randle from Michigan has made genealogy contacts on Prodigy. He had a woman go to her local library in Illinois, while he was in California, to look up some information on his behalf. Similarly, Brother Parkinson from Ogden has researched a special family history lesson on the Net, using resources from family history publishers.

To Renew Friendships

Old college roommates, members of former wards, long-lost high-school buddies, former mission companions—all are keeping in touch now, better than they ever could before, with e-mail.

I'd long ago lost track of my favorite college journalism professor, Ed Eaton from Auburn, Washington. But one day I saw his name on an LDS mailing list, and we were back in contact. I wasn't the only one to get in touch with him. He writes: "I submitted a couple of things to LDS-GEMS [a widely distributed e-mail list], and had old friends and even new acquaintances contact me. My list of members with e-mail addresses is not long, but it is growing."

Bill James, a member of my ward in Pitman, New Jersey, had some success looking up the Web page from his mission in Finland <*http://www.neptune.net/ ~finnmish*>, where he was able to locate contact information for several old friends. (See chapter 5 for more mission pages, and access to other missionary resources.) Brother Randle from Michigan was likewise able to locate old friends and mission companions through the Canada Montreal Mission Web site.

To Make New Friends

This is the heart of the Internet: Bringing together people with similar interests, people who would have been best friends in real life but for the geographic distance. The Internet removes that barrier, and in so doing, makes way for enduring friendships.

Brother Thomas R. Valletta of central Utah has made numerous new friendships through his Internet connections, particularly through his participation in the ZION mailing list.

Sister Julie A. Siler of Inkom, Idaho, has found new friends through her online chat channel (Chapter 8 contains more information on discussion groups.)

Writer Benson Parkinson from Ogden credits the Internet with having given him "more colleagues, critics, and fans during two years on our Mormon literature discussion list than the previous ten years at large."

Online friendships have been invaluable to Brother Matteson from Ann Arbor. He says the friends he's made through various online groups have been "good support" through some difficult times.

Florida's Brother Laflin treasures his online friendships, and laments only that he hasn't the time to build additional relationships. "We are a community of a sort and, if I had more time, I could add so many more Net friends."

To Discuss Ideas

Who hasn't lamented the lack of time to really discuss gospel issues in Sunday School? No more. With 24-hour access to members just as anxious as you are to explore their thoughts and share their experiences, you'll never run out of time again.

The Internet has helped Brother Bigelow from West Valley, Utah, to better appreciate other viewpoints and better explore and express his own ideas.

Brother Anderson from Seattle has had many opportunities over the years to hone his thoughts on numerous gospel-related ideas. He wonders, though, whether his writing has been entirely beneficial. "I'm not sure how helpful the things I've posted in CompuServe, *alt.religion.mormon* and *soc.religion.mormon* have been. They seem to have had a positive effect for some, no effect for others. A very few others seem to have taken offense," he says.

Latter-day Saints say their online discussions help them really think about what they believe. Nashville's Lynne Pike has discussed "many and varied gospel concepts with individuals from *all* walks of life! In the process, we've all gained something from one another. I know that I have personally learned from the Internet dialogues in which I have participated a great deal about my own personal values and about the divergent experiences and attitudes that exist within the culture of the Church."

Brother Burton from Murray, Utah, has a great interest in religious history, scriptural interpretation, and the interaction of science and religion, and has participated in several related e-mail groups. "Those interactions invariably influence my thoughts and comments on/in the Church," he says.

To Keep in Touch

When the Elders assigned to our ward discovered that I had e-mail access, they began making a habit of stopping by on their P-days to send off mass-mailings to extended family members. Thank goodness for transfers!

ON SPEAKING UP

Newsgroups give me a place where I can ask questions of those who are more learned than I, and where I can share concerns I might otherwise be too shy to voice in my local area.

Hilary A Croughton, Ipswich, England

Brother Laflin from Florida is at the receiving end of similar exchanges. "We have a daughter on a Spanish-speaking mission in Texas," he says. "I contact local members from time to time and leave messages with them for her."

Brother Cheney in Prescott, Arizona, keeps in touch over the Net with an LDS student in Jerusalem, a friend of his daughter and member of their stake.

To Prepare for Church Callings

Imagine preparing your seminary or gospel doctrine lesson in half an hour—and doing a far better job of it than you ever did in two hours of preparation in the past. Members say they use the Internet all the time in preparing for Church callings.

Linda Adams, a Latter-day Saint from Kansas City, Missouri, says it is "wonderful" to find so many good LDS sites out there—"people who are striving to live the gospel, like me." It's like having "pen pals," she says. Most useful to her are the "interesting" mailing lists that can help with callings and provide a place for members of the Church to share their lesson ideas. "It's great."

Sister Siler from Inkom, Idaho, has taken things off of the Internet to share with others, particularly material for Primary.

Brother Eaton from Auburn, Washington, often speaks at firesides in his area, and saves ideas from the Internet for his talk file. "I use the material in high council talks in the hope that they won't be 'dry council' talks," he says.

Ardis Parshall from Orem has picked up and filed away some hints on "how I will do such-and-such if it is ever part of my calling."

The resources of the Internet have been useful to Brother Cheney from Arizona in his research on archaeology and the Book of Mormon for Gospel Doctrine class and firesides.

Brother Parkin from Utah has used various cartographic references and some Scouting ideas pages in when he was a Cubmaster for the ward Cub Scout pack.

Brother James from New Jersey finds the online edition of the *Church News*—especially conference issues—useful in obtaining quotes for talks. (See chapter 8 for more on reading the *Church News* and other LDS publications online.)

Brother Cundick from Salt Lake City has occasionally used stories and experiences from the Internet in his Home Teaching messages.

Seattleite Craig Anderson has used online resources from CompuServe and the Web both in Young Men and in Scouts.

To Better Understand Other Members

Sunday contacts and monthly visits in a small geographic area give a narrow view of the membership of the Church. Meeting people with different experiences teaches tolerance.

Brother Burton from Murray, Utah, explains that because of his Internet exposure, he now has "a much broader vision" of the membership of the Church. "I have a better understanding of the differences between doctrine and culture/tradition/policy, and a much more tolerant feeling for those who have very different perceptions of the purpose of the Church," he says.

A Warning

It's not all positive, of course. As with anything good, the Internet can be used for bad, for distracting the members, for encouraging dissension, for enlarging misunderstandings.

Long-time users share their thoughts on the unsavory parts of the Internet, and offer advice for the unwary.

Ardis Parshall from Orem: "I've become aware of how many very vocal people there are out there who do not like the Church or its leaders at all, yet claim membership somehow. They seem to reinforce each other in a kind of negative community."

Kevin Cundick from Ogden, Utah: "The Internet is a prime example of how there is and always will be 'opposition in all things that righteousness might be brought to pass.'"

"There should be a note of caution sounded toward those who enter the Internet fray," says Brother Anderson from Seattle. "There's a ton of anti-LDS stuff out there. If you wade in unprotected, depending on the depth of your testimony, you could find yourself seriously doubting what you have accepted all your life. On the other hand, if you're willing to search a little deeper, there are usually some excellent responses to the junk dealt out by the antis, provided you're willing to withhold judgment on the matter until you've looked beyond the surface to find the larger truth about the situation in question."

Brother Grant from Walnut, California, wonders whether a lot of Latter-day Saints feel out of place or that they do not fit in. These are people who basically believe the Church is true, he says, but have some belief that is contrary to the teachings of the Church. "They use the Net to find people with similar beliefs, which I'm not sure is an entirely healthy thing."

Brother Cundick from Salt Lake City has similar concerns. "While the Cyberworld version of the Church has its benefits, there are certainly drawbacks as well. I learned on CompuServe that there are a vast range of opinions and outlooks. Most people seem to have questions they'd like to resolve. That means the controversial issues such as homosexuality, evolution, and polygamy seem to go round and round as new people come on and, not knowing what has been discussed to date, bring up these issues over and over again. I felt this caused a lot of divisiveness that was wearing and discouraging at times."

Michigan's Brother Randle says the pitfalls are sometimes of a more personal nature—specifically in the area of e-mail messages that don't permit facial expressions or humorous gestures. For example, he says, he was being "dry" (as in dry humor) in a response to the Elders quorum secretary about some home teaching problems, "and he actually thought I was all offended and serious. He then came back with this major apologetic reply."

Brother Parkinson says the Internet can cause relationship problems for people who get overly involved. "I get wind of people who end up spending too much time on e-mail and whose spouses get jealous. It works out around our house, since my wife's just as avid for the Internet as I am."

Brother Matteson from Ann Arbor is concerned that for some members, online activity will become the focus of their religious life. "While I have made some friends on the Internet," he says, "I still feel that the ward I attend is the central community of my Church involvement. In fact I have seen some who have tried to make the electronic forums a substitute for the normative Church involvement, and most of the forum leaders have noted that this is an inappropriate use of these forums. They are not the Church and should not substitute for regular Church activity."

Brother Burton has to remind himself sometimes that the LDS online community is a minority group, and that he must not get a distorted sense of the membership from the limited exposure.

For Brother Randle—and for many other LDS Internet users—the interaction with a broad cross section of the population can be problematic at best. "Most of the groups on AOL and stuff like that are so full of psycho anti-Mormons that they are no fun to participate in," he says.

Cathy Gileadi from Salem, Utah, is the mother of nine children, and has had to deal with the effects of the negative material available on the Internet in her family. "My next child to get ready to go on a mission has been looking, with a friend, at anti-Mormon Internet stuff and getting messed up and confused. Grrr. It's the standard kind of stuff and uncomely."

The Kidds believe that exposure is inevitable. "For good or evil," they write, "for better or worse, an electronic revolution is taking place that will permanently alter the way in which we live. There is much concern that this electronic medium, much like television, will become a new channel to let filth and worldliness into our homes. Indeed, computers should be used with prudence, just as television and other forms of entertainment should be used with discretion. There is no doubt that Satan will use computer communications to spread his message and bring misery into the lives of those who will listen."

The best advice: When it comes to conversing online, remember always that all influence must be maintained "by persuasion, by long-suffering, by gentleness and meekness, and by love unfeigned; By kindness, and pure knowledge, which shall greatly enlarge the soul without hypocrisy, and without guile—Reproving betimes with sharpness, when moved upon by the Holy Ghost; and then showing forth afterwards an increase of love toward him whom thou has reproved, lest he esteem thee to be his enemy; That he may know that thy faithfulness is stronger than the cords of death. Let thy bowels also be full of charity towards all men, and to the household of faith, and let virtue garnish thy thoughts unceasingly" (D&C 121:41–45).

THE INTERNET RESOURCES RATING SYSTEM

I had a college roommate who recalled, with some distaste, a Seminary teacher who graded students on their testimonies. "You can't rate testimonies!" Jackie insisted. Her unwillingness to stand in front of her class, unprompted by the Spirit, ultimately had a rather negative effect on both her grade and her feelings about Seminary.

Jackie, if you're reading this, there'll be no repeating that mistake. Rating Web sites is a difficult exercise, particularly when the sites contain doctrinal material. There's always a risk that a rating might be misperceived as a commentary on the quality of the doctrine or testimonies on the site.

This rating problem is resolved, to some extent, by excluding from the outset sites that don't stand up to minimal standards. All the sites in this book have already passed the preliminary screening. Sites that contain no original material, that contain nothing more than links to other sites, or that are primarily "under construction" are not included. And sites that are overly silly, unfocused, irresponsible, or pointless do not appear on this list.

There was a bit of wrestling with the question of whether or not to include, in the name of being comprehensive, material openly hostile to the Church. Reviewing the actual sites, though, made the decision easy. They tended to be as silly, unfocused, and irresponsible as dozens of the friendly sites we excluded. For that reason, you won't find in this book links to sites that appear to exist solely to trash what Latter-day Saints hold sacred. At the same time, however, it's clear that one person's "honest" is another person's "hostile." These listings do include sites that contain well-researched scholarly materials on Church history and doctrine. Many of these scholarly materials are produced by active, believing Latter-day Saints; others are not. In any event, all contribute something valuable to the pool of knowledge.

So on to the ratings. Highest marks go to sites that are regularly updated, that contain original material, that are easy to use, and that are well edited. Organization, access speed, and readability also contribute to high scores. Low marks go to sites with outdated links, confusing structure, and unsubstantiated doctrine.

By any criteria, though, site evaluation is an inexact science. Your friendly author concedes all debates, acknowledging that her ratings are influenced primarily by how well-behaved her children were at the time she read the page. If you own a low-rated site, direct all hate mail at her kids, who probably poured grape juice on her carpet and roller-skated on her couch the morning she looked at your Web site.

THE RATING SYSTEM

The Internet site evaluations in this text employ a system of stars. Here's what the ratings mean:

★★★★★ Bookmark this site. It's worth visiting at least once a week.

★★★★ Stop by every month or so.

★★★ Information tends to be static, but it's good for background.

★★ Contains minimal information, but worth a visit if you're researching the subject.

★ Site contains at least some worthwhile material, but it may be out of date, of dubious authority, difficult to use, or commingled with ideology hostile to the Church.

☞ No rating. This site contains the text of conference talks, scripture, or doctrinal discourse where a rating simply doesn't apply.

$ Commercial site. Judge for yourself.

☑ A top-twenty pick. The twenty best LDS sites on the World Wide Web. Chapter 13 contains an overview.

2

WHY THE CHURCH HAS A WEB SITE— AND WHY IT'S NOT BIGGER

In 1996 there appeared—almost out of the blue—a Web site at the Internet address *<http://www.lds.org>*. A few experimental souls had been checking that address regularly, so when the official page appeared, the news spread throughout the LDS online community within hours. To the disappointment of visitors, though, the page contained nothing more than a beautifully done piece of artwork and a promise that more information would follow.

Months passed. Then, one day, the page changed. The artwork disappeared, and in its place appeared real information from, and about, the Church. The official LDS Web site was born.

Much excitement ensued. Not only was the Church making an organizational dive into new technology, but it appeared to be giving an official blessing to the electronic communications revolution. Since that time, the official Web site of

The Church of Jesus Christ of Latter-day Saints has grown, albeit at a careful and measured pace, to become one of the best LDS sites on the Web.

It's all part of an increasingly open way of interacting with the outside world. With an expanding missionary effort comes the need to find new tools for reaching out to that world. Leaders have been open and generous with their observations about the place of the official Web site in the Church's overall communication effort.

One in particular, Elder Jeffrey R. Holland of the Quorum of the Twelve Apostles, spent some time in conversation with the author of this book, explaining how the official Web site came into being, and what he hopes it will accomplish.

AN INTERVIEW WITH ELDER JEFFREY R. HOLLAND

I spoke with Elder Holland the day he returned from meeting with the Saints in South America. Although he was still feeling the effects of two weeks in Brazil, Elder Holland spoke candidly about taking the message of the gospel online, and explained what he sees as the obligation of Latter-day Saints who participate in the online electronic community. These are his comments:

Q LAURAMAERY GOLD: *What were the circumstances surrounding the Church's original decision to create a Web site?*

A ELDER HOLLAND: Obviously there's been a lot of awareness of the Internet and of the increasing opportunity for communication it provides. I think the Church was appropriately cautious and measured, not rushing unduly to create a Web site. It was something we wanted to consider and review thoughtfully. I said once in another interview that we weren't "breathless" about using the Internet, but we also weren't unmindful of the potential that it had.

So we determined some basic things that would probably be of interest and at the appropriate time created the home page based on that.

Q *Content didn't appear on site until long after the page was established. What was the source of the apparent delay?*

A   You noted that a page was held before we put much on it. That was done simply to let people know we were aware the Internet was available. While we didn't feel any particular haste or overly urgent need to pursue it, we did want to hold the page, to put out the notification that more information would follow.

Q   *How did you determine what material would appear on the site?*

A   We decided early on that we would begin with materials in two general divisions, divisions that were actually not unrelated. One would be a media guide of sorts, directed at journalists and newsmakers, people who wanted to know about the Church and wanted an easy, convenient way to find that information. We put up resource materials that would be of general use to them—basic policy statements, basic facts about the Church.

The other somewhat-related general division was material to serve the nonmember, investigators who didn't know about us, people who were inquiring. We wanted them to have accurate information. We were aware that there was a lot of inaccurate information being put out by others. We wanted to share our own story with inquiring people not of our faith who were interested in the Church. Those were the two general guidelines that established what we did first.

What's related to that, and what may be obvious, is that we did not feel, and have not felt yet, that the Internet was necessarily the ultimate way to communicate with members of the Church. Members of the Church who have access to the Internet are such a small fraction of our total membership that it will be a very long time before we see it as a major vehicle to communicate with the Church at large. That day may come, but it surely is not upon us right now.

Q   *Generally, how are Latter-day Saints to view technology—as a boon to missionary work, or as a tool for evil?*

A   It is like most things in the world. First of all, there is a wonderful gift in this. God is blessing people in a manner consistent with the spirit of the restoration of the gospel. I love the passage from the Prophet Joel that Moroni quoted to Joseph Smith, in which he said that God would pour out His spirit on all the earth, on all people.

> "And it shall come to pass afterward, that I will pour out my spirit upon all flesh; and your sons, and your daughters shall prophesy, your old men shall dream dreams, your young men shall see visions."
>
> Joel 2:28 (See Joseph Smith History 1:41.)

I think we have to know that the wonderful world we live in is enhanced greatly by all kinds of technology and science and wonders. Those are blessings from God.

But, as with almost anything in life, there can be a negative application of those blessings. Automobiles are a wonderful blessing, but you can do a lot of damage with them. And that would be true with electronic technology. There are certainly a lot of unseemly things on the Internet, real filth. We would want our members to be guarded against that just as they would be guarded against inappropriate material anywhere—in television, movies, or any other medium. Use of the Internet will require judgment, maturity, and faithful responsiveness from Latter-day Saints, just as is required of us in every other aspect of our lives.

Q *How can the Internet play a role in spreading the gospel?*

A I mentioned that it's certainly one way we can tell our story widely—by widely, I mean globally. The numbers online may not be overwhelming, but it gives us a certain global reach that allows us to tell an international audience about the restored gospel.

For those who are attuned to the technology and have Internet access to go along with their interest, we may be able to give facts and tell our story better than we could at any earlier time in history. These people may not have access to the missionaries. To those people, I'm sure the Internet will be a blessing, and there will be a certain kind of missionary effort going forth that way.

We're not overestimating it, but neither are we underestimating the potential missionary influence.

Q *How aware is the leadership of the Church about the Internet and other technology?*

A I think the leadership is very aware of it. But we are also very conscious that it reaches only a fraction, a very small group of the Church. So we are not putting much freight on that, (laughing) on that particular railroad car. It's just too small. But we're very aware of it. We have people who live all day, every day, with it. We have a large investment in technology.

Q *Why isn't the Church's Web site bigger than it is?*

A We're just taking that a step at a time. We've made a modest beginning—an appropriate beginning, but it's been modest. We have not been casual, but we've approached it with caution and a sort of measured step. We're putting online what seems of interest. As that world unfolds, we'll be making comparable developments. We just haven't had much incentive to put a whole host of things online that wouldn't be of interest and wouldn't be of much help to people. But yes, you can expect to see more information in the future for the benefit of the members. If I use the word "research," that might be overstating it at present. But people will want to have more basic Church reference materials, and eventually they'll be able to find many of them there.

Q *What are the dangers for the Church in overemphasizing the Internet? Is there some perception among leadership that the Internet is ultimately more harmful than it is helpful to members?*

A One of the dangers I've already mentioned is to overestimate the number of people it reaches. We'd be foolish to think of the Internet as a mainline delivery system to a Church of 10 million members, only to find out we're reaching 30,000. Obviously that would be foolish and unwise.

There is always going to be a very special human relationship in the Church—missionaries talking face-to-face with people, families in family home evenings, exchanging experiences and laughter. I don't think the Internet is ever going to alter that very much. For example, we would not want fathers to substitute endless isolation watching television for endless isolation surfing the Internet.

We don't underestimate the ability to transmit a wonderful breadth of material. But we don't overestimate its role in substituting or replacing warm personal communication, the spirit-to-spirit contact we have in the Church. We need the goodwill and brotherhood and sisterhood found there. We won't ever expect the Internet to replace much of that.

Q *Members of the LDS online community regularly communicate with investigators about the Church, and there are already many, many instances of people joining the Church because of contacts that originated over the Internet. At the same time, there is a small number of people who say their perspective of the Church changed for the worse because of information they found online. When you hear reports in Salt Lake regarding gospel contacts made over the Internet, what is their general tenor? Do they tend to be more positive than negative?*

> **ON THE IMPACT OF THE INTERNET**
> Whether the Internet is positive or potentially destructive to members of the Church depends on how the members use the Internet. I want the Internet to be a positive influence in my life, so I make sure that the sites I visit are in keeping with the 13th Article of Faith . . . if there is anything virtuous, lovely or of good report . . . well, I think you get the drift.
>
> Tonia Izu, San Jose, California/Provo, Utah
> <Tonialzu@ix.netcom.com>
> Webmaster, LDS Members' Home Pages
> <http://www.netcom.com/~toniaizu/cmembers.html>

A I don't know that we've had enough experience to know much about it. If it's happening, that's great. That's wonderful. We'd like to hear about it. On the other hand, we're always disappointed when people have a negative experience, and that's a risk whether it's the Internet, books, newspapers, or whatever. A lot of people publish a lot of things that really require a response. We would like the privilege—whether it's the Internet, television, or the printed page—we would like the privilege of telling the accurate true story of the Church. We would like our opportunity to tell the truth.

There are some who disagree with the Church, with its premises and purposes, and frankly are determined to do damage to it. That's a risk on the Internet, but it's a risk with other media as well.

Q *What advice would you give to members who are considering getting on line?*

A If that's an affordable way for people to communicate, wonderful. If they're wise and judicious about how they use it, knowing full well what exists out there, then that ought to be their privilege.

Q *Have you any other advice regarding how people should conduct themselves on line?*

A Be worthy and honorable Latter-day Saints. Defend the truth. Be clean. That is good advice for any time, and it is good advice for users of the Internet.

ON THE INFLUENCE OF THE INTERNET

The Internet has broadened my horizons and helped increase my testimony of the Gospel. It's given me an opportunity to share ideas and read the ideas of others, enriching my real life tremendously. I can't imagine the world without it anymore.

Kathy Fowkes, Mesa, Arizona
<rogkat@primenet.com>
LDS Women's Forum
<http://www.primenet.com/~rogkat/index.html>

A TOUR OF THE OFFICIAL WEB SITE

In the next two chapters, you'll learn how to get online, and how to navigate around the Internet. For now, though, feel free to just sit back and watch the guided tour. If you want to follow along from your own computer, and are already connected to the Internet and can find your Web browser software, enter the address *<http://www.lds.org>*. (Internet addresses in this text appear in angle brackets [<>]. Do not enter the angle brackets when you enter an address.)

The first stop is the front page of the official Web site. As with most Web pages, the site contains both text and graphics.

The panel on the left is the title of the page, and has no additional function. In the large panel on the right you'll see an index of the information available at the site (see figure 2.1). In a moment, we'll look at a few of the items in the index, but for now, we'll look around this page. Move to the bottom of the page (by using the

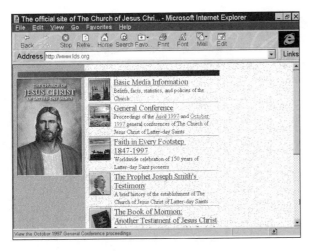

FIG. 2.1

The front page: A list of links to additional pages.

PageDown key on your keyboard, or by clicking with your mouse in the vertical scroll bar at the far right).

In the lower half of the front page, you'll see a couple of additional index items, along with some buttons for other features, and some copyright information (see figure 2.2).

Through the Index

We move back to the top of the page now (see figure 2.3), to begin exploring the site.

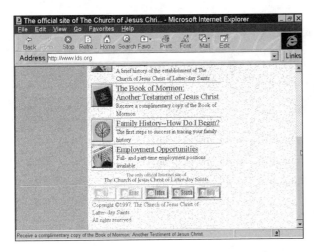

FIG. 2.2

The lower front page: Additional links, plus publishing information.

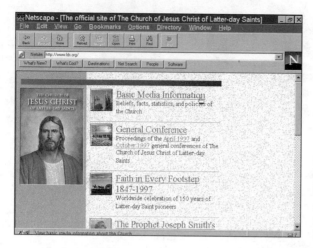

FIG. 2.3

Back to the top: The same page, viewed from a different piece of software. Note that the mouse pointer changes to a hand shape when it passes over the hyperlink.

As you slide your mouse pointer over the first index item, you'll see it change from an arrow to a hand shape as it crosses either the graphic of the Salt Lake Temple, or the underlined words Basic Media Information. The underline, and the hand shape, indicate that the items are *hyperlinked* to other pages on the Web site. (If your own software doesn't underline the hyperlink, you can turn the underline back on from the Options setting.) At the bottom of the page, the Status Bar will display a description of the hyperlink.

Click with your left mouse button on either the graphic or the words (they both execute the same command). A new page, the Basic Media Information page, appears on screen (see figure 2.4).

There you'll find two new links. Click on the first, Global Media Guide (see figure 2.5), to find links to everything from Core Beliefs and Doctrines to the Tabernacle Choir.

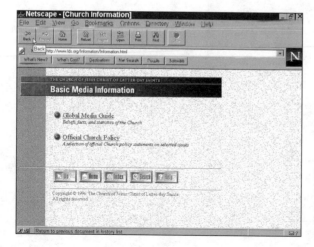

FIG. 2.4

Visiting the first link: The Basic Media Information page works like page two of a newspaper. You have to open it to read.

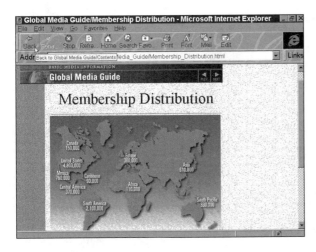

FIG. 2.5

Membership distribution: One of several pages available at the Global Media Guide.

To move back through the levels to the front page, click the Back button, in the upper-left corner until you arrive. Once you arrive back at the front page, explore each of the additional hyperlinks in the same way. Just click through, and back out, to see the entire site.

When you feel comfortable about navigating through Web sites, return to the front page, move to the bottom, and click on one of the five rectangular buttons for additional features. The Up and Home buttons are disabled from the front page. When they appear on other pages, they'll take you back to the front page one step at a time, or in a single giant step.

The Index button takes you to an alphabetical listing of all the information at the site (see figure 2.6).

The Search button lets you search the entire site for information related to a specific search word (see figure 2.7). Just enter a single word, several words,

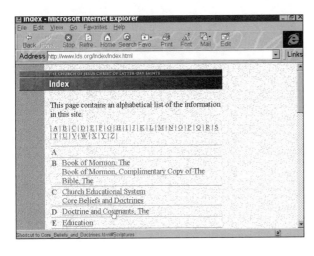

FIG. 2.6

Index: Click a link to go directly to a page.

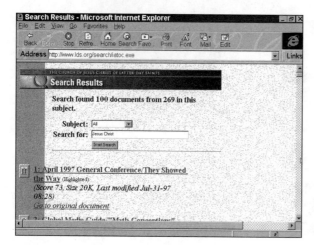

FIG. 2.7

Search: Search the Web site for information on a particular topic.

or a phrase in the Search for: box, then click the Start Search button to begin searching.

Finally, the Help button contains a document that will teach you how to use the Church Web site.

Confused? Relax. Chapter 3 will get you online in no time, and chapter 4 provides additional navigational helps for the rest of the Internet. It's not the Liahona, exactly, but you will be able to use it to find your way through the electronic Deseret.

3

GET ONLINE

Getting online is a simple four-step process. It boils down to this: Set up your equipment, get an Internet account, fire up the software, and go. If you've yet to do any one of those things, read on. If you've done them all, feel free to skip this entire chapter and move along to the good stuff in the rest of the book.

STEP ONE: SET UP THE EQUIPMENT

When purchasing a personal computer, you're faced with essentially two choices: a Macintosh or an IBM-compatible PC (which, ironically, isn't necessarily compatible with IBM's personal computers. You're just as likely to purchase a machine that's Compaq-, Dell-, or Gateway-compatible). In any event, all non-Macintosh home and business computers are grouped together as PCs. (OK, there are exceptions—but those are machines of the Star Trek class, called *workstations;* if you don't know what a workstation is, you don't need one.)

Approximately 80 percent of personal computers in use today are PCs. If you're not sure which to buy, here's one recommendation: Consider buying whichever machine you use at your place of employment. The particular brand of PC is not significant, but do consider the benefits of being able to use the same disks, data, and computing conventions both at home and at the office. Efficiency generally outweighs any other consideration in the Mac/PC war.

If you're genuinely starting from scratch, here's the simple breakdown of considerations.

PC	Macintosh
Less expensive.	Easier to use.
More software available.	Better software available.
Upgrades are cheaper.	Upgrades are easier.
Users are part of a larger community.	Users are part of an elite community.

Computer writers can and do argue about each of these points, but for the most part, that's the way the arguments break out.

Whether you already own, or are looking to buy, this is the minimum configuration you'll need to make good use of your home PC. Any computer made after 1994 probably meets these recommended minimums.

Component	PC	Macintosh
Processor (Chip)	80486—a "486" for short	75MHz PowerPC 603 RISC
Video adapter (card)	640 x 480	800 × 600 (built in)
Monitor	14" color, .28dp	15" color, .27dp
RAM	8M—"8 meg" for short	8M
CD-ROM drive	4×—pronounced "four speed"	4×
Hard drive	500M (1 gigabyte is better)	1 gigabyte

If you're buying now, you'll find that machines being sold today are of the Pentium—think of it as a "586"—class. Hard drives are generally 1 gigabyte (1,024M) and larger. CD-ROM drives are veering toward 16 speed and higher. And video adapters are commonly 1,024 by 768. Rejoice while you can. In a few weeks, *whatever* you buy will be outdated.

The Modem

The modem connects your computer, through a telephone line, to the online world. Most computers sold today include modems as standard equipment.

If you have a notebook PC, or a machine purchased before 1995, you may have to purchase a modem. Virtually all desktop computers sold since then have a modem included as part of the standard equipment. The standard transmission rate for prepackaged modems is still 33,600 baud, or 33.6 kilobits per second, for lower-priced computers. A 33.6-kilobit modem comes standard in some premium computer packages. (*Baud* describes the data speed of the modem. Loosely translated, it means bits of data per second—although purists will dispute that definition. Nod and smile when they do; a more technically precise definition won't change how quickly, or slowly, your modem functions.) For World Wide Web access, don't consider anything slower than a 28.8-kilobit modem. As a general rule: The higher the speed, the better. Speeds of 56 kilobits per second are also readily available.

Another consideration is whether to buy an internal or external modem. An internal modem is the simpler of the two. It consists of a printed circuit board that you plug into an expansion slot in your computer. A telephone cable plugs into a standard jack on the end of the board. If you're reluctant to open your computer, most retailers will be happy to do it for you—for a modest fee.

> **THE CABLE CONNECTION**
> Watch for the newest connection technology: cable modems. Provided by your cable TV company, these super-fast connections will allow you to transfer data at 350 times the speed of 28.8-kilobit modems. You'll find a review and comparison of cable modems at the PC World Web site: <http:// www.pcworld.com/hardware/ communications/articles/aug97/ 1508p158e.html>

Slightly more expensive, an external modem has its own power supply, plastic casing, and blinking lights to tell you when it's communicating. It also has extra cables for connecting to your computer, usually through the serial port. The phone line plugs into a jack on the modem. The advantages of the external modem are that it is easily portable—meaning it can be used on more than one personal computer; you have a visual indicator of the modem status; and when your connection hangs up, you can shut down the modem without shutting down the entire computer.

If you're ready to invest in a modem of your own, spend the extra money on speed rather than the external box. Reduce the clutter in your work area by buying a 33.6K internal modem.

Notebook computer users have different options. You could use an external modem, or you could use a PC Card internal modem. The PC Card is a credit-card-sized unit designed to plug into a PC Card (formerly *PCMCIA*) slot. Most laptop computers sold since 1995 have at least one of these slots. Costs vary, but PC Card internal modems can easily run double that of a standard modem. Buy the fastest speed you can afford.

STEP TWO: GET AN INTERNET ACCOUNT

To get to the Internet and World Wide Web sites, you need an account through a commercial online service, such as America Online or CompuServe, or through a dial-up Internet service provider, called an ISP.

Commercial Online Services

The major commercial services provide excellent Internet access and have adjusted their prices to be competitive with the ISPs. In addition, the commercial services offer something that the ISPs do not—content. Each service provides its own discussion forums, databases, and other features that are available only to its members.

Even if you already have an ISP, a commercial online service may be a worthwhile investment. Besides the additional content, commercial online services organize and categorize the most useful functions of the Internet into easily navigated menus and icons. The amount of time you save searching for data may be enough to offset the extra cost. In addition, commercial services are portable—you can access them toll-free from most large towns and cities around the world.

Connection software is provided by the commercial services free of charge. Get your software by calling the toll-free number listed in the following sections, or from the disks that fall out of any number of computer magazines and unsolicited mailings. In addition, most personal computers sold today include the connection software for at least one of the commercial online services.

America Online and CompuServe are the two most popular services available today. Together they boast a user base of more than 10 million subscribers.

The following list describes the leading commercial online services. In each of these listings you'll find a World Wide Web address, called a *Uniform Resource Locator.* URLs are explained on p. 43.

America Online. America Online (see figure 3.1) features an easy-to-use graphically oriented interface. It has a reputation as a fun, family-oriented service, although the LDS-oriented pickin's are slim. Users interested in getting together for private, invitation only, discussions may appreciate the convenience of AOL's private chat rooms. Contact AOL at (800) 827-6364. *<http://www.aol.com>*

CompuServe. CompuServe (see figure 3.2) was a pioneer in providing online services and had a significant impact on the online LDS community through the Latter-Day Saints section of the Religion Forum. (The section name is another example of long-time moderator Keith Irwin's policy of inclusiveness: The hyphen is for the LDS members, the capital D is for the RLDS members.) Current section leader Arthur Wilde continues Brother Irwin's policies of civilized, inclusive

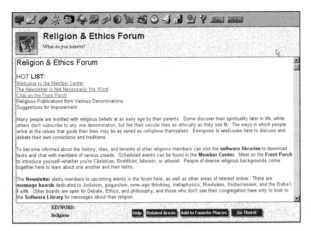

FIG. 3.1

AOL: Mediocre LDS content

discussion, barring ad hominum attacks and welcoming diverse points of view. Contact CompuServe at (800) 848-8199. <*http://www.compuserve.com*>

Other Commercial Services

The definition of what a commercial service is and how it is accessed is constantly changing. Competition has caused some services to readjust their focus. The following services exist in a new, not-yet-fully-explored area between a simple ISP and a full-service commercial online service:

Delphi.   (800) 695-4005 <*http://www.delphi.com*>
Genie.   (800) 638-9636 <*http://www.genie.com*>
The Microsoft Network.   (800) 386-5550 <*http://www. msn.com*>
Prodigy.   (800) 776-3449 <*http://www.prodigy.com*>

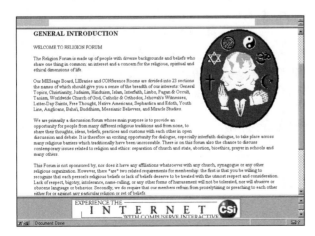

FIG. 3.2

CompuServe: Strong sense of community.

Internet Service Providers

Cheaper (usually), more flexible (sometimes), faster (at least, potentially), and more accessible (unless you travel), Internet service providers are gradually putting the commercial services out of business. ISPs differ from commercial online services in lots of little ways. They tend to be local—except when, like AT&T WorldNet, they're huge. ISPs also tend to be less expensive because they do not provide the additional information resources found on commercial online services. What an ISP does give you is a direct gateway to the Internet. At a minimum, your ISP should furnish:

- toll-free telephone access
- rate discounts for long-term service contracts
- unlimited access
- free telephone support
- a high ratio of access lines to users (You don't want to reach a busy signal when you call in.)
- a software bundle customized for your computer operating system (See the following section on Internet Software Tools for a list of what you'll need.)

To find a provider, check the local yellow pages under Internet Services or Computers—Internet. Read a few local newspapers, watch a few television ads, and make a few phone calls. Every ISP charges about $20 a month for access, and the smaller providers may be willing to negotiate.

Alternatively, choose a carrier that will give you access to your account no matter where you are. Major carriers include:

AT&T WorldNet. (800) 967-5363 *<http://www.att.com/worldnet/wis>*
IBM Internet Connection. (800) 455-5056 *<http://www.ibm.net>*
MCI Internet Dial Access. (800) 550-0927 *<http://www.mci.com/resources/ forhome/index.shtml>*
Sprint Internet Passport. (800) 359-3900 *<http://www.sprint.com/sip>*

Having trouble getting started with your new software? Good ISPs will hold your hand through the set-up process, making sure you're online, trouble free. Take advantage of the support line to get yourself properly set up.

Internet Software Tools

These Internet tools let you do something after you get online. If you're using a commercial online service, most of these tools will be included on a disk with your access software. Check back regularly, though, to be sure you're using a current edition of every piece of software.

Web Browser. Among the pieces of software included with your start-up software will be a thing called a *Web browser.* It's likely that your Web browser will be called either *Netscape Navigator* or *Microsoft Internet Explorer.* You may have heard about the great war between Netscape Navigator and Internet Explorer. To make your own comparison, start with the package you receive from your Internet service provider. Then download the other from Netscape at *<http://www.netscape.com>* or Microsoft at *<http://www.microsoft.com/ie/default.asp>*.

> **ON THE MAGIC OF COMMUNITY**
> In a land where Church members can be tens of miles apart, communication via the Internet brings members together in a way nothing else can. It provides an opportunity to visit with people all over the country, picking up from them ideas to try out in one's own area; an understanding of the diversity of the membership; and the knowledge that one is not alone in one's trials.
>
> Hilary A Croughton, Ipswich, England
> *<hathi@enterprise.net>*

Electronic Mail Reader. Your Web browser has built-in e-mail capabilities, but there are better choices. Your Internet service provider will supply you with an e-mail reader to get you started. After you're online, try a couple of different readers to see which best suits your needs. All readers can read, create, and send mail. The better ones give you advanced features and improved screens. Two popular and often-praised mail readers are Eudora, *<http://www.eudora.com>*, and Pronto 96, *<http://www.commtouch.com>*. Commercial online services such as AOL and CompuServe have built-in e-mail readers.

News Reader. Both Navigator and Explorer contain built-in newsgroup readers. However, you may find that a dedicated newsgroup reader, such as Forte's Free Agent, *<http://www.forteinc.com>*, offers easier-to-use features and greater flexibility. Free Agent has the ability to work off-line, saving you toll charges if you're being metered.

Chat Software. In chapter 8 (see page 187) you'll learn about an Internet feature called Internet Relay Chat (IRC). If your service provider doesn't include chat software in your start-up package, you'll want to pick up a package of your own. One software package that can get you started is mIRC. The latest version requires that after you try it, you register and pay a fee. Older versions are completely free of charge. A fast, clean front-end for IRC, with useful options and tools, can be found at *<http:// www.mirc.co.uk/get.html>*. Download is free.

STEP THREE: START BROWSING

Your first online adventure will be to browse (you've also heard it called *surf*) the Web. As mentioned earlier, your startup software will usually include either Netscape Navigator or Microsoft Internet Explorer. Install the browser as your provider directs, open it, and in the Address or Location box—the only space on the page where you're allowed to type something—type this:

```
http://www.lds.org
```

Press the Enter key, and you'll be transported to the home page for the Church of Jesus Christ of Latter-day Saints (see figure 3.3).

You'll notice that a home page, also called a *Web site* or simply a *page,* looks something like a magazine cover. The line you typed is called an *address* or an URL—pronounced "earl" and short for Uniform Resource Locator. URLs are key to finding every page on the World Wide Web.

Surfin' Safari—Entering URLs

Entering URLs looks a little tricky, but it's actually quite simple. Ninety-five percent of the Internet addresses you run across in your life will begin with the designation `http://`. Another 4.5 percent will begin with `ftp://`. If you run across the other half percent, you'll probably be looking at things so obscure they don't really bear learning about.

As a rule of thumb, the HTTP designations, short for hypertext transfer protocol, indicate an address for a graphically enhanced, magazine-cover-like World

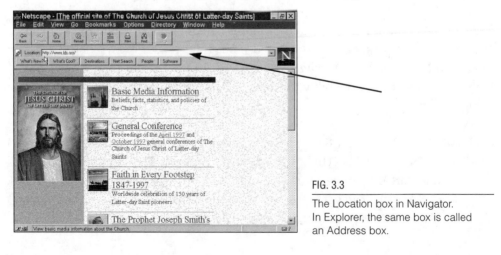

FIG. 3.3

The Location box in Navigator.
In Explorer, the same box is called
an Address box.

Wide Web page. The FTP (file transfer protocol) designations, on the other hand, indicate ugly, nongraphical, nonviewable files that you download to your own computer—at which point they might get installed and become quite pretty after all. FTP is the method by which you will do virtually all of your Net file transfers. When you need a file or a piece of software, chances are good that you will use FTP to get it.

A Faster Surf: Hyperlinks

As you slide your mouse pointer around the Church Web page, you'll notice that it changes shape when it points at certain elements on the page that are underlined and highlighted. These are called *hyperlinks*. A hyperlink is a quicker way to get to another page. Click a hyperlink, and it will automatically enter the URL for you, saving you the trouble of typing. Most hyperlinks appear as underlined text, but they can also take the form of pictures, clickable buttons, logos, and menu bars.

DUKE OF URL

Throughout this text, we designate URLs in this manner:

Page Name <http://address.domain/ filename>

You can manually copy the names from the text to your Web browser, or you can go directly to the pages from *hyperlinks*—clickable words that jump you directly to the correct site—on the *Mormons on the Internet* Registry, a Web site found at *<http://members.aol.com/MormonNet>* You'll find more information about using the Registry in chapter 4, page 47.

To see a menu of other things you can do with a hyperlink, position your mouse cursor over the hyperlink and click the right mouse button (see figure 3.4).

Back and Forth on the Web

To navigate your Web pages, you have three tools.

Toolbar buttons.   The toolbar buttons appear in a row across the top of your browser (see figure 3.5). The left and right arrow keys move you back and forth

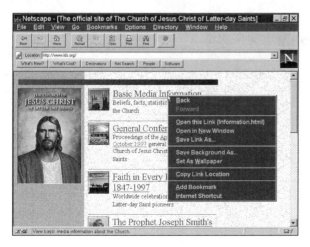

FIG. 3.4

Using a browser to surf.

through pages you've already viewed. The Stop button prevents a page from loading. The Refresh option reloads a page.

Pull-down menus. Select recently used addresses from the pull-down Address box in Microsoft Explorer or from the Location box in Navigator (see figure 3.6). Click the down arrow at the right of the box. Alternatively, go to the Go menu and select a different recently viewed page.

Scroll bars. Pages larger than your screen can be navigated horizontally and vertically from the scroll bars across the bottom and along the right side of your screen (see figure 3.7). If pages are consistently wider than your screen, consider decreasing your display size. (Go to the Control Panel, select the Display tool, then the Settings tab. Change the Desktop Area.)

Beyond the World Wide Web

Once you're comfortable with the whole Internet thing—or at least the World Wide Web portion of it—you're ready to graduate to more complicated features.

E-Mail. The most basic of services provided by ISPs and commercial online services is e-mail. *E-mail* is simply electronic mail sent and received over the Internet. Until recently, e-mail was strictly text-based. Now it's possible to format e-mail and attach audio, graphics, and additional files.

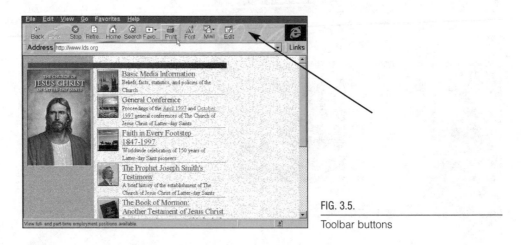

FIG. 3.5.

Toolbar buttons

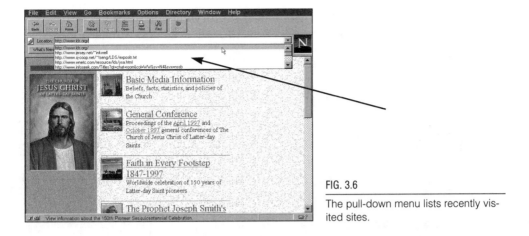

FIG. 3.6

The pull-down menu lists recently visited sites.

Mailing Lists.   These are discussions and information exchanges conducted via e-mail. Discussions are limited to a particular subject, carried on among a group of subscribers. Subscribers e-mail their responses to the mailing list, and the list is then automatically mailed to all subscribers. Some mailing lists are *read-only,* meaning that the discussion is more of a lecture.

UseNet Newsgroups.   *UseNet newsgroups* are open forums for public discussion. Newsgroups can be an effective way to engage a wide variety of people in ongoing correspondence concerning virtually any subject.

FTP Sites.   Files (data, graphics, audio, and software) can be transmitted over the Internet. The method used to *upload,* or send, and *download,* or receive, files is called *FTP,* short for *File Transfer Protocol.* When we direct you to an FTP site, you'll be downloading a file. Files are stored on a remote site. When you want the

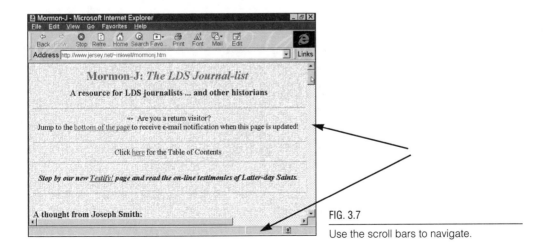

FIG. 3.7

Use the scroll bars to navigate.

file, you enter the URL, which begins with the designation `ftp://`, in the Address or Location box of your browser. Your browser will automatically download the file to your computer.

ON THE INTERNET AS A RESOURCE

Overall, I see the Internet as a resource, rather than a building tool. It is like asking if the library is a building tool. Many individuals go there, but they don't bond. They each go to the library to obtain the information they need.

I suppose I differentiate between two aspects of the Internet: e-mail versus the Web. One involves communication and that in itself may be considered a building tool. The other is basically a resource; and unless communication, via e-mail, occurs, it is basically a library.

Tonia Izu, San Jose, California/Provo, Utah
<Tonialzu@ix.netcom.com>
Webmaster, LDS Members' Home Pages
<http://www.netcom.com/~toniaizu/cmembers.html>

STEP FOUR: GO!

And that's why you've got the remainder of this book. In chapter 4: "Getting Around," you'll begin your online adventure by learning about a thing called "Netiquette" and visiting the Web sites of other Latter-day Saints.

4

GETTING AROUND

Once you're set up on the Internet, you'll need to find your way around. The bulk of this chapter is dedicated to a thing called a search engine—the tool you'll use to find things on the Internet long, long after this book goes out of date.

First, though, a brief introduction to a special feature for buyers of this book: the *Mormons on the Internet* Web site. Then comes a brief section on Netiquette for Latter-day Saints, followed by some Site Finders and People Finders—Internet sites that will help you locate other Latter-day Saints online. The remainder of the chapter consists of a lengthy introduction to Search Engines, information that you'll want to keep handy for all your Internet research.

THE MORMONS ON THE INTERNET REGISTRY

Throughout this text you'll find the addresses, or URLs of hundreds of LDS-oriented Internet sites. While you could enter each of them manually, you're invited to use a simpler Internet tool created just for buyers of this book.

Open your Web browser and enter the URL for the *Mormons on the Internet* Registry, at *<http://members.aol.com/MormonNet>* (see figure 4.1). Bookmark the Registry page (see page 49) so that you can return to the site with the click of a button.

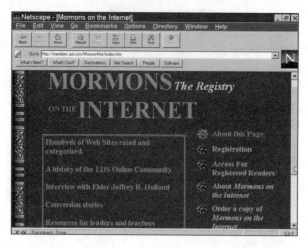

FIG. 4.1

The *Mormons on the Internet* Registry: Most complete listing of LDS sites on the Net.

The first time you visit the Registry site, you'll need to complete a brief registration form. On subsequent visits from the same computer, you'll be able to go directly to the Web site without any intermediate steps. (If you visit from a different machine, you can enter your password to access the site without re-registering.)

Once in the Registry, you'll be able to click on chapter names, section names, and Web sites to get to any site in this book. You can also conduct word searches on the text to find the information you're looking for. Site locations and content change over time, so as LDS sites move or disappear, and new sites appear, the Registry will be updated. The site will be maintained as long as this book, or subsequent editions of this book, remain in print.

The following sites provide some great links to LDS sites around the Net. See page 24 for an explanation of the ratings.

Infobases LDS World.   Great looking site, but it often fails to live up to its promise. Includes links to Gospel Study, News & Events, Missionary Work, LDS Family History Network, Arts & Culture, Mormon Marketplace, LDS WebLinks. Tends to be quite commercial—not surprising, given that Infobases is, after all, a successful commercial enterprise. ★★★★
<http://www.ldsworld.com>

LDS Info Resources. Deseret Book's listing of LDS information, alongside the Deseret's Best LDS Web Sites compilation (see figure 4.2). The search tool is quite limited. ★★★★
<http://www.deseretbook.com/ldsreso.html>

MORMON-INDEX.   The Mormon Internet Resources Distribution List. Receive a weekly message via e-mail about new LDS sites, discussion lists, and organizational information. This is a free subscription service. To subscribe, send an

e-mail to *<majordomo@lists.panix.com>*. In the body of the message type `sub-scribe mormon-index` *<your e-mail address>*. ✍
<http://www.idot.aol.com/mld/production/yiaz1876.html>

Mormons.Org.   A thorough, well-organized site, worth bookmarking. ★★★★★ ☑
<http://www.mormons.org>

Mormons on the Internet Registry.   Absolutely the best site for locating information on LDS Web sites. ★★★★★ ☑
<http://members.aol.com/MormonNet>

Pearls.   Originally a top-ten list, but it's since grown a bit. Contains good links. ★★★
<http://www.cache.net/~john/lds>

Top Ten Mormon Sites.   Very well chosen list, compiled by Nyall R. London. It includes a list of runners-up. ★★★★
<http://www.geocities.com/ Heartland/1830>

NETIQUETTE FOR LATTER-DAY SAINTS

Over the weekend I received—completely out of the blue—an e-mail note from a stranger who was hoping, I suppose, to "save" me from my faith. His note to me came complete with the usual invectives and vituperations. It read, in part: "Also according to the Smythsonian as well as your own BYU, there is no historical data

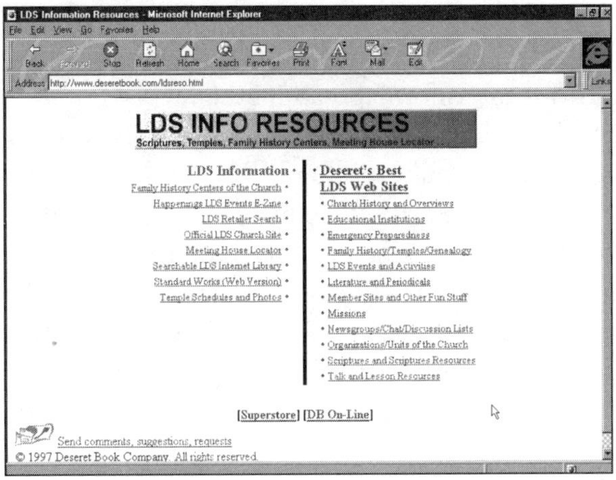

MARK THE SPOT

A Web browser's Bookmark feature makes it easy to return to a favorite site. Whenever you find a great search tool, add it to your list of bookmarks. Here's how: Go to the Web page you want to bookmark.

In Internet Explorer: Go to the Favorites menu, and click the Add to Favorites command. Use the Organize Favorites command to set up folders for grouping your bookmarks by category.

In Netscape Navigator: Use the Ctrl+D key combination to add the command to your bookmark list. Alternatively, go to the Bookmarks menu, and click the Add to Bookmarks command. The Go To Bookmarks command lets you organize your bookmarks by category.

To return to the bookmarked page at a later time, simply click the Favorites (or Bookmarks) menu and select the site from the drop-down list.

FIG. 4.2

Deseret Book: Good list of links to other LDS sites.

to backup the book of Mormon. The above is the TRUTH and I have checked it against Mr. Joseph's Smith's own writing while I was in Utah. You can yell 'FALSE' but it is not. I have not shown you hatred. If I did hate you I would have destroyed your web site. . . . If your are truly willing to look at your own religions teachings seriously, please write back. If not, I hope you like the path you've chosen and that your heaven will be here on earth because once Jesus comes again, this earth will end (2 Peter 3:11–13; Revelations 21:1). I will pray for you." (Spelling and grammar unchanged.) My correspondent signed his full name, appended by "A Christian."

I considered putting some energy into responding to my correspondent's concerns, but in the end, I simply wished him the best, reminded him that destroying Web sites is a bad thing to do, and sent him off to visit Arden Eby's Web site *<http://www.teleport.com/ ~arden/nccj.htm>* censuring anti-Mormon bigotry.

I didn't say this to my new friend, but my heaven really is here on earth. I have a happy life, a wonderful husband, great kids, and a pretty solid relationship with God. And it's for those reasons that I no longer bother trying to bash with the insincere. Bashing throws life out of balance. It requires turning away from God and facing darkness. It saps energy that rightfully belongs to my family and to the twelve-year-olds I teach in Sunday school. And above all, it's not polite.

Over time the Internet has developed a code of conduct, a set of behavioral standards for participants that is known, collectively, as "Netiquette." While there will always be a percentage of participants bent on breaking the "code," most people really do try to be civilized. In the Latter-day Saint online community, in particular, people have managed collectively to adhere to a high standard of conduct.

If you want to be welcome there, here's what you need to know about Internet etiquette—the "rules of the road" for the Information Superhighway.

First, do no harm. Be sure that every place you go is better because you were there.

ON LIVING YOUR FAITH

When it comes to netiquette, there are two things to remember:

One: Live the Thirteenth Article of Faith in what you do, say, and make available on the Internet. I think that's the basis for most etiquette/netiquette rules. If we all remembered to be honest, virtuous, and of good report, a lot of the other rules wouldn't be needed.

Two: In that frame of mind, don't argue with the "anti-Mormons." That's what they want to do, and it doesn't do any edifying for them, you, or the other listeners.

Curtis (Jewell) Whalen, Poplar Bluff, Missouri
<curtis_jewell@bigfoot.com>
Ringmaster, LDS Friends Web Ring
<http://www.geocities.com/Heartland/Meadows/3044/LDSFriends.html>

Second, don't spam. *Spamming* once referred strictly to mass mailings issued to lots of newsgroups. Now it includes the practice of sending irrelevant messages to newsgroups, mailing lists, and even individuals. (Newsgroups are explained in more detail in chapter 8: "The Living Church," page 189.) People gather on the Internet for a purpose. Do not waste "bandwidth" (the finite space on the Internet's "airwaves") by sending information—especially commercial information—to people who didn't ask for it.

Third, remember that the person who reads your words is not a computer, but is a child of God, someone who will make decisions about his or her future in the Church based on your behavior.

Fourth, remember that members of the Church are often just as fragile as nonmembers. Sometimes Latter-day Saints have tended to treat other Saints with a degree of contempt in the impersonal arena of the Internet—and have caused no end of hurt feelings by doing so. Assume that everyone you speak to is feeling vulnerable, and needs your loving words to get through the day. And remember that any disagreement you have with another Latter-day Saint is, ultimately, pretty insignificant.

The following Web sites provide some excellent background information on what you need to do to avoid offending—and being offended by—other members of the community.

> **ON AVOIDING CONFRONTATION**
>
> I personally try to avoid getting into debates with anyone who is confrontational. In many discussion forums online, you'll meet mainline Christians who feel their call is to go save the misled Mormons from damnation, and they do this not by talking about their faith, but rather by lying about ours. I avoid getting into conversations and debates that have no potential to go anywhere or bear any good fruit.
>
> Ronald Conrad Schoedel III, Ontonagon, Michigan
> <schoedel@up.net>

Building Your Integrity Bank Account.   A report carried in BYU-Hawaii campus bulletin. ☞
   <http://websider.byuh.edu/kealakai/archives/news/june12/kongaika.html>
Charter: soc.religion.mormon.   A brief outline of policies for the soc.religion.mormon newsgroup (covered in chapter 8, page 189). Standards by which all participants must abide. ★★
   <http://www.lds.npl.com/special/usenet/srm/index.html>
FAQ About Lists.   (See figure 4.3.) An excellent introduction to mailing lists, particularly to lists of an LDS bent. Explains their advantages and disadvantages, along with some basic netiquette for Latter-day Saints using the lists. Also includes links to a number of mailing lists of interest to Latter-day Saints. ★★★★
   <http://www.netwizards.net/~btphelps/mormon/lds1.htm>
Links to Netiquette and HTML Web Sites.   A good collection of information on Internet etiquette, using the Internet, building Web sites, and more. Includes links to other LDS Web sites. ★★★
   <http://www.netcom.com/~toniaizu/ehtml.html>

PEOPLE FINDERS

One of the first things you'll want to do, once you get online, is look around for other Latter-day Saints.

You'll find us everywhere: building our own Web sites, debating in newsgroups, chatting in chat rooms, engaged in discussions on e-mail lists, offering advice in genealogy forums, sharing stories in online testimony meetings.

The following Web sites are a good place to get started. Here you'll find the BYU Alumni Association, several organized meeting spots, and collections of personal Web pages. If you're looking for information on a particular ward, branch or stake of the Church, you'll find them listed in chapter 8: "The Living Church." Single Adult Saints may be interested in browsing chapter 10: "Interest Groups"—the dating and courtship sites.

Alumni Association.   Helpful links to Brigham Young University's Aspen Grove family camp, Cougar Club, Varsity Club, reunions, much more. If you've ever

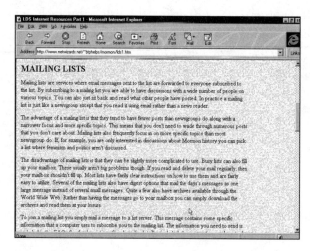

FIG. 4.3

Frequently Asked Questions: A set of instructions for mailing list etiquette.

had any affiliation with the Y, you'll want to return to this site. ★★★★★
<http://ucs.byu.edu/alumni>

LDS Web Ring. The LDS Web Ring is a system for allowing Web surfers to easily jump from one site to the next. Sites that carry the LDS Web Ring logo have links to the next site in the Ring. This Ring is limited to sites that have faithful information. The Ring's Requirement: "Anything on your page regarding the Church, its operation, leaders, and teachings must be as true as the gospel." ★★★★
<http://www.cyberhighway.net/~shwankey/ldsring.html>

LDS Friends Web Ring. A new Web ring for LDS member home pages. Add a bit of coding to your own home page to join the ring. To be included in the ring, a site must be positive about the gospel. ★★★★
<http://www.geocities.com/ Heartland/Meadows/3044/LDSFriends.html>

LDS Friends Worldwide. A great place to find old friends and meet new ones. Because it's also a "dating" site, you'll find more information, and a rating, in chapter 10: "Interest Groups"—Dating and Courtship
<http://www.downtown-web. com/cfw>

LDS Info Central. A Web site with names, locations, and e-mail addresses of Latter-day Saints on the Internet. Quite extensive. ★★★★
<http://www.geocities.com/Heartland/Plains/5537/roster.htm>

LDS Members' Home Pages. A list of more than 200 pages, sorted by last name. ★★★
<http://pw2.netcom.com/~toniaizu/cmembers.html>

Member Sites and Other Fun Stuff. Cute graphics, but navigation is time-consuming. Approach this one only if you've got some free time. ★★★
<http://www. deseretbook.com/ldsinfo/member.html>

Members' Homepages. A list of member pages, along with brief descriptions of the contents. Very well done. ★★★★
<http://www.geocities.com/Heartland/ 4034/content.html#member>

Mormon Ring. Another ring that works on the same principle. This Ring allows any page with Mormon content to join. Many—perhaps most—of the sites are tremendously antagonistic toward the Church. ★
<http://www.california.com/~rpcman/LDS.HTM>

Nauvoo. (See figure 4.4.) Once upon a time, Nauvoo was a forum on AOL. Now everyone can participate—and should. This is easily the best discussion place on the World Wide Web. Orson Scott Card's sponsorship gives it cachet; his *Vigor* newsletter gives it substance. Follow the links to the kids' forum, the Red Brick Store, the Mansion House library, and more. ★★★★★☑
<http://www.nauvoo.com>

World Wide Web First Ward. Virtual ward complete with auxiliaries, gospel, doctrine, and homemaking. Includes columns, testimonials, letters from readers, more. A top-notch site. ★★★★★
<http://www.uvol.com/www1st>

ON CREATING A COMMUNITY
OF SAINTS

One day [Roger Brown and I] were searching the Net in search of a pen-pal service for Latter-day Saints. We were disappointed to find nothing. I suggested that we start one of our own. . . .

In December of 1995, we finally brought the first "Mormon" pen-pal site to the Internet. . . . So far it has been a great success. I estimate that about 30 people have married or gotten engaged as a result of meeting on the site; the number may now be much higher.

We are trying to create a unique environment of community. I think this is a "brave, new world," and the possibilities for good are endless.

Christian Adams, Provo, Utah
<orad@ldsfriends.com>
<friends@ldsfriends.com>
Webmaster and Associate, LDS Friends
Worldwide Page
<http://www.ldsfriends.com/index.html>

SEARCH THE INTERNET

Every time a bell rings, the Internet gets new things—or so we're told. There are hundreds of LDS-oriented Internet sites out there; new locations appear every day. Sites we describe in this book will disappear, they'll move to new locations, they'll get new and better information. Whatever the case, you'll want to have the skills to go out and search on your own for whatever you need on the Internet. Search engines will be helpful in finding not only LDS-oriented sites, but also for searching out Internet sites on virtually any topic that interests you.

Search Engines

Simply put, search engines are akin to a phone book for the Internet. They're free, and they're invaluable for their flexibility and their power to light the darkest corners in order to find the information you're seeking. Use a search engine much as

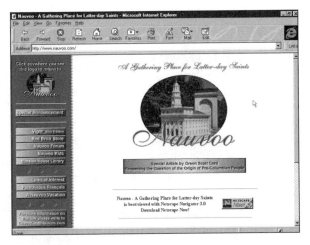

FIG. 4.4

Nauvoo: Best hangout on the Web.

you'd use the index of a book or the yellow pages of a telephone directory. Bookmark them (see instructions on page 49) so that they're easily available.

The search engines discussed in this chapter are much grander in scope than the search vehicles you might find on the individual Web sites featured throughout this book. For the most part, on-site search engines don't reach beyond the archives of their particular site.

Search engines in this chapter index more sites—in some cases the entire Internet—to accumulate information for vast databases. From these search engines you'll get better, more varied tools for querying data and interpreting results.

Although many of the search engines featured here may seem similar, significant differences lie just below the surface. Their primary focuses differ, and the information you generate will likewise be different. Several different types of user interfaces are featured. Some are extremely user-friendly, and others are extremely powerful and better left to the seasoned user.

> **ON TRACKING BYU GRADUATES**
>
> Like all Alumni Associations in the country, one of our biggest challenges is communicating with the large membership of our organization (approximately 300,000). We have used traditional printed materials such as the *Brigham Young Magazine,* flyers and letters, but it is impossible to reach everyone through traditional methods. . . .
>
> We hope that as we develop the Web page and more and more of our alumni have access to the Internet this will be an effective vehicle for communication.
>
> George H. Bowie, BYU Alumni Association
> *<gbowie@ymail.byu.edu>*
> Alumni Association page
> *<http://ucs.byu.edu/alumni>*

A Few Words About Boolean Algebra

Boolean algebra is the backbone of all search engines. It sounds French but isn't. And it's certainly worth knowing about before beginning what could be a lifetime of sweeping Internet searches.

Boolean algebra was developed by the English mathematician George Boole
in 1847. It brings together logical concepts and mathematical representations. A
special set of mathematical *operators,* each having specific characteristics, is used
to define Boolean logic. The basic operators, those used in most search engines,
are AND, OR, and NOT.

This section explains the operators; the next section will show you how to use
them for searching.

The AND *Function*

The AND function requires that all elements within the search term be present. If
you type in a list of words, the search engine will return only the items in its database that include *all* the search words. The AND function in a search engine is
usually represented by placing a plus sign (+) directly in front of a word, without a
space. Some engines ask that you type the word AND in all caps. In a few engines,
the AND is assumed.

The OR *Function*

The OR function requires only one of the elements in the search term to be present for the search to produce a positive result. In other words, if you type in a list
of words, the search engine will return a list of sites containing any of the words in
the list. The OR function is the presumed default function in most search engines.

The NOT *Function*

The NOT function produces a positive result only if the designated element is not
present. Most search engines allow you to designate a NOT by placing a minus
sign (-) directly in front of the search term you want excluded.

what they discuss or put up. Some members put up journals, others talk about their families, still others bear their testimonies or put music up, but they all have the gospel in common.

The idea of "Building an Online Community" is particularly apt when I think about the goal of the ring—to start a small "neighborhood" of linked Web pages from Church members that are "safe for the kids to play," uplifting, and friendly. The idea of any ring is to link together sites with a common interest—in a sense, creating their own neighborhood.

Curtis (Jewell) Whalen, Poplar Bluff, Missouri
<curtis_jewell@bigfoot.com>
Ringmaster, LDS Friends Web Ring
<http://www.geocities.com/Heartland/Meadows/3044/LDSFriends.html>

How to Conduct a Search

All search engines feature an input box where you can enter what are known as *keywords.* The keyword is the beginning of your search. You begin your search when you enter your keyword, click the Search or equivalent button, and wait for the search engine to produce results.

It's not feasible to cover every method of conducting a search in the space allotted here. But it will be possible to touch on the basics—the features common to all search engines.

Unique Word Searches

You can begin your search by entering a single word in the keyword box and clicking the Search button. This is a wonderfully simple way to conduct a search if the keyword you're using is so unique that it is unlikely to produce many results. Searching for the keyword `Zoramite` produces no more than a handful of results. But a less specific term, `religion` for instance, can easily produce better than a million matches.

Don't despair. A million places to look isn't really as hopeless as it sounds. Search engines don't return results in a random order. Using complicated algorithms, the best search engines rank the matches, and list the most relevant sites first.

Combined Word Searches: Using the AND, OR, and NOT Operators

A better method of conducting a search is to combine words. In this way you can easily narrow the field from tens of millions of matches to a much more manageable number. Multiple word searches take advantage of the Boolean operators.

The OR operator is the default condition for most search engines. Type in the keywords without any symbols in front or in between to invoke the OR operation.

As an example, the search string `LDS Mormon` will produce results if either, or both, of the keywords are present.

On the surface this doubling up would seem counterintuitive to your efforts to minimize irrelevant items when you search. If one word produces tens of millions of results, shouldn't two words produce more? They should and do. However, once again, the ranking algorithms come into play. The ranking of sites depends on several factors including, but not limited to, the number of times your word combination appears in a document, at what point—nearest to the beginning—the words appear in the document, how closely the two words appear in a document, and others.

The criteria used for ranking may vary from search engine to search engine. The more words you give the algorithm to work with, the more accurate the resulting rankings will be. Again, the highest-ranked sites are listed first. What this means is that, although you'll likely get millions of matches for multi-word searches, the most relevant matches will be the relatively few that appear at the top of the list.

To further define your search, invoke the AND operator. Although the method for invoking the AND function varies among search engines, the characteristics of the function do not. Currently, the most common way of searching with AND is to place a + sign directly in front of the keyword.

The AND function in the search string `+Mormon +Saints` produces results only when both keywords, Mormon and Saints, are present. (By the way, search engines also tend to be case sensitive. Uppercase letters search only for proper nouns. Lowercase letters return everything, proper or not.)

The NOT function provides an excellent means of eliminating items that may often be present with your keywords, but are of absolutely no interest to you. The NOT function can generally be invoked by placing a minus (-) sign in front of the keyword. The search `+Mormon +Zion -Moab` will return documents containing the keywords Mormon and Zion, but only if those documents do not contain the word Moab.

Grouping Words

Placing your words in groups can further narrow your search. Use this method when looking for "Mormon Zion" but not "Zion Mormon." The method for placing words in groups varies among the search engines. The two most common methods are placing them within quotes (`"Mormon Zion"`), or joining them with a colon (`Mormon:Zion`).

Spelling Counts—Somewhat

Not sure whether it's Rameumton or Rameumptom? Sometimes you're not sure of the exact spelling of a word. Other times, you're looking for several similar words (Mormon, Mormons, Mormonism). In either case a wild card character allows you to enter the part of the word you know and ignore the rest. For instance, try entering `Mormo*` if you're looking for anything on Mormonism. In this case the asterisk (`*`) is the wild card character that tells the search engine to look for all words beginning with the letters M o r m o.

Filters

All search engines employ some sort of "search only" filtering mechanism. As the name implies, you can use a filtering mechanism to force the search engine to consider only pages in a defined category. All other pages are filtered out. Selecting the category Religion, for example, restricts your search to religion-oriented sites. Methods for applying filters vary among search engines, but basically they all involve selecting a primary subject category from a list.

The Search Engines

In this section we list a few of the growing number of search engines on the Internet. With a few exceptions, the search engine home pages consist of a list of topics—to help focus your search, and an input box for your keyword.

Searches on different engines yield different results. There are reasons for this variation, including the frequency with which the search engine database is updated, the algorithms used to determine the most relevant matches, and the different restrictions the search engines place on themselves when listing sites.

The search engines are listed here alphabetically. Each offers unique features, advantages, and disadvantages. Ratings are based on the author's personal likes and dislikes. Because the search engines don't compare with the LDS sites in the rest of this book, this rating system used here is entirely different. Not to worry. You'll pick it up pretty easily.

AltaVista

AltaVista (see figure 4.5) claims to be the largest Web index. The 31 million pages on 627,000 servers, plus 4 million articles from 14,000 Usenet groups, go a long way in supporting that claim. AltaVista is the primary search engine powering many of the subject-oriented search engines on the Internet.

The primary user interface consists of a simple keyword box and a Submit button. AltaVista uses Boolean searches. Detailed search instructions are available by clicking the Help or Advanced Help buttons.

Perhaps because yours truly is an old Luddite who enjoys doing things manually, AltaVista is my favorite search engine. Although it could really use an intuitive user interface, recently added "screen tips" make it a bit easier to navigate.

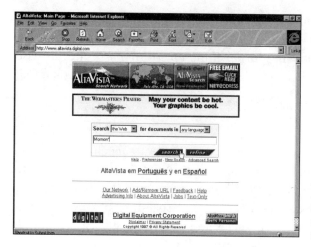

FIG. 4.5

AltaVista: A simple concept. Type in the keyword and click Submit. The new Refine feature narrows the search.

A search on the term `Mormon*` (the * is the wild card that causes the search to return words like Mormonism and Mormonania), returned 39,260 hits. AltaVista gets a rating of **A**. View the site at <*http://www.altavista.digital.com*>.

America Online Mailing List Directory

America Online Mailing List (see figure 4.6) is an easy-to-use directory featuring over 3,200 mailing lists. The search function includes filtered keyword searches. When the Directory locates a mailing list, it provides a synopsis and detailed information on how to subscribe. The home page features links to useful items, including Working with Mailing Lists, Glossary of Terms, and a weekly Top 20 list. Search instructions are found at the bottom of the opening screen.

This is a nice site, more useful than most. A recent search on the term `Mormon*` returned six mailing lists, including the Overland Trails discussion list with refer-

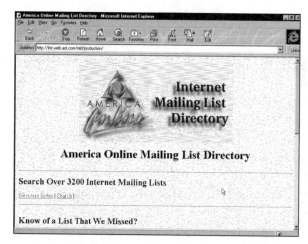

FIG. 4.6

AOL Mailing Lists: Although some of the information on the America Online Mailing List Directory site is restricted to AOL members, there is still plenty for others to choose from.

60

ences to the Mormon trail. This site earns a **B+**. The America Online Mailing List Directory is online at *<http://ifrit.Web.aol.com/mld/production>*.

Deja News

Deja News (see figure 4.7) is a search engine dedicated to newsgroups. (You'll find more information about newsgroups in chapter 8: "The Living Church," page 189.) It employs a Boolean-style search mechanism to weed through what it claims is the largest collection of indexed archived Usenet news available.

A recent search on the word Mormon* turned up 6,734 newsgroup messages. Search features include pattern matching (the use of partial words with wild cards), filtered searches, and time-sensitivity ranking.

For depth and scope as well as ease of use this site gets an **A** rating. Visit Deja News again and again at *<http://www.dejanews.com>*.

Excite

Excite features Boolean Web searches. Filtering selections help to redirect your search from the entire Web to Usenet groups, NewsTracker, or Web Reviews. The home page (see figure 4.8) also includes links to yellow pages, e-mail directories, shareware, maps, and more.

It's worth noting that Excite's search engine has the ability to build relationships between sets of words and concepts. In other words, Excite can equate the term "peace officer" with the word "policeman" when conducting a search.

A search on the term Mormon* brought up only ten hits, but then suggested ten additional search terms such as Mormonism, Nephi, LDS, and, er, humorless, polygamy, and watchtower. Harumph.

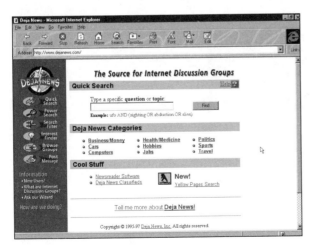

FIG. 4.7

Deja News: A simple search mechanism, but advanced filtered searches can be accessed by clicking Power Search.

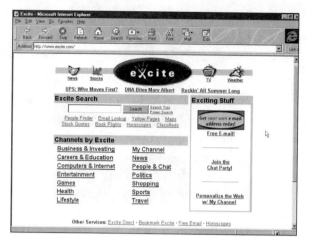

FIG. 4.8

Excite: The Excite page features the standard keyword input box, Search button, and links to other useful locations.

For its limited capacity, despite its ease of use, this site earns only a **C+**. You'll find all this excitement at *<http://www.excite.com>*.

Infoseek

Infoseek (see figure 4.9) is another search engine that attempts to make Web browsing easier by creating hierarchical categories and subcategories to filter searches. Infoseek offers several methods of searching the Web, which the developers have dubbed Ultrasmart and Ultraseek. Ultrasmart offers comprehensive query results plus the ability to drill down through several layers within your query. Ultraseek is a streamlined version of Ultrasmart, aimed at power users who know precisely what they're looking for.

A search on the term `Mormon*` returned 5,191 sites, and notified me of related topics "Church of Jesus Christ of Latter-day Saints" and "Jehovah's Witnesses." Guess it's pretty obvious who provides the greatest volume of sites using the name of the Church.

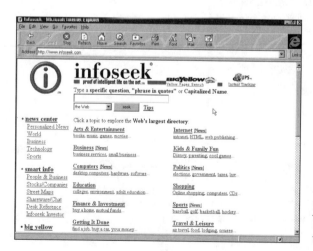

FIG. 4.9

Infoseek: Includes links to news, directories, and other services.

Small problem: With our Internet Explorer content filter on, all our Infoseek searches stalled out, warning us of the presence of "obscene gestures." Whether it's someone's idea of a practical joke, or a protest against self-censorship, it's an annoyance. It's otherwise a fairly useful engine, but because of the annoyances, it gets only a **B-** rating. Infoseek hides out at *<http://www.infoseek.com>*.

InfoSpace

InfoSpace (see figure 4.10) is a comprehensive directory tailored to locating people, businesses, government offices, toll-free numbers, fax numbers, e-mail addresses, road maps, and URLs. You'll be able to locate organizations by city, by address, or by name. Get door-to-door directions, obtain local city guides, access apartment locators, and even check weather and ski conditions.

Directory information is also available for federal, state, and local government offices. The downside? It's awfully slow. But because it appears to do everything it's advertised to do—and that's a lot—this site rates an **A-**. Make space at *<http://www.infospace.com>*.

Liszt

Liszt is another directory of mailing lists. Currently, there are over 70,000 entries compiled from servers around the world. Searches can be conducted using Boolean search methods, or you can choose from a smaller assortment by selecting specific topics (see figure 4.11). Perhaps even more important is the fact the Liszt is updated each week, ensuring against wasting your time with expired mailing lists.

A search on `Mormon*` located ten LDS mailing lists. For its ease of use, depth, and scope, Liszt gets an **A-** rating. You'll find the site listed at *<http://www. liszt.com>*.

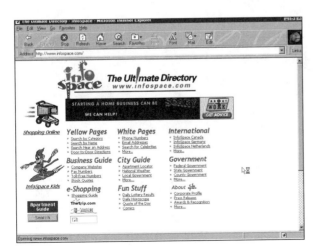

FIG. 4.10

InfoSpace: Locates virtually any organization and draws a map to get you there.

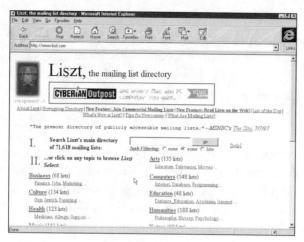

FIG. 4.11

Liszt: Check out the Tips for Newcomers before signing on.

Lycos

Lycos (see figure 4.12) is an especially user-friendly indexed Internet search engine. It features excellent instructional pages for its point-and-click-driven search protocol. Lycos employs a fuzzy search mechanism, finding like words and concepts. If you're looking for a lost roommate, Lycos's People Find feature is probably the best on the Internet.

Searching on the term `Mormon*` turned up 4,933 links. For basic ease and convenience, this is an **A-** rated site. Lycos lies at *<http://www.lycos.com>*.

Magellan Internet Guide

Magellan (see figure 4.13) would be just another entry in the user-friendly, category-oriented search engines if not for the unique filtering options offered on the

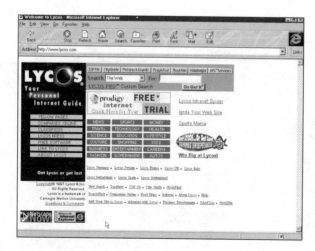

FIG. 4.12

Lycos: Among its many features, the Lycos home page contains links to money sites, a stock locator, and a people finder.

FIG. 4. 13

Magellan: The standard keyword box plus unique filtering options.

home page. Searching the entire Web is one option. Selecting Reviewed Sites Only limits your search to the 60,000 plus Web sites reviewed by Magellan's editorial staff. Select the Green Light option to avoid those sites intended for mature audiences.

Magellan was able to generate 840 hits from the search term Mormon*. Because full access is always a plus and its options are good too, we rate this a **B+** site. Explore Magellan at <*http://www.mckinley.com*>.

Search.Com

C|NET's tool Search.Com (see figure 4.14) is designed to be a user-friendly search vehicle. Features include links to telephone and e-mail directories. Search topics include Arts, Business, Computers, Employment, UseNet, and Web. Search.Com

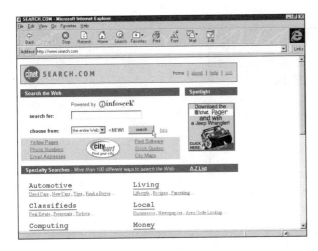

FIG. 4.14

Search.Com: Uses Express Search to find links to other search engines from its home page.

is one of several sites powered by the AltaVista search engine. Searching on the term Mormon* generated 13,053 hits. Search.Com also found related search terms "Church of Jesus Christ of Latter-day Saints," "Parks & Wilderness Areas," and "Museums & Parks in Utah." Sure beats "Watchtower"!

As a high point in a long list of excellent search engines, this site gets an **A** rating. Start your search at *<http://www.search.com>*.

Starting Point

Starting Point (see figure 4.15) provides a standard keyword Boolean search. In addition, Choice Web Sites offers a large assortment of selected Web sites grouped in 12 categories: Business, Computing, Education, Entertainment, Investing, Magazines, News, Reference, Shopping, Sports, Travel, and Weather.

Searching on the term Mormon* generated exactly 0 hits, but the engine did manage to return links to several related sites.

Starting Point's searches require jumping through a lot of hoops. It does have some redeeming features, though: overall ease of use, and an ability to customize. For that it moves up from an **F** to a mere **D**. Get started at *<http://www. stpt.com>*.

WebCrawler

WebCrawler (see figure 4.16) features a comprehensive index of the World Wide Web. The primary user interface supports Boolean search operators. Searches can be aided by selecting one of the 18 categories listed. A help section offers detailed instructions for conducting advanced searches. Click Special to find the Top 100 list and other items of interest.

A search on the term Mormon* returned 1,602 easy-to-read links. However, many of the listings seemed to be dated; the sites no longer exist. In spite of that,

FIG. 4.15

Starting Point: Offers a simple-to-use, no-nonsense approach to search the Web.

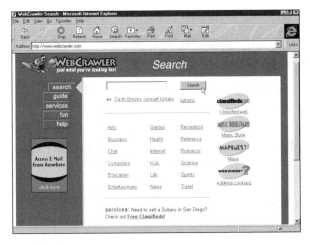

FIG. 4.16

WebCrawler: Flexibility to search from the simple to the complex.

we still rate WebCrawler a **B+** for its ease of use. Crawl over to the site at *<http://www.webcrawler.com>*.

WorldPages

Missing your old mission haunts? WorldPages might be worth a look. It's an online business telephone and fax directory that claims to provide access to numbers in more than 100 countries. At the time of writing, Hong Kong companies were listed, but Europe appeared to be on hold. For that reason, we'll rate this site a **C**. You'll find it at *<http://www.worldpages.com>*.

Yahoo

Yahoo (see figure 4.17) is an indexed search engine, capable of comprehensive searches. Yahoo prioritizes matches and returns the highest-rated 100 matches.

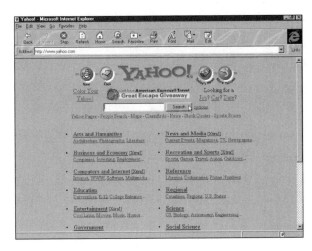

FIG. 4.17

Yahoo: The Religion category is waaaay down there at the end.

Searches can be better focused by choosing from e-mail listings, Usenet groups, or the seemingly endless hierarchy of categories and subcategories. Yahoo offers links to Religion, Genealogy, and other helpful categories. Searches can be as simple or as complicated as you choose.

A search on Mormon* generated only 126 hits, an unhealthy number of which are mean-spirited in nature.

The editorial decisions that go into adding a site to Yahoo make it a tremendously out-of-date, and biased, collection of sites. Add to that the fact that it fails to index the content of the pages it lists, and Yahoo is an all-around non-starter. The hierarchical structure gives it some value, though, so Yahoo rates a grudging **B-**. Do your own whooping at hollering at Yahoo's Web site, at <*http://www. yahoo.com*>.

PART TWO

THE MISSION OF THE CHURCH

5

PROCLAIM
THE GOSPEL

The Church of Jesus Christ of Latter-day Saints is a church on a mission—a three-part mission to be specific. Our task? To proclaim the gospel, to perfect the Saints, and to redeem the dead.

In this chapter, you'll find reviews, histories, and commentaries that address the first part of that mission: proclaiming the gospel. We begin with testimony—the conversion stories and spiritual experiences of Latter-day Saints throughout the world. Following that is an introduction to the Church. You'll find there information about contacting the Church, as well as background, doctrine, and an introduction to the Book of Mormon, the keystone of our religion. Finally, you'll find sections on responding to critics of the Church and doing missionary work.

TESTIMONY PAGES

As noted in the introduction to this book, I'm more than a little fond of the Internet. I perceive it as one giant week-long testimony meeting—albeit, one where there are altogether too many distractions.

Over the past two years, I have become a collector of conversion stories. The stories I was reading at various Web sites were moving—so much so that I eventually was motivated to gather them into a single place in order to share my discovery with the world.

Grant Johnson, Webmaster at the New Jerusalem site, did an even better thing, setting up a site where people could submit their conversion stories, and publishing not just links, but actual stories that would never otherwise have been available for public view.

A handful of other Latter-day Saints have built their own testimony and conversion story sites, giving Net surfers a fine selection of testimony sites worth visiting. If you do nothing else on the Internet, if you study no other LDS-oriented pages, you must at least take a look at these great sites.

Caelum Fides. A very nice collection of testimonies and conversion stories. ★★★★

<http://members.visi.net/~atom/totally/TEST_MAIN.html>

Classic True LDS. Nearly 500 stories from LDS history and personal experiences. This site fascinates. ★★★★★

<http://www.xmission.com/~dkenison/lds/ch_hist>

Donny Osmond Explains His Beliefs. Actually, a very thoughtful page. Worth a read. ★★★★

<http://www.osmond.net/donny/beliefs/home.html>

First Vision Accounts. A delightful collection of accounts of the first vision. Sheds additional light on the events of that day. Well worth reading. ★★★★★

<http://www.primenet.com/~kitsonk/mormon/firstvis.html>

New Jerusalem Testimony Stories. New Jerusalem's conversion stories from Latter-day Saints around the world (see figure 5.1). In just over a year, this site has received more than 100 conversion story submissions, all of which testify of

miracles worked in the lives of investigators, new members, and long-time members. The only site on the Web to earn this rating: ★★★★★★☑
<http://new-jerusalem.com/testimony/stories.html>

Should We Pray About the Truthfulness of the Book of Mormon? And why not? A tremendous response to those who would say no. ★★★
<http://members.visi.net/~atom/totally/Mike.html>

Subscriber Submissions. Personal experiences and essays submitted by subscribers to the popular LDS-GEMS mailing list. Organized in order of submission. ★★★★★

<http://www.xmission.com/~dkenison/lds/gems/arc_subs.html>

Testify! (See figure 5.2.) Conversion stories. Arranged by contemporary individuals, historical individuals, contemporary collections, and historical collections. It's my own page, but I'm tremendously fond of it, and give it a correspondingly high rating. ★★★★★

<http://www.jersey.net/~inkwell/testify.htm>

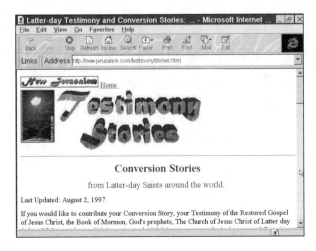

FIG. 5.1

New Jerusalem: Absolutely the best, most uplifting site on the entire Internet.

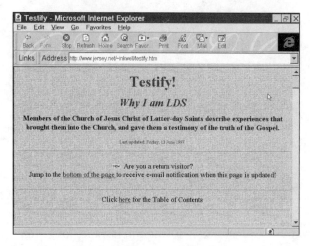

FIG. 5.2

Testify! A runner-up to New Jerusalem for its collection of conversion stories.

Testimonials. A newer collection of conversion stories. Growing. ★★★
<http://www.uvol.com/www1st/testimonies/homepage.html>

Testimonies. A collection of testimonies borne by general authorities. ★★★★
<http://www.mormons.org/testimonies>

Testimony and Knowledge. Answers to questions about the nature of testimonies. What do Latter-day Saints mean when they speak of their "testimonies"? Isn't it just based on emotion? What role does intellect play? What is the gift of the Holy Ghost? How does one "follow the Spirit"? ★★★
<http://www.athenet.net/~jlindsay/LDSFAQ/FQ_Testimony.shtml>

The Prophet Joseph Smith's Testimony. From the official Web site. First vision, visit of Moroni, testimonies of witnesses, more. ★★★★★
<http://www.lds.org/Joseph_Smith_Testimony/0-JS_Testimony_Contents.html>

INTRODUCTION TO THE CHURCH

As you make your way around the Internet, and begin telling people in various chat rooms and mailing lists about your affiliation with Mormonism, you'll often be asked questions about the Church by people who are completely unfamiliar with it. In this section, we present a collection of sites that make a good starting point for introducing the Church.

At these sites you'll find information about contacting the Church, information that includes toll-free telephone numbers, meeting house locations, and other helpful resources. The section on Background information describes the history and teachings of the Church. In the Gospel Doctrine section, you'll discover a large number of Internet sites dedicated to explaining the fundamental principles of the gospel, most of which tend to be thoroughly documented from scriptural sources. After that comes a section introducing the Book of Mormon, followed by a section on other resources for investigators.

Contacting the Church

I was raised in an unenthusiastically LDS family—one where my contact with the Church consisted primarily of Wednesday afternoon Primary, where my busy mom would occasionally drop us off so that she could run errands. But when I was young teenager, a great bishop (probably at the urging of my vastly more enthusiastic grandmother) persuaded me to participate in a temple trip that changed my life. On that temple trip, I discovered the gospel, and returned home with a profound desire to be actively involved in Church.

> **ON CONTACTING THE CHURCH**
> There is a new program in the Church pertaining to missionary work. The program is being operated by the MTC in Provo, in that any name can be submitted by phone or by Internet and missionaries will be notified in the zone the person lives and it is treated as a referral. This is going to be the most important program we have ever done on the Internet.
>
> Joe Laflin, Bradenton, Florida

The very next week, I convinced my parents to take me to Church on Sunday morning. We pulled up just as the building was emptying out. I'd gotten the time all wrong. Someone I recognized from my Primary days straightened me out. A couple of weeks later, I talked my parents into taking me back. It wasn't good. The doors were locked and the building was dark. Later I found out about a thing called Stake Conference.

A short time later, I gave it another shot. They drove me all the way back to the meeting house. The doors were locked. The building was dark. Later I found out about General Conference.

A few weeks passed. They took me back and let me off at the door. This time the building was open, full of people even, but none of them did I recognize. It was a different ward. The meeting schedule had changed.

Eventually, I figured out the system, found a regular ride to church, and got so involved that I became the one other people called to find out what was going on. It certainly would have made life easier back then if I'd have had access to these great Internet resources.

The LDS Meeting House Locator.   Whether you're planning a trip, or moving to a new location, Deseret Book's listing of meeting houses is a worthwhile resource (see figure 5.3). The most complete listings on the Internet. ★★★
<http://www.deseretbook.com/locate>

FIG. 5.3

LDS Meeting Houses: Travel anywhere, and still get to the Church on time.

Get a Free Book of Mormon. Not an official page, but the author is working hard to be a good missionary. ★★★

<http://frontpage.inet-images.com/thebishop/LDS/free_bom.htm>

Other Resources. The Internet isn't the only electronic resource for contacting the Church. For a free copy of the Book of Mormon, in the United States call 1-800-528-2225. For a free copy of the Holy Bible (King James Version), call a different number: 1-800-408-4343. *Together Forever,* a free video, explains Heavenly Father's plan of happiness. Get a free copy by calling 1-888-917-5858. *Family First,* a free video, teaches practical ways to build stronger and more loving families for real home improvement. Order a free copy from 1-800-832-2900. The main operator at Church headquarters can be reached at 1-800-453-3860. The Church may also be contacted at Public Programs, Salt Lake City, Utah, 84150 USA.

Background on the Church

For me, conversion to the gospel was the easy part. The thrill that went through me as I stood on the temple grounds early one evening, at the close of a testimony meeting, and quietly joined in singing "I Know that My Redeemer Lives"—that was the moment I knew it was all true.

The harder part was—and still is, really—learning what it meant to be a practicing Latter-day Saint. When I figured out the joke about the plastic grapes, I knew I was making progress.

Here, online, is the New and Prospective Members class I've always wanted to organize, the one where investigators find out that being Mormon means not only a change of heart, but also a change of life.

Part 3 of this text, Living a Latter-day Saint Life, is devoted to an in-depth discussion of all the facets of the Mormon experience. This section you're reading now just skims the surface, a bit like the dust on the decorative bowl of plastic grapes my gramma—and everyone else's gramma—made at homemaking meeting one afternoon in 1967. Please pass the Jello!

A Brief Introduction. Origin, organization, and doctrines of the Church. Material from teachings of the prophet and *A Marvelous Work and a Wonder.* Includes Joseph Smith and some historical facts concerning the rise of the Church, Church Organization, Common Consent, Other Church Organizations, Scripture, and Some Basic Doctorines. Good information, really unattractive page. ★★★

<http://www.primenet.com/~kitsonk/mormon/introlds.htm>

A Church for All the World. An excellent overview of the Church, its auxiliaries, history, and doctrine. The explanations are accessible by clicking on a topic of interest. ★★★

<http://www.nevada.edu/home/16/blake/www/presskit.html>

An Unofficial Introduction to The Church of Jesus Christ of Latter-day Saints. Answers to common questions about the Church. Are we Christians? Why do we call ourselves "Latter-day Saints"? Why the term "Mormons"? What is the Book of Mormon? Not bad stuff. ★★★

<http://www.athenet.net/~jlindsay/LDS_Intro.shtml>

Basic LDS Church Information. Straightforward, accurate information on the history, beliefs, practices, and organization of the Church. Membership statistics slightly outdated. A good place to point investigators. ★★★

<http://www1.trib.com/SUPPORT/RESTORATION/lds.html>

Church Organization and Priesthood Authority. Articles on the administration of the Church. Includes information on the Contemporary Church Organization, Branch, Districts, Lay Participation and Leadership, Common Consent, Following the Prophets, Priesthood Organization, Auxiliary Organizations, Relief Society, Young Women, Primary, Correlation of the Church, Administration, Church Education System (CES), Church Publications, Record Keeping, Disciplinary Procedures, Organizational and Administrative Church History, Organization of the Church in New Testament Times, and The Worldwide Church. Very thorough. A Mormons.Org page. ★★★★★

<http://www.mormons.org/basic/organization>

Daily Living. A collection of articles and links to other sites describing life as a Latter-day Saint (see figure 5.4). Includes information on Activity in the Church, Agriculture, Attitudes Toward the Arts, Attitudes Toward Health and Medicine, Attitudes Toward Business and Wealth, Callings, Church Organization

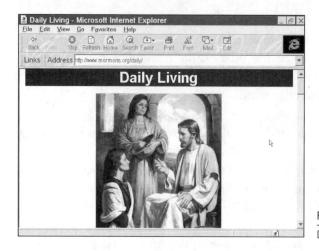

FIG. 5.4

Daily Living: What a scope!

and Priesthood Authority, Dating and Courtship, Education, Family History or Genealogy, Family Home Evening, Church History, Holidays and Celebrations, Interfaith Relationships, Teachings About Law, Lay Participation and Leadership, Meetings and Conferences, Military and the Church, Missionary Work, Parenting, Politics, Teachings About Prayer, Reverence, Sabbath Day, Teachings About Sexuality, Tithing, Welfare and Humanitarian Assistance, and the Word of Wisdom. ★★★★★

<http://www.mormons.org/daily>

Etiquette.   Describes meetings, proper attire, order of service, and other guidelines that will be of great help to new members. Separate pages for Basic Service, Baptisms, Funerals, and Marriage. ★★★★

<http://www.nettally.com/LDS/etiquette.html>

Glossary of LDS Terminology.   Comprehensive, well-presented list of terminology and jargon used in the Church. ★★★★

<http://ldschurch.net/s/danville/sr1/glossary.html>

Gospel Essentials.   Basic information on the mission of the Church, from New Jerusalem. Heavy scripture. ★★★ 🖙

<http://www.new-jerusalem.com/gospel/essentials.html>

Latter-day Saint Guidebook.   Statistics, organizational information, materials, more. ★★★

<http://www.nettally.com/LDS/guide.html>

LDS Evidences Home Page.   An interesting collection of materials providing evidence of the truth of the teachings of the Church. Not necessarily persuasive, but certainly worth reading. ★★★★

<http://www.geocities.com/Athens/Forum/5499/ldsstuff.html>

Meetings and Conferences.   Articles describing the various meetings conducted as part of LDS worship. ★★★

<http://www.mormons.org/daily/meetings>

Mormons—Are We Healthier!   References to medical research on Mormons. ★★

<http://www.nettally.com/LDS/medmor.html>

Overview.   An illustrated overview of the history, name, and organization of the Church. Top-quality information, well documented. ☞

<http://www.mormons.org/overview_eom.htm>

Questions About LDS Worship and Practices.   Well-written responses to basic questions about LDS beliefs and practices. Includes information on fasting, the Word of Wisdom, genealogy, more. ★★★★

<http://www.athenet.net/~jlindsay/LDSFAQ/FQ_practices.shtml>

The Church of Jesus Christ of Latter-day Saints.   A brief introduction to history and some doctrine. ★★

<http://www1.trib.com/SUPPORT/RESTORATION/lds.html>

The Pencil/God Dilemma.   A parable about the gospel. ★

<http://members.visi.net/~atom/totally/Pncl_god.html>

What Mormons Believe.   From Richard Hardison. Facts and figures, a bit of history. Lacks a table of contents. ★★

<http://www.nettally.com/LDS/qa.html>

Gospel Principles

Theology, anyone? Set down that glue gun. It's time now to get some real doctrine. In this section, you'll find links to material that describes fundamental Mormon doctrine, the teachings and background that everyone needs to be able to teach a class of rowdy twelve-year-olds.

Chapter 6, "Perfect the Saints," page 121, moves into more advanced material. Here, though, are all the basics for new and prospective members wanting to understand fundamental Church doctrine:

Basic Beliefs.   Good collection of information on fundamental teachings of the Church (see figure 5.5). Contains the text of articles on Articles of Faith, The Purpose of Life, The Gospel of Jesus Christ, Teachings About Jesus Christ, The Book of Mormon, The Holy Bible, Teachings About the Godhead, Teachings About the Family, Teachings About Temples, Church Organization and Priesthood Authority, Teachings About the Afterlife, Teachings About Our Premortal Existence, and Doctrines of the Gospel. Good background material. ★★★★

<http://www.mormons.org/basic>

FIG. 5.5

Basic Beliefs: Yep, that about covers it.

Does the Father Have a Tangible Body?   Edited extract from the site owner's book *One Lord, One Faith: Writings of the Early Christian Fathers As Evidences of the Restoration.* Heavy. ★★

<http://members.visi.net/~atom/totally/Tng_body.html>

Faith, Grace, and Works.   An insightful theological discourse on the LDS view of the relationship between faith and works. Includes a link to a separate page listing key scriptures for study on this topic. ★★★

<http://www.athenet.net/~jlindsay/faith_works.html>

God, the Father.   Explanation, names, titles. Written by BYU's department of Religious Education. ★★★

<http://reled.byu.edu/books/god_the_father.html>

God.   A statement on the Godhead and the nature of God from BYU's department of Religious Education. A bit thick. ★★★

<http://reled.byu.edu/books/nature_of_god.html>

Gospel Principles Course.   A description of each element of the Sunday School course for new members. ★★★

<http://www.nettally.com/LDS/gospel.html>

Holy Ghost.   An essay on the nature and role of the Holy Ghost. From the Department of Religious Education at BYU. ★★★

<http://reled.byu.edu/books/holyghost.html>

Jesus Christ.   An overview of the life, role, prophecies, ministry, death, and resurrection of Jesus Christ. From BYU's department of Religious Education. ★★★

<http://reled.byu.edu/books/jesus_christ.html>

Premortal Existence.   Accurate representation of the LDS belief in antemortality. Documented and readable. Quite brief. ★★★

<http://www.shire.net/mormon/pre.html>

Questions About Baptism.   Baptism by immersion by authorized ministers of God: nice idea or essential ordinance? The page describes why baptism is essential to salvation.★★★

<http://www.athenet.net/~jlindsay/LDSFAQ/FQ_Baptism.shtml>

Religious Education.   Some of the beliefs of The Church of Jesus Christ of Latter-day Saints, compiled by the Religious Education department at BYU. ★★★

<http://www.byu.edu/rel1/books/ldsinfo.html>

Teachings About Prayer.   A brief collection of articles on LDS beliefs about prayer. ★★

<http://www.mormons.org/daily/prayer>

Teachings About the Afterlife.   A large collection of articles related to LDS beliefs about the afterlife. Includes information on Death and Dying, The Afterlife, The Spirit World, Salvation for the Dead, Final Judgment, Judgment, Resurrection, Exaltation, The Church of the Firstborn, Degrees of Glory, Celestial Kingdom, Terrestrial Kingdom,

Telestial Kingdom, Hell, Heaven, Spirit Prison, Eternal Progression, Everlasting Burnings, Book of Life, Buffetings of Satan, and Damnation. A Mormons.Org page. ★★★★★

<http://www.mormons.org/basic/afterlife>

Teachings About the Godhead.   Articles relating to LDS beliefs about the Godhead. Includes articles on God, The Godhead, God the Father, Jesus Christ the Son of God, The Holy Ghost, Condescension of God, Godhood, and Early Christian Deification. A Mormons.Org page. ★★★★

<http://www.mormons.org/basic/godhead>

Teachings About the Premortal Existence.   Brief collection of articles on antemortality. A Mormons.Org page. ★★★

<http://www.mormons.org/basic/premortal>

The Falling Away and Restoration Foretold.   Quotations, illustrations, explanations of the apostasy and restoration. ★★★★

<http://www.xmission.com/~health/mormon/apostasy.html>

The Family: A Proclamation to the Church and the World.   Text of the 1995 official proclamation from the First Presidency. ☞

<http://www.lds.org/Policy/Family.html>

The Gospel of Jesus Christ.   A collection of some 25 topics on basic gospel-centered themes. Includes articles on The Gospel of Jesus Christ, Joining the Church, The First Principles of the Gospel, The Plan of Salvation, The Plan of Our Heavenly Father (First Missionary Discussion), The Gospel of Jesus Christ (Second Missionary Discussion), The Restoration of the Gospel of Jesus Christ,

Faith in Christ, Repentance, Baptism, Baptism of Fire and the Holy Ghost, Born of God, Conversion, Discipleship, Enduring to the End, Abrahamic Covenant, Gospel of Abraham, Latter-day Covenant Israel, Elect of God, Fall of Adam, Last Days, Dispensations of the Gospel, Fullness of the Gospel, and Missionary Work. ★★★★

<http://www.mormons.org/basic/gospel>

The Immortality & Eternal Life of Man. A discussion of the basic principles of the Gospel. ★★★
<http://www.xmission.com/~pengar/allen/book.html>

The Mormon God and the Problem of Evil. Mormonism's most important contribution to theology. ★★
<http://www.teleport.com/~arden/evilfaq.htm>

The Origin of Man. Text of a first presidency message signed by Joseph F. Smith. ☞
<http://reled.byu.edu/books/origin_of_man.html>

The Plan of Our Father in Heaven. Excellent explanation of the plan of salvation. Illustrated, documented, thorough. ★★★★★
<http://www.new-jerusalem.com/plan/plan.html>.
An equally well-done page by another writer is available at
<http://www.xmission.com/~health/mormon/plan.html>

The Word of Wisdom. The LDS Code of Health. Text of the 1833 revelation to Joseph Smith forbidding the use of tobacco, alcohol, tea, and coffee, and providing nutritional guidelines with an emphasis on grains. A bit of commentary at the end. ☞
<http://www.athenet.net/~jlindsay/WWisdom.shtml>

Welfare and Humanitarian Services. The importance of helping the needy and less fortunate. On the nature and importance of service. A description of the Church's welfare and humanitarian services program. From the Church's official Web site. ★★★★
<http://www.lds.org/Global_Media_Guide/Welfare_and_Humanitarian.html>

Word of Wisdom. Origin and history, with links to medical commentary. ★★★
<http://www.nettally.com/LDS/WofW.html>

The Role of the Book of Mormon

I admit with some chagrin that when I entered the Missionary Training Center, I still hadn't read the entire Book of Mormon. Many chapters, many sections, but never had I read it through cover to cover. The MTC cured that problem in short order.

One afternoon, while the elders were building strong bones and muscles in the MTC gym, my companion and I sat out on the front lawn reading scriptures. I wasn't but a few verses into King Benjamin's address (Mosiah 2–5) when suddenly I realized that my mind was absolutely and completely clear, and that I was being given a perfect understanding of the material I was reading. That sensation continued throughout my reading that day. I was receiving inspiration and guidance from on high, and I knew it without any doubt. That sublime, inspired sensation filled me with awe, and let me know that the Book of Mormon was precisely what Joseph Smith claimed it to be. The experience has never been forgotten, and has only rarely been repeated.

In this section you will find introductory material for the Book of Mormon, suitable for aiding the understanding of the first-time reader.

The complete Book of Mormon text is found in chapter 6, "Perfect the Saints," page 121. And responses to critics of the Book of Mormon, as well as additional study materials, are listed in chapter 11, "Pursuit of Excellence"—Personal Scripture Study, in the Book of Mormon section.

23 Questions Answered by The Book of Mormon.   Poses questions about theology and life, and lists Book of Mormon scriptural responses to those questions. Includes good links to pages on the apostasy, Christ in America, and an explanation of the Book of Mormon. ★★★★
<http://www.xmission.com/~health/mormon>

A Brief Introduction to The Book of Mormon: Another Testament of Jesus Christ. (See figure 5.6.) Jeff Lindsay's very well-documented responses to basic questions about the Book of Mormon. Answers What is the Book of Mormon? What is its purpose? Who wrote it? Who was Mormon? How did we get it? How was it translated? Who else saw the gold plates? How does the Book of Mormon relate to the Bible? Does the Bible say anything about the Book of Mormon—for or against? Who were the Book of Mormon people? What did the Book of Mormon people know of Christ? Why should I read the Book of Mormon? How can I know if it is true? Wait a minute—the Bible says there can be no more scripture! We've already got a Bible! and Other objections to the Book of Mormon. Includes a link to Evidences for the Book of Mormon. ★★★★
<http://www.athenet.net/~jlindsay/BOMIntro.shtml>

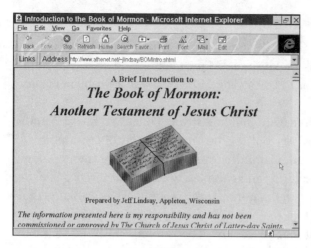

FIG. 5.6

A Brief Introduction: Responds to basic Book of Mormon questions.

Biblical References to the Book of Mormon. Scriptural references and text without commentary. ★★
<http://www.primenet.com/~kitsonk/mormon/bom.html>

Biblical References to the Book of Mormon. A somewhat better list of references, this one with brief commentary. ★★★
< http://www.xmission.com/~health/mormon/bomref.html>

My Favorite Scripture from the Book of Mormon. A discourse on poverty from Alma 32. ★★
<http://www.nettally.com/LDS/favpray.html>

Take the Book of Mormon Challenge. Outlines the conditions under which the Prophet translated the Book of Mormon. ★★
<http://www.primenet.com/~kitsonk/mormon/challang.html>

The Book of Mormon: A Witness of Jesus Christ. A graph of Book of Mormon references to Christ. ★★
<http://www.primenet.com/~kitsonk/mormon/witchris.htm>

The Book of Mormon: An Overview. Chapter-by-chapter descriptions of the content of the Book of Mormon. A Mormons.Org page. ★★★★★
<http://www.mormons.org/basic/bom/overview>

The Coming Forth of the Book of Mormon. History of the work of translation. ★★★
<http://www.primenet.com/~kitsonk/mormon/comingfo.html>

The Testimonies of the Book of Mormon Witnesses. Includes biographical information. Quite thorough. ★★★★
<http://www.primenet.com/~kitsonk/mormon/witness.html>

Items of Interest to Investigators and New Members

Here it is, the inevitable miscellaneous section, a list of basic information that doesn't quite belong anywhere else. You'll find here answers to questions, information lists, and a few other items worth a look.

All About Mormons. (See figure 5.7.) John Walsh's very large site containing texts on virtually anything anyone has ever wanted to know about Mormonism. It's, ahem, encyclopedic in its coverage. In fact, it makes extensive use of the *Encyclopedia of Mormonism* and a few other classic Mormon texts. Good information. I'd be happy to see it stay around. ★★★★★☑

<http://www.mormons.org>

Answers to Frequently Asked Questions. From All About Mormons. What does LDS stand for? Are Mormons Christian? Do Mormons Believe in the Bible? Who Was Joseph Smith? and other questions about distinctive LDS theology, the restoration, plural marriage, the role of women, LDS holidays, crosses, and more. Very thorough responses. A good reference for nonmembers who express curiosity. ★★★★

<http:// www.mormons.org/faq>

Evidences of the True Church. Contains the old legend about a group of nonmembers compiling the list of 17 points. If someone ever substantiates that story, I'll eat the list. (Note: I may have to ready my fork. As this book was going to press, a reviewer provided me with persuasive evidence that the story is true. You'll find his note posted at *Mormons on the Internet* Registry. See chapter 4, page 47 for access information.) ★★

<http://www.nettally.com/LDS/evidence.html>

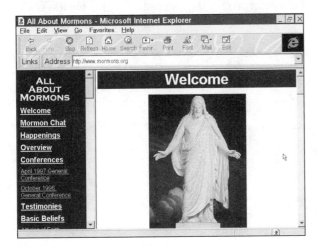

FIG. 5.7.

All About Mormons! The name doesn't mislead.

Evidences of the True Church.   Forty-three of 'em! I distrust these "True Church" lists for the same reason I distrust people who try to appropriate the word "Christian" exclusively for themselves. If I can create a list to define myself as the "True" Church, other people can just as easily create their own opposing lists using their own definitions. The *only* valid evidence of truth, as far as I'm concerned, is the witness of the Spirit. That being said, this list is the most thorough I've seen. Very well documented. ★★

<http://www.nettally.com/LDS/43.html>

Evidences of the True Church.   This time, it's just 41 Points of the True Church. List compiled by Michael T. Griffith. ★★

<http://ourworld.compuserve.com/homepages/MGriffith_2/points.htm>

Got Questions?   A brief listing of questions from visitors to the Cumorah's Hill Web site. A submission form lets visitors ask more questions about the Church. It's tremendously short, but the potential is there for growth. ★★

List of questions and answers:

<http://members.aol.com/cumorahhil/qa.htm>

Question submission form:

<http://members.aol.com/cumorahhil/got_questions.htm>

Frequently Asked Questions about Latter-day Saint Beliefs.   (See figure 5.8.) Jeff Lindsay's common questions and answers about LDS beliefs and practices. Contains links to entire pages that respond to: Are Latter-day Saints a Cult? Are Latter-day Saints Christians? Did Joseph Smith Make Any Accurate Prophecies? Is Baptism Essential? Are we Christians? Why do we call ourselves "Latter-day Saints"? Why the term "Mormons"? What is the Book of Mormon? Also, questions about the Restoration (and the Apostasy), Joseph Smith and Modern Prophets, Joseph's First Vision Accounts, Baptism for the Dead, Testi-

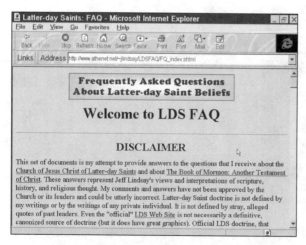

FIG. 5.8

Frequently Asked Questions: Just the FAQs about Mormonism.

mony and Knowledge, the Divine Potential of Man, Relationships Between God and Man, Salvation and Exaltation, Science Fiction, Race, LDS Temples, LDS Worship and Practices, the Book of Mormon, and the Book of Abraham. An excellent site. Many of these pages show up individually throughout this text. ★★★★★
<http://www.athenet.net/~jlindsay/LDSFAQ/ FQ_index.shtml>

New Member Discussions. The seven discussions for new members, along with commentary from a relatively new convert to the Church. ★★★
<http://www.nettally.com/LDS/lesson.html>

Points of the True Church. The old list of 17 your mother probably hung on her refrigerator. ★★
<http://www.primenet.com/~kitsonk/mormon/ points.htm>

Seventeen Evidences of the True Church. In case you've missed it elsewhere. ★★
<http://www.nettally.com/LDS/17+.html>

RESPONSES TO CRITICISM

I lived in Taiwan at the time of the open house and dedication of the temple there. Throughout those events, the members were disturbed by the presence of a handful of vocal protesters who did their disruptive best to interrupt the proceedings. At one point, I spent a bit of time talking with a couple of them. After I accepted their literature, the two became quite forthcoming about their presence. Both admitted they were absolutely unfamiliar with the Church, not even knowing, in fact, which church it was they were objecting to. They said they'd actually been through a quick indoctrination session prior to arriving in Taiwan, where they'd been assured that the Church was a cesspool of iniquity, and that they'd be doing a fine service to raise a ruckus. Their real incentive, they told me, was a free vacation to Asia.

The problem with responding to critics is that it's an unwinnable task. Even if it were possible to win all the big battles, there'd always be a critic arguing that the Book of Mormon is an obvious fraud because the name Sam is too short, and the name Coriantumr is missing a vowel. Respond to these fights, and within moments you find yourself swatting at gnats instead of sharing the gospel. Nevertheless, failing to respond implies inability to respond. So the Natural Man rises to the fore and takes on all comers.

Reponses to critics range from the scholarly and thoughtful to the reactionary and insupportable. Because many of the page authors arrange their responses as a sort of "to do" list, these pages sometimes raise more questions than they answer.

The responses listed in this section are general in nature, and apply to the whole range of LDS doctrine, history, and policy. Specific responses to critics of the Book of Mormon are listed in chapter 11, "Pursuit of Excellence," in the Personal Scripture Study section, page 241.

A Sci-Fi Connection in LDS Theology?   Good responses to a couple of actual questions relating science fiction and Church doctrine. Ooo-oooo. ★★
   <http://www.athenet.net/~jlindsay/LDSFAQ/FQ_SciFi.shtml>
Accusatory Questions.   Responses to 45 questions regularly raised by critics. A Mormons.Org page. ★★★★
   <http://www.mormons.org/response/qa>
Are Latter-day Saints a Cult?   Detailed discussion on many popular topics used to condemn the Church as a cult. ★★★
   <http://www.athenet.net/~jlindsay/LDSFAQ/FQ_cult.shtml>
Are Latter-day Saints Christians?   Another good Jeff Lindsay page. ★★★
   <http://www.athenet.net/~jlindsay/LDSFAQ/FQ_Christian.shtml>
Are Mormons Christians?   Dr. Stephen E. Robinson discusses the specious arguments used to exclude Latter-day Saints from the Christian community. Thoroughly reasoned. ★★★
   <http://199.227.118.92/response/general/christians >
Baptism for the Dead FAQ.   Very lengthy treatment of the historicity of vicarious baptism. ★★★
   <http://www.athenet.net/~jlindsay/LDSFAQ/FQ_BaptDead.shtml>

my dismay, I found myself falling into the same tactics as those I opposed, in that I was using strident denunciations rather than facts to counter the misstatements and innuendoes.

Malin and Stan have provided a vehicle in which the claims of the critics can be answered in a reasonable manner, without the hatred and acrimony present in so many of the venues available online today. They have provided me with the means of learning more of the history and beliefs of the LDS people than I had believed possible. I will always be grateful to them for the gift that they have given me . . . the gift of knowledge.

Gene Humbert, Denver/metro, Colorado
<G.Humbert@worldnet.att.net>
Webmaster, SHIELDS page
<http://www.shields-research.org>

Canon Dates. A table of dates for the canonization of New Testament texts. ★★
<http://www.primenet.com/~kitsonk/mormon/canon-dates.html>

Chattanooga Cheapshot, or The Gall of Bitterness. Review of the anti-Mormon tract "Everything You Ever Wanted to Know About Mormonism." Edges over to cynical, but probably not without cause. ☞
<http://www.farmsresearch.com/frob/frobv5/dcp.htm>

Christian and Jewish Leaders Condemn Anti-Mormonism. Christian and Jewish leaders speak out against the religious bigotry directed at Latter-day Saints. ★★★
<http://www.teleport.com/~arden/nccj.htm>

Christian-bashing. By Pat Buchanan. Ironic. ★
<http://www.nettally.com/LDS/Pat.html>

Church History Criticism. Intelligent responses to issues raised by critics of the Church and its history. Responds to *Mormonism—Shadow or Reality,* and incendiary claims related to divine Adam, occult, freemasonry, blood sacrifice, prophecies, Danites, Mountain Meadows. ★★★★
<http://www.mormons.org/response/history>

Constancy amid Change. FARMS Editor Daniel C. Peterson is nothing if not enthusiastic. He's the Captain Moroni of respondents to critics of the Church, and this review of Ankerberg and Weldon's *Behind the Mask of Mormonism* is in keeping with his generally combative approach. If you disagree with his point of view, you'll find him obnoxious. People who agree will consider him, well, delightful. ☞
<http://www.farmsresearch.com/frob/frobv8_2/dcp.htm>

DCP's Gospel Research InfoNet. Very strongly worded material, and not yet a lot of it. This site is largely under construction. ★★
<http://www.linkline.com/personal/dcpyle/gri>

Evidences for the Book of Mormon.   Responses to common questions raised about the Book of Mormon and its historicity. Includes Geography of the Arabian Peninsula, Writing on Metal Plates, Writing in Reformed Egyptian, Mulek Son of King Zedekiah, The Use of Cement in Ancient America, Chiasmus in the Book of Mormon, Olive Culture, Wars in Winter, Mesoamerican Fortifications, Numerous Hebraic Language Structures, Names in the Book of Mormon, "The Land of Jerusalem," and Volcanism in Book of Mormon Lands. ★★★★
<http://www.athenet.net/~jlindsay/BMEvidences.shtml>

FAQ Alt.Religion.Mormon.   Disturbed by the misinformation he saw being promulgated on the newsgroup alt.religion.mormon, participant John Halleck—who was not a member of the Church—put together a FAQ (frequently asked questions) document to respond to the accusations. Very accurate presentation of material. Interesting footnote: John has since joined the church. ★★★★
<http://www.cc.utah.edu/~nahaj/faq.html>

FARMS Criticism Papers.   Book reviews—or more precisely, responses to critical publications (see figure 5.9). I get a letter every couple of days from Internet users who are either investigating the Church, or bent on saving my soul from evangelical hell. In both cases, these letter writers are posing questions derived from anti-Mormon tracts. What a relief it is to have the Foundation for Ancient Research and Mormon Studies standing out there, waving its arms, so that I can direct my correspondents to a safe landing. If FARMS wrote nothing more than what it posts on this page, it would be a worthwhile institution. Each of the current items is reviewed in this text. Check back for new additions from time to time. ★★★★★☑

<http://www.farmsresearch.com/critic/reviews.htm>

Frequently Asked Questions About LDS Beliefs.   By Jeff Lindsay. A lot of thought went into these pages. Politely and thoroughly covers questions that repeatedly

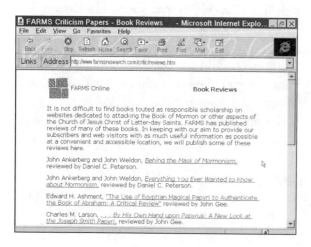

FIG. 5.9

The FARMS criticism page: Reviews of critical texts.

arise from readers of cult classics such as *The God Makers*. Covers the perennial favorites: Are Mormons Christian? Was Joseph a fallen prophet? (and related allegations), Why baptism for the dead? Do Mormons really think they will become gods? Was Satan a brother to Christ? Do Mormons worship Adam? Are LDS temples derived from Masonry? Also covers Book of Mormon questions, questions on the role of Christ in the Church, the Book of Abraham, and faith vs. works. Not to be missed. ★★★★★

<http://www.athenet.net/~jlindsay/LDSFAQ/FQ_index.shtml>

Fulfilled Prophecies of Joseph Smith. Describes prophecies made by Joseph Smith, and their fulfillment. Several examples covering a variety of topics. Ultimately, it's proof of nothing, but if the question even arises, here it is. ★★

<http://www.athenet.net/~jlindsay/LDSFAQ/FQ_prophecies.shtml>

General Criticism. Articles addressing Anti-Mormon Publications, Are Mormons Christians, Are Prophets Infallible, Dealing With Difficult Questions, Anti-Mormon Tactics, Apostates, Blacks and the Priesthood, The Godmakers, A Better House, the RLDS Church, and Mormon Fundamentalists. A Mormons.Org page. ★★★

<http://www.mormons.org/response/general>

Ignoratio Elenchi. The Dialogue That Never Was. A review of White's *Letters to a Mormon Elder*, by L. Ara Norwood, who says "Crafting only his own letters, he controls the content and thereby easily escapes the cross-examinations which would surely be forthcoming from a true dialogue." ☞

<http://www.farmsresearch.com/frob/frobv5/norwood.htm>

Joseph's First Vision Accounts. Responses to questions about varying accounts of the First Vision. Responds to inquiries about timing, contradictions, historical errors, multiple accounts. ★★★

<http://www.athenet.net/~jlindsay/LDSFAQ/FQ_first_vision.shtml>

LDS Critics. A commentary on the nature and motivation of criticism. ★★

<http://www.nettally.com/LDS/allcritics.html>

LDS Teachings on the Divine Potential of Human Beings. Discussion of the ancient Christian concept of "theosis" and its presence in LDS theology. Author Jeff Lindsay answers questions about whether Mormons think they will become gods, whether LDS doctrine teaches that there are multiple gods, the LDS doctrine of deification, early Christian beliefs about the divine potential of humans, and whether LDS people believe God once was a man. ★★★

<http://www.athenet.net/~jlindsay/LDSFAQ/FQ_theosis.shtml>

MASH. Author Mike Ash responds to attacks on the doctrines/beliefs/prophets of the LDS Church. Lots of questions, few answers. What's there is worth reading. ★★

<http://www.xmission.com/~mash/noframe.html#criticism studies>

Mormons and Militias? Jeff Lindsay's response to misinformation linking the Church to militia groups. ★★★

<http://www.athenet.net/~jlindsay/militias.shtml>

No Man Shall Add to or Take Away. Text of a discussion by Howard W. Hunter (President of the Church) on the assertion that the Bible says there will be no additional scripture. Lawyerly. ☞

<http://members.aol.com/ssh81675/ldsrefer/documents/hunter.htm>

Prophets in Latter-day Saint Religion. Answers to common questions about prophets and about Joseph Smith in particular. Responds to questions about what prophets are, the "heresy" of modern prophets, infallibility, imperfections, the role of the prophet, continuing revelation and changes, the character of Joseph Smith, document forgeries, others. Very well done. ★★★

<http://www.athenet.net/~jlindsay/LDSFAQ/FQ_prophets.shtml>

Quest for Eternity. Author Allen Leigh spent several years in online discussions with nonmembers of the Church. In response to the questions of critics, Brother Leigh conducted a great deal of research. Many of his responses to those critics have been compiled into an electronic document that explains the basic teachings of the Church and answers many of the criticisms of Mormonism. Commentary is fairly well documented, and thoroughly scriptural, without being argumentative. ★★★★

<http://www.shire.net/mormon/book.html>

Questions About LDS Views on Salvation and Exaltation. Responses to questions about grace and works, the status of nonmembers, and the potential for godhood. ★★

<http://www.athenet.net/~jlindsay/LDSFAQ/FQ_Salvation.shtml>

Questions About Relationships Between God and Man. Jeff Lindsay responds to questioners who ask if Jesus is our elder brother, and whether we believe that Christ and Satan are brothers, that God was once a man who had a heavenly father, that God the Father and Christ are different beings, that Christ "progressed," and that Mormons believe they can become like God. Answers questions about polytheism, whether Joseph Smith ever said that he was greater than Jesus, an anthropomorphic God, worshipping Adam, and denying the miraculous birth of Christ. ★★★★

<http://www.athenet.net/~jlindsay/LDSFAQ/FQ_Relationships.shtml>

Questions About the Book of Abraham. An LDS FAQ from Jeff Lindsay. Very extensive response to questions about the Book of Abraham, its source, its content, and the Prophet's comments about the facsimiles. Massive. Covers a multitude of questions. ★★★★★

<http://www.athenet.net/~jlindsay/LDSFAQ/FQ_Abraham.shtml> and part 2 at *<http://www.athenet.net/~jlindsay/LDSFAQ/FQ_Abraham2.shtml>*

Response to Criticism. A discussion about criticism, and links to pages of response to critics of the Church and its doctrine. Includes responses to Accusatory Questions, General Criticism, Book of Mormon Criticism, Church History Criticism, and Book of Abraham Criticism. Very thorough. ★★★★★ <http://www.mormons.org/response>

Response to the Mormon Critics. Russell Anderson's very well done responses to polemical attacks on the Church (see figure 5.10). He writes: "This site is not provided to answer the critics. They don't believe there is an answer. This information is for those who have faith in the Gospel of Jesus Christ but don't know how to answer some of the critic's questions."

The site includes responses to Decker's insufferable *God Makers,* as well as his *To Moroni with Love* and *Complete Handbook on Mormonism;* the Tanners' *Mormonism: Shadow or Reality;* Martin's *Maze of Mormonism;* Brodie's *No Man Knows My History;* Marquart and Walters' *Inventing Mormonism;* and Bodine's CRI Paper "Book of Mormon vs. the Bible (or common sense)."

It also includes a comparison of early Christianity and Mormonism, and addresses frequently repeated allegations regarding Joseph Smith, the First Vision, the Book of Mormon, the Book of Abraham, Changes to Scriptures or history, Temples, and Brigham Young. The Internet is a better place for this site. ★★★★★

<http://www.digitalpla.net/~russ/response.htm>

Review: *Ask Your Mormon Friend.* LeIsle Jacobson reviews McKeever Johnson's *Questions to Ask Your Mormon Friend: Effective Ways to Challenge a Mormon's Arguments Without Being Offensive.* Is it any surprise that the reviewer finds the text both ineffective *and* offensive? ☞

<http://www.farmsresearch.com/frob/frobv7_1/lij.htm>

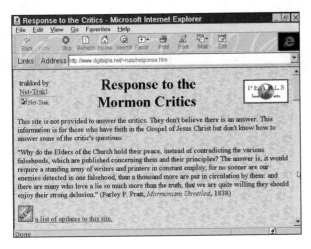

FIG. 5.10

Response to the Mormon Critics: Help for the faithful.

Scholarly and Historical Information Exchange for Latter-day Saints (SHIELDS). A site for responses to issues raised by critics of The Church of Jesus Christ of Latter-day Saints. I had much hope for this site, but there's just not enough content yet to make it worthwhile. The gem here is in a buried page responding to an organization called CARM. For those responses alone, this page gets a rating of ★★★★.

Main page: <*http://www.shields-research.org*>

CARM responses: <*http://www.shields-research.org/CARM.htm*>

Stumpus Team of Missionaries. Take the challenge. ★★★★

<*http://www.new-jerusalem.com/stumpus/questions.html*>

The Book of Mormon Answerman. (See figure 5.11.) Intelligent responses to questions about the Book of Mormon. The submission form at this site allows you to ask questions of your own. The Book of Mormon Answerman has responded to some 1,000 questions. The Book of Mormon Answerman is a fun read; what it lacks in authority, it makes up for in enthusiasm. ★★★★

<*http://www.new-jerusalem.com/bom-answerman*>

The Chapman LDS Resource. A collection of 30-some research papers responding to questions raised by critics, as well as other topics from all over the map. Some of the documents are excellent. ★★

<*http://www.2s2.com/chapmanresearch/side1.html*>

The Gainsayers. Darrick T. Evenson was converted, then apostatized and became affiliated with the anti-Mormon group Ex-Mormons for Jesus. This page documents his eventual return to the fold of Christ. In it, he describes the techniques used by dishonest critics to discredit the Church. ✍

<*http://199.227.118.92/response/general/gainsayers*>

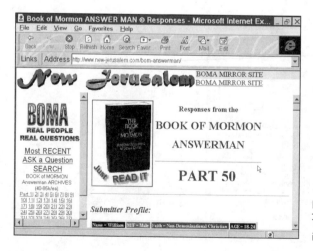

FIG. 5.11

The Book of Mormon Answerman: Bite into it.

Triptych.   Daniel C. Peterson's 1996 Editor's Introduction wherein he describes the anti-Mormon technique of creating, then destroying, straw man arguments. FARMS needs to build a front page for all these sites. ☞ *<http://www.farmsresearch.com/frob/frobv8_1/intro.htm>* See more of Peterson's Editor's Introductions on related themes:

An Embarras de Richesses *<http://www.farmsresearch.com/frob/frobv3/intro. htm>*; By What Measure Shall We Mete? *<http://www.farmsresearch.com/frob/ frobv2/intro.htm>*; Doubting the Doubters *<http://www.farmsresearch.com/ frob/frobv8_2/intro.htm>*; History of the Signature/FARMS Conflict *<http:// www.farmsresearch.com/frob/frobv6_1/intro.htm>*; Human Fallibility *<http:// www.farmsresearch.com/frob/frobv7_2/intro.htm>*; Of Implications *<http://www. farmsresearch.com/frob/frobv7_1/intro.htm>*; Of Paying Attention to the Book of Mormon *<http://www.farmsresearch.com/frob/frobv1/intro.htm>*; Of Polemics *<http://www.farmsresearch.com/frob/frobv6_2/intro.htm>*; Questions to Legal Answers *<http://www.farmsresearch.com/frob/frobv4/intro.htm>*; Traditions of the Fathers *<http://www.farmsresearch.com/frob/frobv9_1/intro.htm>*

You Never Know Who's Watching You.   Writer Teresa Holladay describes her experience in public LDS discussion forums. "It was a jungle! It wasn't hard to see, from the knowledge base, who were the Mormons and who were the non-Mormons, but it *was* hard to distinguish, from the tone, who was on the Lord's side. *Everyone* seemed intent on drawing blood." ★★★ *<http://members.aol.com/itstessie/sngl/aol.htm>*

MISSIONARY PAGES

My high school class reunion takes place this year. What is it, I wonder, that compels people to reunite with faintly-remembered faces they've not seen for more than half a lifetime?

It's not an idle question. I've already bought the plane tickets, and I intend to be there, husband and five of the children in tow. Why am I going?

Part of it is curiosity. So many years spent so far from "home" mean that I've missed seeing what my former classmates have done with their lives. Some of us have kept in touch via e-mail, but we haven't really spent any time together. What, I wonder, do the people who grew up around me look like, work like, live like after twenty years?

Another part is a sociology experiment. I want to know how many high-school romances turned into long-term marriages. Did popularity serve the cheerleaders well in real life? Did the athletes grow up healthier than the chess players? Did the science clubbers end up wealthier than the rod-and-gun clubbers?

AN ONLINE BAPTISM

One of my first electronic missionary experiences involved Beth.

Beth was one of the members of the Hatrack River area on America Online. Her screen name (the name she used online) was "Dorcas Bee." One night, when we were both online together, I asked Beth if her screen name referred to the Dorcas in the Bible. This led to a religious discussion, where Beth told me she was quite interested in finding out what Mormons believed. I told her that I would be glad to answer any questions or let her know more about my religion.

After that, Beth and I exchanged electronic mail on a regular basis.

One day I asked if Beth would be interested in reading the Book of Mormon. After receiving an affirmative reply, I mailed a copy to her and waited for her reaction.

I did not receive any e-mail from Beth for over a week after she received the book. Needless to say, this was a cause for concern. I wondered if she was offended by something she had read, or if her minister had persuaded her not to read it. There is always a risk in sharing the gospel with others. I hoped that Beth hadn't decided to break off our electronic friendship.

When Beth finally renewed our discussion, she sent good news. She had been staying away from the computer because she was reading the Book of Mormon. After the excitement of our discussions, she had been worried that she would find something in the book that was too strange for her to accept. Yet she had found no such doctrine.

About this time my husband became involved in the correspondence with Beth, and we both exchanged e-mail with her on a regular basis to answer her questions and encourage her gospel study. We

For me, though, the biggest motivation may be my need to be the missionary I never was in high school. I grew up in the wilds of the "mission field," not among nonbelievers, but among people who believed differently, and much more publicly, than I did. It was a place where my loudly religious classmates reminded me of nothing so much as the exuberant 1820s revivalists portrayed in *The First Vision*. The Prophet's young confusion there was in proportion to my own teenage awkwardness in the face of my vehemently non-LDS classmates. Their evangelical zeal, their oft-proffered "Praise The Lord" buttons, and their invitations to youth rallies and prayer meetings came to me at every turn.

At one point in my junior year, as I sat in study hall memorizing verses for an upcoming seminary class, an otherwise good friend noticed my reading and began plying me with evangelical tracts she'd collected from her minister. I protested to her their exclusionary definition of "Christian," written not to include all who worship Christ, but to exclude all who come to Him as Latter-day Saints do. I described to her the vast gulf between what the pamphlets proclaimed about LDS belief and what Mormons really believe. My arguments served only to create divisiveness—as arguments always do—so I quietly withdrew from the debate.

suggested that it was time for her to search out her local ward and attend services there. She looked in the phone book, called the bishop of her ward in Grand Rapids, Michigan, and obtained the meeting times and directions to the chapel.

It is an unsettling experience to send someone off on her own to attend her first LDS service. Would she have a good experience? Would she be ignored or welcomed? Would she enjoy the meetings? We glued ourselves to our computers on that first Sunday, waiting for any word from Beth. Fortunately, the Saints in Grand Rapids came through with flying colors. Beth was immediately met by the full-time missionaries, as well as several members of the ward who were serving as greeters that day. One greeter had formerly attended the same church Beth was then attending, and he took Beth under his wing.

Just a few months after our chance meeting in an electronic chat room, Beth took all the missionary lessons and accepted the challenge to be baptized. She wrote us a lovely e-mail that same evening, and I think we felt the spirit of the experience through her words. My husband and I found it ironic that we shared great joy with a good friend that day—yet we had never seen her face, had never heard her voice, and had never been in the same room with her.

After Beth's baptism, we continued our communication and friendship. Her husband Jeff fully supported Beth's decision to be baptized, and finally became a member of the church in April of 1996.

Kathryn H. Kidd <custodian@nauvoo.com>,
Moderator, Nauvoo <http://www.nauvoo.com>,
as told to Clark L. Kidd, Algonkian Ward, Warrenton Virginia Stake

Hers was one of several offensives being made on Latter-day Saints by members of our community at the time. Being then relatively unacquainted with theology and religious history and various points of doctrine, I became rather reticent about publicizing my own religious beliefs. I wish I could say that I finally took courage, stood up in a school assembly and proclaimed my faith. I have to admit, though, that when I graduated, there were probably no more than a dozen people in my entire school who knew I was a Latter-day Saint.

I take no pride in this past, especially when I compare my behavior to the courage shown by another teenager, Priscilla Mogridge Staines,[1] who joined the Church in England in the 1840s—coincidentally at about the same time and place

[1]The Priscilla Mogridge Staines story appeared in 1877 in Edward Tullidge's book *The Women of Mormondom*, reprinted by Truth in the 1970s. Both editions are difficult to find. To obtain a copy, call Benchmark Books (800-486-3112) or Sam Wellers Zion Bookstore (800-333-7269), and ask to be put on the waiting list. Sam Wellers can be contacted via e-mail at <wellers@xmission.com>. Readers with an interest in old LDS books will want to participate in the LDS-Bookshelf mailing list. (See chapter 11 for more on LDS-Bookshelf.)

as my earliest LDS ancestors joined the Church. Priscilla had become dissatisfied with the Anglicanism she'd been raised with, and prayed earnestly to be shown "the true religion." At the age of nineteen she heard the restored gospel preached and was converted. Over the objections of her family, she resolved to be baptized. She said of that experience:

It is proper to here state that baptism was a trial to the converts in England in those days. They had to steal away, even unknown to their friends oftentimes, and scarcely daring to tell the saints themselves that they were about to take up the cross; and not until the ordinance had been administered, and the Holy Ghost gave them boldness, could they bring themselves to proclaim openly that they had cast in their lot with the despised Mormons. Nor was this all, for generally the elders had to administer baptism when the village was wrapt in sleep, lest persecutors should gather a mob to disturb the solemn scene with gibes or curses, accompanied with stones or clods of earth torn from the river bank and hurled at the disciple and minister during the performance of the ceremony.

On the evening of a bitterly cold day in mid-winter, as before stated, I walked four miles to the house of a local elder for baptism. Arriving at his house, we waited until midnight, in order that the neighbors might not disturb us, and then repaired to a stream of water a quarter of a mile away. Here we found the water, as we antici-pated, frozen over, and the elder had to chop a hole in the ice large enough for the purpose of baptism. It was a scene and an occasion I shall never forget. Memory today brings back the emotions and sweet awe of that moment. None but God and his angels, and the few witnesses who stood on the bank with us, heard my covenant; but in the solemnity of that midnight hour it seemed as though all nature were lis-tening, and the recording angel writing our words in the book of the Lord. Is it strange that such a scene, occurring in the life of a Latter-day Saint, should make an everlasting impression, as this did on mine?

Having been thus baptized, I returned to the house in my wet and freezing garments.[2]

Priscilla's family was unhappy over her decision to be baptized, and she was forced to leave them. She prepared to "gather to Zion," leaving England on De-cember 27, 1843. She recorded:

[2]The above excerpt from *The Women of Mormondom* was distributed by David Kenison via LDS-Gems mailing list. LDS-Gems distributes stories from LDS Church history to subscribers by e-mail. Subscriptions are free. You'll find subscription information at <*http://www.xmission.com/~dkenison/lds/gems*>

I was alone. It was a dreary winter day on which I went to Liverpool. The company with which I was to sail were all strangers to me. When I arrived at Liverpool and saw the ocean that would soon roll between me and all I loved, my heart almost failed me. But I had laid my idols all upon the altar. There was no turning back. I remembered the words of the Saviour: 'He that leaveth not father and mother, brother and sister, for my sake, is not worthy of me,' and I believed his promise to those who forsook all for his sake; so I thus alone set out for the reward of everlasting life, trusting in God.

Priscilla married William C. Staines and emigrated to Utah. I, on the other hand, spent a short time at a local college, then packed my bags and went away to BYU, and from there to many other places. And through all the years I've wondered: If I'd been a stronger, more courageous Latter-day Saint in high school—if I'd had the courage of my ancestors, and of people like Priscilla Mogridge Staines—would I have given others the strength to listen to the missionaries when they came, to hear the messages of the gospel, and to find the same joy in serving the Lord that I've had?

Perhaps nothing would have changed. Perhaps I even did the right thing by refusing to enter the fray. But I'll always wonder. And my class reunion will be spent finding out not how people changed after our little high school community disbanded, but how they chose to live.

Allegory of Zenos. Parable of the spreading of the gospel. ★★
<http://www.nettally.com/LDS/olive.html>

Cartoons. Cartoon excerpts from the journal of a returned missionary. ★★★
<http://members.aol.com/pgrundbergcartoon.html>

LDS Mission Resources. A collection of inspirational material for new and prospective missionaries. ★★★
<http://www.xmission.com/~ryanh/missn/index.html>

ON A MEETING PLACE FOR
RETURNED MISSIONARIES

At the start-up of *mission.net* there was a lot of excitement. We were all glad to finally have a common domain where returned missionaries could come and get info on how to locate their mission alumni page. People started to volunteer for all kinds of things. One person decided to make a log of all the messages that had helped get the ball rolling. Another person offered a place to host the domain. Troy Young, who lives in Tucson, Arizona, beat me to the punch and offered to design the Web site. I did a version with frames.

Since that time we have tried to get funding to purchase our own server, rather than just use disk space on another computer. This would allow each mission page maintainer, if they chose, to have a personal account on the *mission.net* server.

Now that we have all of this set up (it took over a year to get the hardware), my next goal is to start writing some simple cgi scripts that will make the main page a little more appealing and interactive. For example, I want to add a random script that will display a "mission of the day" link.

Rob Draughon, Tempe, Arizona
<rob@southwestweb.com>
Maintainer: Mission.net and
Toronto East Mission
<http://southwestWeb.com/mission>

Maps of LDS Missions.   A graphical world map showing the locations of missions and areas. Pretty cool. ★★★

<http://www.vtourist.com/missions>

Mission Alumni Pages.   One of the easier-to-use indices. Click on the mission of your choice. Some 250 missions are represented. ★★★★

<http://www.columbia.edu/~ylee/all-missions.html>

Also try these pages, with similar content: The List of Unofficial Mission Homepages <http://www.sas.upenn.edu/~dbowie/missionpage.html>; Missions <http://www.deseretbook.com/ldsinfo/missions.html>; Missions <http://www.ldschurch.net/lds/missions.html>

Mission Central.   A collection of Mormon Missionary folklore. Urban legends, a few first-person stories, lots of pranks, funny stories, and more. Hysterical. ★★★★

<http://ezinfo.ucs.indiana.edu/~dostlund/mission.htm>

Mission Funnies.   Funny stuff. Great photos. Seeking mail. (Remember that feeling?) ★★★★ <http://www.ysite.com/mission/funnies.htm>

Mission.Net.   Find your mission on the Internet (see figure 5.12). The Mission. Net site lists mission home pages, information about many countries, and help for new missionaries. ★★★★★☑

<http://mission.net>

Missionary Moms.   Space for Missionary Moms to share ideas for sustaining their missionaries while in the field. Delightful. ★★★★

<http://users.ccnet.com/~larson/lds_missionary_mom.html>

Missionary Work.   A collection of articles on topics related to missionary work, mission prep, the MTC, more. ★★★

<http://www.mormons.org/daily/missionary>

FIG. 5.12

Mission.Net: The meeting place for prospective and return missionaries.

Missionary World.   Part of the "Y" site at BYU. Includes links to missionary pages, scriptures, stories, shopping, more. ★★★★
<http://www.ysite.com/mission>

Proclaim the Gospel.   Ward mission projects, mission preparation, other links of interest to member missionaries and full-time missionaries. ★★
<http://www.uvol.com/www1st/proclaim/homepage.html>

Six Discussions.   An expanded summary of new member discussions. The commentary is enlightening. ★★★
<http://www.nettally.com/LDS/diss.html>

Six Lessons.   A brief summary of the formal missionary discussions. ★★
<http://www.nettally.com/LDS/lesson.html>

6

PERFECT THE SAINTS

The second—and probably the most significant—aspect of the Church's threefold mission is perfecting the Saints. And because the Church *is* its members, that means members need to work together to perfect themselves.

It seems an overwhelming task—learning to follow the Savior, to heed the counsel of prophets and apostles, to serve other people, and at the same time build an eternal family, study the scriptures, and continually increase in knowledge and wisdom.

Fortunately, because there's a community of Latter-day Saints out there prepared to help, nobody's on his or her own. So after prayer, after contemplation, after making wise use of all the usual resources available through the associations in your family and your ward, consider turning to the electronic library that is the Internet for further inspiration. The Internet sites listed in this chapter focus on following Christ, seeking inspiration, finding service opportunities, building families, studying the scriptures, and obtaining an education.

COME FOLLOW ME

I have a lot of favorite Primary songs. Very near the top of my personal Mormon Primary Hit Parade, though, is "I'm Trying to Be Like Jesus." It runs through my mind as I drag myself out of bed on Sundays at 5 A.M. I hear the refrain as I drive through the rain to go visiting teaching. It's the song I sing in my head whenever I'm tempted to tie a couple of my contentious children to the roof of the station wagon.

Like every Latter-day Saint, I really am trying to be like Jesus. And so I was startled the other day to realize, for the first time, that the person I'm trying to emulate was several years younger than I am now when He *finished* His mortal mission.

And then it occurred to me that it's now too late even to be like the Prophet Joseph. He'd already done more by the age of twenty than I will be able to accomplish in twice that time. Somehow, I thought I still had some time to get my life straightened out. Guess I'd better move a little faster.

The Life and Mission of Jesus Christ

Knowing the Savior is the foundation of becoming like Him.

Here you'll find a selection of Web sites that describe the life and the mission of Jesus Christ.

A Physician Testifies About the Crucifixion. A doctor's insights on the Crucifixion of Jesus Christ. Valuable medical insight into what was happening to Christ on the cross. ★★
<http://www.konnections.com/kcundick/crucifix.html>

Developing Faith in Christ. Text of an address delivered by Merrill J. Bateman to all Stake Presidents in the Utah North Area. Describes steps in the process of developing faith. ☞
<http://www.vii.com/~nicksl/bateman.html>

How Well Do You Know the Saviour? A parable. ★★
<http://www.konnections.com/kcundick/knowing.html>

Jesus Christ. An overview of the life, role, prophecies, ministry, death, and resurrection of Jesus Christ. From BYU's department of Religious Education. ★★★
<http://reled.byu.edu/books/jesus_christ.html>

PRESIDENT HAROLD B. LEE, QUOTING A BISHOP ON FOLLOWING CHRIST

In response to the Master, "Come . . . follow me," some members almost, but not quite, say, "thou persuadest me almost to be honest but I need extra help to pass a test."

Almost thou persuadest me to keep the Sabbath day holy, but it's fun to play ball on Sunday.

Almost thou persuadest me to love my neighbor, but he is a rascal; to be tolerant of others' views, but they are dead wrong; to be kind to sister, but she hit me first; to go home teaching, but it's too cold and damp outside tonight; to pay tithes and offerings, but we do need a new color TV set; to find the owner of a lost watch, but no one returned the watch I lost; to pass the sacrament, but I've graduated from the deacons now; almost thou persuadest me to be reverent, but I had to tell my pal about my date last night; almost thou persuadest me to attend stake leadership meeting, but I know more than the leader on that subject, so why should I go? Thou persuadest me almost to go to sacrament meeting, but there is going to be such an uninteresting speaker tonight. Almost! Almost! Almost! but not quite, not able quite to reach.

Harold B. Lee, *Stand Ye in Holy Places*, p. 291.

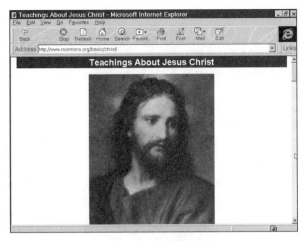

FIG. 6.1

Teachings About Jesus Christ: A vast assortment of authoritative material.

Pictorial Mission of Jesus Christ. The picture and scripture of the day. ★★★★★
<http://www.new-jerusalem.com/jesus/jesus.html>

Teachings About Jesus Christ. A collection of some thirty Christ-centered topics (see figure 6.1). Includes articles on Jesus Christ Our Redeemer, An Apostle's Testimony of Jesus Christ, Come Unto Christ, Christians in Belief and Action, Teachings About Christ, Atonement of Jesus Christ, Head of the Church, Faith in Christ, Testimony of Jesus Christ, An Overview of the LDS View of Jesus Christ, Christology, Jehovah, Prophesies About Jesus Christ, Firstborn in the Spirit, Only Begotten Son of God, Birth of Jesus Christ, Baptism of Jesus Christ, Ministry of Jesus Christ, Crucifixion of Jesus Christ, Resurrection of Jesus Christ, The Forty Day Ministry of Jesus Christ, Appearances of Jesus Christ, Second Coming of Jesus Christ, Fatherhood and Sonship of Jesus Christ, Taking the Name of Jesus Christ Upon Oneself, Names and Titles of Jesus Christ, Types and Shadows of Jesus Christ, Second Comforter, and Sources for Words of Jesus Christ. Most of the material comes from doctrinal sources, and in particular, the Encyclopedia of Mormonism. ★★★★
<http://www.mormons.org/basic/christ>

"And while we meditated upon these things, the Lord touched the eyes of our understandings and they were opened, and the glory of the Lord shone round about. And we beheld the glory of the Son, on the right hand of the Father, and received of his fulness; And saw the holy angels, and them who are sanctified before his throne, worshipping God, and the Lamb, who worship him forever and ever.

"And now, after the many testimonies which have been given of him, this is the testimony, last of all which we give of him: That he lives!

"For we saw him, even on the right hand of God; and we heard the voice bearing record that he is the Only Begotten of the Father—That by him, and through him, and of him, the worlds are and were created, and the inhabitants thereof are begotten sons and daughters unto God."

D&C 76:19–24

The Atonement of Jesus Christ.   A collection of authoritative articles on the subject of the atonement. ★★★

<http://www.mormons.org/basic/christ/atonement>

The Atonement.   Stake conference address on the reality of the atonement of Jesus Christ and its meaning to us. ★★

<http://Webpages.marshall.edu/~brown/atonemnt.htm>

The Book of Mormon: A Witness of Jesus Christ.   A graph of Book of Mormon references to Christ. ★★

<http://www.primenet.com/~kitsonk/mormon/witchris.htm>

The Resurrection of Jesus Christ.   Articles relating to LDS teachings about the resurrection. ★★★

<http://www.mormons.org/basic/christ/resurrection>

The Second Coming of Jesus Christ.   Very small collection of articles on the second coming. ★★

<http://www.mormons.org/basic/christ/second>

Prophets and General Authorities

In this section you'll find a great deal of information about past presidents of the Church, along with biographical information about the prophet, apostles, and other general authorities of the Church.

A Chronology of the Development of Apostolic Succession of the First Presidency.   A well-documented chronology of the development of the apostolic succession from 1831 to 1848. ★★★

<http://Webpages.marshall.edu/~brown/suc-pres.html>

Faust, President James E.   Biographical information about President Faust, Second Counselor in the First Presidency of the Church. ★★

<http://www.byu.edu/rel1/pres/faust.html>

Following the Prophets.   A short collection of articles on prophets and prophetic infallibility. A Mormons.Org page. ★★★★

<http://www.mormons.org/basic/organization/priesthood/prophets>

Gems from the Teachings of the Prophets.   Collection of quotations, arranged by subject. Includes a useful search tool. ★★★★

<http://www.xmission.com/~dkenison/lds/gtp>

General Authorities of the Church.   Scanned-in photo chart from, apparently, the *Ensign.* ★

<http://members.aol.com/cumorahhil/ga/general_authorities.htm>

General Authorities of The Church of Jesus Christ of Latter-day Saints. Pictures, biographies. A slow-loading page, and a bit out of date; it is, nevertheless, a valuable resource (see figure 6.2). Click on any picture to find out more information about that general authority. ★★★

<http://reled.byu.edu/pres/genauth/genauth.htm>

General Authorities of the Church. Statistical information about ages and dates various people have served in various leadership positions (see figure 6.2). Fun. ★★★

<http://www.xmission.com/~dkenison/lds/genauth.html>

General Authorities. Information on the general authorities of the Church. ★★★

<http://www.zarahemla.com/ga.html>

Hinckley, President Gordon B. Background information. ★★

<http://www.zarahemla.com/hinckley.html>

Hinckley, President Gordon B. Brief biographical information and photo. ★★

<http://www.byu.edu/rel1/pres/hinckley.html>

Hinckley, President Gordon B. Stories and lessons from the life of President Hinckley. ★★★

<http://www.indirect.com/www/crockett/gbhlife.html>

In Search of Joseph. Really, really cool site based on one person's search for an accurate image of the Prophet and Hyrum Smith. Must see. ★★★★★

<http://home.fuse.net/stracy>

McKay, President David O. Resources about President McKay relating to his work in education. Contains a biography, symposium links, major addresses, quotes, and a photo album of President McKay's life. Sponsored by the School of Education at BYU. ★★★★

<http://www.byu.edu/acd1/ed/coe/McKay.html>

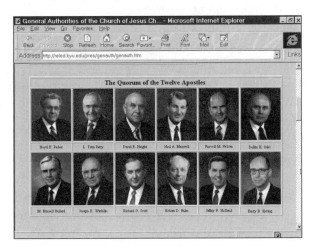

FIG. 6.2

General Authorities: Photos of all the general authorities appear online.

Monson, President Thomas S. Background on President Monson. ★★
<http://www.zarahemla.com/monson.html>

Monson, President Thomas S. Photograph and biographical information about President Monson, First Counselor in the First Presidency of the Church. ★★★
<http://www.byu.edu/rel1/pres/monson.html>

Personal Experiences with General Authorities. Very nice collection of stories submitted by readers of their personal interactions with the apostles. ★★★
<http://www.xmission.com/~dkenison/lds/gems/arc_gena.html>

Presidents of The Church of Jesus Christ of Latter-day Saints. Biographies of Church presidents, their terms in office, pictures, and biographies. From BYU's department of Religious Education. ★★★★★
<http://www.byu.edu/rel1/pres/pres.htm>

Presidents of the Church Trivia. A brief trivia quiz concerning the Presidents of the Church. Cute. ★
<http://Webpages.marshall.edu/~brown/trivia.htm>

Presidents of the Church. Biographies, statistics, illustrations/photos. Very well done. ★★★
<http://reled.byu.edu/pres>

Presidents of the LDS Church. Brief biographical information, illustrations. Just a little less useful. ★★
<http://www.primenet.com/~kitsonk/mormon/presiden.html>

Prominent Persons Associated with the Church. Biographies of about 100 prominent early and modern Latter-day Saints. ★★★
<http://www.byu.edu/rel1/people/people.html>

Teachings of Howard W. Hunter. Quotations organized by subject matter. ★★★
<http://www.indirect.com/www/crockett/hunter.html> (HTML) or
<http://www.indirect.com/www/crockett/hunter.txt> (text)

Teachings of President Gordon B. Hinckley. Quotes from a collection of over 200 talks, organized by subject. ★★★
<http://www.indirect.com/www/crockett/hinckley.html>

The Apostles Arranged by Numerical Position. A listing of Apostles by positions of seniority in the Council of the Twelve. Interesting history accompanies the photos. ★★★
<http://Webpages.marshall.edu/~brown/apostles.htm>

The Living Voice: Continuous Revelation. A chapter from the book by Michael T. Griffith. ☞
<http://members.visi.net/~atom/totally/Rev.html>

The Prophet Joseph Smith. A nice collection of articles on the history, martyrdom, and prophecies of the Prophet Joseph. A Mormons.Org page. ★★★★
<http://www.mormons.org/daily/history/people/joseph_smith>

Messages of Inspiration

I once attended a meeting at BYU where the speaker casually misquoted a scripture, and then proceeded to expound on the errant quote to prove her point.

Being young and stupid, it never occurred to me to actually look up the scripture and try to understand it for myself. Instead, I kept the popular—though inaccurate—misquote in the back of my mind, turning it over and over for—well, let's be honest here—a couple of years.

At about this time, the spring of 1985, the international press began to have a field day with a thing it called the "salamander letter," a troubling document that seemed to cast doubt on the origins of the Church. I was by then living overseas, and my only source of information was the wild exaggeration of the local eight-page English-language newspaper.

With both these difficulties weighing on my mind, late one night I found myself reading the Book of Mormon and wavering back and forth on the edge of sleep. As I was drifting, I'd struggle to read one more verse, then another, while sinking ever deeper into my pillows. As I came to the last verse, I suddenly shot bolt upright in bed, wide awake. For there it was. The answer to the question I'd been puzzling over for two years, the accurate Book of Mormon interpretation of the misquoted Biblical scripture. I'd wrestled all those months over nothing.

And then came to my mind the response to my other "struggle," the clear, ringing words: "There's an answer to everything." I was made to understand that I needed to have patience, and that sometime, somewhere, I'd find all my answers.

I resigned myself to the probability that I'd never in this lifetime understand that document called the salamander letter. Instead, I decided to simply trust in the Lord, and get on with life.

So you'll understand the depth of my interest when, a few months later, the events surrounding the Mark Hofmann document forgeries began to unfold. The discovery of Hofmann's forgeries is a complicated drama that, among other things, uncovered the fact that the so-called salamander letter was just one in a series of bogus, completely fabricated documents without any historical basis.[1]

It seems I got my answer.

It's not often that inspiration is quite so dramatic. God saves the drama for stubborn, obstinate people like me—and like the apostle Paul, whom he had to knock down in the middle of the road in order to be heard.

For better people—those who are teachable and humble—inspiration tends to be a quiet understanding, a peaceful assurance. The following sites provide a vast

---

[1]Additional information on Hofmann, and his murder/forgery scam, is available on the Internet from the Utah Collections Multimedia Encyclopedia at <*http://eddy.media.utah.edu/medsol/UCME/h/HOFMAN,MARK.html*>. The Encyclopedia home page is located at <*http://eddy.media.utah.edu/medsol/UCME*>.

store of inspirational materials—quotes, stories, counsel, and direction. Some are delivered straight to your e-mail box; others require you to do some Web browsing.

Aspiring to Greatness. Poems, quotations, and stories collected by a Latter-day Saint. Ever growing. ★★★★
<http://www.osmond.com/chill/aspiring/index.html>

Characteristics of a Good Mormon. Fourteen standards worth testing yourself against. ★★
<http://www.nettally.com/LDS/17++.html>

Classics in LDS Doctrine. Collection of quotes and excerpts on religious themes. Loosely arranged. ★★
<http://www.xmission.com/~dkenison/lds/lds_quo>

Daily Picture Scripture. A scripture a day. ★★★★
<http://www.new-jerusalem.com/jesus/daily.html>

Especially for Latter-day Saints. Gospel-centered poems and stories, as well as the words to favorite hymns and the text of talks and devotionals (see figure 6.3). ★★★
<http://www.osmond.com/chill/esp4lds>

Faith and Values. Good personal thoughts about faith by a member of the Church. ★★
<http://members.aol.com/kgrant100/faith.html>

Inspirational Stories. Collected by Darrell F. Davis. Lots of material here. ★★★
<http://www.inquo.net/~smudge/stories.html>

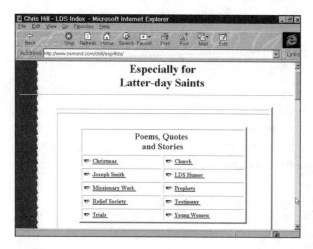

FIG. 6.3

Especially for Latter-day Saints: Stop by for the inspiration.

JOSEPH. Just Ordinary Saints Endeavoring to Promote Harmony. A mailing list for faithful members. To subscribe, send an e-mail request to *<joseph-owner@ bolis.com>*. Digest available. ★★★

<http://www.bolis.com/L/listinfo/joseph>

LDS Spiritual Thoughts Page. Uplifting stories and thoughts. A helpful site managed by David D'Antonio. ★★

<http://www.geocities.com/SunsetStrip/3880>

LDS-GEMS. The best mailing list on the Web. If you have e-mail access, you need to sign up. Daily traffic is about five messages, which includes 150 Years Ago Today, LDS news, stories from Church history, messages from general authorities, and inspiring subscriber submissions. ★★★★★☑ To subscribe: *<http://www.xmission.com/~dkenison/lds/gems/ gemsmail.html>*;

about LDS-GEMS Web site:

<http://www.xmission.com/~dkenison/lds/gems/ gemsarc.html>

LDS-DAILY WOOL. Words Of Our Leaders. Daily quotes from LDS leaders on selected topics, delivered by e-mail. Subscription form available on site. ★★★

<http://www.cybcon.com/~sbirk/wool.html>

PEP. Puente's Electronic Periodical. An inspiring and spiritual electronic newsletter. To subscribe send an e-mail message to: *<intense@acadia.net>*, and in the subject write: Subscribe PEP. ☞

Quotes. Richard L. Evans-style inspirational quotes arranged by subject matter. ★★★

<http://www.inquo.net/~smudge/quotes.html>

Shining moments. A collection of inspirational stories from the *Church News*. ★★★★

<http://www.desnews.com/cgi-bin/libheads_reg?search=%22Shining+ moment%22&limit=999>

SPIRIT. A strictly conservative mailing list of spiritual poems, stories, and experiences. Daily traffic is about five messages. Visit the home page for subscription information. ★★★

<http://seminary.org/spirit>

Weekly Messages of Hope and Inspiration! A page with basic information about the Church, written as messages of inspiration. Maintaining a Web page is an

---

ON INSPIRATION

One day, while I was driving in the car, I had the inspiration for establishing the WOOL—Words of Our Leaders—Web page. I've enjoyed inspiration in my life before and I can tell you this was as much a revelation to me as anything I've had in the past.

The idea was to establish a Web page with an inspirational quote from a leader of the Church, and to offer people the option to sign up for a free mailing list where I would e-mail the quotes to them every day.

Scott Birk, Molalla, Oregon
<sbirk@cybcon.com>
Keeper of "The WOOL"—The LDS Daily "Words of Our Leaders"
<http://www.cybcon.com/~sbirk/wool.html>

ambitious task, so the messages aren't always weekly. But it's a heartening read.
★★★★

<http://www.geocities.com/Heartland/4809/msgTOChtm.htm>

Words of Wisdom.   A mailing list. Sign up to receive, via e-mail, a daily quote from the General Authorities of the Church. This is a free subscription service.
★★

<http://www.ez2.net/users/denis/wow/wow.asp>

WOW-LIVE.   Words of Wisdom Live is a "passively moderated" list of inspirational stories, favorite quotes, missionary experiences, and testimony building stories. Daily traffic is about ten messages.

Subscribe to the regular list or a digest version through a form on the Web site, or send an e-mail request directly to Brian Dorricott, <*brian@net-shopper.co.uk*>, with the message subscribe wow-live. ☞

<http://www.ez2.net/users/denis/wow-live.htm>

Service Opportunities

The Internet came in handy in developing a united effort in the Church's Sesqui-centennial Pioneer Heritage Day service project.

After the First Presidency invited every ward and branch to contribute 150 hours of community service, and about nine days before the scheduled day of service, the LDS-GEMS mailing list asked its more than 9,000 subscribers to report from their home wards on the service activities being planned.

Within a day, GEMS had received nearly 200 reports. Replies came from subscribers around the world. The Hansen Military Servicemen's Branch in Okinawa, Japan, planned work at two local nursing facilities. Costa Rica's Barrio La Loma planned to clean up and paint an elementary school. In the Austria Vienna Stake, Wien 3 said it expected to build a fence around a piece of land in a public park. The Capalaba Ward in Brisbane, Australia, had made plans to door-knock to raise money for Children's Hospital Ronald McDonald House. In Perth, the Mundaring Branch of the Dianella Stake arranged a multitude of projects, including tree planting, sewing for a nursing home, and quilting for charity. From the Brighton Ward of the Crawley, England, stake came plans to feed and entertain the elderly, clear rubbish, and collect items for charity. A ward in Birmingham, England, announced plans to clean up a local nature park. From Heidelberg, Germany's Military Ward came a report of renewing a public park in North Heidelberg.

In a service project of his own, Brother Crockett posted plans for the day of service to his Web site, <*http://www.indirect.com/www/crockett/service/service.html*>, helping to make the day of service a truly united, Church-wide effort.

It should be no surprise that there's not much—short of building your own up-lifting Web site—that you can do on the Internet to serve others. Service necessarily, and properly, is best done in your own geographical community. Nevertheless, if you're looking for a place to serve, there is at least one thing you can do on a larger scale:

FHUnion. FHUnion is an organization established to bring all Family History Center personal holdings online (in the form of catalog listings with detailed descriptions) in a single searchable database. Family History Centers of the Church of Jesus Christ of Latter-day Saints have assembled regionally significant genealogical information that is unique to each FHC. FHUnion needs people to assist in cataloging and submitting FHC regionally unique holdings. The organization needs a Web page construction team, and those who can assist in organizing from national and multistake territories to enter FHC data to the FHUnion Web site. Later local FHC volunteers will be needed to perform look-ups per their schedule. To sign up to assist FHUnion send a message to *<FHUnion-L-Request@emcee.com>* with the subject `subscribe fhunion`. ☞

Welfare and Humanitarian Assistance. Extensive collection of articles on LDS humanitarian service, and the calling of Latter-day Saints to serve others. ★★★★
<http://www.mormons.org/daily/welfare>

> **ELDER HENRY D. TAYLOR ON SERVICE**
> The life span of man is constantly lengthening. More and more elderly citizens are confronted with the problem of properly utilizing leisure time in accordance with their desires, experience, knowledge, and abilities. These sunset years can be rich, rewarding, golden years, filled with work and activity as witnessed by the serene, happy faces of the aging temple workers, and the research people in the Genealogical Library. I was deeply impressed and touched with the look of happiness and contentment on the face of a ninety-two-year-old brother engaged in labeling cans at Welfare Square. Work to him was worthwhile and precious.
>
> Henry D. Taylor, Conference Report, April 1961, p. 125.

BUILDING FAMILIES

It's a tough job, keeping a family together in a busy world where everyone has more commitments than time.

The Internet can help, with tools for improving your parenting, loads of recreational and educational material for families with children, and resources that can help build marriages. You'll find some of them listed here.

Parenting Resources

My husband and I are raising a very non-traditional mix-n-match family of six children, only three of whom I've lived with since their birth. The brood consists of adopted children, stepchildren, and various kinds of biological children. This is what life's like in our house:

A few weeks ago, David, the oldest, decided it was time to pack up and move to Florida. His daddy is pretending not to worry. But Sunday I found Dan still wide awake at three in the morning, waiting for a promised phone call that still hasn't come.

David was about to become a senior in high school when I met him. Because David didn't grow up in my house, because David has never called me Mom, Dan thinks I can't know, that I can't understand who David really is.

In his quiet panic over David's choices, he doesn't see that we're waiting together.

David sits square in the middle of his dad's heart. Fortunately, his soul is kind—like his father's—and he doesn't take advantage of his power. He has a tough exterior, a sulky put-out-teenager mien, a way of walking and dressing and ignoring adults that challenges anyone to like him. Despite his best attempts to prevent it, though, I like David.

And because my view of David isn't overlaid with memories of David-as-a-child, I think I see things in him that his daddy doesn't. Here are the parts of David I find so likeable.

Once on an overnight cross-country trip, in a van packed with sleeping family, David sat up front to help me stay awake while driving. Keep talking, I told him. In my coffee-free world, chatter is the only thing that keeps me on the road. So David talked. From central Ohio to west Indiana, David talked. Told me what he writes, why he likes to write, how to play the dungeons and dragons games I abhor and he loves. (Imagine my surprise when—in building my LDS Authors Web page <*http://www.jersey.net/~inkwell/mjauthor.htm*>—I discovered that one of David's favorite fantasy writers, Tracy Hickman, is an LDS writer from Arizona. Our worlds aren't so far apart as I'd imagined.) Perhaps riding through well-forested roads in the dark of night gave him an alternative to the black clothing he hides in by day, but in any event I found him mature and intelligent and entertaining. Rush and Dr. Laura and all the other voices that populate the airwaves at night have nothing on David.

I gained respect for David as an adult during another conversation, this one between him and his dad. The summer after high school, David was unclear about his future. Dan was worried about David's non-direction, and was gingerly trying to goad him into making some plans. (It's a fun thing to watch, Dan's parenting. It's sometimes quiet, sometimes teasing, but always interesting. He doesn't lecture; he doesn't berate. He just teases and jollies his offspring into acquiescence.) Dan's concern was well-founded. There are members of his own family who, nearing their forties, have yet to leave home and make lives for themselves. As often happens between David and Dad, the conversation turned into a bit of a spar. It came to this: "So, David, you're going to college? Or are you planning to sleep forever on this couch?" David looked at him with adult-sized disdain, and proclaimed "I'm *not* going to turn into my uncle, if that's what you're thinking."

Life's been hard for David these past few years. For a while, it looked as if he actually *might* turn into his uncle. Finally, though, he took his life back, and decided to move to Florida, get a clean start. So now, despite his pride, Dad is worried. David's got no place to live. He's staying with friends. He's sleeping on park benches. He'll be eaten by alligators. His only nutrition is the greasy hamburgers he eats during shift breaks at work.

I hear all of it, and think "David's doing well." He's independent, he's making do, he's struggling, he's making a life. He's working his way to Daytona, looking for college and meaning and friendship . . . all the things he should be doing. And it's hard for him. As it should be. There's no phone, no permanent address yet, so we can't call. We talk about setting up an Internet account for him so that we can exchange e-mail, but he's living without regular access to a telephone. So instead, we wait for those collect calls to come through, progress reports meant to ease Dad's concern. But they seldom do.

So when David called Saturday afternoon and reported that he didn't know where he'd be sleeping that night, Dad panicked. "As soon as you find something, call and tell me where you are." But the call hasn't come.

So we wait.

When parenting feels tougher than it should be, the following Web sites can help:

> ON PARENTING
>
> I had a dream one night about getting together a LDS moms' group with a few of the pen pals I had. So I started an LDS group with three other sisters besides myself, and we went into the Mormon chat room on AOL a few times. From there it was by word of mouth. The group grew so large that I wanted to add more to it, so I created a Web page where I could put thoughts, and links to other things that I thought might be interesting to other moms.
>
> Then we grew, and grew to over 107 women, nationwide, who receive mailings of our daily thoughts, newsletters when we get them together, and general sisterhood. We feel such a spirit and I enjoy everything I do for the women of my group. They are all such a blessing to me.
>
> Faith Minor, Nashville, Tennessee
> <MOMY03KZ@aol.com>
> Webmaster, MomzInZion
> <http://members.aol.com/MOMY03KZ/momzinzion-index.html>
> MomzInZion AOL chat room
> <aol://2719:2-2-momz in Zion/>

A Parent's Guide.   The booklet that discusses LDS parenting. ☞
  <http://www.mormons.org/daily/parenting>
Being a Righteous Husband & Father.   Text of a talk given in the priesthood session of General Conference by President Howard W. Hunter. ☞
  <http://www.inquo.net/~smudge/fathers.html>
FatherWork.   Helping fathers to strengthen family relationships (see figure 6.4). Stories, Ideas, and Activities to Encourage Generative Fathering. ★★★★★
  <http://fatherwork.byu.edu>

LDS E-mail Group for Parents. To subscribe, send an e-mail request to *<karlp@ slcolubs.com>*. ☞

LDS Stay-home Moms Mail Group. To subscribe, send an e-mail request to *<karlp@slcolubs.com>*. Daily traffic is about 30 messages. ☞

Living Through Loss. Materials on surviving the loss of a child. Good help for survivors and those who love them. ★★★★★
<http://members.aol.com/Ethesis/sloss.htm>

Parenting, the Lord's Way. A long, well-documented discourse on parenting, by Allen Leigh. ★★★ *<http://www.xmission.com/~pengar/allen/parent.html>*

Parenting. Articles about parenting children, at Mormons.Org. A very small collection. ★★
<http://www.mormons.org/daily/parenting>

Teachings About Fatherhood and the Role of Men. Being a Righteous Husband and Father, and other addresses and commentaries on fatherhood. ★★★
<http://www.mormons.org/basic/family/fathers>

Teachings About Motherhood and the Role of Women. Conference addresses and written commentaries on motherhood. Static. ★★★
<http://199.227.118.92/basic/family/mothers>

Teachings About the Family. A collection of articles on the Church's strong positions about the importance of family. Includes articles on The Family: A Proclamation to the World, The Family, The Eternal Family, The Joy of Living the Great Plan of Happiness, Teachings about the Family, Teachings About Marriage, Teachings About Motherhood and the Role of Women, Teachings About Fatherhood and the Role of Men, Teachings About Children, Teachings About Sexuality, Brotherhood, and Abuse of Spouse and Child. A Mormons.Org page. ★★★★★
<http://www.mormons.org/basic/family>

The Family Site. Includes the family forum, information on marriage, parenting, health. Sponsored by the Osmond Network. ★★★★★
<http://www.osmond.net/osnet/family>

The Spiritual Foundations of Fathering. A 10-part series from The Church of Jesus Christ of Latter-day Saints on steps to building a strong family. ★★★★
<http://www.osmond.net/osnet/family/sffser.html>

TwinTales. E-mail discussion for the parents of twins and larger sibling groups. Usually has an LDS overtone. Web site includes an archive, a family photo album, and lots of family links and resources. ★★★
<http://seminary.org/twintales>

Values Parenting. A page from Richard and Linda Eyre dedicated to teaching basic values to kids. Includes a discussion page, weekly parenting tip, more. ★★★★
<http://parenting.netpub.com>

Family Resources—
Recreation, Activities, Family Home Evening Resources

Perhaps mine is the only family on the planet where the kids pout and sulk if we *miss* Family Home Evening. I suspect they're only in it for the treats, but hey, whatever works.

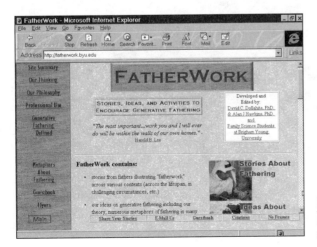

FIG. 6.4

FatherWork: A BYU-affiliated site encouraging good fathering.

If it takes more than a bowl of ice cream to get your family enthusiastic about spending time together, here's help:

Comic Zone. Web site for major nationally-syndicated cartoons. Not specifically LDS. ★★★
<http://www.unitedmedia.com/comics>

Donna's Day. Fun, creative activities for the whole family. ★★★★
<http://www.ktca.org/donnasday>

Family.Com. Disney's page of family activities. Great fun. ★★★★★
<http://www.family.com>

Family Forum. Exchange useful ideas with other LDS families in this new family-friendly discussion forum at Y-site (see figure 6.5). ★★★★★
<http://www.ysite.com/forum>

Family Home Evening. An excerpt from the Encyclopedia of Mormonism. ☞
<http://www.mormons.org/daily/FHE_EOM.htm>

Family Night. Great ideas for Family Home Evening. ★★★★
<http://www.osmond.net/osnet/family/famnite>

Family on a Budget. Low-cost ideas for families rich in everything but money. ★★
<http://www.osmond.net/osnet/family/budget.html>

Family-tested Web Sites. A new site reviewing Web sites for the whole family. Not specifically LDS. ★★
<http://www.geocities.com/Heartland/9530/family.html>

I'll Build You A Rainbow. Words and music to the boo-hooiest song ever written. ★★
<http://www.geocities.com/Heartland/Plains/7717/rainbow.html#rainbow>

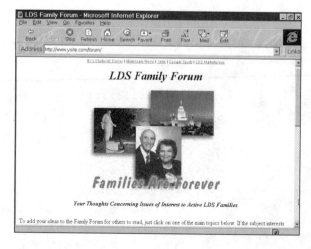

FIG. 6.5

Family Forum: A discussion area for LDS families.

Kids and Parents on the Web.   Resource center for families and schools who want to use the Internet as a tool in children's education. Includes a link to Homework Helper, resources for researching a report, discussion groups for parents and teachers, and project resource lists. ★★★★★
<http://www.respress.com/kids_parents>

Screen It.   Reviews of movies, music, and videos, describing the content and every conceivable (ahem) point of objection. Gives away the endings for too many movies, but worth bookmarking if you're at all concerned about the content of the media you see and hear. ★★★★
<http://www.screenit.com>

The Family Site.   Feature articles, family-oriented cool site of the week. Sponsored by Utah Valley Online. ★★★★
<http://www.uvol.com/family>

Website for Kids of All Ages.   Safe sites for kids and teens. Includes links to Yahooligans, Your Own Newspaper, Teen Net Magazine, Hieroglyphs, Kid-Safe Internet, more. Not specifically LDS. ★★★★
<http://www.yelmtel.com/~mrwizard/kids.htm>

Building Marriages

My husband is perfect. Really. He's absolutely the finest human being I've ever known, and I adore him.

One of his many fine qualities is that he doesn't fight. Oh, he can fight. But he tends not to. It's a good thing, because we're both opinionated, obstinate, and confident of the obvious truth of our own positions—a combination of characteristics that could prove fatal to an otherwise healthy marriage.

Believe it or not, this has something to do with the Internet.

We've finally worked out a system, it seems. When a subject arises on which we can find no agreement, we don't do battle. It's too fraught with emotion, too easy to let loose a volley of careless words.

Instead, we send e-mail. We follow the rules, of course. We try to be kind. But somehow, dancing around a sensitive issue in writing seems to bring out the best in both of us.

Here are some other ways the Internet can help:

After the Wedding Comes the Marriage.   A short page of advice to brides and grooms. ★★
<http://www.osmond.net/osnet/family/marrad.html>

Being a Righteous Husband and Father. By President Howard W. Hunter. Comments on a husband's role in and obligations to his family. ☞
<http://www-leland.stanford.edu/~garyc/pa2/fathers.html>

Cornerstones for Building Homes. President Gordon B. Hinckley's fireside message to young couples. Deals with advice for strengthening and preserving marriage. ☞
<http://www-leland.stanford.edu/~garyc/pa2/17hinc.htm>

Healing the Heartache. A resource for Latter-day Saints and other Christians who are coping with the pain of infidelity. Includes articles on forgiveness, prevention, recovery . . . even STDs. Excellent resources. ★★★★
<http://members.aol.com/itstessie/sngl/adult.htm>

Marriage Skills. Links to *After the Wedding Comes the Marriage* and *I Don't Have to Make Everything All Better.* Limited content. ★★★
<http://www.uvol.com/family/skills.html>

Sanctify. A new mailing list for Latter-day Saints in part-member families. The name comes from 1 Corinthians 7:14, which speaks of "unbelieving" spouses being sanctified by their member spouses. The list offers support, inspiration, and a place to share experiences. To subscribe to Sanctify, send a request to *<majordomo@seminary.org>* with the message subscribe sanctify in the body. Archives are not available. ★★★★
<http://www.seminary.org/sanctify>

Teachings About Marriage. Quotes from various authoritative sources on questions of marriage, eternal marriage, divorce, celibacy, and more. Fairly static; more theory than practice. ★★★
<http://www.mormons.org/basic/family/marriage>

You Believe What?! How to resolve conflicts of faith. Sound advice for part-member families. ★★★★
<http://www.marriagebuilders.com/graphic/mbi5040_qa.html>. Part of the excellent Marriage Builders Web site at *<http://www.marriagebuilders.com>*

Young Married Women. For young married LDS women seeking strength from one another (see figure 6.6). Still in its early stages, but it has potential. ★★
<http://www.geocities.com/Heartland/Ranch/4828>

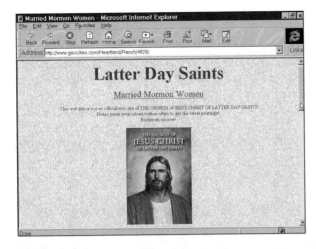

FIG. 6.6

Young Married Women: Recipes, romance, reading

GOSPEL DOCTRINE STUDY TOOLS

Studying the words of the prophets and the apostles—whether written in the form of scripture, or spoken in testimony before the Saints—is fundamental to attaining perfection.

In this section you'll find sites for reading the scriptures online, along with transcripts from conferences and other addresses, and doctrinal texts available online.

Scriptures Online

One of the best things about the Internet is its capacity for making texts—particularly scriptural texts—available online.

This section contains only the online text of each book of scripture. You'll find personal study tools for each of these books in chapter 11: "Pursuit of Excellence."

The scriptures you'll find here take several forms: Web pages where you can read the text straight through, downloadable text files, searchable databases, and more.

The section is organized by individual texts, followed by a list of sites containing multiple books of scripture.

Book of Mormon

The Book of Mormon was introduced in chapter 5: "Proclaim the Gospel." In this section, you'll find the actual text online, in a variety of formats.

Bible II.   A commendable—if entirely misguided—effort to translate the Book of Mormon to American English. Modern copyright law requires the holders of a copyright to defend it, or lose it. The site contains a grudging deposition seeking information on how much of the Bible II was taken from the copyrighted 1981 edition of the Book of Mormon. Somewhere on this site lies the text of the Book of Mormon. Bizarre. ★

<http://www.bible2.com>.

Book of Mormon.   Multiple search tools, in an easy-to-understand format (see figure 6.7). The search hits come up in context. Click on the hyperlinks to read additional surrounding text. ★★★★

<http://members.aol.com/cumorahhil/bom_search.htm>

Book of Mormon.   Straight text, chapter by chapter. Use the Find/Search command on your browser to search any chapter. ★★

*<http://www.math.byu.edu/~smithw/Lds/LDS/LDS-scriptures/
Book_of_Mormon>*

Free Book of Mormon.   Another site for obtaining a free personal copy of the Book of Mormon. See chapter 5 for similar resources. ★★

<http://www.mich.com/~romulans/freebom.html>

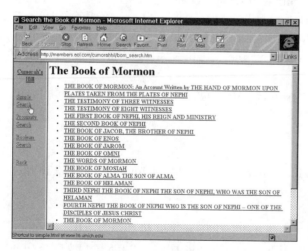

FIG. 6.7

The Book of Mormon: The Cumorah's Hill site incorporates excellent search tools.

copying passages of text to a word processor replace typing the passages or scanning them into the computer; (8) selecting text and applying an electronic highlight replace highlighting text with highlighter pens; (9) attaching pop-up notes to paragraphs of text or to verses of scripture replaces writing in the margins of books; and (10) quick location of text passages that contain certain words and phrases replaces long hours of reading and research.

Alan Ashton in "CD ROM Reviews" <http://www.farmsresearch.com/frob/frobv8_2/ashton.htm>

LDS Newton Books Texts. The Book of Mormon, ready for the Apple Newton Computer. I don't own the computer, so can't evaluate the content. The site itself, though, will be of interest to anyone who does. ★★★
<http://www.coolcontent.com/NewtonBooks>

Mormon's Story. The text of the Book of Mormon in a simpler English. While I'm a great fan of reading scriptures in their original form, I'm an even greater fan of understanding the scriptures—in whatever form generates understanding. Timothy Wilson's rewrite of the Book of Mormon is beautifully done, and it's all available online, at this Web site. If this is the kind of simplification it takes to get a child or a new reader through the Book of Mormon, it's a worthwhile venture. ★★★★★☑
<http://www.enoch.com/voicesfromdust/mormonstory/mormonstory.html>

Search the Book of Mormon. Use the Web to search the Book of Mormon by word or phrase. Great search tools. A Project Gutenberg text, housed at the University of Michigan. ★★★★
<http://www.hti.umich.edu/relig/mormon>

The Book of Mormon. Deseret Book's online text of the Book of Mormon. Very readable. Lacks a search tool. ★★★
<http://www.deseretbook.com/scriptures/bom_home.html>

Bible

The large online community of Christians does a good job of presenting the Bible in electronic form. Most of the following sites contain several versions of the entire Biblical text.

Bible. The text from about 20 Bible translations. Files must be downloaded to your computer to be read. ★★★
<ftp://ccel.wheaton.edu/bible_study_txt>

Bible. Text only. Alphabetized list of chapters of the King James version of the Bible, ready for download. ★★

<http://www.math.byu.edu/~smithw/Lds/LDS/LDS-scriptures/Bible>

Bible Gateway. Full text of six English-language versions of the Bible, plus six non-English translations (see figure 6.8). Includes a very good search engine, and a topical guide. ★★★★★

<http://bible.gospelcom.net>

Bible Text. Includes information on canon dates and Vulgate texts. Great content, absolutely no design, and no search engine. ★★

<http://erdos.math.byu.edu/~smithw/Lds/LDS/Ancient-history-items/Bible>

Free Copy of the Bible (King James Version). Request a copy online. ★★

<http://www.mich.com/~romulans/freebible.html>

The Doctrine and Covenants

You'll find here both text and hypertext (Web language) editions of The Doctrine and Covenants.

The Doctrine and Covenants. Just a smidgen of text here, but keep watching. ★

<http://www.nettally.com/LDS/D&C.html>

Doctrine and Covenants (Text). Available online, the Doctrine and Covenants divided in 14 sections. ★★★

<gopher://wiretap.spies.com/11/Library/Religion/Mormon/Doctrine>

The Doctrine and Covenants. A Deseret Book scripture search site (see figure 6.9). ★★★★

<http://www.deseretbook.com/scriptures/dc_home.html>

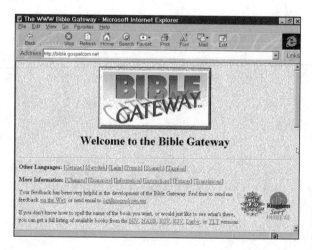

FIG. 6.8

Bible Gateway: This site carries the full Bible text, along with a good search engine.

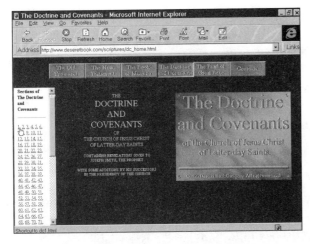

FIG. 6.9

The Doctrine and Covenants: The D&C is just one of several Deseret Book scripture sites.

Index of Scriptures.   The text of the doctrine and covenants. Fixed line lengths. ★★
   <http://www.math.byu.edu/~smithw/Lds/LDS/LDS-scriptures/Doc._and_Cov>

The Pearl of Great Price

The following sites contain both the entire text of The Pearl of Great Price, as well as shorter excerpts—primarily the Articles of Faith—from the full text.

Articles of Faith.   The text, followed by documented commentary and history. ★★★
   <http://www.mormons.org/basic/articles_faith.htm>

Articles of Faith.   The basic doctrines of the Church (see figure 6.10). Graphically appealing, but contains no explanation or insight beyond the text itself. ★★

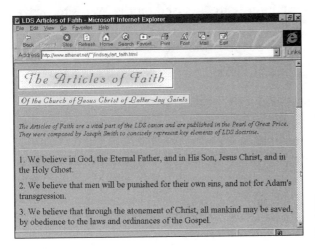

FIG. 6.10

The Articles of Faith: Available electronically from numerous Web sites.

<http://www.athenet.net/~jlindsay/art_faith.html>.
Other well-presented pages for the Articles of Faith are located at
<http://ldschurch.net/s/danville/sr1/aof.html>;
<http://www.deseretbook.com/scriptures/pgp/aof/aof1.html>;
<http://www.primenet.com/~kitsonk/mormon/articles.html>; and
<http://reled.byu.edu/books/artoffai/afaith.htm>

Book of Abraham.   Original texts as found in Times and Seasons. Great content, terrible design. ★★
<http://erdos.math.byu.edu/~smithw/Lds/LDS/Ancient-history-items/Book-of-Abraham>

Index of Scriptures: Pearl of Great Price.   The entire text, listed by book. Difficult to read on screen. ★★
<http://www.nettally.com/LDS/Pearl.html>. Similar site is available at
<gopher://wiretap.spies.com/11/Library/Religion/Mormon/Pearl>

The Pearl of Great Price.   A good Deseret Book site for reading and searching the Pearl of Great Price. ★★★
<http://www.deseretbook.com/scriptures/pgp_home.html>

Standard Works
The complete set of scriptures, online.

Deseret Book.   Scripture search site. Beautifully done. ★★★★★☑
<http://www.deseretbook.com/scriptures>

Index: Standard Works.   Full standard works in text form are also available for download. ★★
<http://www.math.byu.edu/~smithw/Lds/LDS/LDS-scriptures>

LDS Scripture of the Day.   A daily scripture subscription. Send an e-mail request to *<zarahmla@xmission.com>*. Scriptures are archived on the Web site. ★★★
<http://www.zarahemla.com/sotd/sotd.html>

LDS Scriptures.   The Zarahemla Book Shoppe Web site listing numerous links to LDS scriptures (see figure 6.11). Little original content, but the collection is well organized. ★★
<http://www.zarahemla.com/script.html>

Religious and Sacred Texts.   Something from everyone. In addition to links to LDS scriptures, you'll find here links to Apocryphal, Islamic, Hindu, Confucian, Taoist, Bahai, Sikh, Egyptian Book of the Dead, Gnostic, Zen, Early Christian, Zoroastrian, Divrei, Torah, Urantian, Ethiopian, and Medieval texts. Leave a trail of bread crumbs. The page is compiled by Dave Wiley, a Latter-day Saint. ★★★★
<http://webpages.marshall.edu/~wiley6/rast.htmlx>

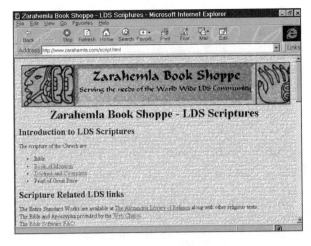

FIG. 6.11

LDS Scriptures: Scripture links available here are top-notch.

The Deseret Book LDS Internet Library.   Search the Standard Works, seven-volume History of the Church, and these gospel classics: Articles of Faith, Autobiography of Parley P. Pratt, Discourses of Brigham Young, Doctrine and Covenants Commentary, Gospel Doctrine, Gospel Standards, Gospel Truth, Jesus the Christ, Lectures on Faith, and Teachings of the Prophet Joseph Smith. Or click on a title and read the entire text on screen. Reading is just a little awkward. ★★★★

<http://library.deseretbook.com>

Messages/Proclamations Online

The following Web sites contain the text of messages and proclamations from the First Presidency.

Continuing Revelation.   The First Presidency Message for the August 1996 edition of the *Ensign,* given by President James E. Faust. ☞

<http://members.aol.com/ssh81675/ldsrefer/documents/reveal.htm>

First Presidency Messages.   Small collection of monthly messages from the First Presidency. ★★★★

<http://members.aol.com/cumorahhil/first_presidency_message.htm>

Proclamation to the Church and to the World.   Text of the 1995 official proclamation on families. ☞

<http://members.aol.com/cumorahhil/proclmtn.htm> The same text is also found at *<http://www.athenet.net/~jlindsay/LDSFamDecl.shtml>*

Proclamations of the First Presidency and the Quorum of the Twelve Apostles.   A commentary on, and links to, the five official proclamations of the Church. ★★★

<http://www.nettally.com/lds/Proc.html>

Strength Through Obedience. The First Presidency Message for July 1996, given by President Thomas S. Monson. ☞

<http://members.aol.com/ssh81675/ldsrefer/documents/obey.htm>

The Doorway of Love. The First Presidency Message for October 1996, given by President Thomas S. Monson. ☞

<http://members.aol.com/cumorahhil/fpm1096.htm>

ELDER NEAL A. MAXWELL ON FIRST PRESIDENCY PROCLAMATIONS

Lamentably, a few Church members say that they want more relevancy but fewer First Presidency pronouncements on issues of current concern. And unfortunately, a few attempt to reshape that which they cannot control, the living Church. By not understanding that it is the true and living Church, they make the mistake of assuming that it is a democracy or just another church. Such a reshaping would be "pleasing unto the carnal mind," for it would suggest that, without the reality of the living Church, there would be no such institutional restraints; people would be "free," like Cain. The church of the living God is the pillar and ground of the truth, as Paul said. (1 Timothy 3:15)

Neal A. Maxwell, *Things As They Really Are,* Introduction

General Conference

It's been just a year now that General Conference has been available online, almost as it happens. In this section you'll find various Conference reports, as well as information about where to go to get the next session of Conference.

Bruce R. McConkie's Testimony. His last Conference talk was one of the most powerful testimonies of Christ ever. This page is maintained by Kevin Cundick. ☞

<http://www.kdcol.com/~kcundick/mcconkie.html>

Deseret News Web Edition. (See figure 6.12.) LDS General Conference site operated by the Church-affiliated Salt Lake City newspaper. Very heavily used during General Conference. ★★★★★

<http://www.desnews.com/confer/main.htm>

General Conference (April '95). Transcripts. ☞

<ftp://ftp.xmission.com/pub/users/z/zarahmla/a95conf.txt>. Transcripts are also available at <ftp://ftp.Webcom.com/pub/gjw1/ftp/lds/cnfapr95> and <ftp://ftp.wnetc.com/lds/cnfapr95>.

General Conference (April '96). Transcripts. ☞

<ftp://ftp.xmission.com/pub/users/z/zarahmla/apr96.txt>

General Conference (April '97). Transcripts of the proceedings. ☞

<http://www.lds.org/General_Conference/97_Apr/97_Apr.html>. Transcripts are also maintained at <http://www.mormons.org/conferences/97_apr>, <http://www.lds.org/General_Conference/97_Apr/97_Apr.html>

General Conference (October '94). Notes from Justin Masters. ☞

<ftp://ftp.Webcom.com/pub/gjw1/ftp/lds/cnfoct94>

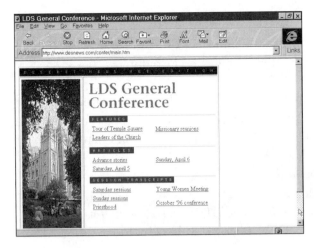

FIG. 6.12

Deseret New Web Edition: This popular site is inundated with visits during General Conference.

General Conference (October '95). Transcripts of the proceedings. 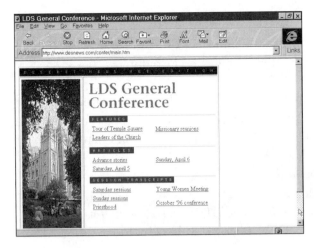 *<http://www.zarahemla.com/ftp://ftp.xmission.com/ pub/users/z/zarahmla/o95conf.txt>*. Transcripts are also available at *<http://www.xmission.com/~dkenison/lds/conf>*

General Conference (October '96). Transcripts of the proceedings. *<http://www.desnews.com/confer/96fall/talks.htm>*. Transcripts are also maintained at *<http://www.mormons.org/conferences/96_oct/index.htm>*

General Conference (October '97). For transcripts of this, and subsequent conferences, visit the official Church site: *<http://www.lds.org>* or the Deseret News site: *<http://www.desnews.com/confer/main.htm>*. Links are also maintained at the Mormons on the Internet Registry. *<http://members.aol.com/MormonNet>*.

General Conference Infobase. An Infobases-formatted compilation of conference talks from 1971 to present. Supplements the missing portions of the commercial LDS Collector's Library CD. This site has no affiliation, however, with Infobases. Requires 50MB of free disk space. ★★★ *<http://www.enol.com/~infobase/conference.html>*. See comparable material at *<http://138.87.135.33/~tellis/conference/index.htm>*

LDS General Conference Talks. A searchable database of talks from 1971 to present. File is also downloadable. ★★★★★ *<http://138.87.135.33/confrenc.htm>*

Pride by President Ezra Taft Benson. Text of President Benson's well-known conference address. *<http://www.nettally.com/LDS/pride.html>*

Talks, Speeches

In this section you'll find the texts of talks and speeches delivered by prominent members of the Church in settings other than General Conference.

BYU Devotional and Fireside Speeches. A listing of the devotional and fireside speeches available at this Web site (see figure 6.13). Includes talks by President Hinckley, Elder Packer, LeGrand Richards, Elder Holland, Hugh Nibley, Elaine Jack, and many more. ★★★★
<http://advance.byu.edu/devo.html>

Fourteen Fundamentals. Downloadable text of address by Ezra Taft Benson. ✍
<ftp://mach.cs.cmu.edu/afs/cs/usr/dba/www/ETBenson-14-Fundamentals>

Seven Deadly Heresies. Transcript of well-known address by Elder Bruce R. McConkie. ✍
<ftp://ftp.sims.net/pub/organizations/zion/documents/heresies>

The 60 Minutes LDS Segment. Transcript of a 1996 television interview with President Gordon B. Hinckley. ✍ *<http://www.nettally.com/LDS/60.html>*. Transcript is also available at
<http://www.xmission.com/~dkenison/lds/gems/60min.txt>

Other LDS Texts Online

In this section you'll find a selection of doctrinal texts written by apostles and other general authorities.

As A Man Thinketh. Treatise on the power of thought, by James Allen. ✍
<http://www.coolcontent.com/TheToolOfThought>

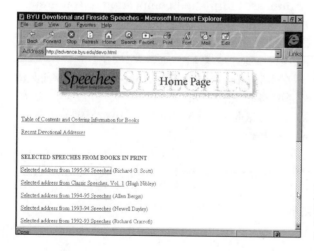

FIG. 6.13

BYU Devotional and Fireside Speeches: Access the best thinking of speakers at BYU.

Doctrinal Books and Other Materials.   A brief list of links. ★★

<http://www.ldsworld.com/links/doct.html>

Gospel Doctrine.   The sermons and writings of President Joseph F. Smith (text appears in sections). ✍

<http://www.math.byu.edu/~smithw/Lds/LDS/Doctrine/Gospel-Doctrine>

History of the Church.   From a 1935 edition of the seven-volume set (text divided into sections). ✍

<http://www.math.byu.edu/~smithw/Lds/LDS/History/History_of_the_Church>

Teachings of the Prophet Joseph Smith.   The 1938 compilation by Joseph Fielding Smith (see figure 6.14). The text is divided into six sections, each one searchable through your browser's "Find" feature. ✍
<http://reled.byu.edu/books/jsteach/jshead.htm>. Another copy is available at *<http://www.byu.edu/Academic-Info/rel1/books/jsteach/jshead.htm>*, and a plain text version is maintained at *<http://www.math.byu.edu/~smithw/Lds/LDS/Joseph-Smith/Teachings>*

The Articles of Faith.   Full text of the book by James E. Talmage. Very well-designed page. ★★★★

<http://www.byu.edu/rel1/books/artoffai/afaith.htm>

The Book of John Whitmer Kept by Commandment.   Typescript of John Whitmer's history of the Church. ✍

<http://erdos.math.byu.edu/~smithw/Lds/LDS/Early-Saints/whitmer,j>

The Encyclopedia of Mormonism.   Order a free copy of the Encyclopedia, along with the Standard Works, on CD-ROM. Pay $4.95 for shipping. $

<http://www.infobases.com>

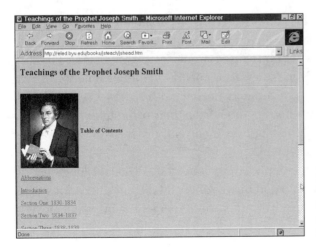

FIG. 6.14

Teachings of the Prophet Joseph Smith: A collection of the Prophet's speeches and writings is available in electronic form.

The History of Joseph Smith.   His own words. Five chapters from the *History of the Church.* ✍

  <http://www.primenet.com/~balexan/pogphst.html>

The Journal of Discourses.   A project to make the discourses available online. Early days. ✍

  <http://www.tlcmanti.org/RefLibraryFolder/JD/refJDMain.html>

EDUCATIONAL RESOURCES: LDS-AFFILIATED COLLEGES, UNIVERSITIES, INSTITUTES

I've been a student at more colleges and universities than I have children—and I have a lot of children. So when I engaged in an online discussion sometime back about the nature of academic freedom at Brigham Young University, I spoke with some authority.

My correspondent had been a BYU student in the '70s, and still took umbrage at the dress codes and honor codes that he considered stifling. There is, he said, no freedom of thought at BYU.

I was the wrong person to pick an argument with that day. I'd had an ugly morning at the University of Missouri. There a journalism professor made the outlandish and contradictory suggestion that all "censorship" should be outlawed. And the entire class of students obediently nodded heads in agreement.

I couldn't stay quiet. "*All* censorship?" I asked. The instructor looked surprised. It was, after all, a graduate journalism course. How dare I think otherwise? "Do you mean to say that nobody, anywhere, should have the right to restrict what any other person reads or views?"

The entire class jumped to his defense. I was a pariah for questioning his judgment.

By the end of the hour I was standing up to argue. Alone, among all the students, I continued to do battle. Nope, they said, nobody should be able to restrict anything. Not communities, not governments dealing with national security, and for that matter, not even parents choosing books for their own children. It was a bloody war, and I was alone. My thinking was incorrect, my speaking out was an affront, and my attitude was unacceptable.

As I left class that day, feeling completely discouraged, I thought longingly of my time at BYU, when I had participated in amazingly intelligent discussions with people who were open-minded, open with their disagreements, and openly loving when they engaged in debate. Is it any wonder, then, that I couldn't agree with my online correspondent that BYU was the school that lacked academic freedom?

I learned at BYU to see the world in all new ways. Sure there's the rare administrator who makes bad, even embarrassing, decisions. But that wasn't the case in the classroom. There I gained perspective, a broader view of man and society that has continued to serve me well through the years. I learned about world religions from James Moss. I gained a macro view of economics and society from Clayne Pope <http://advance.byu.edu/ devo/PopeW97.html>. I learned to write, I learned to really read, I learned to connect all the dots from some of the most free-thinking, broad-minded people in the world.

And I did it all wearing a dress.

Latter-day Saints are regularly admonished to improve their education, to seek wisdom, and learning and understanding.

In this section, you'll find a large number of resources to aid in education. The section begins with information on continuing education, then introduces you to institutes of religion, colleges and universities, and additional educational resources.

> "Teach ye diligently . . . of things both in heaven and in the earth, and under the earth; things which have been, things which are, things which must shortly come to pass; things which are at home, things which are abroad; the wars and the perplexities of the nations, and the judgments which are on the land; and a knowledge also of countries and of kingdoms—
>
> "That ye may be prepared in all things when I shall send you again to magnify the calling whereunto I have called you, and the mission with which I have commissioned you."
>
> D&C 88:78–80

Continuing Education

If full-time college isn't for you, consider expanding your knowledge with continuing education courses.

BYU Continuing Education. Home study, travel study, education week, bachelor's degrees, conferences and workshops, more. An excellent resource. ★★★★★
<http://coned.byu.edu>

BYU Religious Education. Courses offered by Religious Education. Good information. ★★★
<http://reled.byu.edu>

BYU Travel Study. Study in the Holy Land, Central/South America, Europe, Asia, or Nauvoo. (See figure 6.15.) Informative page. ★★★
<http://coned.byu.edu/ts/homepage.htm>

The Church Education System. CES operates religious studies programs in the United States and in over a hundred other countries and territories. Text from the official Church Web site. ☞
<http://www.lds.org/Global_Media_Guide/Church_Educational_System.html>

Institutes

A partial listing of institutes of religion and LDS student associations. You'll find more listings for college-age single adults in chapter 9: "Auxiliaries," the Single Adult section.

> "Set in order the churches, and study and learn, and become acquainted with all good books, and with languages, tongues, and people. And this shall be your business and mission in all your lives, to preside in council, and set in order all the affairs of this church and kingdom.
>
> D&C 90:15–16

California (Riverside) Institute. Class schedules, activities, more. ★★★
<http://members.aol.com/cumorahhil/riversd.htm>

California (Stanford) LDSSA. The LDS student association at Stanford. ★★★★★
<http://www-leland.stanford.edu/group/ldssa>

Illinois (Urbana-Champaign) LDSSA-L. LDS Student Association at University of Illinois. (See figure 6.16) Newsletter, mailing list primarily for the LDSSA at UIUC, but others may join. To subscribe, send an e-mail request to *<listserv@po.uiuc.edu>* or *< ldssa-l-request@postoffice.cso. uiuc.edu>* with the message subscribe `ldssa-l`. More information is available at the very colorful Web site. ★★★★
<http://www.students.uiuc.edu/~sandland>

LDS Student Associations. A good list of links. ★★
<http://www.mich.com/~romulans/ldssa.html>

LDS-GRADS. E-mail discussion list for single LDS graduate students. Send a subscription request to *<tnrands@princeton.edu>* Daily traffic: about 8 messages. ✍

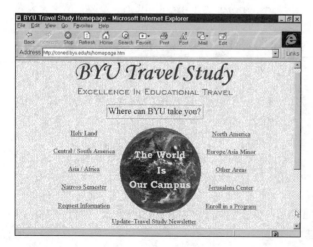

FIG. 6.15

BYU Travel Study: Visit the world via BYU's study abroad programs.

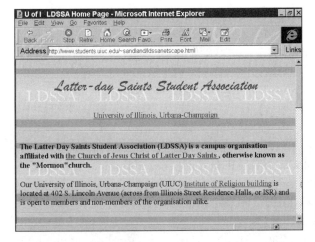

FIG. 6.16

Illinois (Urbana-Champaign) LDSSA: One of several LDS student associations with Web sites.

LDSSA Groups. A list of LDS Student Associations maintained by LDS World. ★★

<http://ldsworld.com/links/ldssa.html>

Louisiana (Baton Rouge) Latter-day Saint Student Association. Includes an intro to LDSSAs. ★★★

<http://members.tripod.com/~moroni>

Massachusetts (Cambridge/MIT) Latter-day Saint Student Association. A substantial amount of information. ★★★★

<http://web.mit.edu/afs/athena.mit.edu/activity/l/ldssa/www/home.html>

Missouri (Columbia) Institute. Activities, courses, more. (But I'm a former student, so ratings may be overstated.) ★★★★

<http://students.missouri.edu/~ldssa>

Missouri (Rolla) LDSSA. Students at the University of Missouri at Rolla. Nice information source. ★★★

<http://www.umr.edu/~ldssa>

Ogden, Utah LDS Institute. The Ogden LDS Institute's home page at Weber State University. ★★★★

<http://www.relia.net/~ldssa>

Sigma Gamma Chi. The national college fraternity for LDS Single Men. Good background information. ★★★

<http://www.cs.utah.edu/~ruefenac/sigma_gamma_chi>

Texas (Denton) Institute. Schedule, leadership, maps, composition. ★★★★

<http://people.unt.edu/~ic09/ldssa>

West Virginia (Huntington/Marshall University) LDS-SA. A short compilation of information. ★★

<http://webpages.marshall.edu/~brown/ldssa.html>

Wisconsin (Eau Claire) Institute.   Schedule, map. ★★
  <http://www.duckpond.com/mormon/institute.html>
Yahoo! List of LDS Student Associations.   Some 250 links. ★★
  <http://www.altavista.digital.com/cgi-bin/
  query?pg=q&what=web&kl=XX&q=ldssa&search.x=38&search.y=3>

Colleges and Universities

This section lists the Web sites of Church-affiliated colleges and universities, along with a handful of Utah schools that no longer have any direct Church affiliation—tho' they do have significant LDS student populations.

Admissions—Brigham Young University.   Applications, forms, and instructions for admission. ✍
  <http://adm5.byu.edu/ar/proj/app_intro.html>
Brigham Young University.   Main site. ✍
  <http://www.byu.edu>
BYU-Hawaii.   Church-owned four-year undergraduate university located in Hawaii. ✍
  <http://www.byuh.edu>
Dixie College.   Two-year college in St. George, Utah. ✍
  <http://www.dixie.edu>
LDS Business College.   Church-owned two-year trade school in Salt Lake City. ✍
  <http://www.ldsbc.edu>
Ricks College.   (See figure 6.17.) Church-owned two-year college in Rexburg, Idaho. ✍
  <http://www.ricks.edu>

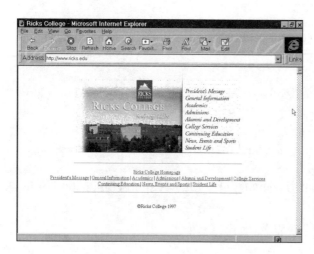

FIG. 6.17

Ricks College: Typical of most college pages, the Ricks Web site provides academic and admissions information to prospective students.

Snow College.   Two-year college in Ephraim, Utah. ✍
   <http://www.snow.edu>
Southern Utah University.   Four-year university in Cedar City, Utah. ✍
   <http://www.suu.edu>
Southern Virginia College.   New two-year college in Buena Vista, Virginia, at the foot of the Blue Ridge mountains. The school is operated by members of the Church, and requires students to maintain academic and behavioral standards comparable to those at BYU. °
   <http://www.southernvirginia.edu>
University of Utah.   The Salt-Lake-City-based university. ✍
   <http://www.utah.edu>
Utah State University.   Four-year university in Logan, Utah. ✍
   <http://www.usu.edu>
Weber State University.   Four-year university in Ogden, Utah. ✍
   <http://www.weber.edu>

Other Education-oriented Resources

You'll find here a list of miscellaneous educational resources oriented toward adult education. Home schooling resources are located in chapter 10: "Interest Groups," page 233.

Aspen Grove Family Camp.   The Alumni Association family camp affiliated with BYU. ★★★
   <http://zeus.byu.edu/alumni/aspengrv.htm>
BYU Alumni Association.   Sponsoring numerous educational events and programs.
   ★★★★★
   <http://www.byu.edu/alumni>
BYU Jerusalem Center.   BYU's Jerusalem-based center for Near Eastern Studies.
   ★★★★
   <http://coned.byu.edu/jc>
BYU Library.   Online searchable card catalog, library info, Web search, course reserve, and more. Everything, in fact, but the books. ★★★★
   <http://www.lib.byu.edu>
Education.   A collection of articles on LDS teachings about education, and educational resources. Includes the history of LDS education and much more. A Mormons.Org site. ★★★★
   <http://www.mormons.org/daily/education>
Caveman Exchange.   A trading post for textbooks, housing, furnishings, more. For Utah Valley-based students. Lacks content. ★
   <http://www.itsnet.com/~rexj/caveman>

Education for Eternity.   A compilation of material on the subject of the eternal nature of education (see figure 6.18). Notable is the collection under the Education and the Gospel link, where the works of apostles and various LDS scholars are found. Lacks a search tool. ★★★

<http://www.byu.edu/tmcbucs/fc/ee/ee.htm>

Y-Site.   A packed page for LDS students. Of particular interest to students at BYU, but there's something there for every college-aged Latter-day Saint. ★★★★★

<http://www.ysite.com/students.htm>

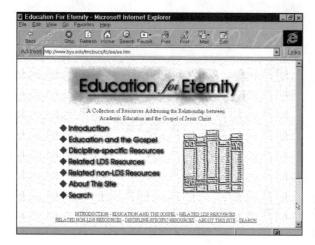

FIG. 6.18

Education for Eternity: A don't-miss page for educators.

7

REDEEM THE DEAD

In the previous chapters you were introduced to the first two elements of the Church's three-fold mission. This chapter looks at part three of that mission: redeeming the dead.

Uniquely among Christian churches, the Church of Jesus Christ of Latter-day Saints holds to the belief that every member of the entire human family will—whether in this life or the next—have the opportunity to hear the gospel of Christ, and to make individual decisions about how to accept that gospel.

Part of accepting the gospel is taking on the name of Christ, and being baptized into the body of the Church. It also involves other necessary ordinances, including the sealing of marriages for eternity, and sealing together family units. All of these ordinances are performed by faithful Latter-day Saints on behalf of deceased ancestors in temples around the world, thus literally fulfilling Malachi's prophecy of Elijah, turning the heart of the fathers to the children, and the heart of the children to their fathers (Mal. 4:6).

In order to perform those services, Latter-day Saints maintain extensive family histories and search out the genealogical records of their ancestors.

This chapter considers Internet resources for researching genealogy and maintaining family histories, takes a brief look at pioneer histories and diaries, and introduces the temples of the Latter-day Saints.

GENEALOGY/FAMILY HISTORY PAGES

Living overseas can sometimes be a struggle. It's not the unfamiliar surroundings or the unusual food or the unaccustomed language. More than anything, it's missing the family that was left behind. And so it happened that while I was living in Hong Kong, and missing my parents and cousins and sibs, I decided to get to work on my genealogy. I hauled a laptop computer and a couple of boxes of pedigree charts into town for a visit to the family history center.

The first order of business was to enter existing names into my computerized family history database. I cracked open the first book and began inputting records, but was dismayed to discover that the books of pedigree charts weren't in very good shape. Fortunately, the computers in the FHC stood ready and waiting. I randomly entered the name of my great-great-grandmother and pressed the enter key.

There she was. Grandma. And Grandpa. And all their kids. Too cool. I was so excited, I decided I'd print out a descendants chart.

The list was four or five pages long. What fun! As I walked back to my seat, I scanned the list. Aunts, uncles, cousins . . .

And then, whoa! There was a name I recognized. I looked, and looked again. Yep. No doubt about it.

I was related to someone I knew. It seems I had a not-so-distant cousin I'd already met . . . a counselor in the bishopric—of my ward in Hong Kong.

Guess I wasn't so far from home as I'd imagined.

You won't need to travel overseas, or even to your local library, to get started with a family history. When you're hunting for your own long-losts, turn to the resources of the Internet.

There are, literally, thousands of genealogy pages on the Internet. They fall into several categories: pages from individual families, pages from family organizations, information from genealogy organizations, research databases, commercial products, LDS-oriented links, and more. Most pages contain links to LDS resources, but few give more than a passing reference to the wealth of information available online.

This section contains a compilation of some of the best starting points for genealogical research.

A Chart for Figuring Relationships.   Can't tell your grand niece from a first cousin once removed? Here's how to figure it all out. ★★★

<http://www.rootsweb.com/~genepool/cousins.htm>

alt.genealogy.   A newsgroup discussing genealogy in very general terms. Low traffic, useful information. See chapter 8, page 189, for instructions on accessing newsgroups. ★★★★

<news:alt.genealogy>

Ancestors.   The family history and genealogy television series, presented by KBYU-TV and PBS. The site contains tips, a resource guide, downloadable charts and software, more. ★★★★

<http://www2.kbyu.byu.edu/ancestors>

Ancestry Home Town.   An entire community dedicated to helping you discover your ancestors. Includes a genealogy library with 108 databases, a community family tree, answers to genealogy questions, genealogy lessons, and commercial links. The genealogy lessons are a tremendous help to beginners. ★★★★

<http://www.ancestry.com>

CompuServe Roots.   The genealogy forum on Compuserve. Worth visiting if you're a member. Very helpful. ★★★★

<http://ourworld.compuserve.com/homepages/roots>

Cyndi's List of Genealogy Links.   Perhaps the best-designed, most thorough noncommercial site on the entire Internet (see figure 7.1). More than 22,000 genealogy sites categorized into 70-some categories, including adoption, biographies, books, microfilm and microfiche, cemeteries, funeral homes and obituaries, census-related sites worldwide, events and activities, family bibles, handy online starting points, heraldry, historical events and people, hit a brick wall?, how to, LDS and family history centers, medieval, genealogy home page construction kit, photographs and memories, preserving your family's treasures, stories and genealogical research, professional researchers, volunteers and other research services, software and computers, terms, phrases, dictionaries and glossaries, and sites for every region, country, and U.S. state. ★★★★★☑

<http://www.oz.net/~cyndihow/sites.htm>

Deciphering Old Handwriting.   An article full of examples and explanations of old handwriting. Very useful. ★★★

<http://www.firstct.com/fv/oldhand.html>

FIG. 7.1

Cyndi's List: Incredibly well-organized collection of genealogy links.

As a result, doing family history research has never been easier than it now is. Through Family-Search, patrons of the Family History Library and Family History Centers have access to the 147 million names in the International Genealogical Index and the growing 9.67-million-name lineage-linked Ancestral File. As name extraction programs convert information from paper records (such as the 1880 U.S. Federal Census and the 1881 British Census) and as people from around the world contribute information to the Ancestral File, the computer resources associated with FamilySearch will make identifying one's ancestors a much simpler task.

David H. Pratt, "Family History, Genealogy," *Encyclopedia of Mormonism*, Vol. 2.

Elijah-L. An LDS Genealogy mailing list. To subscribe, send an e-mail request to *<elijah-l-request@genealogy.emcee.com>*. Daily traffic is about 10 messages. The Web site is an additional source of information. ★★
<http://genealogy.emcee.com/~holdiman/elijah-l>

Everton's Genealogical Helper. A commercial site with a few free databases. Research helps and other tools are tremendously helpful. ★★★★
<http://www.everton.com>

Family History Centers of the Church. Organized by state. Addresses and phone numbers only. The same information is available over the phone at (U.S.) 1-800-346-6044. ★★
<http://www.deseretbook.com/famhis>

Family History. A collection of background information on why Latter-day Saints do genealogy. Includes articles on Family History or Genealogy, Family History Library, Family History Centers, Ancestral File, Family Registry, Family-Search, Family Organizations, Genealogical Society, Granite Mountain Record Vault, and Book of Remembrance. A Mormons.Org site. ★★★
<http://www.mormons.org/daily/family_history>

Family History—How Do I Begin? Information from the Church's Web site on Why family history? Why do members of The Church of Jesus Christ of Latter-day Saints do family history research? What can I do first? What is a Family History Center? and Where is the nearest Family History Center? ★★★★
<http://www.lds.org/Family_History/How_Do_I_Begin.html>

Family Tree Maker. This commercial site includes some excellent noncommercial resources: an online genealogy class, an Internet family name search tool, a how-to guide, biography writing assistant, and much more. ★★★★★
<http://www.familytreemaker.com>

FHL—Brigham Young University. To contact the BYU Family History Library, send an e-mail message to *<FHL@byu.edu>*.

FHL—Salt Lake City. To contact the SLC Family History Library, send an e-mail message to <*famhistlib@aol.com*>.

Gendex. Indexes hundreds of World Wide Web databases containing genealogical data for over two million individuals. Incredibly helpful site with an altogether unattractive format. ★★★★

<*http://www.gendex.com/gendex*>

Genealogy Online. This site is for discussion of genealogy. Includes links to the Genealogy Chat site, events database, the 1880 census, much more. Quite helpful. Little original content. ★★★

<*http://genealogy.emcee.com*>

Genealogy Online's Events Database. Add your own "events" (birth, marriage, death, other) to contribute to the site's 4,000 existing entries. ★★

<*http://events.genealogy.org*>

Genealogy Resources on the Internet. An "obsessive" list of mailing lists, UseNet newsgroups, FTP sites, Gophers, Web, Telnet, and e-mail resources. Ugly but thorough. ★★★★★

<*http://members.aol.com/johnf14246/internet.html*>

Genealogy Software. Reviews of software, links to developers, utilities and add-ons, archives. Very useful if you're looking for a new genealogy package. ★★★

<*http://www-personal.umich.edu/~cgaunt/software.html*>

Genealogy World. This site contains access to both free genealogy information, and a commercial genealogy service (see figure 7.2). The free links include Surname Forums (a search and submission tool for people doing work on any given family name), Genealogy Lady Answers (answers to questions about genealogy research roadblocks), Genealogy Bookstore (books categorized by state, country, and surname, along with books on CD-ROM), monthly genealogy news-

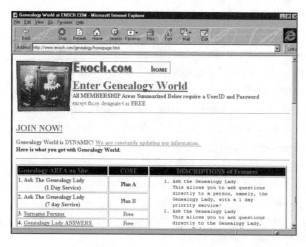

FIG.7.2

Genealogy World: Worth a subscription.

letter (good hints and information sources, also available via e-mail), and more. If you want additional help, Plan A, at $36 a year, and Plan B, at $24 a year, offer professional genealogical assistance. ★★★★

<http://www.enoch.com/genealogy/homepage.html>

GEN-ROOTERS. A mailing list for Latter-day Saints to share ideas and helpful hints on the "how-to's" of genealogy. Send your subscription request to Dianne Morris at <azdee@aol.com>, with a brief description of your Church affiliation and a request that you be added to the list.

How to Gather 1001 Names an Hour from a Family History Center. Robert Ragan, operator of the Treasure Maps site, has written a guidebook for using Family History Centers. Read part of his tutorial—and order the book—at this site. ★★★

<http://www.firstct.com/fv/lds1.html>

Online Language Resources. Translates from 18 European languages to English. Hau bang le! ★★★★★

<http://www.cooklib.org/genlang.html>

The Genealogy Lady. The Genealogy Lady—part of the fantastic New Jerusalem suite of LDS Web sites—answers questions put to her by amateur genealogists. Visit this page to read her responses. ★★★★★

<http://www.new-jerusalem.com/genealogy/questions.html>

Roots-L Surname List Finder. Massive surname search engine. ★★★★

<http://searches.rootsweb.com/cgi-bin/Genea/rsl>

Treasure Maps. Good how-to information (see figure 7.3) compiled by a member of the Church. Numerous Family History Center links and a free monthly genealogy newsletter. ★★★★

<http://www.firstct.com/fv/tmapmenu.html>

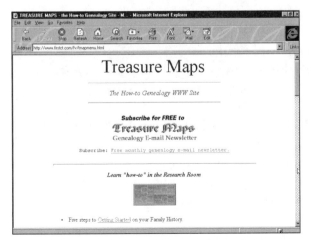

FIG. 7.3

Treasure Maps: Learn how to locate your own ancestors.

U.S. Census Bureau—Genealogy. Disappointingly little information. An Age Search Service that costs $40 per lookup, plus a small amount of information on using Census Bureau information for genealogy. ★
<http://www.census.gov/ftp/pub/genealogy/www>

US GenWeb. Gateway to the huge US GenWeb project. Volunteers across the United States maintain links to information for their states and counties. This page contains information about the project and links to state-level GenWeb sites. ★★★★★
<http://www.usgenweb.com>

World Genealogy Web Project. Your first stop for finding links to international genealogical resources. Adopt a country. Maintain genealogy links for your ancestral home. Nice service project. This page is a very slow load. ★★★
<http://www.dsenter.com/worldgenweb>

FAMILY HISTORIES

Every faithful member of the Church is a pioneer in his or her own right. But if you're among the few who can count Mormon Trail walkers, Nauvoo dwellers, or Mormon Undergrounders among your ancestors, you've got a story worth telling the kids. No matter where your roots originate, your family has a story to match all that genealogy. Here's where you can go on the Internet if you want to write some family history.

Early-Saints. Large collection of biographies of early Latter-day Saints. Really unattractive site, but the information is invaluable. ★★★
<http://erdos.math.byu.edu/~smithw/Lds/LDS/Early-Saints>

Book and Journal Binding. Bind your journal in hard cover for 50 bucks. $
<http://home1.gte.net/rmorgan/bokbind1.htm#bookbinding>

Family History. Articles on the LDS practice of keeping family histories. A small collection. ★★
<http://www.mormons.org/daily/family_history>

Family History Moments. Archived stories from the Church News. ★★★★
<http://www.desnews.com/cgi-bin/libheads?search=family+history+moments&limit=50>

Oral History Questions. A good list of questions for evoking detailed memories during an oral history interview. ★★★
<http://www.rootsweb.com/~genepool/oralhist.htm>

The Family Letter. A service for building a family Web site, newsletter, and history accessible to family members around the world. Great idea. Implementation is a bit rough. ★★★
<http://webols.everton.com/familyletter/fl_welcome.html>

Tracing Mormon Pioneers.   Tips for those tracing their Mormon Pioneer ancestry from Europe to Salt Lake City, Utah. Information regarding online and conventional resources of Mormon pioneer ancestry. Phenomenal page. Well worth reading through if you had ancestors arriving in Salt Lake City from 1847 to 1869. ★★★

<http://www.vii.com/~nelsonb/pioneer.htm>

You Can Publish Your Own Family Keepsakes.   Tips for publishing family records. Excellent. ★★★★

<http://www.rootsweb.com/~genepool/ keepsakes.htm>

TEMPLES

Latter-day Saints are a temple-building people. The temple is the center of our worship, the place we go to find answers and revelation and peace.

The temple is also the place we go to perform service on behalf of those who have gone before, reaping the blessings not only of serving others, but also, in so doing, of being edified and taught of ourselves.

Here you'll find some of the most sacred and important doctrines and experiences being shared among faithful Saints by various means over the Internet. This section includes personal accounts of temple experiences, temple dedicatory prayers, and research on ancient temple building and ceremonies. Also listed here are sites that provide temple schedules and events, as well as information about the history of individual temples.

> **PRESIDENT WILFORD WOODRUFF ON TEMPLE BUILDING**
>
> This is a preparation necessary for the second advent of the Savior; and when we shall have built the temples now contemplated, we will then begin to see the necessity of building others, for in proportion to the diligence of our labors in this direction, will we comprehend the extent of the work to be done, and the present is only a beginning. When the Savior comes, a thousand years will be devoted to this work of redemption; and . . . all the descendants of Shem, Ham, and Japheth, who received not the gospel in the flesh, must be officiated for in the temples of God, before the Savior can present the kingdom to the Father, saying, "It is finished."
>
> "The Discourses of Wilford Woodruff," p. 163, from the *Journal of Discourses,* 19:229–230, September 16, 1877.

Temple Experiences

The Latter-day Saint experience is, at its root, the story of the temple. There is the place where man communes with God. All the work we do in our families, in our communities, and in the world at large has at its root the work of the temple.

It's no surprise that the temple is so elemental to our communication with God. The testimonies and stories associated with the temple are among the most powerful events that Latter-day Saints experience.

In this section you'll find a collection of personal stories about experiences in the temple.

Free the Birdies. The account of a three-year-old child who was involved in a near-fatal accident, and survived to tell the story of what happened during his "death." The story—a powerful testimony of temples and the afterlife—is related by his father, Lloyd Glenn. The experience is tremendously moving, deeply spiritual. A poignant reminder of the importance of temple work. This site also includes an account of my (successful) effort to locate Brother Glenn to confirm the story. ★★★★★

<http://www.jersey.net/~inkwell/testfree.htm>

Temple Dedications. From the LDS-GEMS Archive Index, a compilation of personal experiences associated with the temple, as related by subscribers to the LDS-GEMS mailing list. ★★★★

<http://www.xmission.com/~dkenison/lds/gems/arc_tmpl.html>

Temple Moments. Stories of temple experiences, submitted by readers of the Deseret News. ★★★★

<http://www.desnews.com/
cgi-bin/libheads_reg?search=temple+moment&limit=50>

What the Temple Means to Me. The story of one man's experience with the dedication of the Washington, D.C., Temple. Nicely done page. ★★★

<http://www.wesnet.com/lds-ohio/lds-ohio/temples.htm>

The Story of . . . Just a few of the many conversion stories located at the Testimony Stories Web site. These relate specifically to temple experiences. ☞

<http://www.new-jerusalem.com/testimony/grant.html> and
<http://www.new-jerusalem.com/testimony/deanmacy.html>

About Temples

A collection of information on temple ordinances, dedicatory prayers, ancient temples, and more. Stop and study for awhile.

Mormon Heritage: The Temple Collection. A commercial site for purchasing resin replicas of various temples, including Nauvoo and Kirtland. Photos appear on site. $

<http://webusers.anet-stl.com/~sharon>

Nick Literski's Latter-day Saint Temple Home Page. (See figure 7.4.) From the opening hymn ("The Spirit of God Like a Fire Is Burning") to the closing links, there's not a better place *in the world* for understanding the temple. The site includes temple dedicatory prayers, photos, plans for new temples, and talks and documents related to LDS temples. Be sure to read Nick's newest link: Letters from Visitors to the Home Page. ★★★★★ ☑

<http://www.vii.com/~nicksl>

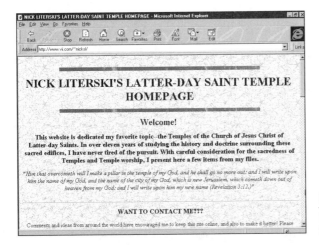

FIG. 7.4

Nick Literski's Page: Marvelous collection of temple-related background.

Questions About Baptism for the Dead. Part of Jeff Lindsay's frequently asked questions suite. Provides answers to several questions: Why do Mormons believe in baptism for the dead? Did early Christians practice baptism for the dead? Where does the Bible advocate baptism for the dead? Well reasoned. ★★
<http://www.athenet.net/~jlindsay/LDSFAQ/FQ_BaptDead.shtml>

Teachings About Temples. A fantastic collection of articles relating to temple worship (see figure 7.5). Includes information on Why these Temples?, Latter-day Saint Temple Worship and Activity, Salvation for the Dead, The Temple and the Atonement, Temple Ordinances, Baptism for the Dead, Washings and Anointings, The Endowment, Temple Sealings, Temple Recommends, Garments, Altars, and Early Christian Temple Rites. A Mormons.Org page. ★★★★★
<http://www.mormons.org/basic/temples>

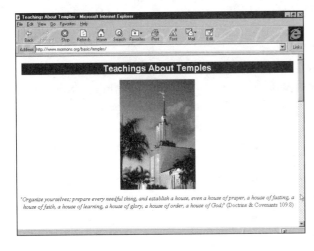

FIG. 7.5

Teachings About Temples: Helpful articles on temple ordinances.

Temple Awareness Fireside.   The program for a fireside on genealogy and raising temple awareness. ★★

<http://www.zarahemla.com/taf.html>

Temple Dedications.   Extremely well-done collection of dedicatory prayers. Site owner Nick Literski describes the prayers given in the dedication of temples as "some of the most valuable doctrinal and historical writings in the LDS Church." Includes prayers in chronological order from the Temple of Solomon to the Temple at St. Louis. ★★★★

<http://www.vii.com/~nicksl/temdeds.html>

Temple Endowment.   Dave Wiley's research on the circumstances that indicate Jesus Christ taught the apostles about the temple after his resurrection. Heavily footnoted. Consider shutting off the dark background before attempting to read. ★★★

<http://webpages.marshall.edu/~wiley6/40_days.html >

Temple Pictures and Dedication Prayers.   Prayers, addresses, and photos of all the temples, including Nauvoo, Kirtland, and Solomon's Temple. A fine collection. ★★★★

<http://www.cs.utah.edu/~ruefenac/lds/temples>

Temple Preparation.   A very good page for new members and others about to go through the temple for the first time. A real "must read." ★★★★★

<http://www.nettally.com/lds/temp.html>

Temple Preparation.   For first-time temple-goers. What to wear when attending the temple. ★★

<http://www.uvol.com/writers/nina/temple.html>

Temples.   Basic temple information from the Global Media Guide of the Church of Jesus Christ of Latter-day Saints. Names, locations, and dedicatory dates for all the latter-day temples. ★★

<http://www.lds.org/Global_Media_Guide/Temples_of_the_Church.html>. The same content, slightly expanded, is available at <http://www.xmission.com/~dkenison/lds/templist.html>

Temples. Guide to temples. A little difficult to navigate, somewhat incomplete. ★★
<http://www.zarahemla.com/temple.html>

The Mormon Temple Ceremony. Describes the temple endowment as a beautiful Christianization of the ancient Hebrew temple rite. Well documented, useful links. ★★★★
<http://www.teleport.com/~arden/temple.htm>

Why These Temples? An essay by President Gordon B. Hinckley. ✍
<http://www.primenet.com/~kitsonk/mormon/templ1.html>

General Temple Information

Check the schedules, use the photos, follow the maps.

Pictures of Temples. A very good collection of temple pictures and operating information. ★★★
<http://www.cs.utah.edu/~ruefenac/lds/temples>

Temples. Schedules, maps, and photos. Each map includes an address and driving directions, along with links to bookstores in various temple districts. A very nicely organized page, by Deseret Book. ★★★★★
<http://www.deseretbook.com/temple>

The Zarahemla Book Shoppe Temple Page. Maps to temples, general temple information, links to temple-related Web pages, a list of temples announced and under construction, and operating schedules for temples in operation. A nice arrangement of "Faith in Every Footstep" plays in the background, but the page is infrequently updated. ★★★

<http://www.zarahemla.com/temple.html>

Individual Temples

The histories of various individual temples.

Boston Temple Page.   Absolutely not to be missed is the history of the temple, written by a member who grew up in the region. Altogether an excellent site, built with an obvious love for both the temple and New England region as the birthplace of the Church. ★★★★

Front page: *<http://acs.bu.edu:8001/~baird/templehome.html>;*
Temple history: *<http://acs.bu.edu:8001/~baird/TempleStory.html>;*
An artist's rendering: *<http://www.deseretbook.com/temple/SCHBSTN.html>*

Herod's Temple: Virtual Reconstruction of the Second Temple.   A reconstruction of Herod's Temple, produced by the Department of Religious Education at Brigham Young University. ★★★

<http://www.byu.edu/rel1/research/temple.htm>

Hong Kong Mission Alumni Home Page.   Includes photos, dedicatory prayer for Hong Kong temple. ★★

<http://www.1source.com/~hop/mission.html>. See schedule and photo at *<http://www.deseretbook.com/temple/SCHHK.html>*

Kirtland Temple.   Tour of the temple. ★★★

<http://www.zarahemla.com/kirtland.html>

Las Vegas Temple.   Background information on the temple in Las Vegas, Nevada. Very thorough. ★★★

<http://www.nevada.edu/home/16/blake/www/LV.temple.html>. See schedule, photo, more at *< http://www.deseretbook.com/temple/SCHLV.html>.*

Logan Temple.   History and early photos of the Logan, Utah, temple. ★★★

<http://cyberfair.gsn.org/usdblhs/ldstemple.html>

Manti Temple.   History of the temple in Manti, Utah, by someone who was married there. Sweet. ★★

<http://www.sisna.com/users/EricSimpson/Manti.htm>

Nauvoo Temple Tour.   Photos, history, diagrams, descriptive tour. Completely fascinating. A valuable document. Worth revisiting. ★★★★

<http://www.indirect.com/www/crockett/nauvoo.html>

Orlando Temple Page.   The Building of the Orlando Temple. Someone should have this much love for every temple. ★★★

<http://www2.gdi.net/~lemuel> Schedules, photo, map, and more are at *<http://www.deseretbook.com/temple/SCHOR.html>.*

Salt Lake Temple, History.   Great page, chock full of explanations and a photographic history (see figure 7.6). An excellent site, and the quality of the historic photographs makes it well worth visiting. It would be nice to be able to click on the pictures and have them expand to fill the entire screen. ★★★
<http://www.nettally.com/lds/hist.html>

Salt Lake Temple, Tour of Temple Square.   Online photo tour of Temple Square, with descriptions and histories of the buildings and monuments located there. ★★★
<http://www.desnews.com/confer/sqtour/tour.htm>

Salt Lake Temple: Max Bertola's Temple Square Tour.   Max Bertola provides a nice tour of Temple Square and nearby historical sites. ★★★★
<http://www.uvol.com/www1st/tsquare>

St. George Temple.   Great history site. Very well done. ★★★
<http://www.infowest.com/Utah/colorcountry/History/Temple/temple.html>

St. Louis Temple.   Building the St. Louis Temple. From the Hammond home page, links to information related to the St. Louis temple.
<http://www.ezl.com/~eggbtr>

Sweden Temple.   In Swedish. Try reading aloud, just for fun. ★★★
<http://www.elfi.adbkons.se/~richard/sdh.html>

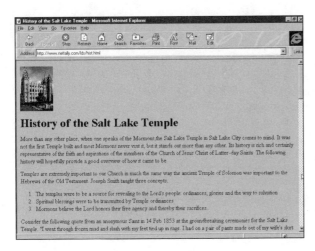

FIG. 7.6

History of the Salt Lake Temple: Page down to see lots of historic photos.

Living a Latter-day Saint Life

8

THE LIVING CHURCH

The threefold mission of the Church describes in a very inclusive way what the Church is all about: reaching out to the world, reaching out to the members, and strengthening family ties.

Part 3 of this book, called "Living a Latter-day Saint Life," is much more narrowly focused. This first chapter in Part 3, "The Living Church," looks at news of the Church in all its forms. The subsequent chapters consider the auxiliaries of the Church, interest groups, the pursuit of excellence, the glory of God, and finally, a roundup of the LDS Internet experience.

Being a member of a living Church can be a bit like catching fish with bare hands. It takes constant vigilance, sensitivity, keen perceptions, a measure of intelligence, and a willingness to act quickly. The reward, of course, is a feast for the soul.

The Church today is a vital force, one that changes—albeit at a marked pace—to accommodate the changing needs of its membership. In the 1970s, an expanded international missionary effort lead to a great deal of prayer over the issue of expanding the priesthood base. In the 1980s, changes in the demographics of member families resulted in a block meeting schedule. In the 1990s, rapid growth led to an expansion in the number and makeup of general authorities. In recent years the number of temples has gone from an easily memorized dozen to more than 50. From a membership of 5 million in the '80s, the Church has again doubled to its present size of 10 million. In our march to the millennium, we as a

Church will continue to find new ways to meet one another's needs. And the Internet will play an ever-increasing part in that outreach.

This chapter lists resources that allow Latter-day Saints—no matter where they live—to keep pace with the change. The first section, the International Church, contains information for members living outside of North America. It's followed by a listing of major events and activities; a large section on news about the Church; a sampling of online wards, branches, and stakes of the Church; and a section on electronic discussion areas that invite member participation.

<table>
<tr><td>

ELDER NEAL A. MAXWELL ON LIVING IN A LIVING CHURCH

It is very nettling to be reminded by the living God, through living prophets, the living scriptures, and the living Church, of one's unfinished work and of one's remaining possibilities. The living God reinforces his promptings by our consciences; the living prophets particularize painfully; the living Church lays heavy duties and responsibilities upon us; the living scriptures add to the stimuli, for the word of God can scarcely be opened without giving us a start, suggesting something that needs to be done or undone. So much livingness does not seem to leave much room for repose.

Neal A. Maxwell, *Things As They Really Are*, p. 35.

</td></tr>
</table>

THE INTERNATIONAL CHURCH

Now that more than half the membership of the Church lies outside the borders of the United States, redirecting the focus internationally is more important than ever before.

Members throughout the world are building Web sites that reflect their own cultures and communities. Together, their sites constitute a diverse, multicultural perspective that fulfills scriptural prophesies of the gospel going to "every kindred, and tongue, and people, and nation" (Revelation 5:9).

Australia: Australian LDS Homepage. Information about The Church of Jesus Christ of Latter-day Saints in Australia. Includes local contacts, Sydney temple information, more. ★★★★
  <http://www.iinet.net.au/~soneil/lds.html>

Australia. Austrialian-operated tour of Church historic sites. $
  <http://www.wm.com.au/ldstour>

Austria: LDS Resources. A bilingual German/English site. Lots of links. ★★★★
  <http://www.ettl.co.at/mormon>

Basque-speaking: Ongi Etorri Mormoi Euskaldunen Etxeko Orrialdera. An introduction to the LDS Church in Basque (see figure 8.1). Includes a history of the Church, the Articles of Faith, Proclamation on the Family. No English. ★★★
  <http://www.cyberhighway.net/~goodies/basque>

Brazil: Página Das Missões Brasileiras. The Church in Brazil, including information on the São Paulo temple. Includes an English translation. ★★★★
  <http://www.xmission.com/~dkenison/brasil>

FIG. 8.1

Ongi Etorri Mormoi: Basquing on the Internet.

Building Zion: The Latter-day Saints in Europe.   Excerpt from Bruce Van Orden's book. History, statistical information, more. ★★★★
<http://fas-www.harvard.edu/~brown5/vanorden.html>

BYU Multicultural Student Services.   Privately collected information regarding the Multicultural Student Services department at BYU. ★★
<http://www.netcom.com/~toniaizu/gmss.html>

Cambodia: LDS Cambodian Connection.   The Church in Cambodia, the Laotian connection, more. In English. ★★★★
<http://www.mormon.org/cambodian-speaking>

Cambodia: The Church in Cambodia.   News, photos, information about the branches of the Church in Cambodia. Very timely. ★★★★
<http://www.orst.edu/~charlesb/sasana.html>

Denmark.   An all-Danish site. History, full text of the Book of Mormon, much more. ★★★★
<http://www.cybercity.dk/users/ccc2343/sdh/sdh.htm>

Eastern Europe Mission Center.   English- and native-language information for missions in the Ukraine, Russia, Lithuania, Hungary, Poland, Romania, and Yugoslavia. ★★★★★
<http://members.tripod.com/~kyiv/>

French-speaking: A multilingual Québecois site for Single Adults/Adultes Célibataires/Adultos Solteros(as). ★★★
<http://www.goldplanet.com/index1.htm>

German-speaking: Das Buch Mormon.   The Book of Mormon in German. ★★★
<http://www.geocities.com/Heartland/Hills/1037/inhalt.htm>

German-speaking: Proclamation on the Family in German.   Read Webmaster Michael Stanek's account of how the proclamation influenced one nonmember.   ✐
<*http://www.ettl.co.at/mormon/deutsch/familie.htm*>

Germany: The Germany Munich Mission Unofficial Homepage.   In English. History of the Germany Munich Mission and its predecessors: the South German/Germany South Mission, the Bavarian Mission, and the West German Mission. Includes an alumni list. ★★
<*http://www.sas.upenn.edu/~dbowie/muenchenmsn.html*>

Holland: De Kerk van Jezus Christus van de Heiligen der Laatste Dagen.   An unofficial Church site, in Dutch. Includes English-language information about the Dutch missions. ★★★★
<*http://www.worldaccess.nl/~collinst*>

Hong Kong: HK Saints.   Bilingual site (but mostly Cantonese) with information about the Church in Hong Kong. ★★★★
<*http://home.netvigator.com/~bonken*>

Japan: Bountiful.   Chat/communication list in Japanese. Uncontroversial. Subscribe with an e-mail request to <*majordomo@iijnet.or.jp*>. Requires Japanese-language computer capability. Daily traffic: 10 messages.   ✐

Japan: Irreantum.   Japanese-language discussion of LDS matters for those who have not been satisfied by formal answers. Subscribe by sending an e-mail request to <*owner-irre@iijnet.or.jp*>. Requires Japanese-language computer capability.   ✐

Japan: LDS-J.   Mailing list for a general discussion of LDS topics. To subscribe, send your request to <*owner-lds-j@iijnet.or.jp*>. Requires Japanese-language computer capability.   ✐

Japan: Plates.   Discussion and information list about PC and data application to gospel study in Japanese. Mainly for those working with data-input, translation,

Braille materials, etc., or Church materials in Japanese. Send a subscription request to *<plates-ml-request@yk.rim.or.jp>*. ✎

Japan: Tokyo English-Speaking. Living overseas means your ward becomes your virtual family. The ties last for life. The Tokyo English-speaking wards have built a fine Web site, of interest to anyone who knows anyone from an Asian expatriate ward. The expat community needs more pages like this. ★★★★★
<http://www2.gol.com/users/franz/index.htm>

Mexico: Benemèrito de las Amèricas. Web site for the LDS-operated school in Colona Juarez, Mexico. Spanish only. ★★★
<http://www.geocities.com/Athens/Acropolis/1789>

Mission.Net. Links to most international missions of the Church. This site is reviewed in chapter 5: "Proclaim the Gospel," page 100. ★★★★★☑
<http://www.mission.net>

Norway: Oslo Stake and the Norway Oslo Mission. Bilingual site, in English and Norwegian, with information about the Church. Links to Scandinavian LDS sites, Norwegian-language information, much more. ★★★★★
<http://www.internet.no/sue/nor/norge.htm> or in English at
<http://www.internet.no/sue/nor/norway.htm>

Our International LDS. Community online LDS Web sites around the world. Links only; no original content. ★★
<http://www.mich.com/~romulans/Intl_LDS_Online.html>

Portugal SUD. No English. History of the Church in Portugal, translations of English-language documents, more. ★★★
<http://www.geocities.com/Athens/Acropolis/2532>

Portugal: Queluz-Portugal Branch. All English, with good general background information on the Church. Very little of specifically Portuguese interest. ★★★
<http://www.geocities.com/Athens/Acropolis/7595>

Puerto Rico.   A few links to good information. ★★★
   <http://home.coqui.net/frankiyl/lds/lds1e.htm>
Regional Church Information.   Links to international sites, arranged by region. No original content. ★★
   <http://www.ldsworld.com/links/geo.html>
Scandinavia: EP Friend.   A mailing list for Latter-day Saints with an interest in Scandinavia. The list operates in Swedish. To subscribe, send an e-mail request to *<Richard.Bruvik@adbkons.se>* 📖
Spanish-speaking: Centro Hispanico de los Santos del los Ultimos Dias.   Basic information about the Church, in Spanish (see figure 8.2). Well-organized site. ★★★★
   <http://duckpond.com/mormon/centro.html>
Spanish-speaking: Creencias de la Iglesia de Jesucristo de los Santos de los Ultimos Días.   Teachings of the Church, in Spanish. Quite brief. ★★
   <http://cc.usu.edu/~slc9d/nicaragua/doctrina.html>
Spanish-speaking: Historia de la Iglesia SUD.   A history of the Church, in Spanish. Includes links to Nicaragua mission. ★★★
   <http://cc.usu.edu/~slc9d/nicaragua/historia.html>
Spanish-speaking: Libro de Mormón.   The Book of Mormon in Spanish. ★★★
   <http://www.duckpond.com/mormon/libro.htm>
Spanish-speaking: Light at the Top of the Mountain.   A monthly e-mail magazine (bimonthly in Spanish) of LDS messages and doctrine. Subscribe by e-mailing a request to *<marda@burgoyne.com>*. 📖
Sweden: LDS Resources.   A list of resources for Latter-day Saints in Sweden. Non-English. ★★★
   <http://130.244.7.117/~richard/sdh.html>

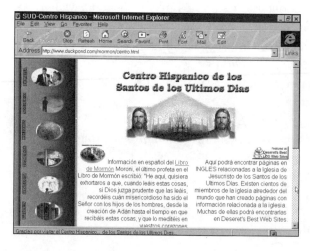

FIG. 8.2

Centro Hispanico: Spanish-speaking members will find much worth reading.

The Worldwide Church.   Articles related to the international Church. Topics include: Community, The Church in Africa, The Church in Asia, The Church in Australia, The Church in the British Isles, The Church in Canada, and Gathering and Colonization. A Mormons.Org page. ★★★
<http://www.mormons.org/basic/organization/world>

WW-LDS.   The home page for Latter-day Saints around the world. Contains an index of articles from Church publications about the international Church, statistical information about the growth of the Church around the world, and a directory of LDS Saints on the Internet who speak non-English languages. Lots of work went into this site. Very well done. ★★★★★
<http://138.87.135.33/ww-lds>

WW-LDS.   A mailing list for discussions about the international Church. To subscribe, send an e-mail request to *<listserv@acadcomp.cmp.ilstu.edu>* with the message "`subscribe ww-lds`" (no quotes). Daily traffic is about three messages. The home page for the World-Wide LDS mailing list includes a directory, statistical information, and an index of international articles in Church magazines. ★★
<http://www.wnetc.com/resource/lds/international.html>

World-wide Church.   A new LDS-GEMS project documenting history and stories from Church members in various countries around the world. ★★★★
<http://www.xmission.com/~dkenison/lds/gems/arc_wrld.html>

EVENTS AND ACTIVITIES

There's no end of events and activities available to Latter-day Saints. In this section you'll find the home pages for activities ranging from the Polynesian Cultural Center in Hawaii to the Hill Cumorah Pageant in New York.

America's Witness for Christ.   Well-done page full of information about the Hill Cumorah pageant, as well as some Historical Church sites in the Palmyra area of New York. Includes links to the Hill, the Pageant, the Sacred Grove, the Smith Home, the Martin Harris Home, the Grandin Printing Shop, the Peter Whitmer Home, and the Fayette Chapel, as well as a map of the area. ★★★★
<http://www.geocities.com/Heartland/6130/hcp.htm>

Art and Culture.   Links to LDS art and entertainment news and other cultural events, compiled by Infobases. Not much to look at, but the information is timely. ★★★★
<http://www.ldsworld.com/ldsarts>

BYU Sports. Stats, coaches, players, and more, for every BYU sport. ★★★★★
<http://sports.byu.edu>

Calendar of Events. Deseret Book's listing of concerts, speakers, and just about anything else you can think of. Readers are invited to submit information about public events for inclusion on the calendar. ★★★★
<http://www.deseretbook.com/events>

Church Pageant Schedules. Schedules and information for Church-sponsored pageants. A schedule for next year would make this a tremendously useful site. ★★★
<http://www.deseretbook.com/pageant.html>

Church Trivia. A fun page. Test yourself. Questions change from time to time. ★★★★
<http://members.aol.com/cumorahhil/church_trivia>

Cougar Sports Network. Headline news for BYU Cougar sports fans (see figure 8.3). ★★★★★
<http://www.ysite.com/csn>

Cougar-Net. Information via e-mail about Brigham Young University athletics. Links to the Cougar-Net and Cougar-Best e-mail lists, plus archives of earlier discussions. ★★★
<http://www.cougar-net.com>

Holidays and Celebrations. Articles on LDS-celebrated holidays and events. Includes commentary on Halloween, Easter, the Hill Cumorah Pageant, more. ★★★
<http://www.mormons.org/daily/holidays>

FIG. 8.3

Cougar Sports Network: The next best thing to being there.

LDS Calendar. LDS events running in the *Church News.* A new entry each Friday. ★★★★★

<http://www.desnews.com/cgi-bin/libheads_reg?search=%22LDS+calendar%22&limit=999&x=47&y=9>

LDS Performing Arts. A list of links to pageants, theater, music, and related events. No original content. ★★

<http://www.mormons.org/happenings.htm>

Lilacs of the Valley. Home page for the pioneer pageant Lilacs in the Valley. Includes music from the presentation. ★★★

<http://208.129.36.5/howard/lilacsplay> or

<http://www.igoshopping.com/lilacsplay>

Mesa Temple Easter Pageant. Information about the Pageant held each year at Easter in Mesa, Arizona. ★★★

<http://www.tcsaz.com/mesapageant.html>

Mormon Arts Foundation. Information on the art gallery and the festival at Tuacahn. ★★★

<http://www.thewatchmen.com/ma>

Mormon Miracle Pageant. The Mormon Miracle Pageant, performed in June on the grounds of the Manti Temple. Free admission. Site hadn't been updated for the next pageant, so the rating looks worse than it deserves to be. ★★

<http://www.manti.com/pageant.htm>

Palmyra Ward's "Hotel Palmyra." The Palmyra Ward sponsors a bed-and-breakfast service for visitors to the area each year. Families and groups are welcome to stay in the homes of members of the Palmyra Ward. Sponsored by the Palmyra Youth, donations are accepted, and breakfast can be provided. Respond by e-mail to Owen Allen at *<oallen@ix.netcom.com>.* ✑

> **ON CREATING UNDERSTANDING**
>
> Aloha! I created the page for the Polynesian Cultural Center to distribute information to a worldwide audience at a minimal expense. I feel the Internet is a wonderful medium to share information about the beautiful cultures of Polynesia. I think world peace can be achieved if people have access, awareness, and understanding of all the world's cultures.
>
> Christian Wilson, Webmaster, Polynesian Cultural Center, Hawaii
> *<http://www.polynesia.com>*

Polynesian Cultural Center. Delightful site full of valuable information for visitors to the Center in Hawaii (see figure 8.4). Contacts, and everything you need to know to make your visit enjoyable. ★★★★★☑

<http://www.polynesia.com>

Question of the Week. Another trivia test, with questions running each week in the *Church News.* ★★★

<http://www.desnews.com/cgi-bin/libheads_reg?search=%22Question+of+the+week%22&limit=999&x=92&y=13>

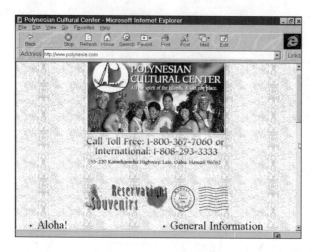

FIG. 8.4

Polynesian Cultural Center: Surf's up!

Tuacahn. An excellent site describing events at Tuacahn, the Mormon art center. Links to information on Tuacahn Events, Ticket Info, About Utah!, and Photos. A very nice page. ★★★★

<http://www.showutah.com>

The Spirit of Nauvoo. Lodge at the Nauvoo House, one day or longer. Available in July and August at $17.50 per day. $

<http://www.nauvoo.com/vacation>

NEWS OF THE CHURCH

The only real difference between living among the main body of the Saints, and living out in what used to be called the "mission field," is access.

During my years living overseas, I found lack of access to be something of a burden. Mail delivery overseas was generally unreliable, and always slow. At one point, I was living on a small island outlying Hong Kong, far away from the other Latter-day Saints in my ward, which meant that even secondhand news was hard to come by.

Going online opened up the world for me. The newsgroup I participated in became my primary—in fact, my only—source of Church news. It was still a form of secondhand information, but Utah-dwelling Saints were quick to announce every bit of Church-related news they came across.

It was, in effect, the very first LDS Wire Service in existence. I was the first in the ward to know about deaths, callings, policy changes, and every other scrap of information that fascinates those who can't get it without some effort.

Now, as you'll see from the resources listed in this section, news about the Church is easy to find. The following resources are divided into three groups: broadcasters, traditional print publishers, and new electronic publishers.

Broadcast

My grandparents had to walk miles to school in the snow—yeah, yeah, yeah, Grandpa, and it was uphill both directions, right? My parents remember when they didn't have television at all—I know, I know . . . and that was before color was invented, right Dad? So the other day, when my husband told our 12-year-old that when we were young we actually had to walk all the way across the room to . . . , our son interrupted and finished his sentence for him—"to push the buttons. I know, Dad."

"No," my husband said. "We didn't have buttons. We had to turn a dial." Our son looked surprised, and then burst into laughter.

Now our son's already got the next round for his children. "When we were young," he'll tell his babies, "we used to stand around the computer and listen to radio broadcasts."

It's Internet radio, and that's what we really do. Whenever I listen, the kids gather 'round and ask, in wonderment, "Where's that coming from?" Ha! I've one-upped them.

To me, this is incomparably the most fascinating part of the Internet: listening to online broadcasts of LDS radio programming.

The following sites offer some great listening through the speakers and sound card on your PC. You'll need a copy of the software that plays the broadcast. It's available for free by clicking on the download icon at each site.

Bonneville International.   Links to all the Bonneville media properties (see figure 8.5). ★★

<http://www.bonneville.com>

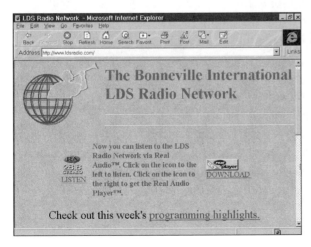

FIG. 8.5

LDS Radio Network: Listen to live LDS programming through the sound card and speakers on your PC.

KBYU Radio/TV. Information-heavy page from KBYU, the BYU media affiliates. Listen to KBYU-FM over the Internet. ★★★★★

<http://kbyuwww.byu.edu>

KSL Radio/TV. Watch KSL TV, and listen to KSL Radio live, over your Internet connection. ★★★★

<http://www.ksl.com>

LDS Radio Network. Twenty-four-hour programming from Bonneville International. Listen to conference talks, uplifting music, Church news, and BYU sports from your desktop. Probably the second-best site on the Internet. ★★★★★☑

<http://www.ldsradio.com>

Print

The sites below are associated with traditional print publications, including magazines, journals, and newspapers.

A few of the publications listed here have no direct LDS affiliation, but do carry a larger-than-average quantity of information either about the Church or about subjects of specific interest to Latter-day Saints.

Alumni Publications. A collection of publications from the Alumni Association at Brigham Young University. Includes links to *Brigham Young Magazine,* Alumni Today, Emeritydings (a newsletter for emeritus BYU-ers) and Passages (the alumni tours newsletter). ★★★★★

<http://ucs.byu.edu/alumni/alum-pub.htm>

AML-List. List of LDS and LDS-affiliated publications. Webmaster Benson Parkinson does a great job of keeping these lists up to date. ★★★★

View a list of newspapers at

<http://cc.weber.edu/~byparkinson/aml-list.html#newspapers>

A list of LDS journals is maintained at

<http://cc.weber.edu/~byparkinson/aml-list.html#journals>

Ancient American Archaeology. No known LDS affiliation, but certainly of interest to members of the Church. Ancient American is a bimonthly, color, popular science magazine, describing with photographs and reports the accounts of overseas visitors to America hundreds . . . even thousands of years before Columbus. ★★★★★

<http://ancientamerican.com>

Brigham Young Magazine. The BYU alumni publication, which is distributed quarterly (see figure 8.6). This site contains the current issue, and archives of several back issues. Great reading. ★★★★★
<http://www.byu.edu/bym>

BYU Public Communications. A great site listing BYU news and events, along with links to the text of selected devotionals, calendars for fine arts productions and conferences and workshops, BYU sports, construction updates, and much more. Maintained by BYU Public Communications. ★★★★★
<http://www.byu.edu/news>

BYU Publications. Includes *BYU Magazine, Clark* (law school) *Memorandum, Exchange* magazine, course catalogs, and more. Documents must be downloaded to an Adobe Acrobat reader, available from a link at the site. ★★★★
<http://advance.byu.edu/pdf.html>

BYU Studies. BYU's scholarly journal. Dedicated to the correlation of revealed and discovered truth and to the conviction that the spiritual and the intellectual may be complementary and fundamentally harmonious avenues of knowledge. This multidisciplinary journal has been published continuously since 1959. Its objective is to publish the best possible LDS scholarly journal, along with one or two major books a year, and occasional smaller monographs or special issues. The Web site contains a subscription form, index to content, and information about events. While the journal itself is fantastic, the site lacks real content. ★★
<http://humanities.byu.edu/BYUStudies/homepage.htm>

Church News. Deseret News' semi-official *Church News.* The site used to be publicly accessible. No more. Access is available only by subscription; and even then, it's not a very accessible site. Your account number is the 10-digit code on

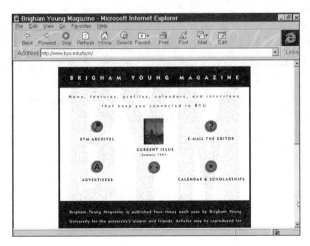

FIG. 8.6

Brigham Young Magazine: The alumni publication is filled with well-written articles on a variety of topics.

the mailing label of your print edition of the *Church News.* The commercialization of this publication is a tremendous loss to the online community. ★
<http://www.desnews.com/cn>

Church Publications. A collection of articles describing publications of the Church. Includes information on *Church News*, Conference Reports, Curriculum, General Handbook of Instructions, Bulletin, Distribution Centers, Doctrinal Works, *The Children's Friend*, Comprehensive History of the Church, and *The Contributor.* A Mormons.Org page. ★★
<http://www.mormons.org/basic/organization/publications>

Deseret News. Good site for staying current on Utah politics or issues. ★★★★★
<http://www.desnews.com>

FARMS Review of Books. Reviews of books on LDS topics. Of particular note is the presence of refutations of critical works. Includes ROB's predecessor, *Review of Books on The Book of Mormon.* ★★★★
<http://farmsresearch.com/frob/main.htm>

Hartmut Weissman's Betrachtungen ("Reflections"). A Euro-*Sunstone/BYU Studies.* Write Weissman at Gartner Platz 10, 61130, Nidderau, Germany, or e-mail him at *<74371.174@compuserve.com>* ✍

Insights: An Ancient Window. The newsletter of the Foundation for Ancient Research and Mormon Studies (FARMS). ★★★
<http://farmsresearch.com/insight/main.htm>

Journal of Book of Mormon Studies. Scholarly journal for Book of Mormon research, published semi-annually by FARMS. ★★★★
<http://farmsresearch.com/jbms/main.htm>

KeAlaka'i. BYU Hawaii's campus bulletin. Not regularly updated, but if you're a BYU-H alum, you'll want to stop by. ★★★
<http://websider.byuh.edu/kealakai/curentkeala/index.html>

Latter-day Messenger. LDS newspaper distributed in Northern California. Missionary news, obituaries, more; but it's infrequently updated. ★★
<http://www.mcmusic.com/ldm.html>

LDS Periodicals. A list maintained at Mormon-J: The LDS Journal-List. ★★★
<http://www.jersey.net/~inkwell/mjldsj.htm#mags>

(Logan) Herald Journal. No archive, no search engine. Sometimes you'll stumble across Church news for Cache County, though. ★★
<http://www.hjnews.com>

ON INTERNET PUBLISHING

The BYU Studies home page was created about two-and-a-half years ago. Our primary goal in creating the page was to enable online access to our comprehensive index (and the inherent searching capability of such), and to have an online version of our catalog. Additional focuses include having subscription information, highlights on our book line, bios of staff members, and info on our writing contests.

I see future offerings from us including perhaps our entire journal on the Net, all searchable and digitally available.

Karl F. Batdorff, Brigham Young University, Provo, Utah
<Karl_Batdorff@byu.edu>
Webmaster, BYU Studies page
<http://humanities.byu.edu/BYUStudies/homepage.htm>

Newsnet @ BYU. The KBYU/*Daily Universe* (BYU student newspaper) page. Campus events, live cam coverage of construction at the Lee Library, sports, Utah news, more. ★★★★
<http://newsline.byu.edu>

(Ogden) Standard-Examiner. Good religion coverage. An excellent newspaper. ★★★★★
<http://www.standard.net>

(Provo) Daily Herald. (See figure 8.7.) Utah Valley's best daily. (Take my recommendation with a grain of salt. This was the paper that trained me up in the way I should go; now that I'm old, I will not depart far from it.) The *Herald* operates a fine religion section that tries too hard to be diverse. ★★★★
<http://www.daily-herald.com>

Salt Lake Tribune. The not-the-*Deseret-News* Salt Lake daily. Articles about the Church are frequent. A very well-done site. ★★★★★
<http://utahonline.sltrib.com>

Speeches. Selected speeches from BYU devotionals. Includes "Do What Is Right" (Richard G. Scott), "Leaders and Managers" (Hugh Nibley), "Psychology and Repentance" (Allen E. Bergin), "And Also by Faith" (K. Newell Dayley), "We'll Sing and We'll Shout: A Mantic Celebration of the Holy Spirit" (Richard H. Cracroft), "One Step Enough" (John S. Tanner), "Of Souls, Symbols, and Sacraments" (Jeffrey R. Holland), and "A Man After God's Own Heart" (Vaughn J. Featherstone). Hasn't been updated in a while. ★★★
<http://advance.byu.edu/devo.html>

Submitting an Article to the Church News. For budding writers. ★★
<http://www.mich.com/~romulans/desnews.html>

Sunstone. The publication is not yet online. There is, however, an e-mail contact at *<SunstoneUT@aol.com>* ✍

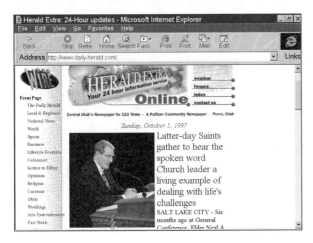

FIG. 8.7
_____

(Provo) *Daily Herald:* Religion from the heart of Happy Valley.

This People. The *People* magazine of Mormonism. Unfortunately, it hasn't been updated in more than a year. ★ *<http://www.ldsworld.com/thispeople>*

Utah Historical Quarterly. A 60-year index, which stops in 1995. No other content. ★ *<http://www.xmission.com/~drudy/ushs/uhq.html>*

Wasatch Review International. A Mormon literary journal. Again, nobody appears to be keeping it up to date. ★ *<http://members.aol.com/itstessie/wasatch>*

Electronic

I'm an old-school journalist, trained from youth to love printer's ink, racks of type, and loud presses. So it's with mixed emotion that I acknowledge the progress that has taken over my profession and made the future of publishing into something composed of electronic bits and bytes.

As happens with all progress, my excitement about the future is tempered by nostalgia over losing the past. That's not to say that progress in publishing is all, or even mostly, bad. It's not. It's mostly good. Electronic publishing has a number of advantages over traditional publishing, advantages that affect both the publisher and the reader. Not only is it less expensive—it eliminates two of the three costs of publishing: paper and postage—but it's also more timely and better focused.

For readers, electronic publications enable research. No more newspaper morgues, clipping services, or tattered library copies on microfilm when you need to search for information. Everything published electronically remains available for as long as the publisher maintains an archive. Readers get their information faster, and at a lower cost, than they've ever had from traditional media.

As you'll see from the following list of electronic periodicals, online publishing also enables anybody—absolutely anybody—to jump into the fray. The quality of information available from "small-press" online periodicals varies with the skill and resources of the publisher, but overall, the world is a better place because of their contribution.

Happenings. Monthly newsletter of LDS events sponsored by Deseret Book. ★★★★
Subscribe to the e-mail service at *<http://www.deseretbook.com/happenings/subscribe.html>*, or view contents online at *<http://www.infobases.com/news/ldsnews.htm>*.

Ketav. BYU's Department of Computer Science's Online Magazine. Essays on computer science, religion, more. Great content. Unfortunately, it's not been updated for months. ★★
<http://lal.cs.byu.edu/ketav/standard/homepage.html>

Latter-day Magazine On-Line. Published irregularly by the Latter-day Foundation for the Arts. Content's good, but it's been neglected for better than a year, as of this review. ★★
<http://www.uvol.com/www1st/ldsmag>

LDS News on the WWW. Regularly updated news briefs not generally seen anywhere else (see figure 8.8). Nicely designed page; easy to read. Unfortunately, the news items are mostly unattributed. ★★★★
<http://www.geocities.com/heartland/6130 /ldsnews.htm>

LDS News E-mail. A weekly mailing of LDS news. ★★★
<http://www.geocities.com/Heartland/6130/ n002.htm>

LDS News Sites. An infrequently updated list of links to various news sites. ★
<http://www.ldsworld.com/links/news.html>

Light at the Top of the Mountain. Free gospel topic magazine, only published on the Internet. E-mail: *<marda@burgoyne.com>*. No Web site. ☞

MORMON-NEWS. A new read-only mailing list containing news of the Church. Average daily volume: 5 messages. Subscribe by sending an e-mail request to *<majordomo@ panix.com>* containing the message subscribe mormon-news. ★★★★

ON NEWS

As a member of the Church, living on the East coast, I found it hard to get up-to-date news in one place about the Church and its activities. . . . That's when I decided to gather the news in one place for others, as a free service.

Since beginning the site, I have added a Church History section, as well as a special Pioneer section. I hope that readers go away with a knowledge of what is going on in the Church, as well as with a bit of historical knowledge. If it helps their testimony to grow that's even better. The site was designed to be a learning experience.

Jordan D. Jones, Naugatuck, Connecticut
<cjones@ctconnect.com>
Site Creator/Editor LDS Virtual Gifts
<http://www.geocities.com/heartland/6130>

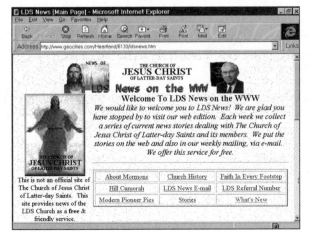

FIG. 8.8

LDS News on the WWW: News briefs about the Church.

News & Events. The Infobases news site. Contains links to the LDS Newswire index of *Church News* and *This People* magazine. ★
<http://www.ldsworld.com/ldsnewswire>

News Posts. An archive of news items posted to the LDS-GEMS mailing list. Items are culled from articles in newspapers and other publications. Makes a great clipping service. ★★★★
<http://www.xmission.com/~dkenison/lds/gems/arc_news.html>

The James Talmage Society Newsletter. A group publishing information about LDS scientists and issues related to science and religion. Chatty. Science Departmental. Sometimes valuable. ★★★★
<http://cpms.byu.edu/cpms/talmage/homepage.html>

The Leading Edge. Science fiction and fantasy magazine produced by an all-volunteer staff at Brigham Young University; featuring fiction, poetry, and art. It's actually quite good. ★★★★
<http://humanities.byu.edu/tle/theleadingedge.html>

The Wasp. LDS journal of news, reviews, and commentary published by Christopher and Deanna Estep. Humor, opinion . . . not nearly so biting as its Nauvoo-period namesake. ★★★
<http://pw2.netcom.com/~estep/index.html>

Vigor. A thoughtful publication of essays edited, and sometimes written, by Orson Scott Card. Published irregularly, but well worth the read. ★★★★
<http://www.nauvoo.com/vigor>

Worldwide LDS FriendsZine. A small collection of stories and poetry. The first issue has been out for an awfully long time. ★★
<http://www.downtown-web.com/cfw/ezine/fall96>

> Now we're starting to implement a full moderated chat. The forum is completely censored, meaning that when people try to crash it with criticism or rude comments, we politely write to them and suggest this is not the forum for that. We're also working on [a] daily devotional that will go out via e-mail, and we're in the process of building a 24-hour-a-day Internet radio station.
>
> The second major item is that we've just added a mall with 640 projects going out. The mall is focused around generating revenues for charitable projects.
>
> Max Bertola, Orem, Utah
> *<editor@uvol.com>*
> Publisher, WWW First Ward
> *<http://www.uvol.com/www1st>*

WWW First Ward.   A daily online publication from Max Bertola. Includes a daily devotional, This Day in History, weekly scripture, letters from readers, weekly Sunday School lesson, columns, Church news, more. A gold mine of information. ★★★★★☑

<http://www.uvol.com/www1st>

Zion's Fiction.   Writer Thom Duncan's fascinating new publishing venture. Works of LDS-themed speculative fiction are available electronically. It's all quite forward-looking. ★★★★

<http://zfiction.com>

Recent Articles About the Church

There are, of course, many more places to find news about the Church and its members. We list a couple here, with the caveat that articles disappear from the Web over time. The *Mormons on the Internet* Registry, described in chapter 4, will be regularly updated with links to articles that appear in major news publications. Visit the Registry at *<http://members.aol.com/MormonNet>* for links to significant articles that appear after the release of this book.

All Things Considered.   A National Public Radio broadcast discussing Mormonism. Includes an interview with Elder M. Russell Ballard, writer Armand Mauss, and author Jan Shipps. ★★★

<http://www.npr.org/ramfiles/970820.totn.02.ram>

Kingdom Come.   The *Time* cover story on the history of the Church. ☞

<http://www.pathfinder.com/@@dsl@FAcAkfl3kQXK/time/magazine/1997/dom/970804/religion.kingdom_come_.html>

Sunday Interview. Text of the 1997 *San Francisco Chronicle* interview with President Hinckley. ☞
<http://www.sfgate.com/cgi-bin/chronicle/
article.cgi?file=SC36289.DTL&directory=/chronicle/archive/1997/04/13>

ONLINE UNITS OF THE CHURCH

Ready to move beyond news from downtown Salt Lake City? If your ward or stake has developed a Web site, you already know where to go for a local calendar of events.

Many units of the Church have created home pages as part of their public communications effort. The following Internet sites will be of interest whether you're building a Web page for your own ward, or just want to keep in touch with friends from a former ward.

Here you'll find links to both branch/ward sites and stake home pages, along with other information about the organization of the Church.

Contemporary Church Organization. An *Encyclopedia of Mormonism* article describing how the Church is organized. ☞
<http://www.mormons.org/basic/organization/
Contemporary_Organization_EOM.htm>

Stake and Ward Home Pages. A great page. Dozens of stakes and wards, organized by country and state. ★★★★
<http://ldschurch.net/s/danville/sr1/lds_pgs.html>

Stakes. The stake listings are buried deep in this long list of good links. ★★
<http://www.geocities.com/Heartland/4034/content.html#stakes>

Units of the Church. A nice listing of wards, stakes, districts, and branches with their own Web pages. ★★★
<http://www.deseretbook.com/ldsinfo/units.html>

Wards. Links to various wards and branches. ★★
<http://www.geocities.com/Heartland/4034/content.html#ward>

DISCUSSION GROUPS

Though you might not know it from the information presented earlier in this book, the Internet is much, much more than a collection of Web pages! In fact, Web browsing consumes only a little bit of the average Internet user's online time.

Far more significant, for most people, is the two-way communication that comes out of discussing the gospel with other members of the Church. Discussions take many forms: Private electronic mail, e-mail lists, real-time chats, newsgroups, and discussion forums. The nature of these discussions ranges from the positive and uplifting, to the scholarly and academic, to the negative and critical, to the downright nasty and loathsome.

No matter what your own inclination, you'll find like-minded Latter-day Saints in various discussion areas eager to hear your point of view—and even more eager to tell you theirs.

Mailing Lists

A mailing list is, quite simply, a small group of people that send e-mail to one another. Mailing lists generally have a theme, some reason for being, which defines the subject matter up for discussion.

Lists create communities—small groups of people who have in common not only their basic religious affiliation, but also some additional interest that binds them together.

To participate in an e-mail list you must first subscribe. To subscribe to a list, send an e-mail request to the moderator or sponsor named in the listings below. The sponsor may write back to you personally acknowledging your request, but more often, you'll be signed up automatically, just because you asked.

Some lists are closely moderated, meaning that off-topic submissions are returned to the sender. Others are barely moderated, and some aren't moderated at all. A caution: Even among otherwise good Latter-day Saints, unmoderated lists sometimes become a bit hot, creating animosity and hurt feelings. Participation requires a thick skin, a sense of humor, a deeply rooted faith, and an ability not to take things personally.

Moderated lists, on the other hand, can degenerate into a sort of sing-song pedantry, unless the moderator has a gift for steering with both patience and faith. The best lists have a very specific purpose, and a light-handed moderator who discourages tangents and encourages discussion.

Lists of Lists
The following sites describe LDS e-mail lists, and are regularly updated.

LDS E-mail Lists. A Web site maintained at Mormons.Org. ★★★
 <http://www.mormons.org/other/EMAIL.htm>
LDS Internet Resources. Clark Goble's very well-maintained list of LDS mailing lists. Clark's compilation is a primary resource for the listings that appear in the next section. ★★★★
 <http://cc.weber.edu/~byparkinson/goble.faq>. Content is mirrored at *<http://www.netwizards.net/~btphelps/mormon/lds1.htm>* and *<ftp://ftp.wnetc.com/lds/lds-resource-faq>*.
LDS Mailing Lists. A somewhat less complete list of mailing lists. ★★★
 <http://www.wnetc.com/resource/lds.lists.html>

The LDS E-mail Lists

The following listing of sites is only a sampling of the many LDS e-mail lists available. Additional lists are found in other chapters, where their focus is directly related to a specific topic addressed elsewhere in this book. The lists are unrated here, but may appear with ratings when they're addressed topically in other chapters.

AML-LIST. A discussion list for members of the Association for Mormon Letters. Welcomes all scholars and fans of Mormon literature. Maximum volume is 30 posts per day. Send subscription request to *<aml-request@cc.weber.edu>* with the message `subscribe aml-list` "Your Name in Quotes" *<your@address.in.brackets>*. Benson Parkinson moderates the list.
<http://cc.weber.edu/~byparkinson/aml-list.html>

AML-LIST Digest. Daily compilation of posts to AML-List. Send subscription requests to Benson Parkinson, moderator, at *<byparkinson@cc.weber.edu>*.

AML-MAG. The low-volume version of AML-List. Includes columns, reviews, and news items on Mormon literature, and selected posts from AML-List. To subscribe, send a request to *<aml-request@ cc.weber.edu>* with the message `subscribe aml-mag` "Your Name in Quotes" *<your@address.in.brackets>*.

COOP.Mormon.Org. The LDS Cooperative School Discussion Page. A discussion area for an LDS-oriented cooperative school, an alternative to Public and Home schooling. Subscribe and read the archives at the Web site.
<http://coop.mormon.org>

COUGAR-BEST. Selected messages from COUGAR-NET. Subscribe with an e-mail request to *<listserv@byu.edu>* with the message: `subscribe COUGAR-BEST FirstName LastName`. Operated by David Kenison *<dkenison@ xmission.com>* and my distant cousin, Newell Wright *<nwright@wcu.edu>*. Archives are maintained at the Web site.
<http://www.zilker.net/~ender/c-net.html>

COUGAR-NET. High-volume list for discussions of BYU sports. Topics include games, recruiting, BYU alumni in the pros, and other WAC teams. Subscribe with an e-mail request to *<majordomo@zilker.net>* containing the message `subscribe cougar-net`. Archives available at the Web site.
<http://www.zilker.net/~ender/c-net.html>

CTR. The self-proclaimed Psychic Mormon Friends Network, a list for LDS students at the University of Washington. Subscribe with an e-mail request to *<listproc@u.washington.edu>* with the message `subscribe ctr your-name`.

DAILYBREAD. A chapter a day from the Book of Mormon, in sequence (see figure 8.9). To subscribe, send e-mail request to *<majordomo@bolis.com>* with the message `subscribe dailybread`.

<http://www.idot.aol.com/mld/production/yiaz1785.html>

DISCIPLES. For those who struggle with issues of same-sex attraction but are committed to obedience to the gospel of Jesus Christ and the teachings of modern apostles and prophets. Anonymous participation is permitted. Charter is strictly enforced, as is confidentiality. The list welcomes parents, spouses, priesthood leaders, and counselors. Subscribe with a request to *<d2moderate@aol.com>*. Charter is at the Web site.

<http://users.aol.com/disciples2>

ELIJAH-L. Genealogy discussion from an LDS perspective. Questions regarding genealogical resources and other helpful information can be found here. Subscribe with an e-mail request to *<ByronDH@aol.com >* with the message `subscribe`. Archives at the Web site.

<http://genealogy.emcee.com/elijah-l>

ELWC. The Electronic Latter-day Women's Caucus, which bills itself as The Ward from Hell. Discussion of feminism and women's issues with an extremely radical, critical bent. Send subscription requests to *<dsmith@princeton.edu>*.

EP-LIST. Scandinavian Saints and those interested in talking about Scandinavia. The list is limited to LDS members, preferably those with some connection to Scandinavia. Subscribe with an e-mail to *<Richard.Bruvik@adbkons.se>* with your name and a little information about yourself. Archives at the Web site.

<http://www.netman.se/adbkons/sdh.html>

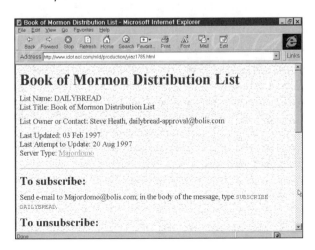

FIG. 8.9

DAILYBREAD: A chapter a day of the Book of Mormon.

EYRING-L. The Mormonism and Science list. Includes discussions on evolution, the ethics of various scientific techniques, and the interplay that scientists have between their disciplines and their religion. Subscribe with an e-mail request to *<majordomo@majordomo.netcom.com>* with the body `subscribe eyring-l` `<your@email.address>`.

FAMILIES. A discussion list for families of LDS members dealing with same-sex orientation. Not negative toward the Church. Subscribe with an e-mail request to *<d2moderate@aol.com>*. More information is available at the Web site. *<http://members.aol.com/disciples2/families.htm>*

FREE-SAINTS. Nonmembers and Latter-day Saints debate the truthfulness of the Church. The list is designed for rigorous discussions, and people who engage in personal attacks are removed. Subscribe with an e-mail request to *<free-saints-request@graceweb.org>* with the body `subscribe`.

GAYMORMON. An e-mail group for same-sex attracted Saints and their friends for the discussion of issues with family, friends, and those trying to become part of the gay community. Made up of SSA Mormons with varying degrees of involvement in the gay community and/or the LDS Church. Similar in tone to Q-SAINTS. To subscribe, send an e-mail request to *<nephi@netcom.com>*.

HANDCART. Genealogy of Mormon handcart pioneers. Discussion area for anyone with interest in the genealogy, journals, and stories of the pioneers who settled in the Salt Lake Valley from 1847 to 1860. Subscribe with an e-mail request to *<MAISER@rmgate.pop.indiana.edu>*, with the message `subscribe handcart`.

JRCLS. An Internet e-mail list for members of the J. Reuben Clark Society, an association of LDS legal professionals. To subscribe, send an e-mail request to *<listserv@lawgate.byu.edu>* with the message `subscribe jrcls-l` `<your name>`.

JOSEPH. This is a moderate mailing group to discuss topics related to the gospel. Political or social issues are not allowed here. The emphasis is on learning to live the gospel and is an attempt to have discussions without the bickering and arguments that are on many other lists. It is moderated to ensure that all posts fit the theme and charter of the list. Subscribe by sending your request to *<majordomo@bolis.com>* with the body `subscribe joseph` `<your@email.address>`. Archives are at the Web site. *<http://www.bolis.com/L/listinfo/joseph>*

LAMPS. Latter-day Saint Association of Mathematical and Physical Scientists (James E. Talmage Society). Send a subscription request to *<carrie@csoffice.cs.byu.edu>*.

LDISABLED. For members of the Church who are disabled, or chronically ill in any way, and their families and friends. To subscribe, send an e-mail request to *<listserv@home.ease.lsoft.com>* with the message `subscribe LDISABLED <your name>`.

LDS-BOOKSHELF. A mailing list designed for those who collect or have a serious interest in collectable books related to Mormon Americana. Subscribe with an e-mail request to *<majordomo@bolis.com>* with the body `subscribe lds-bookshelf`. List operators are Keith Irwin and Hugh McKell. Archives are maintained at the Web site.
<http://www.wenet.net/~kirwin/bshelf.html>

LDSF. A mailing list devoted to speculative fiction from a Mormon point of view. Not limited to LDS authors of science fiction. To subscribe, go to *<http://www.coollist.com>*. At the "Subscribe to a List" section, enter the letters ldsf. Then enter your e-mail address. The list is operated by writer Thom Duncan, who operates the Zion's Fiction Web site.
<http://www.concentric.net/~zfict>

LDS-GEMS. A low-volume, heavily moderated list that includes Church news, excerpts from talks, and more. It also includes the distribution of Dave Kenison's "Church History Stories" and Dave Crockett's "150 Years Ago in Church History." To subscribe, send an e-mail request to *<majordomo@xmission.com>* with the body `subscribe lds-gems`. The list is operated by Dave Kenison and Dave Crockett. Archives are available at the LDS-GEMS Web site.
<http://www.xmission.com/~dkenison/lds/gems>

LDS-GRADS. A chat group for single LDS graduate students or those who are like-minded. The list is primarily for social support and open-minded discussions. While discussions about dating and social concerns are found here, much more is intended. To subscribe, e-mail a request to *<lds-grads-request@cs.umd.edu>* with your name and a little information about yourself.

LDS-IRCD [DIGEST]. The Latter-day Saints' mormon-IRC Mailing list. Subscribe with an e-mail request to *<majordomo@wizards.net>*, with the message `subscribe lds-ircd`.

LDS-NET. The oldest mailing list for LDS discussions. It's often called the Internet First Ward. The list is of a general nature, and includes discussions on social issues, doctrine, scriptures, and general news. It is fairly moderate in tone and volume, though controversies do flair from time to time. Mostly unmoderated. Subscribe with an e-mail request to *<listproc@mainstream.net>* with the body `subscribe lds-net your name`.

LDS-PHIL. The LDS Philosophy of Religion list. Primarily for professional philosophers and those with training in philosophy who happen to be Mormon or interested in Mormon theology. The list presents an opportunity to discuss religious issues within the confines of their technical expertise. The list is not moderated, but subscription must be approved. It is a low-volume list. To subscribe, send an e-mail request to *<listserv@vma.cc.nd.edu>* with the message `subscribe lds-phil` *<your name>*. Archives are at the Web site. *<http://www.nd.edu/~rpotter>*

LDS-POLL.   This is a moderated newsgroup for discussing political issues that affect or interest Latter-day Saints. A wide range of political views are encouraged. News and information about pending legislation can also be found here. To subscribe, send an e-mail message to *<LDS-Poll-owner@bolis.com>* with the body `subscribe lds-poll`.

LDSPRIMARY.   This is a mailing list for parents, teachers, and administrators in the primary organization. It has discussions dealing with teaching the gospel to children, activities for these children, and finding resources related to these topics. It also discusses the responsibilities of those who have been called to work with the primary organization. Subscribe with an e-mail request to *<majordomo@panix.com>* with the body `subscribe ldsprimary` *<your@ email.address>*. Archives are at the Web site. *<http://www.panix.com/~klarsen/ldsprimary>*

LDS-RESEARCH.   A mailing list for scholarly discussions on various LDS subjects. It is for serious research on doctrine, history, society, and culture. The list is moderated. Posts are required to include references and quotations relative to the subject being discussed. To subscribe, e-mail a request to *<majordomo@xmission.com>* with the body `subscribe lds-research`.

LDS Scripture of the Day.   To subscribe, send an e-mail request to *<zarahmla@ xmission.com>*.

LDSSA-L.   A newsletter and information for the LDS Student Association. This is from the University of Illinois, but may contain information for college students at other institutions that are associated with LDSSA. To subscribe, send an e-mail request to *<Listserv@po.uiuc.edu>* with the text `subscribe LDSSA-L` your name. Archives are at the Web site. *<http://www.students.uiuc.edu/~sandland/ www.aquila.com/niuldssa>*

LDS-SEMINAR.   Commentary on each week's Gospel Doctrine lesson. The posts are open to exegesis, textual analysis, historical issues pertinent to the context or application of the scriptures, life applications, and "likening the scriptures unto us" issues. Includes regular columns, plus postings from other participants. To subscribe, send a message to *<majordomo@ldschurch.net>* with the message `subscribe ldss` *<yourname@your.email.address>* or the digest version `subscribe LDSS-D` *<yourname@your.email.address>*.

LDS-SUNDAY SCHOOL. Full text of next week's Sunday school reading assignment. This year's reading assignment is the Doctrine and Covenants. The reading assignment is divided into five messages, one for each weekday. Subscribe by sending your e-mail request to *<anderson@itsnet.com>*. Archives are at the Web site.

<http://www.itsnet.com/~anderson/lds-ssrl.html>

LDS-TREKKERS. For LDS Church members who are also fans of Star-Trek. Subscribe with an e-mail request to *<listserv@muskrat.com>* and the message `subscribe lds-trekkers`.

LDS-YW. LDS-YW is dedicated to the Young Women of the Church and their leaders. It is a way to exchange ideas, testimonies, and experiences. To subscribe, e-mail your request to *<majordomo@xmission.com>* with the body `subscribe lds-yw`.

LIAHONA. Young Single Adults. To subscribe, send a request to *<majordomo@ npl.com>*, with the message `subscribe liahona`. The Web site contains more information. *<http://www.hili.com/~mal/liahona>*

MORM-HIST. Thoughtful discussion of Mormon history. Subscription requests should be addressed to *<majordomo@sara.zia.com>* with the message `subscribe morm-hist`.

MORMON-HUMOR. Mormon-humor is an e-mail list for telling jokes, puns, and amusing stories and anecdotes about Mormons and Mormonism. Almost all aspects of Mormon culture, activities, events, and people worldwide are fair game. However, racist and sexual jokes and jokes that make malicious fun of others should not be sent to mormon-humor. To subscribe, e-mail a request to *<majordomo@lists.panix.com>* with the body `subscribe mormon-humor`.

MORMON-INDEX. List of queries, responses, announcements, and information on Mormon resources on the Internet. If you are looking for information, you can post requests here as well. A very excellent service. To subscribe, send an e-mail request to *<majordomo@lists.panix.com>* with the body `subscribe mormon-index <your@email>`. The list is operated by Kent Larsen. Archives are at the Web site.

<http://www.panix.com/~klarsen/mormon-index>

MORMON-L. Generally considered to be a very liberal, very active mailing list. Subject matter covers all bases and generates a lot of volume. It's also been very controversial and, as a result of some nasty discussion a long time ago, is no longer housed at BYU. As one of the oldest Mormon mailing lists, it tends to be very widely read. To subscribe, send an e-mail request to *<majordomo@catbyrd.com>* with the body `subscribe Mormon-l <your@ email.address>`.

MORMON-NEWS. A mailing list where news about the church and news articles concerning the church are posted. No discussions about the articles are posted here. Send a subscription request to *<majordomo@lists.panix.com>* with the body `subscribe mormon-news`. Archives are at the Web site. *<http://www.panix.com/~klarsen/mormon-news>*

MORMONS-ONLY-L. A forum for members to assist one another in lesson and talk preparation, exchange testimonies, share faith promoting stories, and provide a friendly way for Mormons to get to know each other over the Net. The list is moderated. Subscribe with a request to *<listserv@muskrat.com>* with the body `subscribe mormons-only <your first name> <Your Last Name>`. More information is available at the Web site. *<http://home1.gte.net/pmuskrat/mormons/only.htm>*

MORMONTR. Mormon Trails discussion list. Subscribe with a request to *<listserv@unlvm.unl.edu>* containing the line `subscribe mormontr`.

ORSON-SCOTT-CARD. A mailing list devoted exclusively to discussion of Orson Scott Card's writings. Orson Scott Card is a well-known science-fiction author and has also authored plays and worked on screenplays. To subscribe, e-mail a request to *<majordomo@wood.net>* with the message `subscribe orsoncard`. Archives are available at the Web site. *<http://wood.net/~khyron/card/cardlist.html>*

OVERLAND-TRAILS. Discussions of the emigrant overland trails of the mid-nineteeth century, such as the Oregon, California, and Mormon Trails. Subscribe with an e-mail request to *<listproc@bobcat.tamu-commerce.edu>* with the message `subscribe overland-trails <your name>`. More information is available at the Web site. *<http://www.idot.aol.com/mld/production/yiafzks2.html>*

PARENTS. A general list for LDS parents. Subscribe by sending an e-mail request to *<majordomo@ldschurch.net>* with the message `subscribe parents`.

PEACE. For Latter-day Saints who need a place to discuss issues relating to depression. No archive, moderated. To subscribe, send a request to *<majordomo@ldschurch.net>* with the message `subscribe peace <your e-mail address>`.

ON FORUM MAKING

I was motivated to start the MORMONS-ONLY list by the discouraging conversations on USENET's alt.religion.mormon, where I found mostly anti-Mormon propaganda and some good members involved in "defense" of the faith. I wanted a place where good Latter-day Saints could converse freely without those outsiders causing trouble . . . I also wanted to keep it that way, so the list was moderated from the beginning. MORMONS ONLY is a Mormon social center on the Net!

If a message doesn't meet our standards, it will be returned to sender with a brief explanation and invitation to try again.

Phil Musgrave, Kailua, Oahu, Hawaii
<phil@muskrat.com>
List owner, Mormons Only

LIVING A LATTER-DAY SAINT LIFE

PIONEER-COOKING. A list for information and discussion about all aspects of pioneer life. It focuses in more on practical things such as cooking and recipes. To subscribe, send an e-mail request to *<majordomo@seminary.org>* with the message `subscribe pioneer-cooking`. Archives are at the Web site. *<http://seminary.org/pioneer>*

PREP. A list for discussions and information about disaster preparedness, home storage, and emergency planning, from an LDS perspective. To subscribe, send an e-mail request to *<majordomo@seminary.org>* with the body `subscribe prep`. Archives are at the Web site. *<http://seminary.org/prep>*

Q-SAINTS. E-mail list for lesbian, gay, and bisexual people that come from a Mormon or Restoration background. Family members are welcome. Often takes an adversarial position toward the Church. Sponsored by Affirmation. Subscribe with an e-mail request to *<majordomo@vector.casti.com>*

SAINTS-BEST. Highlights from other LDS lists, maintained by David B. Anderson. Subscribe with an e-mail request to *<listserv@mainstream.com>*, with the message `subscribe saints-best`.

SAMU-L. This group is for more technical discussions about antiquities and how they relate to Mormonism. There are frequent discussions about the historical background of Mormon scriptures, archaeology and the Book of Mormon, and historical symbols. Generally low in volume and most posts contain quite a bit of information. To subscribe, send an e-mail request to *<pacal@bingvmb.cc.binghamton.edu>* or *<mraish@library.lib.binghamton.edu>*.

SANCTIFY. A list for members who have loved ones who are less active, new members, or nonmembers. Designed to function as a support group to share feelings and thoughts on dealing with the spiritual and social issues involved in such relationships. Subscribe with an e-mail message to *<majordomo@seminary.org>* with the body `subscribe sanctify`. Archives are at the Web site. *<http://www.seminary.org/sanctify*

SCOUTS-LDS. A low volume list dealing with the scouting program in the church. Share ideas for activities, describe ways of dealing with the youth, or ask advice on handling your calling. To subscribe, send a request to *<scouts-lds-request@tagus.com>* with the message `subscribe  scouts-lds`. Visit the Web site to review archives. *<http://www.tagus.com>*

SCRIPTURE-L. A discussion of the scriptures. Operated and moderated by Gregory Woodhouse. Volume is moderate. Send subscription requests to *<scripture-l-request@lists.best.com>* with the message `subsingle`. To receive all the day's messages in one post mail, change the message to `subscribe`. Archives available at *<http://www.wnetc.com/scripture-l>*

SEMINARY.   Lesson ideas for teaching seminary, institute, or any other teaching position. Inspiring. A really first-class, useful list. It appears again in chapter 9 as a top-20 Internet resource. The list has just changed ownership. Send your subscription request to *<majordomo@listservice.net>* with the message `sub-scribe seminary`.

SISTERS.   For women to discuss any topic they choose. To subscribe, send an e-mail request to *<MAISER@rmgate.pop.indiana.edu>*.

SISTER-SHARE.   Sister-share operates as an "online Relief Society." Very high volume—so high, in fact, that keeping up could be an all day task. Most posts tend to be chatty, although scriptural topics and ideas for Relief Society lessons sometimes appear. But not often. Subscribe with an e-mail request to *<list-serv@psuvm.psu.edu>* with the message `subscribe sister-share` *<your name>*. Archives are maintained at the Web site.
<http://cac.psu.edu/~mauri/ldssis/ldssis.html>

SPIRIT.   A mailing list for poems, spiritual thoughts, and stories. Discussions are discouraged, but submissions are welcome. Subscribe with an e-mail request to *<majordomo@seminary.org>* with the message `subscribe spirit`. Archives are maintained at the Web site. *<http://seminary.org/spirit>*

STAY-AT-HOME MOMS.   A forum for mothers who have chosen to stay at home. Subscribe from the Web page.
<http://www.utw.com/~kpearson/homemoms.html>

STUDENT REVIEW.   Low-volume general discussion list for alumni of *Student Review* (unofficial magazine at BYU) about *Student Review* and about the Church. Digest available. To subscribe, send an e-mail message to *<major domo@ panix.com>* with the message `subscribe student-review` *<your name>*.

STUDIES.   Discussion of scriptures and reference materials related to Gospel Doctrine lessons. Subscribe with an e-mail request to *<majordomo@bolis.com>* with the message `subscribe studies`. Visit the Web site for archives.
<http://seminary.org/studies>

TEENS.   A general list for LDS youth. Subscribe with an e-mail request to *<majordomo@ldschurch.net>*, with the message `subscribe teens`.

TEENSTOO.   Discussion list for teen members of the LDS Church who experience a same-sex orientation and desire to remain true to the teachings of the church. Not negative toward the Church. Supports LDS concepts. Subscribe with an e-mail request to *<chiefguy@aol.com>*. More information is available at the Web site.
<http://members.aol.com/teenstoo>

UNITED-ORDER.   A fairly mainstream mailing list designed for discussing the doctrines and culture of the Church. Fully moderated. Most articles are posted.

The list limits personal contention but respectful disagreement is acceptable. There is also a digest version of this list. To subscribe, send an e-mail request to <*majordomo@bolis.com*> with the message `subscribe united-order` or `subscribe united-order-digest`. Archives are maintained at the Web site. <*http://www.bolis.com/list-archives/united-order-digest*>

WOMENTOO. LDS Women with a same-sex orientation who seek to follow the Church's teachings. Not negative toward the Church. Subscribe with an e-mail request to <*d2moderate@aol.com*>. More information is found on the Web site. <*http://members.aol.com/disciples2/women.htm*>

WW-LDS. The Church in an international setting. Promotes discussions of the relationship between local cultures, the Church, and Utah Valley culture. It also is for discussing how the ecclesiastical organization and operation is affected by local cultures and the challenges this brings to effective Church service. News about the Church is international settings can also be found here. To subscribe, send a request to <*listserv@acadcomp.cmp.ilstu.edu*> with the message `subscribe ww-lds <your name>`. Archives are found at the Web site. <*http://138.87.151.56/ww-lds/index.htm*>

ZION. A fairly conservative mailing list for discussing the church and the gospel. Many topics or particular orientations on topics are not allowed here. Posts that could be considered critical of either the Church or the leaders of the Church are not permitted. Subscribe with an e-mail request to <*majordomo@bolis.com*> with the message `subscribe zion`. More information is available at the Web site. <*http://www.kdcol.com/~mcgee/zion.html*>

ON THE ADVANTAGES OF CHATTING

My LDS friends and I have found all types of rooms to chat in . . . The most meaningful and fun experiences I've had with other LDS folks in chat rooms were actually in other Christian Chat rooms. In these rooms, some really nice people are chatting about their spiritual and Biblical concerns. Everyone always jumps in and talks to everyone else, especially if there is a concern. . . .

There is also a fair amount of support going on for the lonely and those in mourning, and there are a great many places to have questions answered. . . .

Finally, it's a great way for families across the country to gather and chat in the evening. I have friends with up to six or seven family members, all online. They get into chat rooms and catch up on the events of the day.

Donna Perkins, Eagle River, Alaska
<*perkins@servcom.com*>

Real-time Chats

Me, I'm not a chatter. I used to be, but gave it up after about 20 minutes.

Other people, though, seem to thrive on the genre. They love the noisy, fast-paced, mixed-up conversations that take place in Internet chat rooms, and claim that I'm missing out on the best game in town.

Chatting is the practice of jumping into a live conversation and typing as fast as you can. As soon as you send off a line, other people are reading it and responding to what you wrote. It's all tremendously exciting, and—because the sentences tend to intertwine with the musings of other chat-room participants—it's utterly confusing to new users.

If you're inclined to give it a shot, you'll need to download the free software that makes it all possible. Visit the Web sites in the following chat listings for help getting online.

#LDSYouth.   A heavily used chat area for LDS teens. Includes a Web-based chat area that doesn't require any special software. ★★★★★
<http://www.inetworld.net/kaos/ldsyouth.html>

#mormon.   (See figure 8.10.) This page is dedicated to the many inhabitants of the undernet #Mormon (pronounced "pound Mormon"). A very busy, very popular chat site. Requires special software, but it's all explained at the Web site. ★★★★
<http://www.lds.npl.com/special/irc/mormon>

#mormon.amigos.   A new chat area for Spanish-speaking Saints. Spanish isn't one of my languages, so this site is unrated. ☞
<http://gemstate.net/friends>

#mormon.friends.   The Mormon Friends chat area. Requires special software. ★★★★
<http://gemstate.net/friends>

#mormon.teens.   A fairly new site for teenage chats. News, online dances (really!), more. Safe, moderated. Requires special software. ★★★★
<http://www.geocities.com/Heartland/Hills/6850>

Cumorah's Hill Online Chatting.   An unscheduled chat area. You might find someone online, but probably won't. Requires no special software. ★★
<http://members.aol.com/cumorahhil/chat>

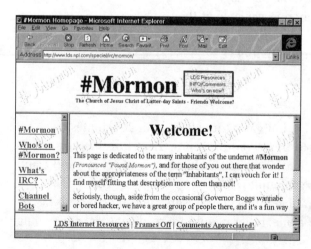

FIG. 8.10

#mormon: Before you chat, stop here for an introduction.

Mormon Chat.   Scheduled chats take place most evenings. Requires no special software. ★★★★

<http://www.mormons.org/chat.htm>

Newsgroups

Somewhere between the stately pace of e-mail lists, and the pure adrenaline rush of real-time chat, lie Internet newsgroups.

Newsgroups are part of a separate portion of the Internet called the UseNet. There are some 20,000 UseNet newsgroups where people debate everything from UFOs to e-coli.

Given the vast number of newsgroups, there are surprisingly few devoted specifically to LDS topics. In fact, only two significant LDS newsgroups exist, one of which is a bit rowdy, and the other of which is a complete madhouse. A third group, focusing on Mormon fellowship, has only a small number of regular participants.

If you're game for a bit of pushing and shoving, open the newsgroup reader on your Web browser (from Navigator, go to the Window menu and click Netscape News. From Explorer, go to the Go menu and click Read News).

If this is your first time reading the newsgroups, you'll need to set some options (call your Internet provider to obtain the appropriate settings for your account), and download the entire list of newsgroups. The process takes about ten minutes on a 28.8-kilobit modem.

> **ON THE ROLE OF S.R.M.**
> The idea behind soc.religion.mormon is to provide an arena for the courteous debate of all issues Mormon, cultural, or religious. This includes all the breakaway sects, such as the RLDS, as well as the main Church of Jesus Christ of Latter-day Saints based in Salt Lake City. We welcome all points of view, as long as they are expressed courteously, but because of the way in which Mormons view Temple matters, as sacred and not to be discussed outside Temple walls, we do not allow any direct quotes of the Temple ceremonies. It is not primarily a fellowship group, although some threads are definitely "fellowship" oriented. It was meant to be a place where Mormons and nonMormons alike can discuss Mormonism with more light and less heat. To promote this, our charter mandates that at least one moderator be nonMormon, that personal insults are not appropriate, and that all posts be regarding Mormonism.
>
> Diana Newman, Smithfield, Utah
> *<bee@utah.uswest.net>*
> Moderator, soc.religion.mormon

Once you're set up, using newsgroups is a snap. Subscribe to a group (search for the word "mormon" to see a listing), and click on it to read the discussion.

Discussions take place in "threads," where all the discussion on a particular topic keeps the same subject name, and continues for as long as anyone is interested in talking.

The following newsgroups are worth stopping by. Just gird up your loins before you wade in.

alt.religion.mormon.   Too much bile stored up? Disgorge it all in alt.religion.mormon. You'll fit right in. This newsgroup is the nastiest LDS site on the Web, though the occasional gentle soul tries—for a few days, at least—to inject a word of kindness. (I wish I could claim to be one of those kind people. I'm not. I behave as badly as anyone when I'm in a.r.m.) Don't jump in without reading it for a week or so first. You're unlikely to say *anything* that hasn't been said dozens of times already. ★

<news:alt.religion.mormon>

alt.religion.mormon.fellowship. A nice place. A quiet place. Except when nastiness spills over from a.r.m. and infects the generally nice conversations taking place in a.r.m.f. ★★★★

<news:alt.religion.mormon.fellowship>

byu.news. For news, discussion, and information related to Brigham Young University. Very little traffic. ★★

<news:alt.religion.mormon.fellowship>

msn.forums.religion.latterdaysaint. For Microsoft Network subscribers, this forum is strictly for LDS fellowship. No bashers allowed. I'm not an MSN user, so this site is unrated. ☞

Section 13. The LDS discussion forum on CompuServe, and accessible only to CIS members. Moderator Arthur Wilde runs a very thoughtful, very tolerant forum. Type go:religion, and log in to section 13. ★★★★★

soc.religion.mormon. Though this group is moderated, it still manages to be tremendously confrontational. Definitely more civilized than the unmoderated a.r.m., however. ★★★★

Web Site Discussion Areas

Finally, we come to the newest sort of discussion group, the Web-based discussion forum.

nonexistent, and that as a nation there is a great lack of people who are willing to adopt or foster children. I had several replies from people who were surprised at the difference between their part of America and Britain. So yes, I do feel that I have an mission/obligation to educate people as to what goes on in the "real" world. It all goes back to helping people understand each other, I suppose.

Hilary A Croughton, Ipswich, England
<hathi@enterprise.net>
ARMF participant
<alt.religion.mormon.fellowship>

Using these sites is a simple, almost self-evident procedure. Some sites require you to register (it's free), some require you to enter a password of your own choosing, and some are just wide open to anyone that stops by.

Some advice, a caution that applies to any discussion group that piques your interest: Before jumping in for the first time, pause to read the existing discussions for at least a day or two. Be sure you understand who's who, and resist the urge to criticize or complain until you've at least introduced yourself and made a couple of positive contributions.

COUGARTALK.   The BYU Cougar sports discussion forum (see figure 8.11). It's talk radio in written form—and the emotions get a little warm-blooded. ★★★★
<http://www.ysite.com/cougartalk>

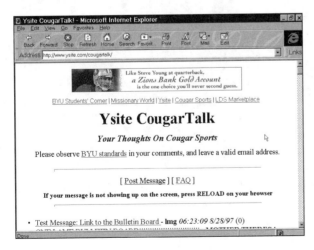

FIG. 8.11

COUGARTALK: Toss the ball around with online sports fans.

Nauvoo.   Once upon a time, Nauvoo was a forum on AOL. Now everyone can participate—and should. This is easily the best discussion place on the World Wide Web. Orson Scott Card's sponsorship gives it cachet; his *Vigor* newsletter gives it substance. Follow the links to the kids' forum, the Red Brick Store, the Mansion House library, and more. ★★★★★☑
<http://www.nauvoo.com>

The LDS Infobase Message Board.   A new forum for posting public questions, information, or requests. Lacks organization, and takes a true bulletin board form, with random, unrelated topics appearing in chronological order. Nevertheless, it has potential as a source of information. ★★★★
<http://www.enol.com/~infobase/wwwboard>

9

AUXILIARIES

I loved going to my grandparents' house for Sunday dinner. A few times a year, we got to dress up in our nicest clothes, then go to Grandma's, where the grownups sat at their table and all the cousins sat at theirs.

After dinner, we'd all head out to the car to go to sacrament meeting. The building where my grandparents' ward met was a wonderful two-story brick meetinghouse built by my grandpa and my dad and the rest of the ward in the early 1950s. There were pictures of Jesus on the walls of the chapel, and it was an altogether different place from the white cinderblock building in my own town, where I attended Primary on weekday afternoons.

When I turned eight, it seemed natural to ask Grandpa to baptize me. He was happy to do so. He and Grandma drove up from their town for the Saturday-night baptism, and came back the next afternoon for fast and testimony meeting, where Grandpa confirmed me. It was a doubly exciting day, not only because I was being confirmed, but because for once, Grandma and Grandpa got to come to *my* church.

During the testimony meeting, two deacons wandered up and down the aisle holding microphones that they gave to anyone who wanted to stand and bear testimony. Grandma, tearful at the baptism and confirmation of her first grandchild, signaled for a microphone. She stood and bore her testimony, then sat down and handed the microphone to me. I stood, and tried for the first time in my life to speak in front of the whole ward. I was dumbstruck, so Grandma whispered the words in my ear. "I am thankful for my family . . ." I repeated the words into the microphone. "I am thankful to be baptized . . ." Nodding to Grandma, I repeated the words. "I am thankful for the Prophet." I nodded and repeated. "And I know this Church is true." I started to repeat, then paused, and said in an embarrassingly loud voice directly into the microphone, "But Grandma, this church isn't true. *Your* church is true."

It wasn't for many years that I was able to understand why the entire congregation burst into laughter.

In later years, when I was only a little bit smarter, I began hearing a different kind of testimony. For some reason, it became fashionable to stand up in front of a congregation and declare: "Actually, it's not the Church that is true; it's the gospel that is true."

I nodded and started to repeat . . . then paused, and said to myself, "No, I don't think so."

True conversion—to any principle—happens at two levels: the theoretical and the practical. When I believe a thing in theory, but don't act on it in practice, I'm not yet converted; I'm merely persuaded. I might believe in theory that education is important, but if I don't encourage my children to finish their homework, if I fail to show up for school conferences, if I don't get an education myself, then I'm not truly converted to the principle of education.

> "Wherefore he saith, When he ascended up on high, he led captivity captive, and gave gifts unto men. . . . He gave some, apostles; and some, prophets; and some, evangelists; and some, pastors and teachers; for the perfecting of the saints, for the work of the ministry, for the edifying of the body of Christ: Till we all come in the unity of the faith, and of the knowledge of the Son of God, unto a perfect man, unto the measure of the stature of the fulness of Christ: That we [henceforth] be no more children, tossed to and fro, and carried about with every wind of doctrine, by the sleight of men, [and] cunning craftiness, whereby they lie in wait to deceive."
>
> Ephesians 4:8, 11–14.

Likewise, to see the gospel as a thing separate from the Church is to be converted in theory, but not in practice.

The word "gospel" is associated with the Greek word *euaggelizo*, meaning the bearing of good tidings. In the scriptures, the word refers specifically to the glad tidings of the kingdom of God. And what is the kingdom of God, on this earth, if not the Church?

Without a foundation, and without a structure, there is no body of Saints that makes up the Church. There is no means by which we create fellowship. There is no mechanism by which we teach. There is no machinery in place for the perfecting of the Saints.

I love being a Latter-day Saint not only because I love God, but also because I love what God organized. I love the Church. I love all its bits and pieces and personalities and programs and policies and practices. I love the sisterhood of Relief Society, the visiting teaching, the homemaking meetings, the working together that can exist only where there is a structure. I love the Sunday School organization, the reasoning together, the insight that comes from actually, physically, sitting in a class together with other Saints and listening to what they have to say. I love Primary, and Seminary, and the Youth Programs. I love the programs for priesthood holders and for single adults. None of these programs is theoretical; nor could they be. They are part of a living organization that demands much, and gives much in return.

So Grandma, I say this for you—and you know I'm old enough now to mean it with all my heart: I am thankful for my family. I am grateful I was baptized. I am thankful for the Prophet. And I know this Church is true.

This chapter lists resources for the heart of the Church: the auxiliaries. You'll find here Internet listings for the Priesthood, the Primary, the Relief Society, the Seminary program, the Single Adult program, the Sunday School, the Young Men, and the Young Women.

> "Now therefore ye are no more strangers and foreigners, but fellow citizens with the saints, and of the household of God; And are built upon the foundation of the apostles and prophets, Jesus Christ himself being the chief corner[stone]; In whom all the building fitly framed together groweth unto an holy temple in the Lord: In whom ye also are builded together for an habitation of God through the Spirit."
>
> Ephesians 2:19–22.

PRIESTHOOD RESOURCES

Helps for priesthood quorums are amazingly difficult to come by on the Internet. In fact, given the ratio of men to women in the LDS online community, the dearth of priesthood resources is downright incredible.

The message? If you're a priesthood holder, and feel compelled to build a Web site, there's a wide-open opportunity to magnify your calling.

The few Priesthood-related sites that do exist do a fine job of covering what they can. You'll find them here:

Aaronic Priesthood.   A collection of articles on topics related to the establishment and powers of the Aaronic Priesthood. Information includes Aaron: Brother of Moses, Aaronic Priesthood: Powers and Offices, Aaronic Priesthood: Restoration, Bishop, Deacons, and History of the Office of Bishop. A Mormons.Org page. ★★★★
   <http://www.mormons.org/basic/organization/priesthood/aaronic>
A Combined Index to the Melchizedek Priesthood Study Guides, 1974–1997. Searchable index of the various Melchizedek Priesthood Study Guides published between 1974 and 1997. ★★★
   <http://Webpages.marshall.edu/~brown/mpsgindx.htm>

Elders Quorum Resources.   Ryan Marchant's priesthood resources page, full of links to scriptures, research, music, and other links (see figure 9.1). Looking forward to seeing some original priesthood-specific material on the site. ★★
<http://www.inconnect.com/~marchant/elders>

Home Teaching Page.   A resource for Elders Quorum Presidencies and home teachers of the Church of Jesus Christ of Latter-day Saints. Very slow loading, with little content, but it's making progress. Additional contributions are welcome. ★★★
<http://www.cnx.net/~kmsiever>

Leaders to Managers: The Fatal Shift.   Brother Nibley's brilliant analysis of the need for leadership. Worth visiting repeatedly, even tho' the material, of course, never changes. ✍
<http://www.farmsresearch.com/cwhn/nibley02.htm>

Melchizedek Priesthood.   A collection of articles on topics related to the establishment and powers of the Melchizedek Priesthood. Includes information on Melchizedek: LDS Sources, Melchizedek: Ancient Sources, Melchizedek Priesthood: Powers and Offices, Oath and Covenant of the Priesthood, Restoration of the Melchizedek Priesthood, and Apostle. A Mormons.Org page. ★★★★
<http://www.mormons.org/basic/organization/priesthood/melchizedek>

Palo Alto 2nd Ward Elders Quorum.   Very clean, professional looking—and parochial—bulletin. Probably not of much interest to anyone outside of the

> ### ELDER JEFFREY R. HOLLAND ON THE INSTITUTION OF THE CHURCH
> This Church, the great institutional body of Christ, is a marvelous work and a wonder not only because of what it does for the faithful but also because of what the faithful do for it. Your lives are at the very heart of that marvel. You are evidence of the wonder of it all.
>
> Elder Jeffrey R. Holland, "Miracles Of The Restoration." Conference Report, October 1994.

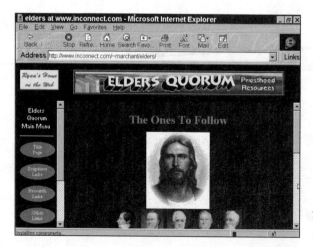

FIG. 9.1

Elders Quorum Resources: Good study links.

Palo Alto 2nd Ward. Currently list events for the week of April 27, 1997 (may not be of much interest to the Palo Alto 2nd ward after all!). ★★
<http://www-leland.stanford.edu/~garyc/pa2>

Priesthood Ordinances. Articles on the ordinances performed both in and out of the temple. Includes information on Ordinances, Ceremonies, Administration of Ordinances, Baptism, Baptism for the Dead, Confirmation, The Endowment, Priesthood Blessings, Blessings, Blessing of Children, Sacrament, Sealing Power, Cancellation of Sealings, Temple Ordinances, Temple Sealings, and Washings and Anointings. A Mormons.Org page. ★★★★★
<http://www.mormons.org/basic/organization/priesthood/ordinances>

Priesthood Organization. A must-read for all priesthood holders. Articles on Following the Prophets, the Priesthood, Priesthood Offices, Priesthood Ordinances, Melchizedek Priesthood, Aaronic Priesthood, President of the Church, First Presidency, Quorum of the Twelve Apostles, Council of the First Presidency, Succession in the Presidency, Bishopric, Mission Presidents, Assistants to the Twelve, Area Presidency, and Power of the Priesthood. A Mormons.Org page. ★★★★★
<http://www.mormons.org/basic/organization/priesthood>

ON A VISION OF HOME TEACHING

My original decision to create the Home Teaching page was out of frustration from lack of similar resources available on the Internet—in fact, I found few sites related at all to the Melchizedek Priesthood. . . .

My vision of the page is to have input from all over the world with ideas and experiences to share with other home teachers throughout the Church. I want it to be a place to share and uplift [and] to aid in the home-teaching effort.

Kim Siever, Surrey, British Columbia, Canada
<kmsiever@cnx.net>
Webmaster, Home Teaching page
<http://www.cnx.net/~kmsiever>

PRIMARY

I have a cousin who is the World's Best Mom. She and her husband raise happy, kind, polite children who love one another and are generous and considerate with others.

But when the family moved to Tacoma last year, her seven-year-old son Jonathan had a difficult time of things. Entering a new school with a tough teacher left him despondent, so much so that he withdrew from life, and even began to shy away from other children. It got so bad that my cousin finally decided to remove him from school altogether and teach him at home.

Things got a little better, but at Church he was shy and withdrawn, refusing to speak to anyone or to answer questions in his Primary or Sunday School classes. My cousin, deeply concerned about his happiness, didn't know what to do.

Then along came Sister White.

Everyone's got a testimony of something, and for Sister White, the best—the only—thing about the gospel is the Primary organization. Sister White loves the Primary.

In this particular Primary there were a handful of "difficult" children. In addition to Jonathan, who refused to speak, there were four tough kids that had scared off a progression of teachers, and a little girl from Russia who spoke no English.

Sister White asked for, and got, a class made up of the six children nobody else seemed able to teach. And she turned them around. Week after week she would visit the children in their homes, read scriptures with them, talk with them, and just generally be their friend.

Somewhere along the line, Jonathan lit up. He began speaking again, started making friends with other children, and developed some self-esteem.

My cousin is so encouraged by the positive changes in his ability to deal with other people that she's decided to re-enroll him in public school. And she gives all the credit to a loving Primary teacher who magnified her calling.

Sister White's not alone in her love for Primary. The following pages were compiled by other Latter-day Saints eager to share their Primary experiences, their sharing time ideas, and their successful activity ideas with other Primary teachers throughout the Church.

LDSPRIMARY.   A mailing list for parents, teachers, and administrators in the Primary organization. Discussions about teaching the gospel to children, activities, and resources. To subscribe, send an e-mail request to *<majordomo@ panix.com>* with the message subscribe ldsprimary *<your@email.address>*. Highly regarded. More information is available at the Web site.
★★★★

<http://www.panix.com/~klarsen/ldsprimary.html>

It was also nice to have an online directory of people's names and phone numbers [and e-mail addresses] since all the moves in and out of the ward made a ward directory close to useless. . . . Because of some privacy issues raised before we started the page, all of the member information and photos are in a password-protected section.

In the course of the page's existence, I received several e-mails from people considering the area or moving into the area and was able to link them up with someone in the ward studying the same thing in school or in a similar line of work.

Gary Coleman, Atlanta, Georgia
<garycoleman@juno.com>
Creator, Elders Quorum Page
<http://www-leland.stanford.edu/~garyc/pa2>

Primarily for Primary People. Very brief selection of ideas, but this page welcomes contributions. ★
<http://www.uvol.com/www1st/primary/primary.html>

Primary. Worth at least one visit. Mailing list information, song books, links to sites that no longer exist. ★
<http://www.zarahemla.com/primary.html>

Primary and Children's Information. Brief list of links to Primary sites. Irregularly updated. ★
<http://www.ldsworld.com/links/primary.html>

Primary Idea Page. A living, breathing specimen. Amusing anecdotes are being submitted and posted. Includes extensive, logical menus, submenus, and sub-submenus. Lot of work here, and regularly updated. ★★★★★
<http://www.primarypage.com>

Primary Matters. A very useful page, with a Sharing Time exchange, Musical Notes for singing time, a discussion forum, and ideas for Achievement Days (see figure 9.2). ★★★★
<http://members.aol.com/chriska1/primary.htm>

Primary Singing Time. Ideas for getting children involved, plus links to pages for the Primary Homepage, Seasonal Games, Teaching Songs, Games, and 1997 Program Songs. A very useful site. ★★★★
<http://cord.iupui.edu/~whansen/singing.htm>

Primary, ETC. Primary ideas to share, things to sample, things to buy, and links. $
<http://w3.softdesdev.com/~debra>

RELIEF SOCIETY RESOURCES

I belong to a mailing list where the subject being debated right now is the role of women in the Church. And as so often happens whenever this particular discussion rolls around again, everyone is on the same side of the debate. The fascinating thing is that all the participants think they're arguing. In fact, none of them seems ever to say anything much different from this:

"Women don't get respect but I respect women. Men have the power but the women make everything happen. Nobody appreciates the contribution that women make, I say with great appreciation for the contribution that women make." (Wouldn't it be amusing to find that mysterious and much-fabled leader who thinks women don't deserve respect, have no power, and don't make a contribution? We could staple a blue light to his head, and have an actual person to point at whenever someone brings up the accusation of misogyny.)

From my perspective, the problem is this: We have all bought into The Great Lie. The Great Lie teaches that public behavior is significant; that private behav-

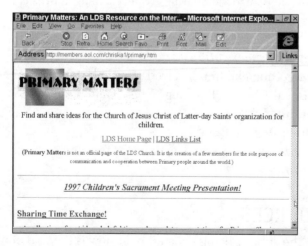

FIG. 9.2

Primary Matters: Talk with other Primary leaders online.

ior matters not at all. The Great Lie grows every time a politician or athlete or any other celebrity is discovered behaving badly, and when voices call out from the sidelines: "Doesn't count! He was doing it in private! Resume play!" The voices get louder, and a society aghast at bad behavior is made to feel as though, somehow, it is the wrongdoer, for having had the temerity to notice.

The Great Lie makes heroes of kings and presidents and football players and all manner of physically attractive people, while at the same time making goats out of impoverished mothers raising decent children, hardworking fathers who leave work at quitting time to spend the evenings with their families, and teenagers who deliberately choose chastity and sobriety. We live in a world where the very worst behavior, behavior that violates every social more, is treated as though it is, somehow, utterly courageous.

The Great Lie has its origins in the innocent history lessons from elementary school, where the public behavior of heads of state was seen as more significant than the private behavior of, say, the wives of heads of state. Choosing to launch a bloody war generates respect. Choosing to show restraint, to spend time helping a child, to pay one's debts, to aid the elderly and infirm, to do any of the thousands of little acts of courage and bravery and kindness that good people do privately each day—those things don't deserve comment. They don't get mentioned, let alone get recorded and passed along to later generations.

It's the cult of celebrity that defines most of the Western world. (And the Eastern one, for that matter . . . but that's for another day.) Worship goes to people whose most notable life skill is an ability to skip meals and curse. To have the triple talent of skipping meals, cursing, and removing one's underwear is the sure road to wealth.

How does The Great Lie apply to the gospel? We perpetuate The Lie every time we make heroes out of people who contribute a tiny percentage of their billions to a charity, and scorn the widow's mite. When we take personal pride-by-affiliation in a professional athlete who made a career choice to dishonor the Sabbath, and overlook the equally talented athlete who decides not to become a professional because he holds the Sabbath sacred. It's perpetuated when a ward knows every detail of a bishop's life, and can't remember the name of his wife.

It's public versus private, and it's the thing we obsess over each time we engage in debate about the role of women in the Church. It's time to give up the debate. Women and men have one role: To live like Christ. If we live Christ-like lives in private, if we teach our children that private behavior is all that matters, then we find that who does which public job is of absolutely no consequence. The goal is not to be watched, but to watch. Not to be seen doing, but to do. And in this— only this—there is safety; in this there is peace.

Relief Society

These general Relief Society sites contain a wealth of ideas and suggestions for women in the Church.

Kirkland Washington Second Ward RS Newsletter. Updated monthly. It's much less parochial than the name would imply. It does include this month's birthday listing, but of more general interest are the monthly message from the President, messages from the General Relief Society President, plus other articles local in content but universal in applicability. (My husband's observation: Also note that there are many fine new recipes to keep homemakers busy for the coming month. I don't mean to be sarcastic, but the recipes are dominated by desserts that the Beaver would find just dandy! Come back here once a month, and after a year or two of these fattening recipes you could search out the Widows Forum.) ★★★★★
<http://members.aol.com/Cballd/k2legacy.html>

Relief Society. Not a great deal of information, and what's there is irregularly updated. ★★
<http://members.aol.com/cumorahhil/rspage.htm>

Relief Society. Ideas for homemaking meeting, education, visiting teaching, and activities, along with e-mail contacts of sisters holding various Relief Society–affiliated callings (see figure 9.3). Operated by Zarahemla Book Shoppe. The site is a little crowded and difficult to read, but the ideas are worth the visit. ★★★
<http://www.zarahemla.com/rs.html>

FIG. 9.3

Relief Society: Read the history of Relief Society, and find lots of teaching ideas on the Web.

Relief Society. Brief list of links to Relief-Society–related sites. Not regularly updated. ★

<http://www.ldsworld.com/links/rs.html>

SISTER-SHARE. Relief Society discussion list. Tends to be tremendously chatty, without a lot of depth. If you've got the time . . . To subscribe, send an e-mail request to *<listserv@psuvm.psu.edu>*. Sisters only. More information is available at the Web site. ★★★

<http://cac.psu.edu/~mauri/ldssis/ldssis.html>

SISTERS. For women to discuss any topic they choose. To subscribe, send an e-mail request to *<MAISER@rmgate.pop.indiana.edu>*.

Homemaking

Plastic grapes, wooden wall things, first aid classes . . . This could be a whole 'nuther book. Just a smattering:

Homemaking. A brief list of ideas. ★★

<http://www.zarahemla.com/rs.html#Homemaking>

Homemaker Herald. Popular monthly newsletter. Features include: Family Fare (thoughts and tips on feeding the brood), Recipes to Save, Homemaker Tips (from keeping eggs fresh to ridding your tub of mildew), plus other feature articles. Not specifically LDS. ★★★★

<http://www.homemakerherald.com>

Relief Society Rest Stop. Links to Morale Boosters, Recipes, Housekeeping Hints, Making a House a Home, and Homemaking Night Ideas. Somewhat useful, tho' the housekeeping hints would be better located on a Priesthood site. ★★★

<http://www.mormons.org/rs>

Sue's Block of the Month. Enter your quilt block in the Block of the Month contest. Participants work together to build a quilt, all the pieces of which go to the winner of a name drawn from among the participants. Might be worth adopting as a ward project. ★★★★

<http://members.aol.com/sewquilty>

The Country Cottage. Good links to country crochet, country knits, charity crafts, down home cookin', writing a family history, taking care of kids, more. ★★★★

<http://www.osmond.net/osnet/family/ccpals>

Women of the WWW 1st Ward, Unite! Not so radical as it sounds. Links to crafts, recipes, *A Woman's Touch* online magazine, and *A Woman's Perspective* newsletter for women. ★★★★

<http://www.uvol.com/www1st/sisters>

World Wide Quilting Page. Basic quilting techniques, diagrams and directions for many traditional quilt blocks, a collection of foundations for paper piecing, the block of the month (actually two new blocks every month). Lots of other stuff here also, so much that it requires, and has, a search engine. Not specifically LDS. ★★★★

<http://ttsw.com/MainQuiltingPage.html>

SEMINARY

Almost by definition, Seminary teachers are the best-organized people in the Church. The high quality of these seminary resources are good evidence of that.

Brother Smedley Pages. From the Timpanogos Seminary in Orem, Utah. Pages on Scripture, Scripture Mastery, Reading, Calendar, Thought of the Day, Thought Archives, Scripture of the Week, Chatroom, Monthly topics, more:

<http://burgoyne.com/pages/wes/seminary.htm> Also Brother Smedley Pages: *<http://burgoyne.com/pages/wes/bspages.htm>*

Scripture Mastery List.   All 100 scriptures used in Seminary. Commentary and memorization helps would make this site more useful. ★★★
<http://www.coolcontent.com/ScriptureMastery>

Seminary.   Sponsored by Zarahemla Book Shoppe. A good teacher resource (see figure 9.4). Includes attention-getters, reference material, and a link to a list of teaching ideas. ★★★★
Attention-getters: *<http://www.zarahemla.com/seminary.html>*
Teaching ideas: *<http://www.zarahemla.com/cesideas.html>*

SEMINARY.   Lesson ideas for teaching seminary, institute, or any other teaching position. Inspiring. A really first-class, useful list. The list has just changed ownership. Send your subscription request to *<majordomo@listservice.net>* with

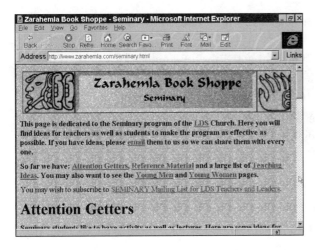

FIG. 9.4

Seminary: Instructional materials are available for Seminary teachers.

the message subscribe seminary. The list now has more than 600 subscribers. ★★★★★☑

<http://www.bolis.com/L/listinfo/seminary>majordomo@listservice.net>

SINGLE ADULT RESOURCES

There's hardly a member of the Church, anywhere, who either hasn't or won't spend some time as a Single Adult. It's no surprise that the Single Adult Internet sites are the most popular, active locations in the entire LDS online community.

In this section you'll find sites for Single Adults, sites specifically for Young Adults, and sites developed by various LDS student associations. None of these sites is specifically focused on dating or courtship; those appear in a later section in this chapter.

Single Adults

Both general sites for all single adults, and sites strictly for older single adults.

Arizona Mormon Single Adults. Current activities for single adults in the Phoenix/ Mesa area of Arizona over the age of 25. Includes activities all over Arizona and refers to some activities in other parts of the country. ★★★★
<http://gn2.getnet.com/~bnesbit/azldssa>

Around the Punchbowl: LDS Single Adult Resources. Very complete LDS Single Adult resource list. ★★★★★
<http://www.itstessie.com/sngl>

LDS Singles Activities for the Houston Area. Upcoming activities, recurring activities, and area hotline numbers. A good site for Texas single adults. ★★★★
<http://www.infohwy.com/church/lds/houston.htm>

It was run to see the e-mail roll in. Some just dropped a line; others wrote essays. One young man, inactive for years, found my Web site and asked how he could find out which ward he went to. He happened to be in my stake, so I put him in touch with his ward rep. Six months later, he wrote to tell me that he was "teaching Course 12 to the worst kids who ever walked the earth, just renewed my Temple recommend, and am getting active in all the Single's stuff."

Teresa Holladay, Dallas, Texas
<ItsTessie@aol.com>
Webmaster, Around the Punchbowl
<http://members.aol.com/itstessie/sngl/index.htm>

LDS Single Adult and Young Single Adult Groups. Links to LDS single adult sites throughout the world. ★★★★
<http://www.mich.com/~romulans/ldssaysa.html>

LDS Singles Connection. Currently listed as the #1 LDS Web site for singles and growing very fast. Nearly 6,000 new Date-A-Base profiles in less than a year. Good advice galore at this site. ★★★★
<http://www.singles.lds.net>

LDS Singles Resources. (SA/YSA) A good list of links, but it lacks original material (see figure 9.5). ★★
<http://www.ldsworld.com/links/sa.html>

LDS Web—San Francisco Bay Area. Information about LDS-sponsored singles activities in the San Francisco Bay Area. Includes activities schedules for Bay Area singles wards and branches; maps, information for the Oakland Temple, visitors center, and the Oakland Interstake Center; links to home pages of and

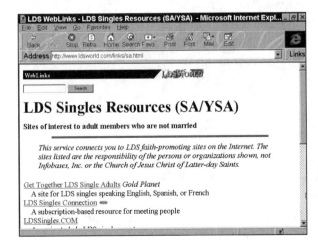

FIG. 9.5

LDS Singles Resources: A starting point for Single Adult links.

Web sites administered by Stanford Third Ward members; and links to other LDS-related sites. ★★★★

<http://www.best.com/~aeroundy/lds>

LIAHONA. Singles mailing list. Not a dating service. For young, single-adult members of the Church of Jesus Christ of Latter-day Saints, but accepts subscriptions from tolerant, truth-seeking individuals who may not fit into one of those categories. To subscribe, send an e-mail request to *<majordomo@cheek.com>* with the message `subscribe liahona`. More information available at the Web site. ☞

<http://www.hili.com/~mal/liahona>

Monument Park 19th Single Adult Ward. Single adults in Salt Lake City. Features a ward calendar and Bishopric message as well as links to other wards. ★★

<http://www.aros.net/~wenglund/mp19th.html>

Single Adults and Young Single Adults. Fairly comprehensive list of links to Web sites posted by numerous single adult groups, as well as Single Adult events. No original content, but it's a good gathering spot to access each of dozens of single adult groups. By Zarahemla Book Shoppe. ★★

<http://www.zarahemla.com/sa.html>

Single Adults Listings. Nearly 100 sites for single adults. The best collection of single adult sites on the Net. Unfortunately, the address is a bear, so once you find it, bookmark the site. ★★★★★

Go to *<http://www.deseretbook.com/ldsinfo/units.html>* and click the link to Single Adults, or try going directly to the site at *<http://www.deseretbook.com/ldsinfo/~lds.cxi?cat=12.15.@&template=level1.html&-main=Organizations/Units of the Church&-url=units.html&-subcat=Single Adults>*

Single Adults, Arizona. Text-based newsletter. Very local. ★★★

<http://www.infohwy.com/church/lds/flagstaf.htm>

Single to the Glory. A column for LDS single adults and leaders. Topics range from the role of the ward SA rep to the law of chastity. ★★★★

<http://members.aol.com/itstessie/sngl/column.htm>

Young Single Adults

Sites for college-age single adults.

Australian YSA Home Page. Well done page. Includes activities, Institute, e-mail addresses, and LDS Links. ★★★★

<http://www.wm.com.au/ysa>

Melbourne YSA Homepage. All the YSA activities in Melbourne in an interactive format. YSA News, Fireside schedules, and links. ★★★★

<http://yoyo.cc.monash.edu.au/~chompy/ysa>

Psychic Mormon Friends Network. Seattle-area YSA network (see figure 9.6). Information and discussion list for Young Adults in the Puget Sound area. To subscribe, send an e-mail request to *<listproc@u.washington.edu>*. ★★★
<http://weber.u.washington.edu/~youngg/pmfn.html>

Riverside Y.S.A. Local activities. ★★★
<http://members.aol.com/cumorahhil/rysa.htm>

Rockhampton: LDS Young Single Adults Page. Rockhampton (or RockVegas as it is known to the locals) is in the tropical north of Australia. Few LDS single adults, but they apparently have fun. Includes links and announcements. ★★★
<http://www.geocities.com/Heartland/3139>

The Field Is White. For the Young Single Adults of the Manchester England Stake to let other Young Single Adults around the world know what goes on in the Church in Manchester and the rest of Britain. Well maintained, good links. ★★★★
<http://www.geocities.com/Athens/Acropolis/8825/index2.html>

Young Single Adults. Features over 20 links to single young adult sites. ★★
<http://www.geocities.com/Heartland/4034/content.html#single>

Young Single Adults. Minimal links. ★
<http://www.wnetc.com/resource/lds/ysa.html>

SUNDAY SCHOOL

For teachers of adults and older youth, this list of Sunday School resources will prove invaluable. You'll find here all kinds of lessons resources, including gospel doctrine lesson outlines, reading lists, and several other practical teaching tools. (This section doesn't begin to touch the entire range of scripture study resources. For online scriptures, talks from general authorities, and commentaries, go to

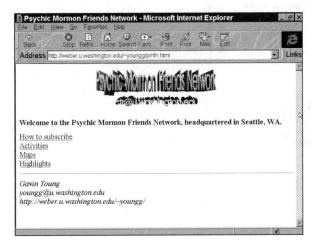

FIG. 9.6

Psychic Mormon Friends: Why bother with written messages?

chapter. 6: "Perfect the Saints," page 121. You'll find additional personal scripture study resources in chapter 11: "Pursuit of Excellence.")

Gospel Doctrine Lessons.   Extremely thorough research. Good background for teachers. Presentation could be a little more readable. ★★★★
<http://www.uvol.com/www1st/barton/index.html>

The Gospel Doctrine Class.   Handouts, lesson schedules, history, more for a ward in Federal Way, Washington. Tremendous! ★★★★★
<http://pw1.netcom.com/~bbeard1/gospdoct.html>

Gospel Teacher's File Cabinet.   This Web-site discussion forum lists new ideas for teaching the gospel, and includes a good list of links (see figure 9.7). Very nicely done. ★★★★★
<http://www.srv.net/~jam/fc.html>

Index to 1997 Church History/Gospel Doctrine Lessons.   Excellent collection of lesson materials from Barton M. Golding, a former Nauvoo resident who now resides in Orem, Utah. Relevant scriptures with commentary and history. ★★★★★
<http://www.uvol.com/www1st/barton>

LDS-SEMINAR.   A mailing list for teachers and students of LDS Gospel Doctrine. Messages address upcoming lessons with commentary on the scriptures assigned for each lesson. To subscribe, send an e-mail request to *<kurtn@ ocean.rutgers.edu>*. Part of the Scripture-L mailing list, except by special request. 📖

LDS-SUNDAY SCHOOL.   Full text of next week's Sunday School reading assignment. This year's reading assignment is the Doctrine and Covenants. The reading assignment is divided into five messages, one for each weekday. Subscribe

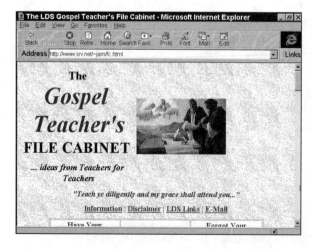

FIG. 9.7

Gospel Teacher's File Cabinet: New lesson ideas posted regularly.

by sending your e-mail request to <anderson@itsnet.com>. Archives are at the Web site. ★★★★★

<http://www.itsnet.com/~anderson/lds-ssrl.html>

LDS Teachers' Resources on the Internet. A small collection of stories and class handouts arranged by topic. ★★★

<http://www.lds.npl.com/special/teachers>

SCRIPTURE-L. A discussion of the scriptures. Operated and moderated by Gregory Woodhouse. Volume is moderate. Send subscription requests to <scripture-l-request@lists.best.com> with the message `subsingle`. To receive all the day's messages in one post mail, change the message to `subscribe`. Archives available at the Web site. ☞

<http://www.wnetc.com/scripture-l>

STUDIES. Discussion of scriptures and reference materials related to Gospel Doctrine lessons. Subscribe with an e-mail request to <majordomo@bolis.com> with the message `subscribe studies`. Visit the Web site for archives.

<http://seminary.org/studies>

Sunday School Page. Links to other teachers, teaching ideas, much more. One of the best Zarahemla Book Shoppe pages. ★★★★

<http://www.zarahemla.com/ss.html>

ON BEING A YOUTH LEADER

The time we spend with the youth is very precious. We must do all we can to make it fun and educational. The more resources we have access to, the better the chance we have at making that time just that.

Mike Pearce, Wichita, Kansas
<mpearce@dtc.net>
Webmaster, Mike Pearce's LDS Scouters Resource Page
<http://www2.dtc.net/~mpearce/scouts/scouts.htm>

YOUNG MEN

Thonk, thonk, thonk . . . Is that a basketball I hear?

If you're looking for something *different* for your Young Men's program, turn to these Internet sites for ideas.

Better yet, take the, ahem, ball into your own hands, and consider letting the Young Men in your ward build a site of their own.

LaVerkin Utah Priests Quorum. Little content, so far, but it's a great class project. ★★

<http://www.axi.net/fourthward>

LDS-Activity-Scoope. Ideas for Young Men's program activities, compiled by German member Thomas Mueller. ★★★★

<http://members.aol.com/ldsscoope/welcome.htm>

Providence Rhode Island Stake YM. Providence Rhode Island Stake Young Men's Home Page (see figure 9.8). One of the best auxiliary-created sites on the Web. Very nicely done, and worth emulating for your own stake or ward. ★★★★

<http://www.geocities.com/heartland/1948>

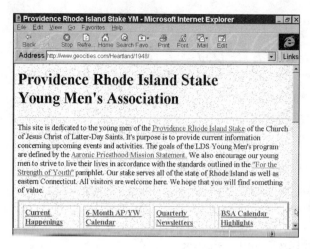

FIG. 9.8

Providence Stake YM: A great local resource.

Young Men. Teaching ideas, letters, more. A growing page. ★★★
<http://www.zarahemla.com/ym.html>

Young Men and Their Leaders. A small number of links to Young Men's resources. ★
<http://www.ldsworld.com/links/ym.html>

YOUNG WOMEN

These sites provide resources for leaders in the Young Women's program.

LDS-YW. LDS-YW is dedicated to the Young Women of the Church and their leaders. It is a way to exchange ideas, testimonies, and experiences. To subscribe, e-mail your request to *<majordomo@xmission.com>* with the body `subscribe lds-yw`.

Marquette Branch Young Women. A sweet page of doctrine and background material produced by the Marquette Branch program. ★★★
<http://members.tripod.com/~1Molly/Mormon.html>

Young Women and Their Leaders. Links to Young Women's resources. ★
<http://www.ldsworld.com/links/yw.html >

Young Women. The Young Women's Pledge/Oath, along with handful of references on ideas for activities, faith, individual worth, and other subjects. Lots of room for expansion. ★★
<http://www.uvol.com/www1st/youngwomen/youngwomen.html>

Young Women. Very extensive list of ideas for Young Women's program. Includes a commercial product list, frequently asked questions about the program, teaching ideas, fireside and lesson ideas, LDS youth page, #LDSYOUTH IRC home page, a Young Women's mailing list, and home pages from several Young Women's groups. ★★★★

<http://www.zarahemla.com/yw.html>

Young Women's Corner. Ideas relating to young women and the Young Women's program (see figure 9.9). Includes leaders, activities, New Beginnings, standards night, firesides, dates, camp, and good clean fun. A tremendous resource. ★★★★★

<http://www.mormons.org/ywc>

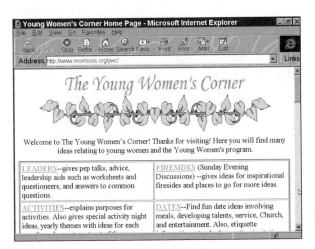

FIG. 9.9

Young Women's Corner: Fun ideas for all YW leaders.

10

INTEREST GROUPS

For Latter-day Saints, religion isn't just something to join, and Church isn't just something to attend. Church and religion and faith and action and work and life are all intertwined, one giving substance to the other. Devout Mormons believe—and live—the scriptural injunction that faith, without *work*, is dead.

For Latter-day Saints, it is part of one's duty to God to be anxiously engaged in parenting, in marriage, in temple work, in callings, in service, and in the community. Indeed, the Saints try to follow the example of King Benjamin, who in his last great address reminded his people: "And even I, myself, have labored with mine own hands that I might serve you, and that ye should not be laden with taxes, and that there should nothing come upon you which was grievous to be borne . . . I do not desire to boast, for I have only been in the service of God. . . . Behold ye have called me your king; and if I, whom ye call your king, do labor to serve you, then ought not ye to labor to serve one another?" (Mosiah 2:14–18)

Labor is a part of every moment of LDS life. Whether it's scout leaders, choir directors, sisters working to build fellowship, or youth who socialize in school and other activities, Mormons make a life's work out of life's work.

Chapter 9 described a number of Internet resources related to the auxiliary organizations of the Church. In this chapter, you'll be introduced to resources for Saints working to blend their religion, their families, their callings, their employment, and their personal interests into one great whole.

The first section covers Youth resources, much of which will be of interest to Youth leaders. That's followed by a separate section on Dating and Courtship. The next section covers Internet resources to help in various Church callings, including Scouts, Music, Activities Committee, Public Communications/Ward Newsletter, and Teaching. Then come sections on resources for Women, for Professionals, for Home Schoolers, for Disabled Saints, and for Saints dealing with same-sex attraction. The final section in this chapter is a list of commercial sites selling products and services designed for Latter-day Saints.

Ready? Then let's Do It.

LDS YOUTH RESOURCES

I was a good teenager. Really. I was respectful, hardworking, clean, and sober. I got good grades, I participated in dozens of organizations and activities at school, I was the president of my Laurel class, I had a part-time job, and I ran the stake dance committee. I got up early every morning all on my own, and found my own ride to Seminary. In short, my children hate me.

Despite all my otherwise good behavior, I had an inexplicable need to "hang" with my friends. Where I grew up, "hanging" meant driving to the next town and cruising in endless slow circles around the "loop," an eight-block rectangle in the center of town. Somewhere around midnight, the police would block the streets, at which time everyone would head toward the parking lot at Jack-in-the-Box, and stand around eating French fries 'til the wee hours.

And that's what the *good* girls did.

That's why I'm glad my own kids have an alternative—a place to "hang" with good kids who love the Church, who are excited about the gospel, who want to be the best people they can be.

Here's where you'll find them:

#LDSYouth. A heavily used chat area for LDS teens. ★★★★★
  <http://www.inetworld.net/kaos/ldsyouth.html>
#mormonteens. This is the #MormonTeens Web site for #MormonTeens chatters, visitors, and nonmembers (see figure 10.1). The chat room has activities such as Cyber-Dances, Food Fights, and Church-related discussions. Meet people from all over the world, or in your own town. Meet cyber-couples, return missionaries, and future missionaries. There's even a Cyber-Prom. ★★★★
  <http://www.geocities.com/EnchantedForest/Dell/3610/Tmp5.htm>

#mormonteens IRC teen chat channel. #mormonteens is a teen chat channel for kewl teens. Come on in and enjoy clean chat!
<http://www.geocities.com/heartland/hills/6850>

EFY Memories. EFY Memories is a collection of pictures and descriptions from participants in Especially For Youth. Accepts submissions. Register to receive e-mail updates. ★★★
<http://users.vnet.net/rabbanah>

For the Strength of Youth. Text of the pamphlet on standards. ☞
<http://www.npl.com/~jradford/soy/strength.html>

How to Write a Sacrament Meeting Talk. An inspirational essay—serious in tone—about speaking at sacrament meeting covering four basic principles. Also tacked on is a humorous piece: Recipe for Cooking Up a Sacrament Meeting. ★★★
<http://www.dayton.net/~dalleyj/bvrcrkward/talk1.htm>

LDS Youth Homepage. Youth-oriented page with thought of day, Seminary scripture mastery scriptures, discussions, and more. ★★★
<http://www.inconnect.com/~bytheway>

Peter D. Coyl Homepage. Peter's a high school student who's built a fine page with information of interest to other youth (see figure 10.2). ★★★★
<http://www.geocities.com/heartland/plains/2999>

The LDS Youth Leaders Page. A collection of ideas for combined youth activities, Young Men's activities, Young Women's activities, Scouts, service, Eagle projects.

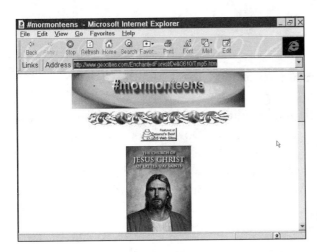

FIG. 10.1

The #mormonteens home page: Start chatting!

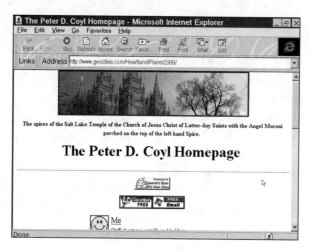

FIG. 10.2

Peter D. Coyl Homepage: Locate teen-oriented links.

Leaders and parents forums accept input from guests. Comments tend to be short. ★★★★

<http://www.ldsyouth.com/leaders>

The LDS Youth Page. Large collection of youth-oriented topics. Dating, pictures, links, books, missionary stories. The guest book is active. ★★★★★

<http://www.LDSyouth.com>

What We Do for Fun. A short list of activities. Not regularly updated. ★★

<http://members.tripod.com/~1Molly/Fun.html>

DATING AND COURTSHIP

Lots of resources here, some for teens, some for single adults. I long for the day when somebody builds a dating and courtship site designed for Happily Married Men.

Youth Oriented

The how-tos and the where-fores of teenage dating for Latter-day Saints.

Dates. A teen-oriented site with good reading on Answers to Dating Questions, Invitations, and Places to Go and Things to Do. Lots of information here. ★★★★

<http://www.mormons.org/ywc/dates/dates.htm>

Dating Ways. How to (eeekkk!) ask someone out on a date (see figure 10.3). Lots of fun suggestions. ★★★

<http://members.aol.com/cumorahhil/dateway.htm>

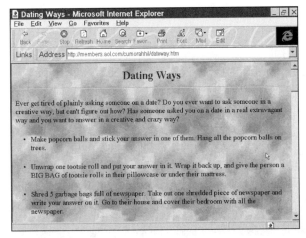

FIG. 10.3

Dating Ways: Gird up your strength.

Good Clean Fun. Younger, and more friends-oriented, but lots of good ideas for group activities. ★★★
<http://www.mormons.org/ywc/gcfun/fun.htm>

LDating and Courtship. *For the Strength of Youth*, plus quotations from other authoritative sources on dating for youth. ★★★
<http://199.227.118.92/daily/dating/index.htm>

LDS TEENS. A mailing list for, well, LDS teens. The list started in January 1997, and sees daily traffic of about three messages. E-mail subscription request to *<karlp@slcolubs.com>.* ☞

Single Adult Oriented

Bemoaning the lack of marriageable singles in your area? Problem solved.

The Internet not only expands your opportunities for meeting the love of your life; it also improves the chances that you'll be able to create a good marriage when you do. E-mail is a boon to relationships, a far better method for sharing and learning about another person than anything that has ever gone before. Grandma and Grandpa mailed long letters; Mom and Dad courted over the telephone; older siblings hung their heads in shame and met at discos and more disreputable places, rationalizing that they'd be able to "make over" the mates they found there. Modern courtship, online, is the best of all worlds: the real sharing and permanence of letters, the immediacy of the telephone, and the shelter—and enforced distance—of online communications. In that environment, real, honest, deep, and eternal love blooms.

Some advice to those who are corresponding over the Internet, from someone who's been there, and who is now happily married because of it: Be completely honest. Be tremendously careful if you find you're corresponding with someone who is *not* completely honest. If you're uncomfortable, trust your feelings. Be open to the promptings of the Spirit.

But while you're being careful, be happy. Ignore people who think it's shocking that you'd correspond with someone as part of a courtship. Remind them that until a few years ago, that's the way all permanent relationships began. Enjoy the opportunity for developing real emotional intimacy with another person. And save all those letters!

April Fools: A Look at LDS Cyber-Love.   A cautionary tale, with advice for single adults meeting others over the Internet. An article from Teresa Holladay's Around the Punchbowl page. ★★★
   <http://members.aol.com/itstessie/sngl/qa970401.htm>

Dating and Courtship.   A collection of articles on dating. Includes *For the Strength of Youth*, Dating and Courtship, Dating Nonmembers, Teaching Adolescents: From Twelve to Eighteen Years, Mature Intimacy: Courtship and Marriage, and President Benson's Teachings About Dating. A Mormons.Org site. ★★★★
   <http://www.mormons.org/daily/dating>

Bear says he never intended to find a wife and children again. "I had no intention of fighting my way back to activity in the Church," he says. "I just happened upon LuJane's personal and immediately knew that she was the one—the only one—for me."

LuJane was quite surprised to get her first e-mail from Bear, as she received it just as she was done posting her personal. "It was as if he was just waiting for me to post it so he could contact me," she says. "I had three teenagers and three adopted young boys, the youngest being only three years old. I had basically given up looking for a worthy priesthood holder who would be willing to take on a family of six kids and a headstrong wife who doesn't want to give up her newspaper business and extremely active lifestyle. . . .

After a two-week visit by Bear, in which much time was spent in family prayer and scripture searching, we were wed at the Potlatch, Idaho, Branch August 8 and are now looking forward to our sealing in the Seattle Temple, hopefully next April.

Let no man or woman disclaim the words of the Prophets. Modern-day technology is leading many lost souls back into Heavenly Father's blessings, and Internet services such as LDS Friends Worldwide are His tools to bring about miracles like we have experienced. Just ask us if this isn't so.

Brujo Bear and LJ Nisse, Palouse, Washington
<lujane@palouse.com>
Publishers, Boomerang!
<http://www.palouse.com/business/boomerang>

Get Together. The Canadian edition of the other sites found here. Multilingual, infrequently updated. ★★★★ <http://www.goldplanet.com/index1.htm>

LDS Friends Worldwide. (See figure 10.4.) Nearly 9,000 members at last count, evenly distributed between brothers and sisters. Very well liked. ★★★★ <http://www.ldsfriends.com>

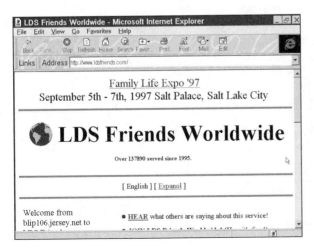

FIG. 10.4

LDS Friends: Meet, greet, have a seat.

LDS Singles Connection.   The dating service is $5.99 a month (see figure 10.5). This is a true computerized matching system. Claims more than 5,700 members. For the curious—and for your amusement—the site does post true success stories from clients. Regularly updated, and fun to read. ★★★★
<http://www.singles.lds.net>

LDS Singles Online.   Basically the same as the LDS Singles Connection except there are only 2,000+ members. One advantage is that they offer cheaper rates for a longer-term commitment. ★★★★
<http://www.lds-singles.com>

Of Souls, Symbols, and Sacraments.   Elder Jeffrey R. Holland, then President of Brigham Young University, discusses why sexual relations are so sacred. ☞
<http://199.227.118.92/daily/sexuality/Holland_SSS.htm>

Teachings About Marriage.   LDS beliefs about marriage. Articles include Eternal Marriage, Covenant Marriage, John and Mary, Beginning Life Together, Plural Marriage, Social and Behavioral Perspective of Marriage, Divorce, and Celibacy. A Mormons.Org page. ★★★
<http://www.mormons.org/basic/family/marriage>

Teachings About Sexuality.   This page offers links to the LDS perspective on such topics as Procreation, Abortion, Adultery, Birth Control. Mostly quotes from the *Encyclopedia of Mormonism.* ★★★
<http://www.mormons.org/daily/sexuality>

The Single Mingle.   Made up primarily of five sections: The Mingle (browse the home pages of many Latter Day Singles), the Barter Board (an online classified Ad Board especially for singles), the Chatter Box (an LDS singles forum), the Funny Bone (a daily dose of humor and inspiration), Singles Travel (a discount

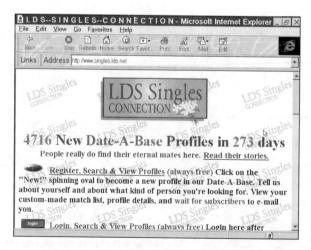

FIG. 10.5

LDS Singles: Check out the Date-A-Base.

travel center for LDS singles). There's a lot of material to read. Participation requires registration, and a maintenance fee of $1.50 a month. ★★★
<http://www.ysite.com/singles>

MANY ARE CALLED

Many, many are called, actually. It's the best thing about the organization of the Church. Whatever your calling, you'll find in this section some tools to help out. Here you'll discover resources for Scouting, music, activities committees, and the ward newsletter. (Separate sections for each of the auxiliaries are found in chapter 9.)

Callings. A talk given at a 1995 Ward Conference by Lisle Brown. Explains the meaning of callings. ★★
<http://webpages.marshall.edu/~brown/callings.htm>

Church Callings. How much shall I ask? How much shall I accept? Allen Leigh attempts to strike a balance between meeting the demands of callings and being reasonable. In other words, if you kill yourself today, you ain't gonna be much good tomorrow. So relax, pace yourself, and do what you can without compromising your own ability to prosper. ★★★
<http://www.xmission.com/~pengar/allen/callings.html>

The Scout Committee

My middle son had his first taste of Scout camp this summer. A few days before his twelfth birthday, it was, so he didn't get to sleep over. So guess who got to make the twice-a-day trip out to Camp Farfaraway, to pick him up and drop him off?

I'm glad I did. It was a real treat to see a group of fine, sturdy young men—the same crowd of rowdy 12-year-olds I teach in Sunday School—pulling together, working as a team, and getting their first real experience at becoming young men.

I have a real tender spot in my heart for the fine scoutmasters who have worked so hard with my own boys, training them, teaching them, demanding their best.

For all of you hard-working scoutmasters, here's some help:

Brad's Book. Excerpts from the book on Scouting written by Brad W. Constantine. Chapter 10: Does Scouting Work Better Inside or Outside the Church? ★★
<http://pages.prodigy.com/PHJF79A/scouts.htm>

Explorer Post 612. News and photos about recent, and not-so-recent, events. Take a peek at the scouting life. Hasn't been updated in awhile though. ★★
<http://www.coolcontent.com/ExplorerScouts>

Exploring Training in the LDS Church.   Slide-show presentation. Of interest to new Explorer leaders, or potential Explorers who might want to steal a glimpse of what lies ahead. ★★★
<http://pages.prodigy.com/PHJF79A/index.htm>

Grant's Scouting Resources.   Primarily for folks interested in scouting in Australia, but *Grant's Scouting Songs and Skit Links* should have universal appeal. Regularly updated. ★★★★★
<http://student.curtin.edu.au/~poneilgdo/scouts/index.html>

Mike Pearce's LDS Scouters Resource Page.   Includes links to scoutmaster minutes and other inspirational messages, leadership helps and ideas, games, stories and poems, songs, spiritual material, and additional scout links (see figure 10.6). Generally considered one of the best Scouting resources on the entire Net. ★★★★★
<http://www2.dtc.net/~mpearce/scouts/scouts.htm>

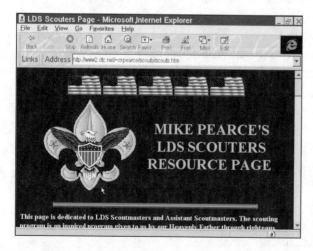

FIG. 10.6

Mike Pearce's LDS Scouters Resource Page: Endless help for scoutmasters.

program for the young men and have seen my troop grow from just four or five boys regularly attending troop meetings to over 30 boys, and thought I should share some of my ideas with others. . . .

On the site, I have posted links to other quality sites that offer good resources. I am also open to posting others' ideas on the page and have offered space on the page to many scoutmasters who have e-mailed me their ideas.

Mike Pearce, Wichita, Kansas
<mpearce@dtc.net>
Webmaster, Mike Pearce's LDS Scouters Resource Page
<http://www2.dtc.net/~mpearce/scouts/scouts.htm>

NJ Region Scouts.   Mailing list for LDS Scout leaders in Northern New Jersey. To subscribe, send an e-mail request to *<rbiddulph@attmail.com>*. ☞

Scout Links.   Sorted alphabetically, by nationality, newsgroups, new sites, and the ability to request that sites be included among the links. Over 500 scout-related sites. ★★★

<http://www.daimi.aau.dk/~arne/ScoutLinks>

Scouting in Utah.   A bit parochial, but it does feature good links to other Scout resources. ★★★★

<http://www.uvol.com/scouts/homepage.html>

Scouting.   Strictly links. ★

<http://www.zarahemla.com/scouting.html>

Scouts-LDS Scouting Resources Home Page.   Mostly under construction, but the owner says it "will contain Scouting resources that are specific to troops sponsored by local units of the Church of Jesus Christ of Latter-day Saints." For now you'll have to settle for links to the Scouts-LDS FTP Archive and Scouts-LDS Mailing List. ★

<http://198.240.118.1/scouts-lds>

SCOUTS-LDS.   A low-volume list dealing with the scouting program in the church. Share ideas for activities, describe ways of dealing with the youth, or ask advice on handling your calling. To subscribe, send a request to *<scouts-lds-request@tagus.com>* with the message `subscribe scouts-lds`. Visit the Web site for additional information. ★★★

<http://www.tagus.com>

The Telegraph.   (See figure 10.7.) A Sea Scouting newsletter published by Bill James, a Latter-day Saint in New Jersey. ★★★★

<http://www.jersey.net/~wrjames>

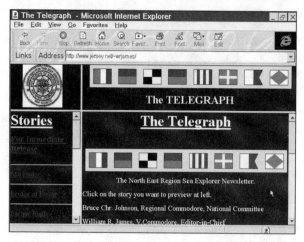

FIG. 10.7

The Telegraph: Scouts Ahoy!

Youth Advancement and Activity Software for LDS Stakes, Wards & Families. Advancement and Activity Software for Cub Scouting, Boy Scouting, Varsity Scouting, Explorers, Sea Explorers, and the YW advancement programs of the LDS church. A commercial site. $
<http://home.utah-inter.net/sbf/sb01001.htm>

Wadsworth Ohio Branch Boy Scouts of America Troop 400. A potential source of pride for Troop 400. A good resource if you're looking for ideas for your own Web pages. Otherwise there's not much here outside of local interest. ★★
<http://junior.apk.net/~jmf/scouts>

The Music Chairman

When I was in the first grade, my younger sister and I came home one day to find a huge piano in our living room. We danced around it in excitement, wondering aloud what it was. As I lifted the lid to look at the strings, my sister made a triumphant shout. "It's *mine*," she announced, waving the red John Thompson beginner's manual my mother had purchased. "See? It came with a Kindergarten book!"

A year's worth of piano lessons later, as the piano became more of a chore than a joy, my grandma caught me plodding, grudgingly, through the second-grade book of piano lessons. "You don't have to be a concert pianist," she whispered in my ear. "Just be good enough to play Church hymns."

So much for my mother's dream of raising brilliant children.

Children's Songbook. The Children's Songbook MIDI page. Sound files of some of the Primary songs. New selections are being added. ★★★
<http://www.uleth.ca/~anderson/csb.htmlx>

LDS Hymns. Good selection of hymns in MIDI format, from Doran Anderson. ★★★

<http://www.uleth.ca/~anderson/midi.htmlx>

The Danish Tabernacle Choir Society. A musical association with the object of diffusing knowledge of the Mormon Tabernacle Choir. This is a history tour. Very informative. Roll up, roll up for this history tour. But purchase the CDs listed if you plan on hearing music. ★★★★★

<http://www.mtc.dk>

Music. Very few links. ★

<http://www.wnetc.com/resource/lds/music.html>

Music to Heal the Soul. Sheryl Bagwell's uplifting collection of hymns and other music (see figure 10.8). Requires a sound card. ★★★★★

<http://ourworld.compuserve.com/homepages/sbagwell/music.htm>

Russ Josephson's Salt Lake Mormon Tabernacle Choir Page. More on history, discography, and information on videos and tours. ★★★

<http://www.geocities.com/SunsetStrip/7158/mtchoir.htm>

ON MUSIC

I have always been a very musical person and always had musical callings. I wanted to be able to share my music with the world and I have found the perfect place on the Internet. I did some investigating and found that there were plenty of sites that had the hymns, but none that had some of the other songs that LDS members like, or even had the hymns in arrangements different from the hymnbook, so I decided to provide that.

Sheryl Bagwell, Salt Lake City, Utah
<PCSBAGWE@ihc.com>
Webmaster, Music to Heal the Soul
<http://ourworld.compuserve.com/homepages/sbagwell/music.htm>

The Activities Committee

"May the road rise up to meet you, may the wind be at your back, and may you never have to serve on an activities committee" (an old Lamanite prayer).

FIG. 10.8

Music to Heal the Soul: Plays in the background.

Christmas and New Year Traditions in the UK.   A wonderful page describing
   English holiday traditions. Some ideas worth contemplating. (Not an LDS
   page.) ★★★
   <http://www.rmplc.co.uk/eduweb/sites/wickham/xmas/xmastory.html>

Planning Calendar.   Holidays, commemorations, events. Everything from National
   Handwriting Day to Be Kind to Animals Week. Not LDS. ★★★
   <http://www.innov-ad.com/event.htm>

Ward Activities.   Very abbreviated collection of successful ward activities. This site
   welcomes reader input. ★★
   <http://www.uvol.com/www1st/perfect/wardact.html>

Ward Activities.   Very brief list of Christmas party ideas. ★★
   <http://www.uvol.com/www1st/perfect/wardact.html>

The Newsletter Editor/Public Communications Specialist

A few Sundays ago I was walking down the hallway at Church when a member of
the mission presidency—someone with whom I regularly exchange e-mail jokes—
stopped me to explain how to get in touch with a third person we'd been discussing. "Just e-mail me his contact," I said. He nodded, then paused a moment,
looked me dead in the eye and said with a smile, "You know, LauraMaery, there
are some people in this world who actually don't have e-mail."

While I don't expect there'll ever be a thing we call the paperless office, the
time is coming when units of the Church will begin publishing their newsletters
online. If you're not quite there yet, you can at least use these online resources to
do a better job at the low-tech paper newsletter you still publish.

Highland Graphics—Clipart.   Over 150 images; specializing in religious and holiday themes. Commercial. $
   <http://www.itsnet.com/~highland>

Jim Radford's LDS Art Gallery.   A large collection of LDS-related artwork and images (see figure 10.9). Tons of stuff. ★★★★
   <http://www.npl.com/~jradford/lds/artgallery.html>

LDS Graphics.   Temple pictures. All of 'em. ★★★
   <http://www.npl.com/~jradford/lds/artgallery.html>

Mike Pearce's LDS Graphics.   Pictures of Jesus, prophets, general authorities, temples, artwork, scriptures (categorized by book), scouting, historical pictures,
   much more. ★★★★★
   <http://www2.dtc.net/~mpearce/graphics.htm>

New Church Logo Announced.   Text explaining/announcing the new logo. It is not
   a graphics download area. The logo does not even really exist on this page to be

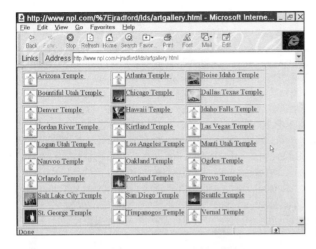

FIG. 10.9

Jim Radford's LDS Art Gallery: Page through the lists of graphics.

captured; it's superimposed over a picture of Jesus Christ. ★★

<http://members.aol.com/cumorahhil/newlogo.htm>

The Life of Christ.   Beautiful collection of artwork from the life of the Savior. Arranged in categories: The pre-mortal Christ, Annunciation, Nativity, Adoration of the Shepherds, Adoration of the Magi, the Holy Family, Youth, Ministry, Children, Parables, Healing, Apostles, Miracles, Mary, Gethsemane, Crucifixion, Ministry in the Spirit World, Resurrection, Appearance in the Americas, Restoration, The Last Judgment. Stunning. ★★★★★

<http://members.aol.com/itstessie/christ>

RESOURCES FOR WOMEN

You may have noticed that chapter 9 had substantially more Relief Society–sponsored sites than Priesthood-sponsored sites.

Guess what? This is the Resources for Women section. The corresponding Resources for Men section consists of exactly no sites. Get busy, boys. The ladies are running you off the road.

Arta Johnson's Home Page.   A good index of publications by and about Mormon women. ★★★

<http://www.ucalgary.ca/~ajohnson/index.html>

Errand of Angels.   To support and encourage all women, but especially those belonging to the Church of Jesus Christ of Latter-day Saints. Includes teaching moments, humor, teenagers, pioneers, cleaning and organizing tips, holidays, and more. ★★★

<http://www.geocities.com/Heartland/Plains/6358>

For the Sisters.   An essay by Krista Holle on her perceptions of the role of women in the church. ★★

<*http://members.visi.net/~atom/totally/Sisters.html*>

LDS Women's Forum.   Lots of writerly resources, and a good place to share essays, poetry, and thoughts (see figure 10.10). ★★★★★

<*http://www.primenet.com/~rogkat*>

Relief Society Meeting.   Transcripts from the most recent Women's Conference, along with articles related to women. ★★★★

<*http://www.desnews.com/confer/97fall/women.htm*>

SISTERS.   A mailing list for women to discuss any topic they choose. To subscribe, send an e-mail request to <*MAISER@rmgate.pop.indiana.edu*>.

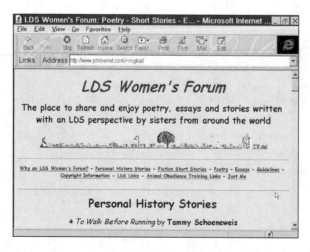

FIG. 10.10

LDS Women's Forum: Share your creative side.

many are online. My site isn't what most would call "literature." It's for the average LDS woman to express her own feelings about her life and her testimony, and to read what others have to say. If it's heartfelt and sincere, I include it, even though it wouldn't win a Pulitzer prize (unless it is extremely negative or anti-Mormon). The site is not fancy, and the graphics are limited on purpose to make it easier to download. From the e-mails I've received, it seems to meet a need.

I think we need to spend more time feeding our Spirits and focusing on the positive, striving for happiness and the ability to rejoice in life regardless of our circumstances, and I want my site to help do that.

Kathy Fowkes, Mesa, Arizona
<rogkat@primenet.com>
LDS Women's Forum
<http://www.primenet.com/~rogkat>

Sister-Share Home Page. This list has been created as a place for LDS women to talk with one another, share stories and experiences, ask and give advice, and get to know one another in a gospel context. More than 400 participants, and a lot of chatter. To subscribe, send an e-mail request to *<listserv@lists.psu.edu>*, with the message `subscribe sister-share`. More information is available at the home page. ★★ *<http://www.omnicron.com/~fluzby/sister-share>*. Additional information is located at *<http://cac.psu.edu/~mauri/ldssis/ldssis.html>*.

The LDS Stay-Home-Moms Home Page. An e-mail group for Mothers who have decided to stay home with their children. Supportive. ★★★
<http://www.utw.com/~kpearson/homemoms.html>

Women's Conference Homepage. Features selected talks about time management (About Time), becoming a disciple of Christ (Becoming a Disciple of Christ), and searching diligently in the light of Christ (The Beacons of His Light). ★★★
<http://coned.byu.edu/cw/womens.htm>

LDS PROFESSIONAL GROUPS

When I lived in Hong Kong, a few of the male members of the Victoria ward organized a thing they wanted to call the LDS Businessmen's Group—until the two women in the ward who wanted to attend the meetings raised some objections. So then it became the LDS Professionals Organization, or the LDS Business Council, or the Mormon Business Group—depending on who typed up the ward bulletin that week. Never mind. Not much business was ever conducted. But I'm here to tell you, it was a really good lunch.

Fortunately, there are some real LDS professional organizations where the members have more in common than close proximity to a great restaurant.

Association of Mormon Counselors and Psychotherapists (AMCAP). Not yet on the Internet, though several of its members, particularly those affiliated with BYU and other universities, are. Search the AltaVista database *<http://www.altavista. digital.com>* using the search term "`mormon counselors and`" (with quotes) to locate people who have published with AMCAP, and who are presently members of the Association.

Collegium Aesculapium. A professional association for LDS physicians, health professionals, and students who approach medical service with high ethical and moral values and with open hearts (see figure 10.11). It welcomes members of The Church of Jesus Christ of Latter-day Saints, alumni of BYU, and other interested persons who desire to grow in mind and spirit as they partake of opportunities to improve human health. The association publishes *The Journal of Collegium Aesculapium,* which focuses on articles dealing with moral, ethical, and religious issues. A very readable page. ★★★
<http://ucs.byu.edu/alumni/collaesc.htm>

J. Reuben Clark Law Society. An association of legal professionals operated by the JRC Law School at BYU. Includes a new e-mail list. ★★★
<http://wwwlaw.byu.edu/JRCLS/Main.html>

JRCLS. An Internet e-mail list for members of the J. Reuben Clark Society, an association of LDS legal professionals. To subscribe, send an e-mail request to *<listserv@lawgate.byu.edu>* with the message `subscribe jrcls-l <your name>`. ☞

Management Society. An organization of individuals from a wide variety of businesses and professions. The Society is associated with the Marriott School of Management at BYU. ★★★
<http://msm.byu.edu/alumni>

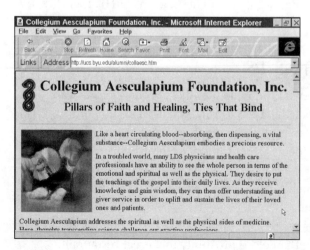

FIG. 10.11
Collegium Aesculapium: Serving LDS health professionals.

The Latter-day Saint Association of the Mathematical & Physical Scientists (LAMPS).
The James E. Talmage Society, the Latter-day Saint Association of Mathematical and Physical Scientists (LAMPS for short) is sponsored by the Brigham
Young University College of Physical and Mathematical Sciences. They publish
a newsletter three times a year. Membership in this association is free and open
to anyone who is studying or working in any of the fields represented by the de-
partments of the College: chemistry/biochemistry, computer science, geology,
mathematics, physics/astronomy, or statistics. ★★★★
<http://cpms.byu.edu/cpms/talmage/homepage.html>

HOME SCHOOLING

Everybody ought to home school their children—even if the kids attend public
school during the day. These sites are useful for anyone who cares about improving their children's education.

COOP.Mormon.Org.   The LDS Cooperative School Discussion Page. A discussion
area for an LDS-oriented cooperative school, an alternative to Public and
Home Schooling. Subscribe and read the archives at the Web site. ★★
<http://coop.mormon.org>

Home Schooling Daily.   The links at this site are organized to encourage use of the
Internet as a curriculum tool. Includes a "play" area and a spot to submit contributions to the cyberworld. Parents will find information on home schooling,
sites to use in a home school, and numerous lesson plans. Includes some of the
best sites on Family Living and Family Entertainment. ★★★★★
<http://www.infinet.com/~baugust>

Izu Early Childhood Education.   A site for home schoolers. Owner Tonia Izu writes:
"Individuals have often asked why and how our children were able to begin first
grade when they were four years old. This page explains our family educational
philosophy. There are several advantages to sending sixteen-year-olds to an out-
of-state university." A very slow load. ★★★★
<http://www.netcom.com/~toniaizu/eiedu.html>

Latter-day Family Resources.   Newsletters and resources for home-schooling. It's
the shopping network of home schooling. Updates quarterly. $
<http://www.itsnet.com/~family>

LDS Home Education E-mail Group.   E-mail group for parents who want the joy of
watching their own children grow and learn. Good resources. ★★★
<http://www.utw.com/~kpearson/LDSHomeEd.html>

LDS Home Schooling.   This site strongly advocates home schooling for everyone (see figure 10.12). A good resource for LDS-oriented links, it includes an

excellent list of home schooling information and links to support groups, Web pages, mailing lists, and curricula. ★★★

<http://www.midnightbeach.com/hs/lds.htm>

LDS Home Schooling Page.   Another great page on LDS home-schooling re-sources. Includes articles on subjects related to home schooling, including par-enting, socialization, dealing with criticism of home schooling, and a history of education; LDS home schooling organizations, curriculum resources, and re-gional contacts; quotes from the Brethren on education, public schools, parental responsibility, socialization, and more. ★★★★★

<http://home1.gte.net/shannon2/index.htm>

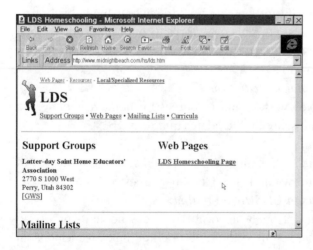

FIG. 10.12

LDS Home Schooling: Support for edu-cation in the home.

what clip-art to use to enhance the page. She also helps me review the links we use on our page. The activity ideas on the page are mostly hers. She creates and edits her own family newsletter each month, which is titled "The Cousin's Paper," and she distributes it to all of the cousins in our family. We use e-mail to accept submissions to her newsletter from her cousins, and so she is learning to type and use the computer for more than just games.

We have found that home school has brought us closer together as a family. We spend more time together, and all of our time is quality time since we are learning together. We plan to home school our younger daughter when she is ready, also.

Julina Mills and Shandalyn Mills, Mesa, Arizona
<pawsed@doitnow.com>
Webmasters
<http://www.doitnow.com/~pawsed/homeschl.html>

DISABILITY, MEDICAL, AND COUNSELING RESOURCES

There's an unfortunate dearth of LDS-oriented Internet information for people dealing with various disabilities. Fortunately, these few sites are unusually well done.

Blain Nelson's Abuse Pages. Counseling resources for people in abusive relationships. Blain Nelson is a Latter-day Saint who established the pages as part of his recovery process. ★★★★
<http://www.pacificrim.net/~blainn/abuse/index.html>

LDISABLED. For members of the Church who are disabled, or chronically ill in any way, and their families and friends. To subscribe, send an e-mail request to <listserv@home.ease.lsoft.com> with the message subscribe LDISABLED <your name>. ☞

LDS Deaf Connection. A tremendously well-done site, with helpful resources for deaf members (see figure 10.13). Features include a message board, news, visitors center, and mission information. ★★★★★☑
<http://www.bolingbroke.com/LDC>

Materials for the Blind and Deaf. An article about materials available to disabled Saints. ☞
<http://www.mormons.org/daily/health/Deaf_Materials_EOM.htm>

PEACE. A mailing list for Latter-day Saints who need a place to discuss issues relating to depression. No archive, moderated. To subscribe, send a request to <majordomo@ldschurch.net> with the message subscribe peace <your e-mail address>. ☞

S.A.V.E.   Substance Abuse Volunteer Efforts helping LDS people overcome substance abuse. A page for Mormons dealing with substance abuse. It is designed to aid people in overcoming these problems through God and respects the spiritual principles of the Church, AA, Al-Anon, and ACOA. ★★★★
<http://www.nicoh.com/IMIS/SAVE>

The Stress Relief Page.   Feeling stressed about life? Overcome with guilt? These scriptures are worth contemplating. ★★★
<http://www.athenet.net/~jlindsay/stress.html>

FIG. 10.13

LDS Deaf Connection: Resources for Deaf members of the Church.

be viewed by others, including those of my own faith, if I pursued the path of being open about my struggles with SSA, or of trying to help others in the same struggle. (At the time, I was using a fake name, afraid a bit of opening that door of admitting my feelings of SSA without shame or guilt.)

There were a few years in which I was actually more in the lifestyle than I was in the Church. I still was administrator of the lists during this time. Often the truth would be spoken through people sharing their struggles and their successes as they were obedient to the laws of God, and I was touched. The lists were an anchor for my soul. I have found that much of what I do with the mailing lists . . . has helped me to find my balance and get myself more grounded in the Gospel and what the Lord has in mind for my life. I am presently very out of the lifestyle and very in the Church. Watching others as they find peace and happiness through obedience has been a blessing and a glorious privilege to watch. I am often filled with the Spirit as I serve in this capacity.

Kim Mack, Ogden, Utah
<SykoBabbel@aol.com>
Webmaster, Disciples
<http://members.aol.com/disciples2>

RESOURCES FOR SAINTS DEALING WITH SAME-SEX ATTRACTION

There's no way to write about this subject without offending someone. So this time around, I'll let two people holding widely divergent views describe their Internet experience as it relates to the issue of dealing with same-sex attraction (see sidebars on pages 236 and 238).

DISCIPLES.   A mailing list for those who struggle with issues of same-sex attraction but are committed to obedience to the gospel of Jesus Christ and the teachings of modern apostles and prophets. Anonymous participation is permitted. Charter is strictly enforced, as is confidentiality. The list welcomes parents, spouses, priesthood leaders, and counselors. Subscribe with a request to <d2moderate@aol.com>. Charter is at the Web site. ★★★★
<http://users.aol.com/disciples2>

Evergreen International.   A Web page for the Evergreen International organization. It tries to help members who struggle with homosexuality. Includes articles on Finding Forgiveness, Finding the Way Back, Healing Your Damaged Life, Obtaining Help from the Lord, Same Gender Attraction, To Be Healed, Trust in the Lord, Happiness. ★★★★
<http://members.aol.com/evergrn999>

FAMILIES.   A discussion list for families of LDS members dealing with same-sex orientation. Not negative toward the Church. Subscribe with an e-mail request

to *<d2moderate@aol.com>*. More information is available at the Web site. ★★
<http://members.aol.com/disciples2/families.htm>

GAYMORMON. An e-mail group for same-sex attracted Saints and their friends for the discussion of issues with family, friends, and trying to become part of the gay community. Made up of SSA Mormons with varying degrees of involvement in the gay community and/or the LDS Church. Similar in tone to Q-SAINTS. To subscribe, send an e-mail request to *<nephi@netcom.com>*. ☞

Q-SAINTS. E-mail list for lesbian, gay, and bisexual people that come from a Mormon or Restoration background. Family members are welcome. Often takes an adversarial position toward the Church. Sponsored by Affirmation. Subscribe with an e-mail request to *<majordomo@vector.casti.com>* ☞

Stephen Rex Goode. Among his many interests, Rex has become a fairly prominent leader in the movement for adhering to gospel standards in the struggle with same-sex attraction. This page contains some of his excellent essays on the subject. ★★★★
<http://www.coil.com/~rexg>

TEENSTOO. Teen members of the LDS Church who experience a same-sex orientation. For those who desire to remain true to the teachings of the church. Not negative toward the Church. Supports LDS concepts. Subscribe with an e-mail request to *<chiefguy@aol.com>*. More information is available at the Web site. ★★
<http://members.aol.com/teenstoo>

WOMENTOO. LDS Women with a same-sex orientation who seek to follow the Church's teachings. Not negative toward the Church. Subscribe with an e-mail

sense of him being there, of leaving me to pick my way through life, at times smiling and approving, and at other times grimacing in a bit of pain and hoping I'll do better the next time.

I'm not the most spiritual of people, but my Internet life, because it is almost all LDS, gives me the feeling—no, the reality—that almost every day I'm living in the midst of a large group of friends, all members of the Mormon community, all talking more or less about the Gospel and life—many critical (possibly even the majority)—but they are still talking and I am still responding. And some have very important things for me to hear. How can daily exposure to this kind and quality of people not make my Heavenly Father a more constant reality in my life? And it has shown me that, in spite of what many might say, it is possible to be gay and spiritual, to be gay and Mormon . . . although for me this has nothing to do with being a formal member of the Church. But even if I were excommunicated, I'd hope my sense of the reality of these things would still be there.

Robert J. Christensen, Eugene, Oregon
<robertjc@darkwing.uoregon.edu>

request to <d2moderate@aol.com>. More information is found on the Web site. ★★

<http://members.aol.com/disciples2/women.htm>

COMMERCIAL SITES FOR LDS PRODUCTS AND SERVICES

Pull out your credit cards, boys and girls. Electronic commerce is here to stay. Here you'll find links to LDS bookstores and a mind-numbing array of products designed for a Mormon audience.

Commercial Sites. A good list of links to commercial sites. ★★★★
<http://www.ldsworld.com/links/com.html>

Commercial Sites. Links to 24 commercial sites including: MTC Cookies, Deseret Book, Covenant Books, LDS Music in Spanish, and more. ★★
<http://www.wnetc.com/resource/lds/commercial.html>

Commercial LDS Sites. Links to 16 commercial LDS sites including: Infobases, Iron Rod Bookshop, Cumorah Hill Publishing, Latter-Day lifestyles, Music Store, and more. Somewhat outdated. ★★
<http://www.nettally.com/LDS/commerlds.html>

LDS Retailer Search. A Deseret Book list of retail outlets for LDS products. ★★★
<http://www.deseretbook.com/retail_search.html>

11

PURSUIT OF EXCELLENCE

The pursuit of excellence. If it wasn't a Latter-day Saint who coined the term, it was certainly a large body of Latter-day Saints that made it popular. We learn from an early age to pursue excellence in all our endeavors. To strive to be the very best people we can be, to contribute to our families, our communities, our Church, and our world. To serve God in serving others. We take as our example not only Christ, from whom we learn service and charity, but also King Benjamin, who labored all his days among his people, building and creating, and serving God.

In this chapter, we use the Internet as a resource in several areas of the pursuit of excellence. The first, and largest, section looks at Internet tools for personal scripture study. In the second section, we cover Mormon arts and letters, the literature and fine arts that help define us as a community. We wouldn't be excellent people if we couldn't keep ourselves in perspective; the third section provides some great resources on Mormon-oriented humor. Finally, we address the last temporal concern: emergency preparedness.

SCRIPTURE STUDY

The Internet is a fantastic tool for studying the scriptures. Not only will you find the complete text of all the standard works online; you'll also find commentary, criticism, history, and other insights that can expand your understanding of the gospel. Latter-day Saints are often advised not only to read the scriptures, but to search them and ponder them, to "feast" on the words of Christ.

In this section, we look at Internet resources that are suitable for personal scripture study, but probably go beyond the scope of Gospel Doctrine class. Here each book of scripture has its own heading; the Book of Mormon tools warrant three heads: Book of Mormon Study Tools, Responses to Critics of the Book of Mormon, and Chiasmus Studies. Following the Book of Mormon sections are sections on the Bible, The Doctrine and Covenants, The Pearl of Great Price, and multiple books of scripture.

Book of Mormon Study Tools

In chapter 4 we introduced the Book of Mormon for investigators and new members. Chapter 6 contains links to the text of the Book of Mormon. You'll find historical Book of Mormon links in chapter 12: "Church History," page 278. In this section, you'll study excerpts from the Book of Mormon, along with textual analysis of those excerpts.

Walk through the following sites for a taste of the Book of Mormon insights available on the Internet:

2 Nephi 25. Describes Nephi's prophetic vision of the Messiah, and the relationship between Grace and Works. Includes links to an introduction to the Book of Mormon, and Jeff Lindsay's discourse on Faith and Works. ★★★
<http://www.athenet.net/~jlindsay/2Nephi25.html>

3 Nephi 11. Christ visits the Americas. Includes useful background information lending context to the chapter. Full text of chapter 11. ★★★
<http://www.athenet.net/~jlindsay/3Nephi11.html>

A Book of Mormon Parable. By Hugh Nibley. An insightful read. ☞
<http://www.primenet.com/~kitsonk/mormon/parable.html>

A Chronology of the Book of Mormon. Very cool hyperlinked chart with a timeline and a description of what was going on at any given time in the Book of Mormon. ★★★
<http://werock.com/granite15/bom-chrn.htm>

Alma 32. Alma's missionary text. Background information lends good context to the quoted material. ★★★

<http://www.athenet.net/~jlindsay/Alma32.shtml>

Alma 36. Alma's beautifully told conversion story. One of the most poetic Book of Mormon passages, this passage is one of the best examples of Chiasmus. The page contains interesting background material, and the full text of the story. ★★★

<http://www.athenet.net/~jlindsay/Alma36.html>

Book of Mormon. Commercial site with numerous texts and other products related to the Book of Mormon. 💲

<http://www.zarahemla.com/bofm.html>

Book of Mormon Lecture Series. A page from the Foundation for Ancient Research and Mormon Studies containing important lectures on the Book of Mormon (see figure 11.1). Catalog-y, but includes full text of Richard Anderson's "Book of Mormon Witnesses"; Dahl's "Faith, Hope and Charity"; Susan Easton Black's "Christ in the Book of Mormon"; James Faulconer's "How to Study the Book of Mormon"; Ludlow's "The Covenant Teachings of the Book of Mormon"; Millet's "The Nature of God in the Book of Mormon," "The Fall As Taught in the Book of Mormon," "The Doctrine of the New Birth," "The Atonement in the Book of Mormon," and "The Destiny of the House of Israel"; Nyman's "Is the Book of Mormon History?"; Ed Pinegar's "Missionary Work and the Book of Mormon"; Stephen Ricks' "The Translation and Publication of the Book of Mormon"; Royal Skousen's "The Critical Text of the Book of Mormon"; James E. Smith's "A Study of Population Size in the Book of Mormon"; Sorenson's "The Book of Mormon in Ancient America"; Catherine Thomas' "Zion and the Spirit of

> **RICHARD CRACROFT ON MARK TWAIN'S BURLESQUE OF THE BOOK OF MORMON**
>
> If Twain read the Book of Mormon at all, it was in the same manner that Tom Sawyer won the Sunday School Bible contest—by cheating.
>
> Richard H. Cracroft, *BYU Studies,* Vol. 11, No. 2, p. 119.

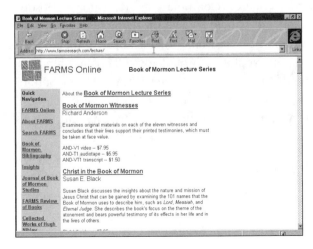

FIG. 11.1

Book of Mormon lecture series: Text from several of FARMS' best lectures.

At-one-ment"; and Tvedtnes' "Hebraisms in the Book of Mormon." You can order these and other items in the series through FARMS. ★★★★

<http://www.farmsresearch.com/lecture>

Book of Mormon Studies.   Research on Book of Mormon Historic Parallels, Geography, Revisions, Joseph as Seer and Translator, Doctrinal Parallels, Authorship, Solomon Spalding's manuscript, Witnesses, and full text of *View of the Hebrews,* 1830 Book of Mormon, and Book of Commandments. Great stuff.

<http://home.sprynet.com/sprynet/chatm>

Brant Gardner's Self-Published Papers Page.   A collection of essays about Mesoamerican issues (Quetzalcoatl's "Fathers" and "The Impact of the Spanish on our Record of Native Oral Tradition") and commentary on the Book of Mormon along with other interesting essays. Lacks authority, but the thinking is worth a read. ★★★

<http://www.highfiber.com/~nahualli>

The Historicity of the Book of Mormon.   A 1993 address to the FARMS annual dinner, by Elder Dallin H. Oaks. ☞

<http://www.primenet.com/~kitsonk/mormon/oaksonb.html>

Journal of Book of Mormon Studies.   Contents for every issue of the *Journal,* but only a handful of full-text articles are available online. Unfortunately, there's no easy way to view a single listing of all the online articles. Click through the contents links to find hyperlinks to the online text of "Lehi's Jerusalem and Writing on Metal Plates," "Three Days of Darkness," "The Prophetic Laments of Samuel the Lamanite," "The Design of the Liahona," "Notes on Korihor and Language," "The Mortal Ministry of the Savior," "The Jewish Lectionary and Book of Mormon Prophecy," "New and Old Light on Shawabtis from Mesoamerica," "The Historiography of the Title Page," "The Economics of the Book of Mormon," "The Tree of Life," "The Book of Mormon, Historicity, and Faith," "Thus Saith the Lord," "Secret Combinations Revisited," "Joseph Smith's Receipt of the Plates and the Israelite Feast of Trumpets," "The True Points of My Doctrine," "Translation of the Book of Mormon," "Others in the Book of Mormon," "Comments on Nephite Chronology," "The Jaredite Exodus," "Destruction at the Time of the Crucifixion," "Jewish and Other Semitic Texts Written in Egyptian Characters," "The Influence of Lehi's Admonitions," and "The Plan of Redemption As Taught in the Book of Mormon." Sterling research, but the table of contents is rather unorganized. ★★★★

King Benjamin's Farewell Address.   If you had to choose one section of the Book of Mormon to send out to all the world, this would be it. Brother Lindsay includes some background information putting the discourse into its historical context. The full text follows. ★★★

<http://www.athenet.net/~jlindsay/KBenjamin.html>

LDS and RLDS Book of Mormon Comparison.   A handy reference comparing the Book of Mormon used by The Church of Jesus Christ of Latter-day Saints and that used by the Reorganized LDS Church (see figure 11.2). This site makes great use of Internet frames technology to allow a side-by-side comparison of both works. One scrollable text is on the left; the other appears on the right. Unfortunately, the site suffers from a lack of commentary, as well as a lack of highlighting. Other than that, it's a fantastic resource. ★★★★

<http://www.dailynews.net/support/restoration/bofm/index.html>

Mormon's Story.   The text of the Book of Mormon in a simpler English (see figure 11.3). While I'm a great fan of reading scriptures in their original form, I'm an even greater fan of understanding the scriptures—in whatever form generates understanding. Timothy Wilson's rewrite of the Book of Mormon is beautifully done, and it's all available online, at this Web site. If this is the kind of simplification it takes to get a child or a new reader through the Book of Mormon, it's a worthwhile venture. ★★★★★☑

<http://www.enoch.com/voicesfromdust/mormonstory/mormonstory.html>

People in the Book of Mormon.   Articles on prominent people in the Book of Mormon, including Book of Mormon Peoples, Abinadi, Alma the Elder, Alma the Younger, Amulek, Benjamin, Brother of Jared, Moroni, Son of Mormon. A Mormons.Org page. ★★★★

<http://www.mormons.org/basic/bom/people>

The Atonement in the Book of Mormon.   Text of an essay by Robert L. Millet, wherein he says it's not possible to appreciate the salvation of Christ until you know why you need Christ. And the Book of Mormon helps establish that. ☞

<http://www.farmsresearch.com/lecture/MIL-VT4.HTM>

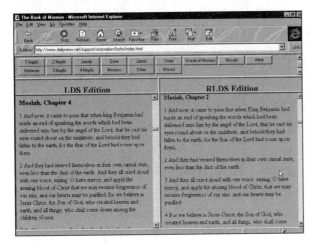

FIG. 11.2

LDS and RLDS Book of Mormon Comparison: Side-by-side view of both editions.

FIG. 11.3

Mormon's Story: An easy-to-read retelling of the Book of Mormon.

The Book of Mormon—Artifact or Artifice? By Orson Scott Card. Adapted from a speech he gave at the 1993 BYU Symposium on Life, the Universe, and Everything. An eye-opening commentary on the Book of Mormon as an impossible work of fiction, by someone who should know. It'll permanently alter the way you understand the Book of Mormon.

<http://www.nauvoo.com/library/bookofmormon.html>

The Book of Mormon: Another Testament of Jesus Christ. Very well done collection of articles on Book of Mormon topics. Includes information on Come Unto Christ, An Overview, Biblical Prophecies About The Book of Mormon, Government and Legal History, History of Warfare, Authorship, The Book of Mormon in a Biblical Culture, Chronology, Commentaries, Economy and Technology, Editions (1830–1981), Geography, Language, Literature, Manuscripts, Names, Near Eastern Background, People in The Book of Mormon, Plates and Records, Religious Teachings and Practices, Studies, Translation by Joseph Smith, Translations, Witnesses, Allegory of Zenos, Anthon Transcript, Archaeology. A Mormons.Org page. ★★★★★

<http://www.mormons.org/basic/bom>

Who's Who in the Book of Mormon. Rick Owen. A list of all the people in the Book of Mormon with biographical sketches. Very helpful. ★★★

<http://www.srv.net/~rlo/bomchar.html>

Responses to Critics of the Book of Mormon

Some of the most heated discussion in the LDS online community surrounds the Book of Mormon: its truthfulness, its historicity, its meaning.

As the keystone of our religion, it is perhaps natural that the Book of Mormon should be the focus of a great deal of discussion, both within the Church, and from without.

Latter-day Saint defenders of the Book of Mormon have produced a remarkable volume of literature in support of the book, responding with scholarly and disciplined answers to each issue raised by detractors.

A good number of the best, most scholarly responses to critics come from the Foundation for Ancient Research and Mormon Studies—FARMS. Accordingly, FARMS studies are well represented in this list of responses to critics of the Book of Mormon. While FARMS also publishes reviews of LDS-authored books on its Web site, the responses to critics are, quite frankly, more interesting, and so are documented here individually.

While the battle continues to rage, the following sites continue to provide good clean help for readers who need additional background on the Book of Mormon.

A Look at Book of Mormon Authorship. L. Ara Norwood's dispassionate review of Holley's *Book of Mormon Authorship*. Very readable, void of polemics. ✍
<http://www.farmsresearch.com/frob/ frobv1/norwood.htm>

A Look at Covering Up the Black Hole. Tom Nibley's rather amusing dismissal of Jerald and Sandra Tanner's 1990 book. ✍
<http://www.farmsresearch.com/frob/frobv5/nibley.htm>

A Modern Malleus Maleficarum. Daniel C. Peterson's review of *The Best Kept Secrets in the Book of Mormon*, a polemic he describes as "New Age anti-Mormonism." ★★★
<http://www.farmsresearch.com/frob/frobv3/dcp.htm>

Abracadabra, Isaac and Jacob. John Gee's well-documented rebuttal to Ashment's *The Use of Egyptian Magical Papyri to Authenticate the Book of Abraham.* ✍
<http://www.farmsresearch.com/frob/frobv7_1/gee1.htm>

Apparent Book of Mormon Problems. Responds to objections about the weight of the plates, coins, the use of the word "adieu," metals, and more. Very thorough

---

THE BOOK OF MORMON MODERNIZED
Isaiah's own cleansing and commission . . .

"In the year that King Uzziah died, I, Isaiah was in the temple. I saw the Lord sitting upon an exalted throne. Angels stood nearby, each with his covering and with power to move about, calling out to each other, 'The Lord of Hosts is most holy, for the whole earth is full of His glory.' As the angels spoke, a door opened and the temple was filled with smoke so that I could no longer see the Lord. Then I realized that I had seen the Lord and exclaimed, 'I am cursed, for I have unclean speech and live among people with unclean speech, yet I have seen the King, the Lord of Hosts!' Then one of the angels came to me, holding a live coal that he had taken from the altar with a pair of tongs. Touching my mouth with it, he said, 'This coal has touched your lips. Your sins are taken away and have been atoned for.'"

2 Nephi 16, from Timothy Wilson's Mormon's Story.
<http://www.enoch.com/voicesfromdust/ mormonstory/mormonstory.html>

answers to questions commonly raised by critics of the Church. ★★★★

<http://www.athenet.net/~jlindsay/LDSFAQ/FQ_BMProblems.shtml>

Archaeology and Book of Mormon Evidence. Jeff Lindsay's thoughtful responses to questions on archaeology and the Book of Mormon. Responds to sixteen real queries from readers. Covers questions such as: Have non-LDS scholars confirmed that the Book of Mormon is true? Does the Book of Mormon have the expected level of historical confirmation for true scripture? Is there evidence that Lehi existed? Why is there lots of archaeological evidence for the Bible but little for the Book of Mormon? Why hasn't a single Book of Mormon site been identified? Is there evidence that the golden plates ever really existed? How can we believe the Book of Mormon without having the original plates? Haven't archaeologists and geneticists refuted the Book of Mormon? Hasn't it been proven that all Native Americans are of Asian (Mongoloid) origin, not Jewish origin? Brother Lindsay's responses are always well documented and thorough. ★★★★

> **PRESIDENT EZRA TAFT BENSON ON THE BOOK OF MORMON**
>
> There are three ways in which the Book of Mormon is the keystone of our religion. It is the keystone in our witness of Christ. It is the keystone of our doctrine. It is the keystone of testimony.
>
> *Teachings of Ezra Taft Benson, p. 53.*

<http://www.athenet.net/~jlindsay/LDSFAQ/FQ_BMEvidence.shtml>

Basic Methodological Problems with the Anti-Mormon Approach to the Geography and Archaeology of the Book of Mormon. "Proofs" of the Book of Mormon. Addresses the nature of "proof," Misconceptions, Witnesses, Understanding of Arabia, Book of Mormon Names, Hebrew writing styles and idioms, Chiasmus, Annual Great Assembly, Modern Stylemetry Analysis, Claims for origin of Book of Mormon, Discussions about the Book of Mormon, and Additional Sources of Information. ★★★★

<http://mercury.digitalpla.net/~russ/bofm.htm>

Biblical References to the Book of Mormon. A brief list of biblical scriptures that prophesy the Book of Mormon. ★★★

<http://www.primenet.com/~kitsonk/mormon/bom.html>

Birthplace of Jesus Christ. FARMS favorites Peterson, Roper, and Hamblin respond to critics who claim Alma 7:10 impugns Joseph Smith. ☞

<http://www.farmsresearch.com/critic/critic02.htm>

Book of Mormon. Critics of the Church and of the Book of Mormon often use a questionable set of assumptions. Bill Hamblin takes a look at the arguments and patterns of assumptions. ★★★

<http://www.farmsresearch.com/critic/critic04.htm>

Changes to the Book of Mormon. Well-done summary of textual changes in a table format. Demonstrates that assertions of "thousands" of changes are overwrought. ★★★

<http://www.primenet.com/~kitsonk/mormon/changes.html>

Comments on the Book of Mormon Witnesses: A Response to Jerald and Sandra Tanner. Tremendously well-documented article by Matthew Roper that challenges the Tanners' representations about the witnesses of the Book of Mormon. ★★★

<http://www.farmsresearch.com/critic/critic03.htm>

Evidences for the Book of Mormon. Jeff Lindsay is the Energizer Bunny of the Mormon Internet. In this page of responses to questions posed by readers, Brother Lindsay describes Excellent Printed Resources, Geography of the Arabian Peninsula, Writing on Metal Plates, Writing in Reformed Egyptian? Mulek, Son of King Zedekiah? The Use of Cement in Ancient America, Chiasmus in the Book of Mormon, Olive Culture, Wars in Winter? Mesoamerican Fortifications, Numerous Hebraic Language Structures, Names in the Book of Mormon, "The Land of Jerusalem" question, and a new page, The Great Catastrophe: Volcanism in Book of Mormon Lands. ★★★★

<http://www.athenet.net/~jlindsay/BMEvidences.shtml>

ON RESPONDING TO CRITICS OF THE BOOK OF MORMON
None of these [response pages] will change the minds of hardened critics, but I honestly have found that there are good answers to most common questions. There are also good reasons not to reject the Book of Mormon in cases where we don't yet have the answers. Intellectually, I find the book to be authentic. Spiritually, I have found it to contain the words and teachings of Christ, the Savior and the Son of the Living God. To me, it is a convincing and powerful book that brings people to Christ, acting as a second witness with the Bible.
Jeff Lindsay, from *A Brief Introduction to the Book of Mormon.* *<http://www.athenet.net/~jlindsay/BOMIntro.shtml>*

Have There Been Thousands of Changes in the Book of Mormon? Very readable explanation of the changes made over time to the text of the Book of Mormon. ★★★

<http://www.athenet.net/~jlindsay/LDSFAQ/FQ_changes.shtml>

Is the Book of Mormon a Fraud? Interesting passages from the works of Hugh Nibley. ★★★

<http://www.athenet.net/~jlindsay/nibley_bom_fraud.html>

Is the Book of Mormon Really an Ancient Book? Modern discoveries that turn the tables on Book of Mormon critics. What seemed a joke in 1830 has become accepted as legitimate today (naming conventions, Hebrew idioms, ancient writing on metal plates, much more). Pages load quickly. Very thorough. ★★★★

<http://www.primenet.com/~kitsonk/mormon/bomanc.htm>

Just the Facts Please. Joseph Smith scholar Richard L. Bushman's evaluation of Marquardt and Walters' *Inventing Mormonism: Tradition and the Historical Record.* Excellent. ★★★

<http://www.farmsresearch.com/frob/frobv6_2/bushman.htm>

Metals, Weapons, and the Book of Mormon. Responds to queries about steel in ancient America, swords, weight of the plates, size of the plates, brass, sources of metals, ancient writing on metal plates, more. There's no end of possible

responses. Jeff Lindsay covers the basics.
<http://www.athenet.net/~jlindsay/LDSFAQ/FQ_metals.shtml>

New Approaches. Reviews of Brent Metcalfe's *New Approaches to the Book of Mormon: Explorations in Critical Methodology.* ☞ Responses from Davis Bitton *<http://www.farmsresearch.com/frob/frobv6_1/bitton.htm>*, John A. Tvedtnes *<http://www.farmsresearch.com/frob/frobv6_1/tvedtnes.htm>*, and Daniel C. Peterson *<http://www.farmsresearch.com/frob/frobv6_1/text_c.htm>*.

Notes on Changes in the Book of Mormon. A site by Kitson Kelly. ★★★
<http://www.primenet.com/~kitsonk/mormon/changes.html>

On Alma 7:10 and the Birthplace of Jesus Christ. Was it really a translation error on Joseph's part when he placed Christ's birth "at Jerusalem which is the land of our forefathers?" A FARMS study. ★★★
<http://www.farmsresearch.com/critic/critic02.htm>

Plagiarism and the Book of Mormon. If you're a nonbeliever, it's tough to account for the Book of Mormon. Critics go to extraordinary lengths to find non-divine sources for the text. This page responds to common charges that the Book of Mormon was plagiarized. Answers three questions: Did Joseph Smith plagiarize from *View of the Hebrews?* Did Joseph Smith plagiarize from Shakespeare? Did Joseph Smith plagiarize from the King James Bible? ★★★
<http://www.athenet.net/~jlindsay/LDSFAQ/FQ_BMProb3.shtml>

Plants and Animals in the Book of Mormon. Jeff Lindsay's answers to objections raised by critics regarding seeming anachronisms in the Book of Mormon. Good introductory material, thorough responses to several specific questions. ★★
<http://www.athenet.net/~jlindsay/LDSFAQ/FQ_BMProb2.shtml>

Proof The Book of Mormon Is True. Show Me a Sign! There are better ways to prove it! ★★
<http://www.nettally.com/LDS/prove.html>

Reformed Egyptian. William J. Hamblin's response to critics who maintain that there is no language known as "reformed Egyptian." ☞
<http://www.farmsresearch.com/critic/critic01.htm>

Review of *A Sure Foundation: Answers to Difficult Gospel Questions.*   This review includes fourteen of the questions and answers included in the book. Worth a read. ☞

<http://www.farmsresearch.com/frob/frobv2/gillum.htm>

Review of *Are the Mormon Scriptures Reliable?*   Diane E. Wirth's examination of the Ropp and Walters' text. She writes: "This book is, perhaps, rather better than the average anti-Latter-day-Saint book." The review responds to oft-repeated allegations about Mormon Christianity, archaeology, reformed Egyptian, Kinderhook, geography, textual changes and inconsistencies, plural marriage, Book of Abraham, scriptural interpretation, and quality of scholarship. ☞

<http://www.farmsresearch.com/frob/frobv2/wirth.htm>

Review of Ethan Smith, *View of the Hebrews.*   Be ready to wave this one next time someone says the Book of Mormon was plagiarized. ☞

<http://www.farmsresearch.com/frob/frobv9_1/hedges.htm>

Review.   Daniel C. Peterson's assessment of Bartley's *Mormonism: The Prophet, the Book and the Cult.* He describes Bartley's haphazard scholarship. (Bartley at one point quotes Brigham Young from a nineteenth-century novel as though the prophet had actually spoken the fictionalized words.) ☞

<http://www.farmsresearch.com/frob/frobv2/dcp.htm>

Review.   Daniel C. Peterson's well-written review of Van Gorden's *Mormonism.* Responds to usual critical controversies such as archaeology, coins, hieroglyphics, birthplace of Christ, Professor Anthon, witnesses, priesthood. ☞

<http://www.farmsresearch.com/frob/frobv8_1/dcp1.htm>

Review.   L. Ara Norwood persuasively refutes David Persuitte's *Joseph Smith and the Origins of the Book of Mormon,* in which Persuitte alleges a *View of the Hebrews* origin for the Book of Mormon. ☞

<http://www.farmsresearch.com/frob/frobv2/norwood.htm>

"Secret Combinations" Revisited.   Daniel C. Peterson article originally published in *Journal of Book of Mormon Studies,* wherein he responds to allegations that the term "secret combinations" casts doubt on Book of Mormon authorship. ☞

<http://www.farmsresearch.com/jbms/jbmsv1_1/dcp.htm>

Some 23 Questions Answered by the Book of Mormon.   One-line questions with relevant scriptural references. ★★

<http://www.nettally.com/LDS/quest.html>

The Book of Mormon and Archaeology FAQ.   Arden Eby's collection of responses to questions raised about Book of Mormon archaeology. Includes a beautiful retelling of the Mayan creation story. Worth a visit. ★★★

<http://www.teleport.com/~arden/mormfaq.htm>

The Book of Mormon and Metal Plates.   Research conducted by William J. Hamblin for FARMS provides powerful modern evidence for the authenticity of the Book of Mormon. ★★★

<http://www.athenet.net/~jlindsay/LDSMetal.shtml>

The Book of Mormon Challenge.   One of those lists that gets passed around Sunday School without attribution. But it's an interesting way to view the Book. ★★

<http://www.primenet.com/~kitsonk/mormon/challang.html>

The Book of Mormon Challenge.   Hugh Nibley's challenge to critics (see figure 11.4). The title is the same as the site above; the content is entirely different. ★★

<http://www.athenet.net/~jlindsay/BOMchallenge.shtml>

Various Editions of the Book of Mormon.   A New Jerusalem site. Text from an *Encyclopedia of Mormonism* article comparing editions. ✍

<http://www.new-jerusalem.com/bom-answerman/changes.html>

Chiasmus Studies

A new and fascinating line of inquiry into the Book of Mormon is the field of Chiasmus Studies. Chiasmus is an ancient poetic and structural form found in both the Old and New Testament, as well as in the Book of Mormon and the Doctrine and Covenants. Its presence in the Book of Mormon is considered by many to be evidence of the Book of Mormon's divine origin.

Several Web sites address the issue of Chiasmus, in particular as it relates to comparisons between the Book of Mormon and the Bible.

Chiasmus in Mosiah 3.   Lacks commentary, but it's a fine resource if you're reading Mosiah anyway. ★★

<http://deathstar.rutgers.edu/people/kurtn/exegesis/mosiah3x.txt>

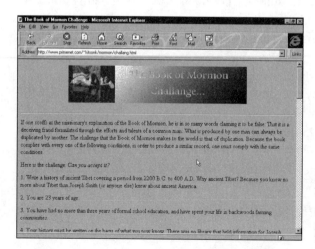

FIG. 11.4

The Book of Mormon Challenge: Description of the difficult circumstances under which the Book of Mormon was translated.

Chiasmus in the Book of Mormon. Another Jeff Lindsay page, with careful explanations of how Chiasmus is structured. Contains many examples of the form. ★★★★

<http://www.athenet.net/~jlindsay/chiasmus.shtml>

Davidic Chiasmus and Parallelisms. A governing literary structure for messianic literature (see figure 11.5). Here you'll find more than 100 examples of chiastic patterns. The page describes the chiastic structure and illustrates it through many examples. Some of the chiastic structures here are controversial, so ponder it carefully. ★★★★

<http://www.geocities.com/CapitolHill/3500/index.html>

Chiasmus on the Brass Plates. A brief introduction to Chiasmus. ★★

<http://www.mormonism.com/chiasmus.htm>

Structure and Outline of Zephaniah. Certainly not a Book of Mormon site, but nevertheless a very compelling resource on chiasmic structure, as illustrated in the book of Zephaniah (see figure 11.6). Compiled by a Rev. Ralph A. Smith, who writes: "The entire book of Zephaniah is constructed as a chiasmus, the purpose of which is to emphasize the character and certainty of the judgment about to fall upon Judah and Jerusalem. Zephaniah alludes to well-known historical events—the Noahic deluge, the Exodus, and the Conquest—to structure his book. The central and most emphatic portion of the book is the call for repentance (2:1–3). The promise of salvation also, breaking the chiastic structure at the end of the book (3:9–20), has particular force." ★★★★

<http://www.berith.com/English/ZEPH001.html>

Bible Study Tools

Two subjects compete for the title of Taking Up the Most Space on the Internet: Religion and Pornography. Naturally, then, there's no shortage of information to

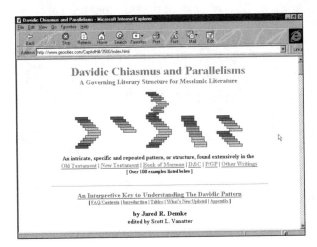

FIG. 11.5

Davidic Chiasmus and Parallelisms: Chiasmus in the Bible has clear parallels in the Book of Mormon.

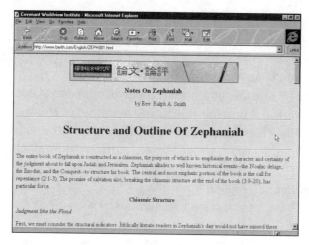

FIG. 11.6

Structure and Outline: The Old Testament book of Zephaniah exhibits the chiasmic structure.

be found on biblical topics—or anti-biblical ones, if that's your inclination. In this section, we list some of the Bible-oriented sites that have a particular interest to LDS readers, but remind you that if you're searching, you'll find literally hundreds of Bible sites of a more general nature. To compare these sites, we looked at a biblical verse that has a great deal more meaning for Latter-day Saints than it has for most other Christians: 1 Cor. 15:29, the reference to vicarious baptism.

The Bible. Links to LDS- and a few non-LDS-authored sites related to the Bible. ★★★

<http://www.cyberhighway.net/~vchopine/ldsbible.htm>

The Bible Browser Advanced Home Page. A tremendously useful comparison of nine popular versions of the Bible (see figure 11.7). Here's what the browser turned up in a comparison of various translations of 1 Cor. 15:29:

American Standard Version (1901): "Else what shall they do that are baptized for the dead? If the dead are not raised at all, why then are they baptized for them?"

Bible in Basic English (1965): "Again, what will they do who are given baptism for the dead? if the dead do not come back at all, why are people given baptism for them?"

Darby (1884/1890): "Since what shall the baptised for the dead do if [those that are] dead rise not at all? Why also are they baptised for them?"

Jerome's Latin Vulgate (405 C.E.): "alioquin quid facient qui baptizantur pro mortuis si omnino mortui non resurgunt ut quid et baptizantur pro illis"

254

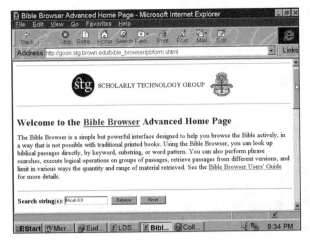

FIG. 11.7

The Bible Browser: Use the Bible Browser to compare nine versions of the Bible.

King James Version: "Else what shall they do which are baptized for the dead, if the dead rise not at all? why are they then baptized for the dead?"

Noah Webster (1833): "Else what will they do, who are baptized for the dead, if the dead rise not at all? why are they then baptized for the dead?"

Revised Standard Version: "Otherwise, what do people mean by being baptized on behalf of the dead? If the dead are not raised at all, why are people baptized on their behalf?"

Weymouth New Testament (1909): "Otherwise what will become of those who got themselves baptized for the dead? If the dead do not rise at all, why are these baptized for them?"

Young's Literal Translation (1898): "Seeing what shall they do who are baptized for the dead, if the dead do not rise at all? why also are they baptized for the dead?"

Altogether easy to use, with useful background information on each version.
★★★★★

<http://goon.stg.brown.edu/bible_browser/pbform.shtml>

Bible Gateway. Another good page for comparing various editions of the Bible (see figure 11.8). This one compares the NIV, NASB, RSV, KJV, Darby, and YLT versions. That same 1 Cor. 15:29 verse looks like this in its other translations:

New International Version: "Now if there is no resurrection, what will those do who are baptized for the dead? If the dead are not raised at all, why are people baptized for them?"

FIG. 11.8

Bible Gateway: Compare six Bible versions.

New American Standard Bible: "Otherwise, what will those do who are baptized for the dead? If the dead are not raised at all, why then are they baptized for them?"

Includes a topical search tool. Lacks the background material found on the Bible Browser site, but still worth investigating. ★★★★
<http://bible.gospelcom.net/bible>

Bible Commentaries

The reference to baptisms for the dead gets a lot more useful when it comes to analyzing the bias of various biblical commentaries. Here's a sampling of what you'll find:

Blue Letter Bible Project.   Multiple commentaries, some very well done (see figure 11.9). Commentator Ray Stedman provides tremendous context for 1 Corinthians, but avoids the baptism for the dead issue altogether. "If Jesus Christ was not raised from the dead, then, as the apostle says in this chapter, we are hopeless, and not only that, we are the most to be pitied of all people—we are nuts, we are fools, we ought to be locked up somewhere, if Christ be not raised from the dead." Very readable.

Another commentator, Chuck Smith, goes for the jugular: "Baptism for the dead is a practice that was common in the pagan religions of Greece and is still practiced today by some cults; but it doesn't change a person's sentence, for that is determined while he lives." Yeah, sez you!

And the last, David Guzik, prefers the "best defense is a good offense" strategy: "What was being baptized for the dead?" he asks. "It is a mysterious passage, and there have been more than thirty different attempts to interpret it.

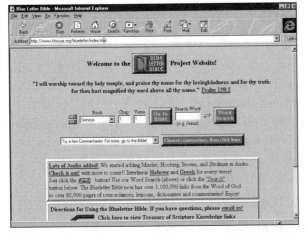

FIG. 11.9

Blue Letter Bible Project: Select any of a number of commentaries.

"i. The plain meaning of the Greek in verse 29 is that some people are being baptized on behalf of those who have died—and if there is no resurrection, why are they doing this?

"ii. Either Paul is referring to a pagan custom (notice he uses they, not 'we'), or to a superstitious and unscriptural practice in the Corinthian church of vicarious baptism for believers who died before being baptized.

"iii. Either way, he certainly does not approve of the practice; he merely says that if there is no resurrection, why would the custom take place? The Mormon practice of baptism for the dead is neither scriptural or sensible."

Choice i. works for us. Occam's razor gives a pretty close shave.

Overall, the site is a bit difficult to use. But it's worth visiting if only for the Ray Stedman backgrounders. ★★

<http://www.khouse.org/blueletter/index.html>

Easton's Bible Dictionary. Here's Easton's take on baptism for the dead: "This expression as used by the apostle may be equivalent to saying, 'He who goes through a baptism of blood in order to join a glorified church which has no existence [i.e., if the dead rise not] is a fool.' Some also regard the statement here as an allusion to the strange practice which began, it is said, to prevail at Corinth, in which a person was baptized in the stead of others who had died before being baptized, to whom it was hoped some of the benefits of that rite would be extended. This they think may have been one of the erroneous customs which Paul went to Corinth to 'set in order.'" Or maybe not. Quite a number of useful definitions, nevertheless. ★★

<http://ccel.wheaton.edu/easton/ebd/ebd.html>

The Concise Matthew Henry Commentary. Regarding 1 Cor. 15:29, the author says: "What shall those do, who are baptized for the dead, if the dead rise not at all? Perhaps baptism is used here in a figure, for afflictions, sufferings, and martyrdom, as Matthew 20:22,23. What is, or will become of those who have suffered many and great injuries, and have even lost their lives, for this doctrine of the resurrection, if the dead rise not at all? Whatever the meaning may be, doubtless the apostle's argument was understood by the Corinthians." Yeah, doubtless. Lots of good stuff anyway. ★★★

<http://ccel.wheaton.edu/henry/mhc/mhc.html>

The Executable Outline Series.   A very well-organized series of documents describing the history and text of books of the Bible. Not LDS, but useful nevertheless. The 1 Cor. verse on baptism is glossed over completely. ★★★

<http://ccel.wheaton.edu/contrib/exec_outlines>

EZRA TAFT BENSON ON THE SIGNIFICANCE OF THE DOCTRINE AND COVENANTS

The Book of Mormon is the "keystone" of our religion, and the Doctrine and Covenants is the "capstone," with continuing latter-day revelation. The Lord has placed His stamp of approval on both the keystone and the capstone.

Conference Report, April 1987.

Virtually every page of both the Doctrine and Covenants and the Book of Mormon teaches about the Master—His great love for His children and His atoning sacrifice—and teaches us how to live so that we can return to Him and our Heavenly Father.

Teachings of Ezra Taft Benson, p. 42.

Miscellaneous Bible Sites

A Bible site, a Bible site. We have got a Bible site. And there cannot be any more Bible sites. These resources will keep your brain bubbling along when you've got nothing else happening—yeah, like *that* ever happens!

Bibles, Bible Resources, and Commentaries.   Good links to Bible translations. ★★

<http://www.igs.net/~vfl/bible-resources.html>

Bible Analysis for Scholars.   A nicely designed site for computer-assisted Bible analysis, located at UC Berkeley (who'd've guessed?). Contains links to downloadable Greek and Hebrew fonts, software links, and an essay on using software to conduct Biblical research. Sounds better than it really is. ★

<http://www-writing.berkeley.edu/chorus/bible/index.html>

Bible Study FAQ.   Answers to questions about how to effectively study the Bible. Assumes Biblical inerrancy, and works hard to account for textual contradictions. ★

<http://www.storm.ca/~sabigail/studyfaq.htm>

Bibles.   List of links to Bibles in various languages. ★★

<http://www.newcreation.org/tcbible.html>

People in the Bible.   A collection of articles on biblical people whose lives had a significant impact on the ancient Church. A Mormons.Org page. ★★★

<http://www.mormons.org/basic/bible/people>

The Hebraeus Foundation.   A charitable foundation funding the Isaiah studies of LDS scholar Avraham Gileadi. Minimal content, but the site includes Dr.

Gileadi's lecture schedule. ★★

<http://www.homestar.net/hebraeus>

The Holy Bible. A collection of LDS teachings on the historicity and role of the Bible. Includes articles on the Bible, LDS Belief in the Bible, King James Version, People in the Bible, LDS Publication of the Bible, Bible Dictionary, Bible Scholarship, Abrahamic Covenant, the Beatitudes, Biblical Prophets, Covenants in Biblical Times, Fall of Adam, The Creation, and the Prophesies of Daniel. A Mormons.Org page. ★★★★

<http://www.mormons.org/basic/bible>

Virtual Jerusalem's Torah and Tradition. For understanding Judaism and its traditions, this is a fantastic site (see figure 11.10). Holidays, doctrine, prayer, Sabbath, the Torah, much more. ★★★★

<http://www.virtual.co.il/depts/torah>

Doctrine and Covenants Study Tools

Because its all so braided into Church history, most of the sites that might otherwise be Doctrine and Covenants–related are actually found in chapter 12: "The Glory of God Is Intelligence"—Church History section.

In this section you'll find study tools specifically related to the text of the Doctrine and Covenants.

Development of the Doctrine and Covenants. A chart outlining the development of the Doctrine and Covenants from the 1833 Book of Commandments to the present. ★★★

<http://www.ham.muohio.edu/~hobbsaf/develop.htm>

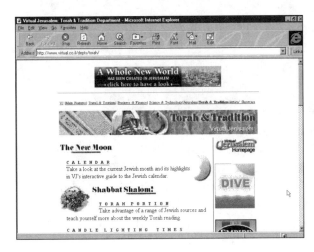

FIG. 11.10
_____
Virtual Jerusalem: A fascinating site for studying Judaism.

Doctrine and Covenants Resource Page. Extensive collection of documents relating to the D&C, revelation, Lectures on Faith, Book of Commandments, mysteries, various discourses. Invaluable study tool. ★★★★★
<http://www.ham.muohio.edu/~hobbsaf/dc_main.htm>

Doctrine and Covenants. Articles related to studying the D&C. Includes an Overview, Doctrine and Covenants Commentaries, Doctrine and Covenants Editions, Doctrine and Covenants as Literature, and Book of Commandments. A Mormons.Org page. ★★★
<http://www.mormons.org/basic/doctrines/scripture/dc>

Doctrine and Covenants. Very brief history. ★
<http://www.nettally.com/lds/D&C.html>

Doctrine and Covenants Mastery Scriptures. Scripture mastery selections from the Doctrine and Covenants, assembled by John Bytheway. ★★
<http://www.inconnect.com/~bytheway/dcmast.html>

People Mentioned in the Doctrine and Covenants. Fantastic collection of thumbnail sketches of people mentioned in the Doctrine and Covenants. The author finds "those who remained faithful made significant impact on Church." ★★★★
<http://www.ham.muohio.edu/~hobbsaf/dcpeople.htm>

Some Historical Notes. Selected verses in Doctrine and Covenants 107. Notes on the amalgamation of this revelation between 1831 and 1835. Good background. ★★★
<http://webpages.marshall.edu/~brown/dc107.htm>

The Second Comforter of Promise and the Second Comforter of Presence. A Commentary on Doctrine and Covenants 88:1–4 by Lisle Brown. ★★
<http://webpages.marshall.edu/~brown/dc88-1-4.htm>

Word of Wisdom. Background information and full text of the Word of Wisdom. Little you haven't seen before. ★★
<http://www.athenet.net/~jlindsay/WWisdom.shtml>

The Pearl of Great Price

The smallest book of the canonized LDS scripture, The Pearl of Great Price was compiled and published by Elder Franklin D. Richards, of the Council of the Twelve Apostles, when he was in Liverpool, England in 1851. Elder Richards was at the time presiding over the British mission.

Elder Richards collected together the items that comprise the Pearl of Great Price: the Book of Abraham, the Book of Moses, the History of the Prophet Joseph Smith, and the Articles of Faith, along with some additional material, and published them in a single volume.

That small book has since been the subject of a great deal of study and thought. Some of the best research is available on the Internet.

Abracadabra, Isaac and Jacob. A John Gee response to Ashment's "The Use of Egyptian Magical Papyri to Authenticate the Book of Abraham." From FARMS Review of Books. Clarifies much controversy. ★★★

<http://www.farmsresearch.com/frob/frobr7_1/gee1.htm>

The Articles of Faith. James E. Talmage. Online hypertext version of the original book. ★★★

<http://reled.byu.edu/books/artoffai/afaith.htm>

Book of Abraham. Facsimile, plus articles on the subject of the Book of Abraham. A Mormons.Org page. ★★★★

<http://www.mormons.org/basic/doctrines/scripture/abraham>

Book of Abraham: Origin and Content. Good treatment of the history and contents of the Book of Abraham. ★★★

<http://www.nettally.com/LDS/abrahamall.html>

Book of Abraham Project. Dr. William Smith's long-running project on Book of Abraham studies. Major effort to coordinate research on the Book of Abraham. Associated with one of the earliest and largest Mormon-oriented Internet sites, the BOAP is showing its age. ★★

<http://mathnx.math.byu.edu/~jet/BOAP.html>

The Book of Moses. The Book of Moses is an extract of several chapters from Genesis in the Joseph Smith Translation of the Bible (JST) and constitutes one of the texts in the Pearl of Great Price. An *Encyclopedia of Mormonism* text. ☞

<http://www.mormons.org/basic/doctrines/scripture/moses_eom.htm>

Notes on the Book of Abraham. Historical information, translation notes, illustrations. A very well-done site. ★★★★

<http://www.primenet.com/~kitsonk/mormon/abraham.html>

Questions About the Book of Abraham. Jeff Lindsay responds to questions about the Book of Abraham, its sources, content, and historicity. An excellent resource. Massive. ★★★★

<http://www.athenet.net/~jlindsay/LDSFAQ/FQ_Abraham.shtml>

ELDER FRANKLIN D. RICHARDS ON COMPILING THE PEARL OF GREAT PRICE

Most of the revelations composing this work were published at early periods of the Church, when the circulation of its journals was so very limited as to render them comparatively unknown at present, except to a few who have treasured up the productions of the Church with great care from the beginning. A smaller portion of this work has never before appeared in print; and altogether it is presumed, that true believers in the divine mission of the Prophet Joseph Smith will appreciate this little collection of precious truths as a Pearl of Great Price, that will increase their ability to maintain and to defend the holy faith by becoming possessors of it.

Preface, 1851 edition of The Doctrine and Covenants.

A Tragedy of Errors. John Gee's review of Larson's critical work, *By His Own Hand upon Papyrus: A New Look at the Joseph Smith Papyri*. A FARMS publication. ✍

<http://www.farmsresearch.com/frob/frobv4/gee.htm>

Multiple Books of Scripture

In this list you'll find study tools related to all or most of the standard works.

The Hebraeus Foundation. Excerpts from the writings of Isaiah scholar Avraham Gileadi. Primarily a commercial site. $

<http://www.homestar.net/hebraeus>

Grant O'Neil's Scripture References. Brief commentaries on the significance of various verses of scripture. ★★

<http://student.curtin.edu.au/~poneilgdo/scripref.html>

LDS Scripture Commentary Archive. A rough collection of scripture commentaries. LDS Seminar topics examine historical and textual material for The Doctrine and Covenants. The Isaiah commentaries are extensive, and broken out chapter by chapter. Dozens of additional commentaries are found under the Assorted, Miscellaneous, and General headings—who can tell which is which? The Bible commentaries at the very end are a tremendous resource. The content is fantastic. If the headings were just a bit better organized, this site would get a solid five stars. ★★★★

<http://deathstar.rutgers.edu/people/kurtn/exegesis/exegesis.html>

LDS Scripture of the Day. To subscribe, send an e-mail request to *<zarahmla@xmission.com>*. ✍

LDS-SEMINAR. Commentary on each week's Gospel Doctrine lesson. The posts are open to exegesis, textual analysis, historical issues pertinent to the context or application of the scriptures, life applications, and "likening the scriptures unto us" issues. Includes regular columns, plus postings from other participants. To subscribe, send a message to *<majordomo@ldschurch.net>* with the message subscribe ldss *<yourname@your.email.address>* or the digest version subscribe LDSS-D *<yourname@your.email.address>*. ✍

LDS-SUNDAY SCHOOL. Full text of next week's Sunday school reading assignment. This year's reading assignment is The Doctrine and Covenants. The reading assignment is divided into five messages, one for each weekday. Subscribe by sending your e-mail request to *<anderson@itsnet.com>*. Archives are at the Web site. ★★★★★

<http://www.itsnet.com/~anderson/lds-ssrl.html>

Miller Eccles Study Group Page. Directions, contact information for a study group conducted in La Canada, California. ★★

<http://www.geocities.com/Athens/2245>

Online Scriptures Website. Ronald Conrad Schoedel's collection of and commentary on the Standard Works. Also includes information about the Apocrypha, Pseudopigrapha, and other non-canonical but nonetheless interesting works. ★★★★

<http://online-scriptures.base.org>

Scriptural Writings. A collection of pages for each of the canonical works, and more. Includes The Book of Mormon: Another Testament of Jesus Christ, The Holy Bible, The Doctrine and Covenants, The Book of Moses, The Book of Abraham, Apocalyptic Texts, Apocrypha and Pseudepigrapha, and Scriptual References to Astronomy. A Mormons.Org page. ★★★★

<http://www.mormons.org/basic/doctrines/scripture>

Scripture Commentaries. A resource for LDS scriptorians. The archive is frequently updated and edited. The material is largely authored by Kurt Neumiller, but he invites all scriptural commentators to submit material. Vast libraries of commentary and other textual material, including in-depth treatments of The Doctrine and Covenants, Isaiah, and numerous gospel-centered topics. An excellent resource. ★★★★

<http://deathstar.rutgers.edu/people/kurtn/exegesis/exegesis.html>

Scripture Mastery. All 100 of the Scripture Mastery verses that Seminary students are asked to memorize. ★★★

<http://www.coolcontent.com/ScriptureMastery>

SCRIPTURE-L. A discussion of the scriptures. Operated and moderated by Gregory Woodhouse. Volume is moderate. Send subscription requests to *<scripture-l-request@lists.best.com>* with the message `subsingle`. To receive all the day's messages in one post mail, change the message to `subscribe`. Archives available at the Web site, along with other scripture resources. ★★★★

<http://www.wnetc.com/scripture-l>

STUDIES. Discussion of scriptures and reference materials related to Gospel Doctrine lessons. Subscribe with an e-mail request to *<majordomo@bolis.com>* with the message `subscribe studies`. Visit the Web site for archives.

<http://seminary.org/studies>

MORMON ARTS AND LETTERS

If we didn't have a culture, we wouldn't be a People. Nothing creates a culture, describes a culture, inculcates a culture so thoroughly as does its visual art and its literature.

As you might hope, the Mormon arts and letters Internet sites are about the most civilized in the entire LDS online community.

For that, credit goes to two people: Benson Parkinson, moderator of AML-List, and Keith Irwin, moderator of LDS-Bookshelf. AML-List, a discussion group for LDS literature, is peopled largely by writers, but also by fans of Mormon literature. AML-List is a model of what an online community ought to be: intelligent, inspired, and entertaining.

Keith's LDS-Bookshelf has generated a whole new level of awareness and appreciation for "the best books," old and rare volumes of Mormon literature.

AML-LIST.   A discussion list for members of the Association for Mormon Letters. Welcomes all scholars and fans of Mormon literature. Maximum volume is 30 posts per day. Send subscription request to *<aml-request@cc.weber.edu>* with the message `subscribe aml-list` "Your Name in Quotes" *<your@address.in.brackets>*. Benson Parkinson moderates the list. The Web site is a tremendous resource for LDS writers. ★★★★★
<http://cc.weber.edu/~byparkinson/aml-list.html>

AML-LIST Digest.   Daily compilation of posts to AML-List. Send subscription requests to Benson Parkinson, moderator, at
<byparkinson@cc.weber.edu>

AML-MAG.   The low-volume version of AML-List. Includes columns, reviews, and news items on Mormon literature, and selected posts from AML-List. To subscribe, send a request to *<aml-request@ cc.weber.edu>* with the message `subscribe aml-mag` "Your Name in Quotes" *<your@address.in.brackets>*.

ANWA.   A support group for LDS women who love to write. Includes a list of authors, and other material of interest to members. ★★★
<http://www.netzone.com/~pegshumw>

Attitudes Towards the Arts.   A collection of articles on the subject of Mormonism and the arts. Illustrates the importance of arts and letters in LDS lives. ★★★
<http://www.mormons.org/daily/arts>

ON WRITING MORMON LITERATURE

I believe that the best purpose of storytelling is hope. In our reading we hope for love, for order, for the possibility that things can work out right—because so often in life, it is not easily so. Perhaps the darkness of modern literature is an admission that we have given up as a people—America. That we don't really believe that things will work out. That ultimately, we are doomed to be alone and desperate.

But we read for hope. Things come together. People get married. Bad guys get caught and punished. Or seemingly mean people repent and are actually kind in the end. We get our stuff back, our hearts healed, more pay, less taxes. Replicators. Hopeful things.

From "Happy Endings," part of a discussion on AML-List, published November 12, 1996. Reprinted by permission of the author. Kristen Randle, Provo, Utah *<randlehouse@earthlink.net>*

Coming from the Light. In this book, author Sarah Hinze shares 35 inspiring testimonials of parents and others who have encountered children before they were conceived or born. $
<http://www.primenet.com/~shinze/index.html>

Hajicek Mormonism.com. A site for collectors of rare LDS books. $
<http://www.mormonism.com/Portrait.htm>

Hatrack River. The official Web site of author Orson Scott Card. Includes helpful links to writers groups for adults and youth. ★★★★
<http://www.hatrack.com>

LDS Arts. Visual, musical, and performing arts with an LDS orientation. ★★★★
<http://www.itsnet.com/~kingc>

LDS Creations. Online gallery exhibiting fine art by Latter-day Saint artists from around the world.
<http://www.ldscreations.com>

LDS Culture and the Arts. Abbreviated list of links. ★
<http://www.ldsworld.com/links/culture.html>

LDS Hymns MIDI Page. Music from hymns, LDS songs, and other musical works. Requires a speaker and sound card. ★★★
<http://www.uleth.ca/~anderson/midi.htmlx>

LDS Women's Forum. Stories, essays, and poetry written with an LDS perspective by sisters from around the world. Uplifting. ★★★
<http://www.primenet.com/~rogkat>

LDS-BOOKSHELF. A mailing list designed for those who collect or have a serious interest in collectable books related to Mormon Americana. Subscribe with an e-mail request to *<majordomo@bolis.com>* with the body `subscribe lds-bookshelf`. List operators are Keith Irwin and Hugh McKell. Archives are maintained at the Web site. Great resources. ★★★
<http://www.wenet.net/~kirwin/bshelf.html>

LDSF. Sci-fi writer Thom Duncan's LDS Science/Speculative Fiction list. The list isn't limited to Mormon authors of science fiction, but includes discussions of other books as related to Mormon literature. Sign up to participate in the e-mail list via the Web site, with the key word `ldsf`. If you don't have a browser, Thom will process your sign-up via e-mail at *<tduncan@zfiction.com>*. The list tends to be a little slow-moving, but it's growing. ★★
<http://www.coollist.com>

ON BUILDING A COMMUNITY OF ARTISTS

As artists often we are laboring in isolation. As LDS artists many of us have a deep desire to use our talents in our hearts to help the cause of Zion; to be a leavening influence in a wicked world. It's often times discouraging to work in isolation. I think a symposium . . . and a festival (which we will have annually from here on out) can be a very beneficial thing to each of us as a community of artists, as we come together to discover and explore new directions and celebrate old directions and accomplishments.

Robert Paxton, Moderator of a Panel Discussion at the Mormon Arts Festival,
<http://www.thewatchmen.com/ma/ma95/panel1.html>

Liahona Developmental Systems.   Promoting LDS Literacy. Collection of LDS literature and learning resources for Spanish-speaking members. Guidelines for using forwarding agencies to distribute LDS products across borders. $
<http://www.liahona.com>

Mormon Arts Foundation.   A festival held each year near St. George, Utah. The Web site focuses on dance, theater, music, literature, film and media, and visual arts. The page includes an art gallery, contest information, and transcripts from previous festivals. A very readable page. ★★★★
<http://www.thewatchmen.com/ma>

Mormon Literature Web Site.   Gideon Burton's comprehensive links to LDS literature. Includes a Mormon literature sampler, a bibliography of Mormon literature, information on Mormon criticism, a "Who's Who" and a "What's Where" of Mormon literature. ★★★★
<http://128.187.38.118/MLDB/mlithome.htm>

Mormon Literature.   Very brief list of literature links. ★
<http://www.wnetc.com/resource/lds/literature.html>

Mormon Tabernacle Choir Discography.   A list of Mormon Tabernacle Choir recordings and related resources. Very, very thorough. ★★★
<http://www.geocities.com/SunsetStrip/7158/mtchoir.htm>

Mormon-J: The LDS Journal-List.   A resource page for LDS journalists, journal-keepers, and other historians. Differs from the literature pages in its emphasis on the journalism profession and the role of journalists as historians. But then, I can say that; it's my own site. View this rating with suspicion: ★★★★★
<http://www.jersey.net/~inkwell/mormonj.htm>

MostlyMormon.   Another site for collectors of used and rare LDS books. $
<http://www.mostlymormon.com>

Museum of Art.   (See figure 11.11.) Durned copyright laws (except when they benefit me). Wouldn't it be great if this page actually contained some art? Ah, well. The background information on museum exhibits make it a worthwhile stop. ★★
<http://www.byu.edu/moa>

ORSON-SCOTT-CARD.   A mailing list devoted exclusively to discussions of Orson Scott Card's writings. Orson Scott Card is a well-known science-fiction author and has also authored plays and worked on screenplays. To subscribe, e-mail a request to <majordomo@wood.net> with the message subscribe orson-card. Archives are available at the Web site. ★★★
<http://wood.net/~khyron/card/cardlist.html>

Review of Orson Scott Card's Science Fiction.   What a treat. Eugene England reviews the science fiction of Orson Scott Card. If you're a fan of either writer, you'll want to read this review. ☞
<http://www.farmsresearch.com/frob/frobv2/england.htm>

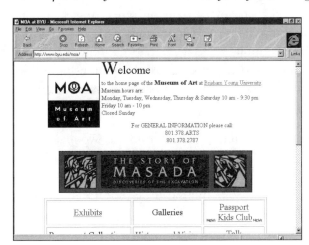

FIG. 11.11

Museum of Art: Information on exhibits at the BYU art repository.

Saints in Review.   Reviews of LDS-authored books, and books on LDS topics. This page is affiliated with Mormon-J: The LDS Journalist. ★★★★
<http://www.jersey.net/~inkwell/review.htm>

STUDENT REVIEW.   Low-volume general discussion list for alumni of *Student Review* (unofficial magazine at BYU) about *Student Review* and about the Church. Digest available. To subscribe, send an e-mail message to *<majordomo@ panix. com>* with the message `subscribe student-review <your name>`. ☞

The C. S. Lewis Home Page.   Yeah, yeah, so he wasn't technically LDS. But his personal theology continues to speak to LDS beliefs to such a degree that he certainly deserves the status of honorary member. This Web site introduces Lewis' works, along with anecdotes, studies, photographs, and much more. Worth diving into. ★★★★
<http://www.cache.net/~john/cslewis/index.html>

Zion's Fiction.   Electronic publishers of LDS science fiction. Operated by author Thom Duncan. The site provides downloadable LDS speculative fiction. Fascinating stuff. $
<http://www.zfiction.com>

MORMON HUMOR

Anyone who thinks Mormons lack a sense of humor hasn't listened to a gloomy congregation singing "There Is Sunshine in My Soul Today."

Latter-day Saints have a great tradition of humor. Sometimes it's spontaneous, as anyone who has listened to President Gordon B. Hinckley—or many of the past presidents of the Church—will attest.

Other times, it's a great set-up. Latter-day Saints love to retell stories of their favorite humorist, J. Golden Kimball, the son of President Heber C. Kimball. The colorful general authority is reputed to have said, among other things, that he couldn't go to hell for swearing, because he repents too damn fast.

Latter-day Saints on the Internet continue to carry on that tradition of Mormon humor, with their own Web sites replete with cartoons, jokes, and amusing stories.

The following sites contain some of the best—and cleanest—humor on the Internet.

Lightness Challenge Page.   Chill out with amusing posts from the two major LDS newsgroups, *alt/soc.religion.mormon.* Twice a year, site owner David Bowie (no, they're not related) conducts a vote for the best postings on the two newsgroups. The messages are always funny, sometimes caustic. ★★★★★
<http://www.sas.upenn.edu/~dbowie/armlc/armlc.html>

Brion Zion.   Cleverly drawn characters evoke a sense of Mormon history and an affection for the geographic wonders of the Great Basin (see figure 11.12). ★★★
<http://www.wp.com/BrionZion/who-what.htm>

Alpha List.   Did you know that the Book of Mormon saved a man's life? He carried it in his shirt pocket over his heart. During the war a piece of shrapnel hit the book, but stopped at 2 Nephi. Alpha is the home page for the alpha mailing list of nonoffensive humor hosted by seminary.org, and residing at the University of Arizona. The list operators are not LDS, but the humor appeals. ★★★★
<http://www.seminary.org/alpha>

CultMaster 2000 Software.   All the power you need to prove that you're the only real Christian around (see figure 11.13). Irresistible. But then, I've been hearing a little too much of the "C" word lately. ★★★★★
<http://www.athenet.net/~jlindsay/CultMaster.shtml>

Bible.   My favorite, from a top-ten list of How the Bible Would Have Been Different If Written by College Students: "Five commandments, but double-spaced and written in a large font, they look like ten." ★★★
<http://www.mormons.org/humor/bible.htm>

Book of Mormon.   Don't miss four-year-old Jonathan's 2,000 Stricken Lawyers. ★★★
<http://www.mormons.org/humor/bom.htm>

On the Bright Side.   A collection of humorous stories that run in the *Church News.* Cute. ★★★★
<http://www.desnews.com/cgi-bin/libheads_reg?search=%22
On+the+bright+side%22&limit=999&x=49&y=12>

Humor, Jokes, Urban Legends, and Myths.   Mostly funny stuff. The unfunny stuff makes jokes at the expense of non-Mormons. ★★★
<http://pw2.netcom.com/~estep/humor.html>

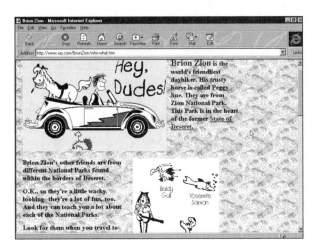

FIG. 11.12

Brion Zion: An amusing side trip.

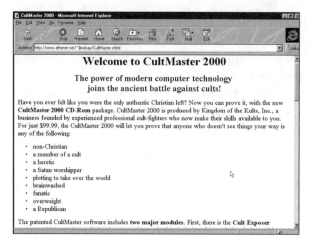

FIG. 11.13

CultMaster 2000 "software": An irreverent swipe at name-callers.

LDS Humor. Includes Bible Humor, Book of Mormon Humor, Mormon Culture Humor, and General Religious Humor. ★★★

<http://www.mormons.org/humor>

> **INSIDER HUMOR**
>
> Orson F. Whitney addressed the October 1918 General Conference on the courage of Columbus, saying "Columbus was one of a number of learned men who held that the earth was a sphere. While not the first to hold that theory, he was the first to put it into practice. He believed that he could reach India by sailing westward. Accordingly, he sailed for India, and found America on the way."
>
> President Smith, from his seat behind the speaker, piped up: "He could hardly have missed it."
>
> Conference Report, October 1918, p. 39.

General Religious. Who can resist: "An Agnostic and an Atheist were married and had a real moral problem on their hands. You see, they couldn't decide which religion not to raise their children in." ★★★

<http://www.mormons.org/humor/general.htm>

Mormon Culture. Jokes that shouldn't be funny. "*Joe:* My home teacher is so good he comes on the first day of every month! *Henry:* Oh Yeah? My home teacher is so good he comes the day before that!" ★★★

<http://www.mormons.org/humor/culture.htm>

10 Reasons to Not Become a Mormon. Forewarned is forearmed. And there's no mention at all of green Jell-O, casserole patrols, or plastic grapes. Must reading for everyone contemplating baptism. ★★

<http://www.nettally.com/LDS/10.html>

10 Nonreligious Benefits of Being a Latter-day Saint. Having an off day? Here are 10 good reasons to be a good Mormon, even when you're not feeling particularly Christ-like. ★★

<http://www.nettally.com/LDS/10yes.html>

Horrible Humor. Visit Jeff Lindsay's Cracked Planet humor pages. Articles on National Lawn Care Now! Commercial Ninja Services. The Citizens Union for

Safe Smoking. The Higher Institute for Safe Shooting. Sci-Cops. More. A crack-up. ★★★★

<http://www.athenet.net/~jlindsay/MyPages.shtml#humor>

MORMON-HUMOR. A new e-mail list for telling jokes, puns, and amusing stories and anecdotes about Mormons and Mormonism. At press time, the list was just getting under way. List owner Kent Larsen says: "Almost all aspects of Mormon culture, activities, events, and people worldwide are fair game. However, jokes that are racist, sexual, or make malicious fun of others should not be sent to mormon-humor. . . . Be prepared to take a light-hearted look at Mormonism and put up with a swear word or two. Don't take offense easily, and we'll all be better off." A once-a-week digest version of the list will also be available. To subscribe, send an e-mail request to *<majordomo@lists. panix.com>*. In the body of the message write `subscribe mormon-humor`. To subscribe to the digest, write `subscribe mormon-humor-digest`. This list is great fun, except when participants debate whether something is funny. ★★★★

> **THE HUMOR OF J. GOLDEN KIMBALL**
> What can God do for a man who is not honest? You may baptize him every fifteen minutes, but if he does not repent, he will come up out of the water just as dishonest as ever. . . . Baptising him in water will not settle the trouble, unless you keep him under.
>
> J. Golden Kimball, Conference Report, April 1909, p. 37.

Facetious (?) Questions. Includes discussions of Mormon ownership of Pepsi, planets, polygamy, and more. Author Jeff Lindsay has written numerous pages of answer to questions about the Church. The answers on this page respond—often flippantly—to questions too bizarre for the serious pages. Good fun. ★★★

<http://www.athenet.net/~jlindsay/LDSFAQ/FQ_Facet.shtml>

EMERGENCY PREPAREDNESS

The sites found here can be of help only *before* the emergency—unless, of course, you're already set up with a generator for your PC and a ham-radio-based modem. Yeah, like you'd then use it to browse the Web, right?

Emergency Communications

It's what to do if the phone goes out.

Ham Radio Outlet. Supplier of amateur radio equipment. $
<http://www.hamradio.com>

W3BNR's Home Page.   Excellent amateur radio links. Amusing links to conspiracy theories. (One hopes the site author also finds them amusing, but given the nature of the subject matter, that's not likely.) ★★★★
<http://www.worldlynx.net/w3bnr>

Disaster Preparedness

When my grandma passed away a few years back, I had to fight hard not to inherit the cans of dried cheese and Textured Vegetable Protein she stored under her bed. Um, yummy. TVP: the perfect filling for tacos, lasagna, and road surfaces. Finally, a noble cousin squared her shoulders and took on the task.

It turns out my grandma's food storage was actually a disaster prevention program. As we hauled out the cans and boxes, we realized that, more than anything, food storage kept the bed from falling down.

72-Hour Emergency Kits.   Make your own 72-hour emergency kit for every member of your family. Includes suggested contents and instructions for use. ★★
<http://www.micronet.net/~searcy/72Hour.htm>

Country Harvest.   Mostly commercial listing of information on food storage. $
<http://www.uvol.com/harvest/homepage.html>

Emergency and Disaster Preparedness.   Courtesy of the Municipality of Anchorage, Alaska. Brief instructions for what to do in the event of an emergency—at which time you'd probably find an online list inaccessible. ★★
<http://www.ci.anchorage.ak.us/Disaster/index.html>

Emergency Essentials.   Mostly commercial, with products for preparedness equipment, camping supplies, and food storage. But it's worth visiting regularly for the Insights column. ★★★★
<http://www.beprepared.com>

Emergency Preparedness.   A storage list, along with basic instructions for use. ★★★
<http://www.uvol.com/www1st/foodstor.html>

Emergency Preparedness.   An almost inconsequential list of links. ★
<http://www.deseretbook.com/ldsinfo/emergency.html>

Emergency Storage.   Latter-day Saints have been counseled to prepare to care for themselves and their families in time of need. Provident living involves being wise, frugal, prudent, and making provision for the future while attending to immediate needs. This site lists the amounts needed for one adult for one year, and provides a number of suggestions for effective storage. ★★★
<http://www.uvol.com/www1st/foodstor.html>

FEMA.   The Federal Emergency Management Agency. The site contains excellent information about emergency preparedness and disaster management. ★★★★★
<http://www.fema.gov>

Food Storage Online. Mostly commercial, but the World Watch column is a pessimist's dream. ★★★★

<http://www.foodstorage.net/world.htm>

Food Storage Planner. Software for estimating, budgeting, and planning your food storage. Between natural, political, and personal disasters, there's nothing but wisdom in storing food and fuel, says the site author. A commercial site. $

<http://www.revelar.com/fsp.html>

Kitchen Science. A great site for food storage, preparedness, tips, recipes, more (see figure 11.14). ★★★★

<http://www.bizcom.com/kitchenscience>

PREP. A list for discussions and information about disaster preparedness, home storage, and emergency planning, from an LDS perspective. To subscribe, send an e-mail request to *<majordomo@seminary.org>* with the body `subscribe prep`. Archives and excellent links to disaster sites are at the Web site. ★★★★

<http://seminary.org/prep>

The Epicenter. A good collection of links to disaster relief, emergency preparedness, and even search and rescue resources. ★★★

<http://theepicenter.com/emerg.html>

The National Food Safety Database. Tips on food safety and home food storage. ★★★

<http://www.foodsafety.org>

West Coast Emergency Supplies. Tips on home safety, water storage, 5 Steps to Family Preparedness, more. Mostly commercial. $

<http://www.open.org/wces/contents.htm>

FIG. 11.14

Kitchen Science: Recipes and tips.

12

THE GLORY OF GOD IS INTELLIGENCE

My first year of college was a tremendous lot of fun. I was finally beginning to comprehend the vast scope of the gospel; the discovery was hugely exciting. Fortunately, my college classes were easy that year, and my job allowed me time to study, because I barely had time for school.

Theology was the driving interest in my life. It seemed as though I couldn't learn fast enough. I signed up for classes at two different institutes of religion, just so that I could inhale more knowledge, ask more questions, listen to more ideas. I was reading voraciously, getting up early to drive my sibs to Seminary, and attending Sunday meetings both in my own ward and with my grandmother in her ward.

After a few months of it, I realized I was never going to discover everything I wanted to know from the pint-sized library at my community college, so I sent in my application to Brigham Young University.

I was overjoyed when I got the acceptance letter. I continued throughout the summer in my mad pursuit of knowledge, determined that some day, I would know everything there is to know.

The final Sunday before I was to go to BYU, I attended Church with Grandma. Among the speakers that week was a sour, balding, middle-aged man, who stood up to the podium and began to drone. On and on he went, exploring the minutiae of some inconsequential subject of absolutely no interest to anyone other than himself. His talk was peppered with unexplained technical jargon and obscure scholarly references; heads throughout the congregation were bobbing and weaving as members of the ward fought off sleep.

My normally patient grandmother peered at him over the tops of her glasses, an inscrutable look on her face. I tried to listen, but between the monotony of the talk, and the expression on Grandma's face, I was able to absorb not a thing.

Mercifully, the talk finally ended, and the meeting closed.

On the way home, Grandma finally spoke up. "Did you find that interesting?" she asked me.

"Well, um, sort of," I hedged.

"Would you like to be able to speak that way?"

"Um, I guess."

"Promise me you won't."

"Why not?"

"That young man has spent the last twenty years doing nothing but going to college," she told me. "He doesn't work, he doesn't go out, he doesn't have any friends. All that education, and he still doesn't know the first thing about life." Then she paused.

"I'm proud of you for getting an education," she said slowly. "But honey, don't you ever lose sight of life."

So stand warned. Grandma's caution applies to all the carnage you'll tear through in this chapter. You'll find here research resources on every topic that's ever made you curious. Church History is treated in great detail. It's followed by sections on Research Projects and Research Groups, Science and Religion, The Church in Society, Doctrinal Issues, and Comparative Theology.

And to Grandma's caution, I add my own. If I've learned any wisdom in twenty years of serious gospel study, it's this: Prayerfully obtained knowledge is the only kind worth having.

CHURCH HISTORY

The Internet is awash in Church history . . . the whole Church, from its original establishment, to its reestablishment in each dispensation. You'll find there information about the Church's growth in the New World, as well as its modern manifestation in the latter-day dispensation.

In this section you'll find Internet sites tracing the Old Testament foundation of the Church, the Church in the New World, the Pre-Christian Era, the New Testament Church, the Interregnum, and finally, the Modern Church.

The Old Testament Church

Latter-day Saints have a profound love for the Church founded at the beginning of man's sojourn on earth, and carried on through a series of prophets and dispensations. The Saints also feel a deep appreciation for their brothers and sisters who maintained—in the face of great tribulation—the history, doctrine, records, and traditions that form the foundation of the gospel.

Latter-day Saints feel an even greater kinship with the children of Israel because of a heritage of shared experiences. The persecution, the pioneer exodus, the temple worship, the belief in Elijah, the faith in the Messiah . . . indeed, all of Mormonism shares a common heritage with the Church founded with Adam; the Semitic roots of the Book of Mormon bind those ties forever.

In this section, you'll find valuable resources for studying the history of the original Church, a key to comprehending the roots of Mormonism.

Additional Old Testament study materials focusing on the doctrine and the text of the book are located in chapter 6: "Perfect the Saints," and chapter 11: "Pursuit of Excellence"—the personal scripture study section.

Jewishness of the Book of Mormon. Page maintained by a Rabbi Yosef, apparently not LDS. The page demonstrates connections linking the Book of Mormon and Judaism for Messianic Jews (see figure 12.1). ★★★
<http://deathstar.rutgers.edu/people/kurtn/rabbiyosef/rabbiyosef.html>

Judaism. Arden Eby's list of resources on Judaism, as it interests Latter-day Saints. ★★★
<http://www.teleport.com/~arden/religium.htm#jewish>

King Saul, the Egyptian Version. An illustrated history compiled by Richard Hardison, a member of the Church. ★★★
<http://www.nettally.com/LDS/saul.html>

Pharaohs and Kings. Summary of a TV series tracing biblical history. ★★
<http://www.nettally.com/LDS/rohl.html>
A more official site is available at
<http://www.knowledge.co.uk/xxx/cat/rohl>

Sukkot and King Benjamin's Message. Interesting Book of Mormon parallels with the Jewish Feast of Booths/Tabernacles. ☞
<http://deathstar.rutgers.edu/people/kurtn/rabbiyosef/sukkotbenj.txt>

A Guide to Polygamy in the Bible and Jewish Law. History, religion, and law. Discusses mostly ancient Hebrew polygamy. Useful background on the practice of plural marriage. ★★★
<http://www.teleport.com/~arden/polyg.htm>

YHWH, the Name of God. Tracing the name Jehovah and its ancient usage. ★★★
<http://www.nettally.com/LDS/YHVH.html>

The Church in the New World

Book of Mormon scholarship has undergone some significant advances in recent years. This section examines new physical evidence for the Book of Mormon and discusses the historicity of the text.

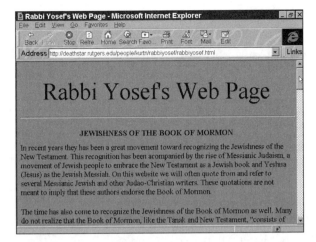

FIG. 12.1

Jewishness of the Book of Mormon: Interesting connections.

Find additional Book of Mormon study materials in chapter 5 (Introduction to the Church); chapter 6 (Gospel Doctrine Study Tools), and chapter 11 (Scripture Study).

A Key for Evaluating Nephite Geographies. Three reviews of Hauck's *Deciphering the Geography of the Book of Mormon.* ★★★
Clark: *<http://www.farmsresearch.com/frob/frobv1/clark.htm>;*
Hamblin: *<http://www.farmsresearch.com/frob/frobv1/hamblin1.htm>;* and
Withers: *<http://www.farmsresearch.com/frob/frobv1/withers.htm>*

Book of Mormon Archaeology FAQ. Answers to frequently asked questions on the origin, geography, population, mythology, archaeology, language, and etymology of the Book of Mormon. Written by Arden L. Eby. ★★★
<http://www.teleport.com/~arden/mormfaq.htm>

Book of Mormon As History. A brief discourse on faith and history and archaeology. ★★
<http://www.nettally.com/LDS/realfake.html>

Brant Gardner's Self-Published Papers Page. A collection of essays about meso-American issues and the Book of Mormon, along with other interesting essays. Tracing Quetzalcoatl-related materials, Multi-Dimensional Commentary on the Book of Mormon, Examining the Historical and Cultural Context of the Book of Mormon, and more. These commentaries examine the Book of Mormon from a number of perspectives. ★★★
<http://www.highfiber.com/~nahualli>

Historicity of the Book of Mormon. From a 1993 talk by Elder Dallin H. Oaks. ☞
<http://frontpage.inet-images.com/thebishop/LDS/historicity_of_bom.htm>

Also available at
<*http://erdos.math.byu.edu/~smithw/Lds/LDS/Oaks-on-BoM-critics*>

Journal of Book of Mormon Studies.   FARMS Scholarly journal for Book of Mormon research. This page lacks a table of contents, so you'll have to dig through each issue to find what you need. ★★★★
<*http://www.farmsresearch.com/jbms/jbms.html*>

Lehi in the Desert.   Multiple reviews of the definitive Nibley text on the Book of Mormon. 📖 Reviews by Compton:
<*http://www.farmsresearch.com/frob/frobv1/compton.htm*>;
Stephen Ricks: <*http://www.farmsresearch.com/frob/frobv2/ricks1.htm*>;
Honey: <*http://www.farmsresearch.com/frob/frobv2/honey.htm*>

Maya Harvest Festivals and the Book of Mormon.   Allen J. Christenson's 1991 FARMS lecture draws parallels between Mayan traditions and Book of Mormon events (see figure 12.2). 📖
<*http://www.farmsresearch.com/frob/frobv3/annual.htm*>

Plates of the Book of Mormon.   A mostly undocumented explanation of the history of the plates associated with the Book of Mormon. ★★
<*http://www.nettally.com/LDS/plates.html*>

Pre-Christian Era Apocrypha and Pseudopigrapha

When the Prophet Joseph Smith was preparing to commence work on the Inspired Version of the Bible, he asked the Lord for instruction on the apocryphal portion of the text.

The revelation he received in response to his question was clear: Some is true, some is not true, and Joseph need not produce the translation.

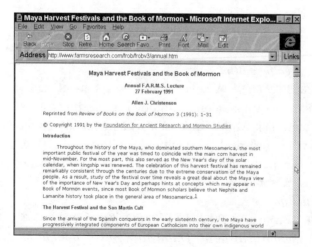

FIG. 12.2

Maya Harvest Festivals: This site includes photos.

It's the job of the reader, said the Lord, to seek individual understanding through the Spirit.

In this section we pull together references on pseudopigraphal and apocryphal texts, along with a number of resources specifically focused on the Dead Sea Scrolls.

Apocrypha and Pseudepigrapha. Background and explanation of apocryphal texts. An *Encyclopedia of Mormonism* article. ☞
<http://www.mormons.org/basic/doctrines/ scripture/apoc_pse_eom.htm>

Background for the Testaments. Stephen Robinson's discourse on apocryphal and pseudopigraphal material of interest to Latter-day Saints (see figure 12.3). ★★★★
<http://www.primenet.com/~kitsonk/ mormon/backgrou.html>

Dead Sea Scrolls. An introduction to the Scrolls as they relate to the literary and sectarian diversity of Judaism at the time of Jesus, evidence relating to the history and preservation of the biblical text, advances in the science of dating Hebrew and Aramaic documents based on changing styles of script, and valuable additions to the corpus of Jewish texts and text genres. An *Encyclopedia of Mormonism* article. ☞
<http://www.mormons.org/basic/doctrines/scripture/dead_sea_eom.htm>

THE DOCTRINE AND COVENANTS ON THE APOCRYPHA

"Verily, thus saith the Lord unto you concerning the Apocrypha—There are many things contained therein that are true, and it is mostly translated correctly; There are many things contained therein that are not true, which are interpolations by the hands of men.

Verily, I say unto you, that it is not needful that the Apocrypha should be translated.

Therefore, whoso readeth it, let him understand, for the Spirit manifesteth truth; And whoso is enlightened by the Spirit shall obtain benefit therefrom; And whoso receiveth not by the Spirit, cannot be benefited. Therefore it is not needful that it should be translated. Amen."

D&C 91:1–6

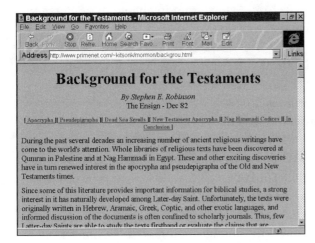

FIG. 12.3

Background for the Testaments: History, maps, an interesting read.

Dead Sea Scrolls, Nag Hamadi, and Josephus. Commercial products for sale, along with links to good Scrolls sites. ★★
<http://www.zarahemla.com/deadsea.html>

Noncanonical Homepage. Apocryphal and pseudopigraphal texts. These are documents that date from around the Christian period. Many are quite interesting from a Mormon point of view, particularly those—such as 1 Enoch, the Testament of the Twelve Patriarchs, and the Assumption of Moses—which are referenced, but not cannonized, in the New Testament. ★★★
<http://wesley.nnc.edu/noncanon.htm>

Scrolls from the Dead Sea. Very comprehensive collection of pages on the Dead Sea Scrolls. If you're at all interested in the subject matter, this is a can't-miss site. Not an LDS page, but the Dead Sea Scrolls in general are of tremendous interest to students of Mormonism, for they cast light on some of the attitudes, practices, and beliefs presented in the Book of Mormon for a Semitic people prior to the coming of Christ. ★★★★
<http://lcweb.loc.gov/exhibits/scrolls/toc.html>. A similar site is located at *<http://sunsite.unc.edu/expo/deadsea.scrolls.exhibit/intro.html>*

The Dead Sea Scrolls. A commentary on why the scrolls are of particular interest to Latter-day Saints, along with a good link to information on the history and geography of the Dead Sea Scrolls. ★★★
<http://www.enoch.com/voicesfromdust/deadsea/deadsea.html>

The New Testament Church

Focusing primarily on LDS-specific New Testament resources, the following sites provide a glimpse into the history of the New Testament period of the Church.

You'll find additional materials for studying the text, and the doctrine, of the New Testament in chapter 6: "Perfect the Saints," and in chapter 11: "Pursuit of Excellence," the personal scripture study section.

Ancient Evidence of Baptism for the Dead. A study by Michael T. Griffith, from a newly published book (see figure 12.4). ☞
<http://www.nettally.com/LDS/proxy.html>

Apocalyptic Texts. An introduction to the genre of literature that contains visionary or revelatory experiences. An *Encyclopedia of Mormonism* text. ☞
<http://www.mormons.org/basic/doctrines/scripture/apocalyptic_eom.htm>

Barry's Early Christianity and Mormonism Page. Barry Bickmore provides a very large collection with many essays showing that LDS theology is much closer to early Christianity than is modern orthodox Christianity. Addresses apostasy, cosmology, requirements for salvation, the temple, references, resources, more.

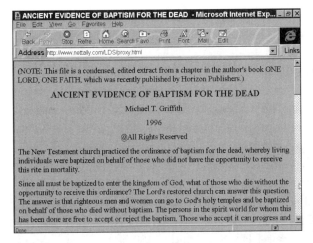

FIG. 12.4

Ancient Evidence: The digest version.

Takes a combative approach, which keeps it from being a top-twenty site. ★★★★★

<http://www.vt.edu:10021/B/bbickmor/EC.html>

Christian Polytheism.   An interesting treatise on the notion of multiple gods. ★★

<http://webpages.marshall.edu/~wiley6/poly.html>

Early Christian Deification.   The standard Christian term for salvation was *theopoiesis* or *theosis*, literally, "being made God," or deification. An *Encyclopedia of Mormonism* article by Keith E. Norman. ☞

<http://www.mormons.org/basic/godhead/Deification_EOM.htm>

Early Christian Temple Rites.   Scholarly articles on temple practices in the early Church. Includes information on Early Christian Temple Rights: Ancient and Modern Parallels, The Doctrinal Exclusion: Lesser Arguments, Baptism for the Dead in Ancient Times, and Ancient Sources for Baptism for the Dead. A Mormons.Org page. ★★★★

<http://www.mormons.org/basic/temples/Early_Home.htm>

Early Christian Works.   Early Christian texts of interest to Latter-day Saints. Tremendous content (Augustine, Creeds, Gnostic-works, Lost-Books, Plotinus, the Problem-of-Evil, and Tertullian works), but it's not yet an HTML (Web) page. Takes some digging to find the information. ★★★

<http://erdos.math.byu.edu/~smithw/Lds/LDS/
Ancient-history-items/Early-Christian>

Early Christianity.   A collection of essays and links from Arden Eby. Some bizarro links, but interesting if you've got nothing else to read. ★★

<http://www.teleport.com/~arden/religium.htm#earlychrist>

Early Church Fathers.   The writings of the Early Church Fathers—from the apostles through Augustine and Anastasius the Librarian. These writings are very early Christian documents dating from between A.D. 50 to around the third century. Many have very interesting items concerning Mormon doctrine. Lacks a search engine. ★★★★

<http://wesley.nnc.edu/noncanon/fathers.htm>

Forty-Day Teachings of Christ.   An investigation into possible remnants of temple ceremonies in the Early Church. The writer asks: What exactly did the Lord say to His disciples during the forty days spent among the apostles after the resurrection? Very thought-provoking. ★★★

<http://webpages.marshall.edu/~wiley6/40_days.html>

Good Works in the Early Church.   From the book by Michael T. Griffith. Primarily a collection of quotes, without commentary. ★

<http://www.nettally.com/LDS/works.html>

Israel Revealed.   By Daniel Rona, an LDS tour guide in Israel. A commercial site. ⑤

<http://www.ysite.com/israelrona>

Organization of the Church in New Testament Times.   An *Encyclopedia of Mormonism* article. 📖

<http://www.mormons.org/basic/organization/
Organization_NTtimes_EOM.htm>

Origin of the Bible.   Loosely documented essay on biblical origins. ★★

<http://www.nettally.com/LDS/Biborig.html>

The Works of Flavius Josephus.   The complete works of Josephus, a historian who wrote at the end of the first century. A valuable source for early Christian history, especially concerning the destruction of Jerusalem. ★★★

<http://wesley.nnc.edu/josephus>

Why There Will Never Be Another Bible.   An insightful examination of the history of the canonization of scripture, from Dave Wiley. 📖

<http://webpages.marshall.edu/~wiley6/bible.html>

The Interregnum

You'll find in this section a large volume of materials on the period following the death of the Apostles, tracing the religious movements that fostered the latter-day restoration of the gospel.

Anglicanism.   Historical and modern documents on this branch of Protestantism, collected by Arden Eby. ★★

<http://www.teleport.com/~arden/religium.htm#cofe>

Ante-Nicene Fathers.   A 38-volume collection of writings from the first 800 years of the Church. This collection is divided into three series, Ante-Nicene,

Nicene, and Post-Nicene Series. Not an LDS page, but of interest for its historical value. ★★★

<http://ccel.wheaton.edu/fathers>

Apostasy. Traces the history of the early Christian apostasy, prophecies of a falling away, changes in doctrine, early Church councils, and controversies. In an unattractive FTP format, but it's tremendously valuable nevertheless. ★★★★

Part 1: <http://erdos.math.byu.edu/~smithw/Lds/LDS/Apostasy.pt1>;
Part 2: <http://erdos.math.byu.edu/~smithw/Lds/LDS/Apostasy.pt2>

Early Christian Online Encyclopedia. Texts, history, writings of the Church from Adam through the fifteenth century AD. Graphics, texts, histories. Phenomenal resource. ★★★★

<http://www.evansville.edu/~ecoleweb>

Medieval Christianity. Brief list of links from Arden Eby. ★★

<http://www.teleport.com/~arden/religium.htm#medieval>

Questions About the Restoration. Despite its name, this site focuses on questions about the apostasy (see figure 12.5). ★★★

<http://www.athenet.net/~jlindsay/LDSFAQ/FQ_Restoration.shtml>

Reformation Era Studies. Links to good historical information on the Protestant reformation. ★★

<http://www.teleport.com/~arden/religium.htm#reformed>

History of the Modern Church

From the Restoration to the international expansion, you'll find every "era" of the latter-day Church represented in this section.

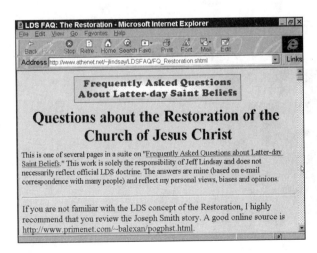

FIG. 12.5.

Questions About the Restoration: And the Apostasy.

This section begins with resources on the Restoration period of the Church, followed by materials on the Church in New York, in Ohio, in Missouri, and in Nauvoo. It continues with information on the pioneer period, the California period, the Deseret period, the Utah statehood period, and finally multiple periods on the expanding Church.

Restoration

These resources focus specifically on the pre-1830 history of the Church.

Chronology of the Coming Forth of the Book of Mormon. The publication history. ★★

<http://www.primenet.com/~kitsonk/mormon/comingfo.html>

Coming Forth of the Book of Mormon. A site examining the history of the publication of the Book of Mormon (see figure 12.6). ★★★

<http://frontpage.inet-images.com/thebishop/LDS/coming_of_bom.htm>

Organizational Chronology of the Church of Jesus Christ. A timeline describing the organization of the Church from 1829 to 1836. ★★

<http://webpages.marshall.edu/~brown/chu-org.html>

Restoration of the Gospel. A collection of articles on the history of the Restoration. Includes information on The Restoration of the Gospel of Jesus Christ, Why did the true Church of Christ need to be restored?, Apostasy, First Vision, Joseph Smith—History, Visitations of Moroni, Faith Once Delivered to the Saints—What Happened to it?, Cumorah, and Christopher Columbus. A Mormons.Org page. ★★★★

<http://www.mormons.org/basic/gospel/restoration>

The History of Joseph Smith. His own words, extracted from the *History of the Church*. 📖

<http://www.primenet.com/~balexan/pogphst.html>

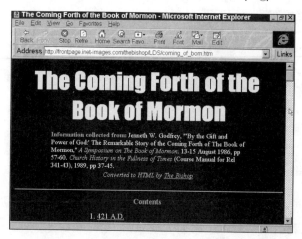

FIG. 12.6

Coming Forth of the Book of Mormon: Historical journey.

The Need for the Restoration. A heavily footnoted discourse by Elder Mark E. Peterson. ☞
<http://www.new-jerusalem.com/stumpus/restoration-need.html> Similar information is found at *<http://wymple.gs.net/~gene/mark.html>*

New York Period
This information concerns the Church from 1830 to the Kirtland exodus.

America's Witness for Christ. An excellent introductory site to the Hill Cumorah pageant, with links to information about the Hill, the pageant, the Sacred Grove, the Smith Home, the Martin Harris Home, the Grandin Printing Shop, the Peter Whitmer Home, and the Fayette Chapel. Includes a map of the area. This site is also notable for its LDS News, and for its Heartland family page. ★★★★★☑
<http://www.geocities.com/Heartland/6130/hcp.htm>

New York Period. Part of Dave Crockett's magnificent suite of Church history resources. Links to articles on the Joseph Smith Home in Palmyra, Accounts of the First Vision, Martin Harris Conversion, Book of Mormon Witnesses, Restoration of the Priesthood, the Urim and Thummim, Timeline for Restoration of Ordinances, and more. ★★★★
<http://www.indirect.com/www/crockett/newyork.html>

History of the Mormon Church in New York City. Kent Larsen's fine collection of information on the Church in New York. Includes a Chronology, links, Personal Recollections and Oral Histories, and General New York City History Information. ★★★
<http://www.panix.com/~klarsen/nyc_lds_history>

Ohio Period
The Kirtland, Ohio, history of the Church has little representation on the Internet. Fortunately, these sources tend to be of good quality.

Josiah Jones. Text of the document Jones, Josiah. "History of the Mormonites, Kirtland, 1831." *The Evangelist* 9 (June 1, 1841):132-36. ☞
<http://erdos.math.byu.edu/~smithw/Lds/LDS/Early-Saints/jones,j>

Kirtland Temple Tour. A guided tour (sorry, no pictures) of the Kirtland temple. Tremendously interesting. ★★★
<http://www.zarahemla.com/kirtland.html>

Kirtland Elders' Quorum Record 1836-1841. Text of the historical record. ☞
<http://erdos.math.byu.edu/~smithw/Lds/LDS/Early-Saints/Kirt-eq-rec>

Kirtland, Ohio Period. Excellent links. ★★

<http://www.indirect.com/www/crockett/kirtland.html>

Ohio. Text of *The Ohio Experience And Joseph Smith And The Restoration.* ☞

<http://erdos.math.byu.edu/~smithw/Lds/LDS/Early-Saints/smith,j-ohio>

WW Phelps. Text of Phelps, William W. Excerpts from Letters from Kirtland, 1835-1836. Microfilm, Family History Library. ☞

<http://erdos.math.byu.edu/~smithw/Lds/LDS/Early-Saints/phelps,ww>

Zebedee Coltrin. The text from Recollections (1833–1836) of Spiritual Experiences in Ohio recorded in Minutes, Salt Lake School of the Prophets, Church Archives. ☞

<http://erdos.math.byu.edu/~smithw/Lds/LDS/Early-Saints/coltrin,z>

Missouri Period

When I moved to Missouri for graduate school, my bishop called me into his office to give me the scoop.

"Welcome to Missouri," he told me. "The Extermination Order has finally been rescinded, and we aren't being treated so badly anymore."

Whew.

Expulsion of the Mormons. Text of an 1839 document describing the extermination order. ☞

<http://erdos.math.byu.edu/~smithw/Lds/LDS/Early-Saints/green,jp>

Far West Cemetery. A project to locate the names of early members of the Church buried at Far West. ★★★

<http://www.sunflower.org/~ronromig/mmffpp.htm>

Historian Recounts Mormon Ouster. A recent news article on Missouri Gov. Lilburn Boggs, published in the Jackson County, Missouri, *Examiner.* ★★

<http://examiner.net/stories/042597/boggs.html>

Missouri: Mormon History Sites. Text of an article from the *Deseret News* describing the Missouri era. ★★★

<http://www.desnews.com/cgi-bin/libstory?dn97&9704270123>

Missouri Mormon Frontier Foundation. A page of Restoration history. Fun. ★★

<http://oz.sunflower.org/~ronromig/mmffhp.htm>

Missouri Period. First rate list of links. ★★★

<http://www.indirect.com/www/crockett/missouri.html>

Persecution. Text of the document Pratt, Parley P., *History of the Late Persecution Inflicted by the State of Missouri Upon the Mormons.* Detroit: Dawson and Bates, 1839. ☞

<http://erdos.math.byu.edu/~smithw/Lds/LDS/Early-Saints/pratt,p-prs>

Willard Richards.   Text of Richards, Willard. "History of Willard Richards"(1836–1839). The Latter-day Saints' *Millennial Star.* ✒
<http://erdos.math.byu.edu/~smithw/Lds/LDS/Early-Saints/richards,w>

Nauvoo Period

Nauvoo is a magical place for me. It seems almost insolent to drive through Nauvoo. When I go there, I park my car on the outskirts of town and walk.

I walk to the temple grounds, wander through the streets, stroll down the hill, and out to the river. As I wander, I can almost hear echoes of voices, of children playing, long skirts brushing against the dust of the ground, laughing, and living. I sometimes think I hear more. Sometimes there's a hurrying of footsteps, an anger, a rushing about. There's weeping, a solemn quiet. I can hear whispers of a meeting in the bowery, a determined clanging of blacksmith iron, a creaking of wheels, then silence.

Nauvoo leave me in awe, it gives me a sense of reverence. It gives me hope.

If you can't be there yourself, the information on these Web sites might give you some of the same sense of history and wonder about that miraculous period in Church history.

Allyn House in Nauvoo.   A commercial site with some interesting Nauvoo history. ★★
<http://www.outfitters.com/com/allyn/nauvoo.html>

Brion Zion's Nauvoo Temple.   Frequently asked questions about the Nauvoo Temple, story of the destruction of the temple by arson, and the making of the film *The Mountain of the Lord.* ★★★★
<http://www.wp.com/BrionZion/homenauv.htm>

Carthage.   Location of the martyrdom of the Prophet Joseph Smith. A non-LDS site. ★★★
<http://www.outfitters.com/illinois/hancock/carthage.html>

George Moore.   The text of Moore, George. Diary excerpts in Donald Q. Cannon, "Reverend George Moore Comments on Nauvoo, the Mormons, and Joseph Smith," *Western Illinois Regional Studies* 5 (Spring 1982)):6-16. ✒
<http://erdos.math.byu.edu/~smithw/Lds/LDS/Early-Saints/moore,g>

History of Hancock County, Illinois.   Additional background on LDS historical sites in the county. ★★
<http://www.outfitters.com/illinois/hancock/history_hancock.html>

Hosea Stout.   Text of Stout, Hosea. Diary (1844–1846). Holograph, UHI. Typescript, BYU-S. ✒
<http://erdos.math.byu.edu/~smithw/Lds/LDS/Early-Saints/stout,h>

In Search of Joseph. One man's project to find a correct image of the Prophet Joseph Smith. The subject is treated with reverence. A fascinating read, with lots of good information about the interment of the Prophet, Hyrum, and Emma. ★★★

<http://home.fuse.net/stracy>

Joseph Smith Daguerreotype. History and replica of the only known photo of the Prophet Joseph Smith Jr. (see figure 12.7). ★★★★★

<http://www.comevisit.com/lds/js3photo.htm>

Josiah Quincy. Text from Quincy, Josiah. "Joseph Smith at Nauvoo: Figures of the Past From the Leaves of Old Journals." Boston, 1883. 📖

<http://erdos.math.byu.edu/~smithw/Lds/LDS/Early-Saints/quincy,j>

Members of the Anointed Quorum. Anointings and endowments performed in Nauvoo from 1842 to 1845. 📖

<http://webpages.marshall.edu/~brown/aq-list.htm>

Nauvoo Expositor. Partial text, transcribed from the only edition of the *Expositor*. Unformatted, difficult to read on screen. Unfortunately, the text does not include the inflammatory Prospectus. ★

<http://www.sj-coop.net/~tseng/LDS/expositr.txt>. The same document is also available at *<http://www.blueneptune.com/~tseng/LDS/expositr.txt>*

Nauvoo Temple Tour. Photos, history, diagrams, descriptive tour. Completely fascinating. A valuable document. Worth revisiting. ★★★★

<http://www.indirect.com/www/crockett/nauvoo.html>

Nauvoo, Illinois Period. Some good links. ★★

<http://www.indirect.com/www/crockett/nauvoop.html>

Nauvoo. Historical background and good links. Of particular interest is the link to the Virtual Tour of the Temple Site. ★★★

<http://www.outfitters.com/illinois/hancock/nauvoo.html>

FIG. 12.7

Daguerreotype: Possibly the only photo ever taken of the Prophet.

Plural Marriages in Nauvoo.   An undocumented list of a few names overlooked in George D. Smith's "Nauvoo: Roots of Mormon Polygamy." Questionable resource. ★

<http://webpages.marshall.edu/~brown/pl-nauv.htm>

Ponderings.   Journal entries and thoughts describing a visit to Nauvoo. ★★★

<http://www.zarahemla.com/ponder.html>

The William Clayton Nauvoo Diaries and Personal Writings.   A chronological compilation of the personal writings of William Clayton while he was a resident of Nauvoo, Illinois. A very, very good resource. ★★★★

<http://www.code-co.com/rcf/mhistdoc/clayton.htm>

Tour of Nauvoo.   Pictures and descriptions, sponsored by the Religious Education department at BYU (see figure 12.8). Fantastic history, beautiful photos. ★★★★★☑

<http://www.byu.edu/rel1/tour/tour.htm>

Pioneer Period

After all the recent interest generated by the Pioneer Sesquicentennial, the Web is abuzz with pioneer sites. This is one of the most popular topics for new LDS Web site builders.

150 Years Ago Today in Church History.   Walking in the footsteps of the pioneers. After tracking the pioneer journey for two years, day by day, the series has now cut back to a weekly report. Very, very well done. ★★★★

<http://www.indirect.com/www/crockett/today.html>

97 Ways to Celebrate in '97.   Great ideas for pioneer day. Most will be just as effective in coming years as they were in '97. ★★

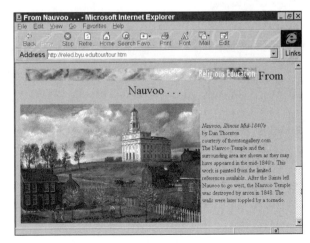

FIG. 12.8

Tour of Nauvoo: Building-by-building tour of restored Nauvoo.

<http://www.ce.ex.state.ut.us/history/sesqui/97ways.htm>

Come Follow Me. A tremendous collection of nationwide newspaper articles relating to the pioneer trek. Worth an afternoon. ★★★★

<http://www.standard.net/~followme>

Heritage Gateway Pioneer Page. Pioneer Trail project sponsored by Utah State Office of Education (see figure 12.9). Campaign for it to stay, as it's the best site anywhere for learning about the Pioneer Trek. ★★★★★

<http://heritage.uen.org>

History. A brief outline of the history of the Church at the Church's official web site. ★★★

<http://www.lds.org/Global_Media_Guide/History.html>

Mormon Diaries/Journals and Biographies. Another tremendous collection of historical links from Dave Crockett. Pioneer biographies and—most fascinating of all—links to some historical audio clips of Wilford Woodruff, Joseph F. Smith, and Heber J. Grant, maintained by BYU. ★★★

<http://www.indirect.com/www/crockett/bios.html>

Mormon Pioneer National Historic Trail. Sponsored by the National Park Service. History, reference materials. ★★★

<http://www.nps.gov/mopi>

Mormon Trail. Discussion of the development and history of the Mormon trail and the celebration of the Mormon Trek. To subscribe, send an e-mail request to *<mormontr@unlvm.unl.edu>*. Sponsored by the University of Nebraska at Kearney. ☞

Pictures of Parley P. Pratt's Grave Site. With text from the grave marker. ★★

<http://www.cswnet.com/~ramona/ppratt.html>

Pioneer Cooking. Discussions, stories, recipes, techniques related to all aspects of pioneer life, with an emphasis on pioneer cooking. Subscribe with an e-mail

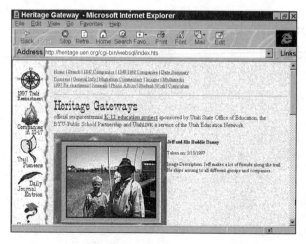

FIG. 12.9

Heritage Gateway: Stop by to see the Pioneer Trail project.

request to *<majordomo@seminary.org>* with the message `subscribe pioneer cooking`.

Pioneer Information.   A brief list of pioneering links. ★★
<http://www.uvol.com/www1st/also/pioneers.html>

Pioneer Moments.   A collection of inspiring pioneer stories from the *Church News*. Worth reading. ★★★★★
<http://www.desnews.com/cgi-bin/
libheads_reg?search=%22Pioneer+moment%22&limit=999>

Pioneer Period.   A very good list of links from David Crockett. Excellent sites, many of which were written by Brother Crockett. ★★★★
<http://www.indirect.com/www/crockett/pioneer.html>

Pioneer Trails from U. S. Land Surveys.   A collection of information about the Western frontier in general, with several sites related specifically to Mormon experiences on the Pioneer Trail. ★★★
<http://www.ukans.edu/heritage/werner>

The Gathering.   Clips and excerpts from the book *Mormon Pioneers on the Trail to Zion,* by Maurine Jensen Proctor and Scot Facer Proctor. Commercial, but interesting. $
<http://www.deseretbook.com/gather>

The Mormon Pioneer Story.   Information on the Pioneer Trail State Park and the This is the Place Monument. Good history. ★★★
<http://www.uvol.com/pioneer>

The Mormon Pioneer Trail.   An incredible site detailing the pioneer trail, with photos, journal entries, maps of each major point on the trail. From the official LDS page. ★★★★
<http://www.lds.org/Pioneer/Pioneer_Trail/00_Trail_Main.html>

The Mormon Pioneer Trail.   An unbelievably well done page . . . sponsored, interestingly, by the Douglas-Sarpy (Nebraska) Counties Mormon Trails Association. History of the trail, history of the Church, history of anything of interest, in an easy-to-navigate page. A late find, or it would have been in the top-twenty list. ★★★★★
<http://www.omahafreenet.org/ofn/trails>

The Mormon Pioneer Trail.   Describes the Wyoming portion of the Trail. Schedules, historical fact sheet, campgrounds. Quite nice. ★★★
<http://www.wy.blm.gov/wyomorindex.html>

The Mormon Trail.   Sponsored by the Elkhorn, Nebraska, Middle School. Excellent collection of information. Kudos. ★★★★
<http://www.esu3.k12.ne.us/districts/elkhorn/ms/curriculum/Mormon1.html>

The Spirit of Pioneering.   Utah Pioneer Sesquicentennial Council Page, the State of Utah's contribution to the commemoration. Includes information about the

pioneer trek, a detailed calendar of events, suggestions for celebrations, educational materials, more. Ironically, the Nebraska-sponsored sites are better. ★★★
<http://www.ce.ex.state.ut.us/history/sesqui>

Trail of Hope. The story of the PBS broadcast on the Mormon Trail. Includes stories and photos. ★★★
<http://www.trailofhope.com>

California Period

A fascinating period in Church history, it's one only just coming to light, and these sites prepared mostly by California-dwelling Saints do a great job of pulling together some of the disparate pieces.

Brion Zion's Mormon Battalion. History of the Battalion, drafted from the pioneer trek to fight in the war with Mexico. ★★★
<http://www.wp.com/BrionZion/homebatt.htm>

The Route of the Mormon Battalion. A gallery of maps, logs, and more on the Battalion. ★★★
<http://uvol.com/maps/morbat.html>

Mormon Colonization of San Bernardino. Fascinating research on the history and results of California colonization. ★★★
<http://sd.znet.com/~covalt/mormon.htm>

The Huntington Library. A collection of Mormorabilia called "Latter-day Saints in El Dorado: The Mormon Presence in California, 1846–1856." Features letters, diaries, and drawings from California's first Mormon immigrants. The San Marino–based library owns and sometimes displays what it claims is the finest collection of manuscript diaries and journals outside of Utah. ★★
<http://www.huntington.com>

Voyage of the Brooklyn. Amazing account of the Pioneer Saints who traveled by sea to California. By David Crockett. ★★★★
<http://www.indirect.com/www/crockett/brooklyn.html>

Deseret Period

It was one of those niggling little questions that has been worming its way up through my subconscious for several years now. Today, it ate its way through to the top, and when it did, I realized I had the answer.

Many years ago, my grandma told me that it's easier to learn things now, in mortality, than it will be in the future, when we don't have these bodies clothing our spirits.

My grandma's wisdom has generally proven sound, so I took her at her word. I never understood the concept, though. Why would learning now be *better* than learning after death? Why faster? Why easier?

Then this week, during sacrament meeting, I had one of those flashes of insight that suddenly make everything clear. The speaker talked about the United Order and the necessity of being willing to share all that we have with our brothers and sisters when the need arises. We will, he suggested, be required to live the United Order during the millennium.

And it occurred to me that sharing will be much easier when we don't worry about starving to death.

Then I realized that many of the things we struggle with here have much to do with bodies that die. We immerse ourselves in jobs to get money to stave off starvation and homelessness. People get angry at being cut off on the freeway, develop unkind stereotypes about people they consider dangerous, overeat, overworry, overreact—all because they have bodies that *might* die.

And so, when we inhabit bodies that might die, the lesson of charity is both real and lasting. Without the risk of death, the notion of charity is merely theoretical, and much more difficult to assimilate. Self-control, without a body subject to temptation, is easy in theory. But to in*corp*orate it would be very difficult.

And yet, perfection requires learning—really learning, not just theorizing—principles of godliness. Faith, charity, love, control of self, compassion, justice, mercy—it's in front of veil that all these principles have reality.

And so, you see, my grandma was right. Now is the time, the best time, to learn and to exercise charity and compassion and all the other qualities necessary to live again in a United Order.

The following Web sites examine a unique period in Church history—that safe place between the pioneer trek and Utah statehood, when members had the peace and freedom to live a higher law.

A Descriptive Tour of the Old Endowment House, Temple Square, Salt Lake City, Utah.
A brief tour of the Endowment House that once stood on Temple Square. ★★★
<http://webpages.marshall.edu/~brown/end-hous.htm>

Brion Zion's Deseret Alphabet. (See figure 12.10.) Enroll in Deseret University, and learn the Deseret alphabet. Includes an FAQ, an alphabet tutorial, books written in the Deseret alphabet, fonts, and more. ★★★★★
<http://www.wp.com/BrionZion/homealph.htm>

Cove Fort. History, photos, and maps of historic central Utah site. I'd visit. ★★★
<http://infowest.com/covefort>

Jacob Hamblin Home. A thumbnail tour, and history lesson, through the Jacob Hamblin Home in Santa Clara. ★★
<http://www.infowest.com/Utah/colorcountry/History/
JHamblin/JHHome.html>

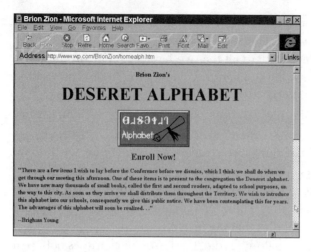

FIG. 12.10

Brion Zion's Deseret Alphabet: Everything you need to learn Deseret.

Old Deseret Living History Museum. Pioneer life is recreated in Old Deseret, where 13 authentic pioneer homes and buildings combine with typical pioneer guides in authentic pioneer dress and animals. Old Deseret represents any of the hundreds of Mormon villages that popped up all around the State of Deseret between 1847 and 1869. An online guided tour. ★★★★
<http://www.uvol.com/pioneer/olddeshm.html>

Polygamy and Mormon Persecution. Very quick look at the history of plural marriage. You'll have to look elsewhere for any depth. ★★
<http://www.nettally.com/LDS/polygamy.html>

POLYGAMY. A mailing list for the discussion of the practicality of living the law of celestial plural marriage. Not a forum to debate the doctrine of Polygamy, or the apostasy of any particular church or group of churches. To subscribe, send an e-mail request to *<majordomo@lofthouse.com>* with the message `sub-scribe polygamy`.

Sons of the Utah Pioneers. Thumbnail sketches of Mormon pioneer history, from the trail to the first years in the Utah Territory. Includes some worthwhile artwork, but otherwise not very substantial. ★★★
<http://www.uvol.com/sup>

St. George. Photos and brief descriptions of historic sites in St. George, the Southern Utah headquarters of the Church during the administration of Brigham Young. ★★★★
<http://www.so-utah.com/zion/stgeorge/homepage.html>

The Deseret Alphabet. Proposal for making the Deseret Alphabet part of the Unicode. Very good historical information and background on the use of the alphabet. ★★★★
<http://www.blueneptune.com/~tseng/Deseret/Deseret.html>

The State of Deseret. A brief history of Deseret, along with a map of the territory. ★★

<http://www.wp.com/BrionZion/who-what.htm#deseret>

UNITED-ORDER. The United-Order mailing list began in January 1997. To subscribe, send an e-mail request to *<majordomo@bolis.com>*, with the message `subscribe united-order`. Subsequent postings go to *<united-order@ bolis.com>*.

Utah Statehood Period

After a period of retrenchment, the collective Church was finally able to square its shoulders and take on the world once again. The period of Utah statehood covers the time frame from the completion of the transcontinental railroad to World War II.

A Tour of Temple Square. See photos and descriptions of historic Temple Square in Salt Lake City. ★★★★

<http://www.uvol.com/www1st/tsquare>

History of the Salt Lake Temple. Very well done, with historic photos of the work in progress, and a history of the building of the Temple. ★★★

<http://www.nettally.com/LDS/hist.html>

Utah Historical Quarterly. Table of Contents only, but the site promises to make back issues available on line. ★★

<http://www.ce.ex.state.ut.us/history/etext.htm>

Utah History Home Page. Links to information on Utah history (see figure 12.11). No original content. ★

<http://www.xmission.com/~drudy/histpage.html>

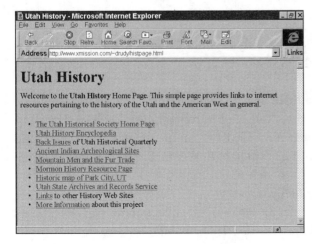

FIG. 12.11

Utah History Home Page: Brief list.

Utah History Home Page.   Learn the four "Are's" of Utah: Archeology. Architecture, Archives, and Artifacts. It's a deep site with lots of sublinks. The depth of the data is not overwhelming, though the site does offer more than the standard *USA Today* factoids. Warrants repeat visits only because you're not likely to take it all in at one time. ★★★★

<http://www.ce.ex.state.ut.us/history/welcome.htm#>

Utah Period.   Another page of Utah history links but these all have definite LDS connections: History of the Salt Lake Temple, Australian Saints Shipwreck, Godbeites, and more. About twenty in all. ★★

<http://www.indirect.com/www/crockett/utah.html>

Multiple Periods

The following sites cover multiple periods of Church history and provide good overall historical links to online LDS resources.

Church History.   Eclectic collection of articles on various Church history subjects. Includes Richard Ballantyne, Biography and Autobiography, Beehive, Ezra Taft Benson, Blacks, Building Program, Christus Statue, Colesville New York, Council Bluffs (Kanesville) Iowa, Nineteenth-Century Ecclesiastical Courts, Oliver Cowdery, and Joseph Smith. ★★★

<http://www.mormons.org/daily/history>

Dave Kenison's Church History Stories Collection.   A collection of over 400 stories each chronicling events in Church history. Titles include Lorenzo Snow's Intro-

I'm working with a man at Apple Computer who is submitting my Deseret alphabet font for encoding by the International Standards Organization. The biggest reason the alphabet was never very widespread was the tremendous cost of translating and printing books with the new alphabet. Today, with the font and computers and the Internet, it's possible to translate and distribute Deseret alphabet material very cost effectively. Just think—it's now possible to be the first author in over 100 years to publish original material in Deseret alphabet!

I hope that this Deseret alphabet page (and the others linked to Brion Zion's State of Deseret) will remind people of a better time, when the bottom line wasn't always the bottom line, when people cooperated a little more and were satisfied with a little less if it helped the group, when the phrase "all you need is love" wasn't just a slogan but an ideal that people at least tried to believe in. If not in 1860 or 1960, then maybe by 2060 we'll get there.

Ron Bodtcher (a.k.a. Brion Zion), North Hollywood, California
<*BrionZion@aol.com*>
Webmaster. Brion Zion's State of Deseret
<*http://www.wp.com/BrionZion*>

duction to the Church, the Death of Alvin Smith, William Geddes—The Boy Preacher, Brigham Young Talks to Norwegian Oxen, and more. A remarkable collection. ★★★★★
<*http://www.xmission.com/~dkenison/lds/ch_hist*>

Gathering and Colonization. Histories of various LDS Pioneer settlements. A Mormons.Org page. ★★★
<*http://www.mormons.org/basic/organization/world/gathering*>

General Church History Resources. One of several well-done pages from Dave Crockett. Links to history sites, no original content (see figure 12.12). ★★★
<*http://www.ldsworld.com/links/hist.html*>

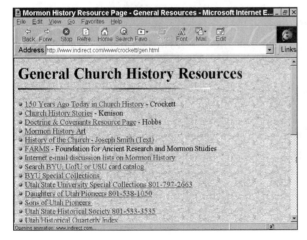

FIG. 12.12

General Church History: A large collection of good links.

History. Very brief list of links. ★

<http://www.wnetc.com/resource/lds/history.html>

Into the Western Country. A fantastic collection of photos and historical items related to Nauvoo, Iowa, pioneer companies, and the Utah Territory. Sponsored by BYU. ★★★★★

<http://www.lib.byu.edu/~imaging/into/poster.html>

LDS Historical Information. William Smith's excellent collection of papers and original diaries and texts. Includes Teachings of the Prophet Joseph Smith, History of the Church, all the versions of the First Vision, and much, much more. Unfortunately, there isn't a search engine, but it is a very good—albeit unattractive—site. ★★★★

<http://erdos.math.byu.edu/~smithw/Lds>

LDS Resources. Arden Eby's list of links to LDS historical resources. Includes other links. ★

<http://www.teleport.com/~arden/religium.htm#mormon>

Mormon History & Doctrine. An outstanding collection of historical analysis. Includes the William Clayton journals, a critical text of all variations of the Book of Abraham, and the Egytian Alphabet and Grammar. ★★★

<http://www.code-co.com/rcf/mhistdoc/mhistdoc.htm>

Mormon History Resource Page. Over 150 links covering all periods of LDS history. An outstanding, well organized collection. ★★★

<http://www.indirect.com/www/crockett/history.html>

MORMON-HIST. A discussion list for LDS historical subjects. To subscribe, send an e-mail request to *<majordomo@sara.zia.com>* with message `subscribe mormon-hist`.

MORMON-J: The LDS Journal History Page. The history page is part of the Mormon-J site for everyone who keeps a written record of Mormon history—public or private. This particular page lists links to journals and biographies, as well as links to a number of other historical documents available online. This

page was created by yours truly, so be skeptical of this rating. ★★★
<http://www.jersey.net/~inkwell/mjhist.htm>

Mormonism Researched. Kerry Shirts's new page of essays on the Book of Abraham, the Bible, the Book of Mormon, and archaeology. Extensive. Compative. ★★★
<http://www. cyberhighway.net/~shirtail/momronis.htm>

Worldwide Church Period. A page of over twenty links. The central theme is building zion. Links include: Postwar Europe, Africa, Mexico, and more. ★★
<http://www.indirect.com/www/crockett/world.html>

Zarahemla Book Shoppe's LDS History Links. Very small collection of links. ★
<http://www.zarahemla.com/ldshist.html>

RESEARCH PROJECTS AND RESEARCH GROUPS

LDS scholars and academics join forces to undertake a number of research pro-jects at these Internet sites.

BOAP Web Page. An organization doing scholarly research on the Book of Abra-ham. In need of an update. ★★★
<http://mathnx.math.byu.edu/~jet/BOAP.html>

BYU Religion Department. Information on upcoming symposiums; a collection of texts, talks, and other material. ★★★
<http://www.byu.edu/rel1/relhome.htm>

Recent Publications from Religious Education Faculty. Books edited or written by faculty of the Department of Religious Education at BYU. Features recent book titles which might be of interest. ★★★★
<http://reled.byu.edu/relstctr/recent.htm>

BYU Religious Studies Center. From BYU Religious Education. Losing its former greatness for lack of a regular update. Worth visiting for the back issues of the newsletter. ★★★
<http://reled.byu.edu/relstctr>

BYU Studies: A Multidisciplinary Latter-day Saint Journal. "Dedicated to the correlation of revealed and discovered truth and to the conviction that the spiritual and the intellectual may be complementary and fundamentally harmonious avenues of knowledge." Whatever. There's not much material at this site. ★★
<http://humanities.byu.edu/BYUStudies/homepage.htm>

Center for the Study of Christian Values in Literature. Publishes *Literature and Belief,* a semiannual journal of scholarly critical articles, interviews, personal essays, book reviews, and poetry focusing on moral-religious aspects of literature. Sponsored by the BYU Humanities Department. Vanishingly little information here. ★
<http://humanities.byu.edu/DeansOffice/CSCV.html>

Chapman Research Group. A private effort to address many LDS topics. An eclectic mixture of subject matter. ★★★
<http://www.2s2.com/chapmanresearch>

Essays on the Gospel. An extensive collection of essays on a wide range of gospel topics, written by author Ron Cappelli. Contains more than 40 essays on the Foundation of Faith, the Plan of Salvation, the Nature of God, Man, and Heaven, and the Doctrines of Christ. Essays are thoughtful, but lack documentation. ★★
<http://www.erols.com/crest/menu.htm>

Foundation for Ancient Research and Mormon Studies (FARMS). FARMS is a nonprofit educational foundation that encourages and supports research about the Book of Mormon and other ancient scriptures independent of all other organizations. Research areas include ancient history, language, literature, culture, geography, politics, and law relevant to the scriptures. As a service to teachers and students of the scriptures, research results are distributed both in scholarly and popular formats. ★★★★★
<http://farmsresearch.com>

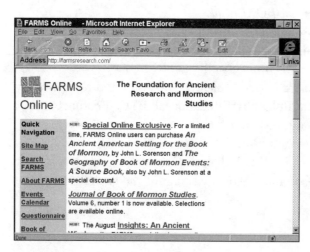

FIG. 12.13

FARMS: Ongoing research on Book of Mormon themes.

James E. Talmage Society—The Latter-day Saint Association of the Mathematical & Physical Scientists. Includes an infrequent newsletter. ★★★
<http://cpms.byu.edu/cpms/talmage/homepage.html>

John Whitmer Historical Association. An independent scholarly society housed at Graceland College, the RLDS educational institution. The Association is composed of individuals of various religious faiths who share "a lively interest" in the history of the Restoration Movement. Not much information available at this site. ★★
<http://www.sunflower.org/~tems03/jwhahp.htm>

LDS-RESEARCH. A mailing list for the serious scholar researching various LDS subjects, including doctrine, history, society, and culture. Not intended to be a forum for sermonizing either for or against the LDS faith. It is intended, instead, to be used for serious, deliberate, and dispassionate scholarship. Subscribe with an e-mail request to *<lds-research@xmission.com>*

Mormon History Association. An independent scholarly society composed of individuals of various religious faiths who share an interest in the history of the Restoration Movement. This page is small, but growing. ★★★★
<http://www.mhahome.org>

Mormon Studies Series. Excellent collection of Mormon studies, published by the University of Illinois Press. Many of these books have won awards. ★★★★
<http://www.press.uillinois.edu/sub/MOR.html>

SAMU-L. This group is for more technical discussions about antiquities and how they relate to Mormonism. There are frequent discussions about the historical background of Mormon scriptures, archeology and the Book of Mormon, and historical symbols. Generally low in volume, and most posts contain quite a bit of information. To subscribe, send an e-mail request to *<pacal@bingvmb. cc.binghamton.edu>* or *<mraish@library.lib.binghamton.edu>*

Sidney B. Sperry Symposium. Annual LDS research conference at BYU. ★★★
<http://reled.byu.edu/sperry/sperry95.html>

The LDS Second Coming of Christ Research Group. A collection of Scripture references regarding the nearness of the Second Coming. ★★★
<http://users.aol.com/clintg777/private/lastdays.html>

SCIENCE AND RELIGION

For nearly 60 years, Dr. Richard T. Wootton (second president of the BYU-Hawaii Campus) has been researching Mormonism and scientists. In a recent "Life, the Universe, and Everything" presentation at BYU, Wootton, author of *Saints & Scientists* (EduTech, Mesa, Arizona, 1992), noted that on a per capita basis, Utah is the leading producer of scientists of any state in the Union and has been since at least 1938, when the statistics were first tracked.

In each case, Dr. Wootton found, Utah had more than double the average state production of scientists.

Dr. Wootton surveyed the Utah-produced scientists in 1955, and again in 1992, with the same questionnaire. Of the scientists produced in Utah, 76 percent were Latter-day Saints. Of that population of LDS scientists, 81 percent had "very strong convictions" of Mormonism (up from 38 percent in 1955).

The number of 1992 LDS scientists with No or Weak convictions was only a third of its 1955 percentage.

According to Dr. Wootton, almost all the recent group of Mormon scientists believe the Church was responsible for Utah's lead and contributed significantly to their own achievements. He said that 85 percent of self-described Strong Mormons believe they harmonize their religion and science.

At least two other studies have corroborated Dr. Wootton's findings (compiled from information provided by Lee Allred *<LeeX_Allred@ccm.ut.intel.com>*. Brother Allred, an organizer for the presentation, will post expanded information at his Web site in the near future.)

On the following Web sites you'll discover what it is these LDS scientists and their armchair cheerleaders are doing:

Constancy in the Midst of Change.   A discussion of entropy and the gospel, from Jeff Lindsay (see figure 12.14). Very thoughtful. ★★★
   <http://www.athenet.net/~jlindsay/entropy.html>

Evolutionism vs Creationism: There's a Third Choice?   An opinion piece on the evolution vs. creationism debate. The viewpoint expressed here is not officially sanctioned by the LDS church. A link on the page will take you to the church's official position statement. A Richard Hardison page. ★★★
   <http://www.nettally.com/LDS/evol.html>

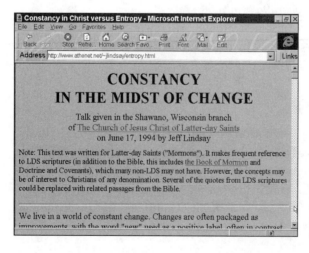

FIG. 12.14

Constancy in the Midst of Change: Change and decay in all around I see . . .

Eyring-L (Mormonism & Science List) FAQ. Frequently asked questions about Mormonism and science. A very short list of responses to questions about the Church's position on various subjects. From the Eyring-L mailing list. ★★★
<http://www.frii.com/~allsop/eyring-l/faq>

EYRING-L. The Mormonism and Science List. Includes discussions on evolution, the ethics of various scientific techniques, and the interplay that scientists have between their disciplines and their religion. Subscribe with an e-mail request to <majordomo@majordomo.netcom.com> with the body `subscribe eyring-l <your@email.address>`.

Faith and Reason—A Christian/LDS Perspective. Author Jeff Lindsay writes "Faith and reason need not be exclusive. Indeed, true faith is intelligent faith, and benefits from the intelligent application of the scientific method, in which hypotheses are tested and used as experimental stepping stones toward further knowledge." ★★★
<http://www.athenet.net/~jlindsay/Experiment.shtml>

Great Quotes from Great Skeptics. "[W]hen the Paris Exhibition closes electric light will close with it and no more be heard of." Fifteen other equally insightful quotes to amuse you. ★★★
<http://www.athenet.net/~jlindsay/SkepticQuotes.html>

Is Human Population Really the Problem? Jeff Lindsay's thoughts on the myth of the overpopulation crisis. ★★★
<http://www.athenet.net/~jlindsay/Overpop.shtml>

LDS Evidences. A collection of evidence supporting the doctrinal and historical claims of the Church. ★★★
<http://www.geocities.com/Athens/Forum/5499/ldsstuff.html>

LDS-PHIL. An e-mail discussion group for the contemplation of philosophy of religion, philosophical theology, and others issues of religion and philosophy from within the context of Mormonism. Subscribe with an e-mail request to <listserv@vma.cc.nd.edu> and the message `subscribe lds-phil`. ★★
<http://www.nd.edu/~rpotter>

Mormon Scientists. A reply to a query originally posted on America Online concerning the output of scientists from LDS regions of the country. By Alan Denison. ★★★
<http://www.nettally.com/LDS/scientists.html>

My Opinion: The Bursting of the Big Bang. Jeff Lindsay's thoughts on the origin of the universe. Very brief. ★★
<http://www.athenet.net/~jlindsay/BigBang.shtml>

Reasons to Believe. The traditionalist-Christian form of FARMS. Not nearly as good, but worth a visit for its insights into evolution, creation, age of man, and other standard areas of controversy. ★★★
<http://www.praisenet.com/rtbweb>

Science and Religion.   Allen Leigh's new essay explaining why science and religion sometimes seem to conflict, and how Latter-day Saints should respond to apparent discrepancies. His views are worth understanding. ★★★★
<http://www.shire.net/mormon/science.html>

Science and Scientists.   The position of scientists in the LDS community. Research by Robert Miller. ★★★
<http://www.nettally.com/LDS/science2.html>

Science: Pro God, Anti God, or Neither?   Thoughts on the understanding that science does not deny God. Posted without attribution. ★★
<http://www.nettally.com/LDS/science.html>

The Lack of Design in Nature?   A response to those who would argue against a Creator based on the notion that organisms have design flaws. Well reasoned. ★★★
<http://www.athenet.net/~jlindsay/DesignFlaws.shtml>

The Origin of Man.   An undated, unattributed statement purportedly from the First Presidency. ★★
<http://reled.byu.edu/books/origin_of_man.html>

THE CHURCH IN SOCIETY

The latter-day Church has had a tumultuous relationship with the world at large. At times, it's been a relationship of mistrust or worse. Other times, it's been entirely positive.

deal, ranging from pretty much constant, to maybe just setting up initial conditions in the Big Bang, but some form of the belief is there for the great majority of list members. It's just that these specific Creationist beliefs are widely considered to be both scientifically untenable and not at all required by our faith. Those who come to the list looking for support for Creationist ideas are thus usually disappointed and tend not to stick around.

However, these subjects are hardly the only ones discussed. Much interesting discussion has been prompted by such scientific discoveries as possible Martian bacteria fossils in a meteorite, or the creation of the first cloned sheep. Some philosophical issues such as dualism and the materialistic nature of Mormon theology have been examined as well.

I think Eyring-L is a great success at what it's intended to be: a forum for the discussion of the issues of science and Mormonism in an open and friendly environment.

Colin Robertson, Redmond, Washington
<colinr@netcom.com>
List owner, Eyring-L: The Mormonism and Science List

The Internet sites in this section examine politics and other social issues that receive a great deal of attention from Latter-day Saints.

Attitudes Toward Business and Wealth. Articles describing the Church's financial investments. ★★★
<http://www.mormons.org/daily/business>

Faith and Morality. An undocumented essay—opinion, really—about choosing right and wrong. ★★
<http://www.nettally.com/LDS/whychur.html>

LDS-POLL. Discussion of political issues of interest to members of the Church. Subscribe with an e-mail request to <lds-poll-owner@bolis.com>. Digest available. More information and a subscription form are available at the Web site. ★★
<http://www.bolis.com/L/listinfo/lds-poll>

Military and the Church. A collection of articles on the military and the Church, War and Peace, Chaplains, and Conscientious Objection. A Mormons.Org page. ★★
<http://www.mormons.org/basic/doctrines/military>

Mormons—Are We Healthier! Abstracts of studies on health codes and longevity. Updates would make this site even more useful. ★★★
<http://www.nettally.com/LDS/medmor.html>

Politics. Teachings of the Church with regard to political issues. Quotations, overviews, doctrine, and other resources on political issues and Mormonism.

Articles cover D&C 134, Civic Duties, Church and State, Diplomatic Relations, Political Teachings, Political History, Political Culture, Contemporary American Politics, and The Council of Fifty. ★★★

<http://www.mormons.org/daily/politics>

Teachings About Law. A collection of articles on LDS beliefs about civil law. Includes information on D&C 134, An Overview, Divine and Eternal Law, Constitutional Law, Constitution of the United States of America, Murder, Capital Punishment, and Civil Rights. A Mormons.Org site. ★★★★

<http://www.mormons.org/basic/doctrines/law>

Working For the Church. An article on why members of the Church are so involved, from the St. Paul Pioneer Press. ★★★

<http://www.nettally.com/LDS/news.html>

Write. Send an e-mail to the President of the United States at <president@whitehouse.gov>. Or visit the White House. ★★★

<http://www.whitehouse.gov/WH/Welcome.html>. You can also get politically involved via Thomas Legislative Information Online.

<http://thomas.loc.gov>

DOCTRINAL ISSUES

This section examines most of the doctrinal issues that generate controversy among the Saints. For the most part, the content on these sites tends to be positive and thoughtful.

Arden's "Mormon Racism" FAQ. A very intelligent, forthright response to questions about the priesthood issue. By Arden L. Eby. ★★★★

<http://www.teleport.com/~arden/mormrace.htm>

A Discussion of the Book of Hebrews and its Relationship to the Melchizidek Priesthood. Arden Eby's response to questions about transferability of priesthood. A bit obscure. ★★

<http://www.teleport.com/~arden/hebrews.htm>

Adam/God Doctrine. A page of intelligent discussion on controversies surrounding questions of the divinity of Adam. Includes articles on Adam-God's Last Stand, Exclusion by Misrepresentation, John A. Widtsoe's statement, Van Hale's perspectives, Comments from President Joseph Fielding Smith, Statement from Elder Bruce R. McConkie, LDS Sources, and Ancient Sources. A Mormons.Org page. ★★★

<http://www.mormons.org/response/history/adam_god>

Attitudes Toward Health and Medicine. Articles describing LDS teachings about medicine and doctrinal issues. Includes information on Attitudes Toward Health, Abortion, Abuse of Drugs, AIDS, Alcoholic Beverages and Alcoholism, Artificial Insemination, Autopsy, Birth Control, Blood Transfusions, Burial, Cremation, Hospitals, Organ Transplants and Donations, Materials for the Blind and Deaf, Maternity and Child Health Care, Medical Practices, and Word of Wisdom. A Mormons.Org page. ★★★

> "And the disciples came, and said unto him, Why speakest thou unto them in parables?
> He answered and said unto them, Because it is given unto you to know the mysteries of the kingdom of heaven, but to them it is not given."
>
> Matthew 13:10–11

<http://www.mormons.org/daily/health>

Blacks and the Church. A brief account of the controversy over priesthood. Sometimes inaccurate, not very comprehensive, and probably misses the point. It's a good shot at a misunderstood topic, but Arden Eby's "Mormon Racism" (opposite) is a better work. ★★

<http://www.nettally.com/LDS/blk.html>

Blacks and the Priesthood. An entirely different perspective on the priesthood issue, drawing parallels with ancient priesthood and proselyting prohibitions, by D. Charles Pyle. Ain't free agency great? ★★★★

<http://www.linkline.com/personal/dcpyle/reading/Blksprst.htm>

Disputed Mormon Texts Archives. A depository for various texts that some have claimed are authentic Mormon texts and others claim are not. Mostly amusing. ★★★★

<http://www.sas.upenn.edu/~dbowie/dispute/dispute.html>

Doctrines of the Gospel. An eclectic collection of authoritative writings on popular gospel-related issues. Includes information on Accountability, Agency, Amen, Angels, Anti-Christs, Apostasy, Authority, Blasphemy, Calling and Election, Charity, Chastening, Commandments, Confession of Sins, Consecration, Contention, Covenants, Cursings, Source and History of Doctrine, Grace, Justice and Mercy, Teachings About Law, Martyrs, Military and the Church, Murder, Patriarchal Chain, Remission of Sins, Repentance, Revelation, Scriptural Writings, Sexuality, Soul, Spiritualism, Stillborn Children, Suicide, Temptation, Testimony, Testimony Bearing, and Unpardonable Sin. A Mormons.Org page. ★★★★★

<http://www.mormons.org/basic/doctrines>

Fall of Adam.   An excellent collection of information related to the Fall. Includes articles on the Fall of Adam, LDS Sources, Ancient Sources, Adamic Language, Adam-ondi-Ahman, and the Atonement. A Mormons.Org page. ★★★★

<http://www.mormons.org/basic/gospel/fall>

God, the Father.   Explanation, names, titles. Written by BYU's department of Religious Education. ★★★

<http://reled.byu.edu/books/god_the_father.html>

God the Father.   Doctrinal beliefs about God. Includes articles on An Overview of Beliefs About God the Father, Names and Titles of God the Father, The Glory of God, The Work and Glory of God, Mother in Heaven, and Ahman. A Mormons.Org page. ★★★★

<http://www.mormons.org/basic/godhead/father>

Grace, Works, and Eternal Life.   The relationship among the principles. Well-written discourse with useful hyperlinked references (see figure 12.15). ★★★

<http://www.athenet.net/~jlindsay/faith_works.html>

Inventing Mormonism.   A collection of controversial historical documents maintained by H. Michael Marquardt. (Find a response to Marquardt's book of the same title at *<http://www.digitalpla.net/~russ/inventing.htm>*.) Documents found here include a bibliography, Books Owned by Joseph Smith, Egyptian Alphabet and Grammar, Family of Joseph Smith, Sr., Family of Joseph Smith, Jr., 1823 Assessment Roll, 1826 Bill of Justice Albert Neely, Affidavit of Isaac Hale (1834), Interview of Martin Harris (1859), Joseph Smith Jr.'s first recorded revelation (1828), Independence Temple of Zion, *Inventing Mormonism: Tradition and the Historical Record,* Journal entries of November–December 1832 by Joseph Smith, List—Early Documents Relating to Joseph Smith Jr. (1825–1831), News items, Patriarchal Blessings, Some Interesting Notes on Succession

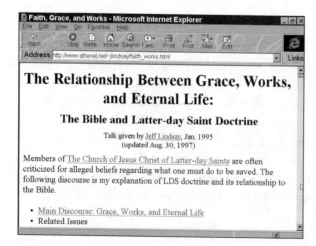

FIG. 12.15

Grace, Works, and Eternal Life: Analysis of the relationship.

at Nauvoo in 1844, Visual Images of Joseph Smith, Writings of Joseph Smith. Sorely lacks images or other documentation that would lend credibility. ★

<http://www.xmission.com/~research/about>

Jesus Is Jehovah.   Evidence that Christ was the God of the Old Testament, extracted from a book by Michael T. Griffith. Heavy scripture. ★★★

<http://www.nettally.com/LDS/jesus.html>

Masonry and Mormonism: The Differences.   A respectful discussion about how the endowment differs from the Masonic ceremony, with an examination of the root of similarities. Includes a good reading list. ★★★

<http://www.teleport.com/~arden/mason.htm>

Nature and Characteristics of God.   Text maintained by the Religious Education Department at BYU. ★

<http://reled.byu.edu/books/nature_of_god.html>

Question and Answer.   Real questions about problematic and difficult doctrines, posed by members and non-members. Growing. ★★★★★

<http://www.mormons.org/qa>

Questions about the LDS Temple and Masonry.   Very long, very thorough investigation into similarities between Free Masonry and the LDS endowment. By Jeff Lindsay. ★★★

<http://www.athenet.net/~jlindsay/LDSFAQ/FQ_masons.shtml>

Scholarly Research.   A brief list of slightly outdated links. ★★

<http://www.ldsworld.com/links/res.html>

Selected Material on Callings and Elections.   Quoted material from authoritative sources. No commentary. ★★

<http://members.aol.com/ssh81675/ldsrefer/documents/election.htm>

Selected Material on Prayer.   Once again, good quotes, no commentary. ★★

<http://members.aol.com/ssh81675/ldsrefer/documents/prayer.htm>

Selected Materials on Heavenly Visitations.   Authoritative quotes on the subject of angelic ministers and heavenly messengers. ★★

<http://members.aol.com/ssh81675/ldsrefer/documents/visits.htm>

Signs of the Times.   Lists numerous scriptural prophecies about the last days. Little explanation. ★★

<http://www.zarahemla.com/signs.html>

Teachings about Children.   Articles about children and the Church. Includes information on Caring for the Souls of Children, The Role of Children in the Church, Born in the Covenant, Adoption of Children, Blessing of Children, and Salvation of Children. A Mormons.Org page. ★★★

<http://www.mormons.org/basic/family/children>

Teachings about Sexuality.   A collection of articles on various teachings about sexuality. Includes "Of Souls, Symbols, and Sacraments," "A Parent's Guide," Abortion,

Adultery, Artificial Insemination, Birth Control, Law of Chastity, Homosexuality, and Sexuality. A Mormons.Org page. ★★★★

<http://www.mormons.org/daily/sexuality>

Teachings about the Holy Ghost. A collection of articles on the subject of the Holy Ghost. Includes information on Always Have His Spirit, His Peace, The Holy Ghost, An Overview, The Holy Spirit of Promise, The Gift of the Holy Ghost, Gifts of the Spirit, Baptism of Fire and the Holy Ghost, Spirit of Prophecy, Confirmation, and The Sign of the Dove. A Mormons.Org page. ★★★★

<http://www.mormons.org/basic/godhead/holy_ghost>

The Bookman's Files on Mormoniana. A large collection of articles on LDS history (succession in the first presidency, the endowment house, chronology of church organization), doctrinal issues (fullness of the priesthood, calling and election made sure, second comforter, progression between kingdoms, the Father and the Son), study helps, talks (everlasting covenant, resurrection, begotten sons and daughters of God, Church of the First Born, women and the priesthood), and more. Author Lisle Brown seems to be the only Latter-day Saint undertaking the effort to post her talks. For the well grounded. Lots of meat, not much milk. ★★★★

<http://webpages.marshall.edu/~brown/lds-lgb.html>

The Creation. Small collection of authoritative articles addressing Creationism. Includes information on Creation Accounts, Animals, Mankind, Worlds, and The Atonement. A Mormons.Org page. ★★★

<http://www.mormons.org/basic/gospel/creation>

The God of Philosophers. Kerry A. Shirts's explication of notes on the theology of various ancient philosophers. There's probably something to this, but it's difficult to see what, exactly, the point is. ★

<http://members.visi.net/~atom/totally/The_God.html>

The Holy Ghost. A text on the Holy Ghost maintained by the Department of Religious Education at BYU. ★

<http://reled.byu.edu/books/holyghost.html>

The Issue of Race. History of the priesthood issue, responses to questions about racism. Lots of documentation, but Arden Eby's "Mormon Racism" site (page 308) is a bit better. ★★★

<http://www.athenet.net/~jlindsay/LDSFAQ/FQRace.shtml>

The Mormon God and the Problem of Evil. Brother Eby posits that only Mormonism has a valid response to the fundamental question of why God permits bad things to happen. ★★★

<http://www.teleport.com/~arden/evilfaq.htm>

The Relationship Between Us, Christ, and God. Answers to common questions about the LDS understanding of God. Responds to: Do you believe that Jesus is your elder brother? Do you believe that Christ and Satan are brothers? Was God once man like us? Did God once have a heavenly father like we have him now? Do you think God and Christ are different beings and that Christ "progressed"? Aren't God and Christ one? If you believe the Father and the Son are separate beings, doesn't that make you polytheistic? Do Mormons believe they will become perfect and that they will be gods? Didn't Joseph Smith even say that he was greater than Jesus? Isn't belief in an anthropomorphic God unchristian? Do Mormons worship Adam? Have they ever? Did Brigham Young deny the miraculous birth of Christ? Quality of responses is generally, but not always, pretty good. ★★★★

<http://www.athenet.net/~jlindsay/LDSFAQ/FQ_Relationships.shtml>

The Top Twenty-five.   Author John W. Redelfs claims these talks, essays, and articles are the most discussed documents in the Mormon Internet community. He's probably correct, which doesn't speak well of our priorities in life. The controversies center on minutiae. ★★★★

<http://www.iperform.net/jwr/top25.htm>

Word of Wisdom.   History, text, and some supportive medical studies. There's much, much more that could be written on this subject. ★★★

<http://www.nettally.com/LDS/WofW.html>

YHWH, the Name of God.   A quick look at the name Jehovah and its history. ★★

<http://www.nettally.com/LDS/YHVH.html>

COMPARATIVE THEOLOGY

In the following list you'll find a number of resources comparing Latter-day Saint beliefs with the beliefs of other faiths. As in the previous section, authors of these sites tend to be positively enthusiastic about the gospel.

A Mormon Reply.   A frustrated reply to bashers. ★

<http://sd.znet.com/~covalt/bashing.htm>

Arden Eby's Religious Studies Center.   A phenomenal collection of links, categorized into Philosophy, General Christianity, Early Christianity, Medieval Christianity, Reformation Studies, Anglicanism, Mormonism, Judaism, Islam, World Religions, General Religion, and Anti-Religious Servers. Brother Eby is a Latter-day Saint, and this collection is world class. Unfortunately, it's not maintained as frequently as one would like, and several of the links have expired. ★★★

<http://www.teleport.com/~arden/religium.htm>

Are You Saved?   A well-written discourse on LDS belief in the New Testament doctrine of salvation. ★★★

<http://www.athenet.net/~jlindsay/grace_def.shtml>

Christ, Jehovah, and the "Witnesses".   Text of President Mark E. Petersen's letter to a sister questioning the Church in view of the teachings of Jehovah's Witnesses. Quotes Witnesses' scriptures to defend LDS doctrine. ★
<http://www.xmission.com/~ryanh/missn/mep_letter.html>

Church Differences.   A discussion of the differences between other major Christian faiths and Mormonism. ★★
<http://www.nettally.com/LDS/diff.html>

Did You Know?   Interesting trivia about religious history. ★★
<http://www.nettally.com/LDS/huh.html>

Divergent Paths of the Restoration.   Dedicated to exploring the diversity of Restoration Churches. With links to official Web sites of other Restoration churches claiming Joseph Smith as founder. Includes other Latter Day scripture, links to Restoration e-mail lists, essays, and other sites illustrating the variety of Latter Day churches. ★★★★
<http://www.angelfire.com/ky/inquiry>

Does the Father Have a Tangible Body?   Edited extract from the site owner's book *One Lord, One Faith: Writings of the Early Christian Fathers As Evidences of the Restoration.* Heavy. ★★
<http://members.visi.net/~atom/totally/Tng_body.html>

Facets of Religion.   A religion library, with documents from all major religious faiths. Material on Mormonism is found under Christianity. ★★★
<http://sunfly.ub.uni-freiburg.de/religion>

Father, Son, and Holy Ghost.   A brief discourse attempting to refute the doctrine of Trinity. ★★
<http://www.nettally.com/LDS/trinall.html>

Frequently Asked Questions.   Addresses questions about basic beliefs of the Church, as compared to teachings of other religious traditions. Responds to What is "Mormonism"? What does LDS stand for? Are Mormons Chris-

modern Prophets. I've discovered an even more solid and clear picture of who we are and where we are going, and even why we are here. My testimony is more solid than ever, and at the same time I have journeyed to a greater tolerance and understanding of others' beliefs, without compromising my own. I'm better able to stand as a witness of God than I was before, because I'm standing on a firmer foundation based on knowledge and backed by an unwavering testimony, and so have virtually no fear of what others may do or say to me because of my beliefs.

Kathy Fowkes, Mesa, Arizona
<rogkat@primenet.com>
LDS Women's Forum
<http://www.primenet.com/~rogkat/index.html>

tian? Do Mormons believe in the Bible? Do Mormons believe in the Trinity? How is LDS theology different from other Christians?" What are some distinctive LDS teachings? Do Mormons believe in the virgin birth? Why don't Mormons have crosses on their buildings and temples? What is the LDS conception of Hell? Also responds to Who was Joseph Smith? Who are your present Church leaders? Can you help me with Family History (or genealogy) research? What are some common policies, practices, and procedures of the Church? Do Mormons worship Joseph Smith? Why did the true Church of Christ need to be restored? Can Mormons have more than one wife? Why is a temple recommend necessary to enter the temple? What is the role of women in Mormon society? Do Latter-day Saints date outside the faith? Do Mormons celebrate holidays and birthdays? What are the Church's policies on divorce? Are Church leaders considered infallible and free from error? Do Mormons wear special undergarments? Do Mormons believe that God is married? ★★★★
<http://www.mormons.org/faq>

Interfaith Relationships.   A collection of articles on the Church's relationship with other faiths. Includes articles under the headings of Christianity, Judaism, and Other Faiths. Very extensive, and covers most prominent religious faiths. A Mormons.Org site. ★★★★★
<http://www.mormons.org/daily/interfaith>

Mormonism, the "Cult"?   A sane, well-documented discourse responding to disparaging language used to describe the Saints. ★★★
<http://www.nettally.com/LDS/cult.html>

Questions About Salvation and Exaltation.   Responds to questions about commandments and works, Mormon exclusivity, attaining godhood, and instant salvation. Fair amount of documentation. ★★★

<http://www.athenet.net/~jlindsay/LDSFAQ/FQ_Salvation.shtml>

Religious and Sacred Texts. A collection of links to religious texts for all major world religious traditions. ★★

<http://webpages.marshall.edu/~wiley6/rast.htmlx>

Reorganized Church of Jesus Christ of Latter Day Saints. The more Trinitarian form of Mormonism. A well-done page explaining RLDS theology. ★★★★

<http://www.rlds.org>

Restoration Churches. A quirky listing of news and introductions to faiths that trace their origins back to the Prophet Joseph Smith. With few exceptions, all of these churches use the Book of Mormon. Information is supplied by the various churches, and no attempt is made on the site to bash or even to draw conclusions. ★★★★

<http://www.dailynews.net/support/restoration>

Restoration Theology. A guide to churches claiming Joseph Smith as founder. A bit out of date, but site author David Bowie did his homework. An excellent compilation. ★★★

<http://www.sas.upenn.edu/~dbowie/restore/restoration.html>

Restoration.org. A relatively new site with a wealth of early LDS history, as well as history from other Restoration groups (see figure 12.16). Excellent resources, much of which takes a perversely Strang-ite point of view. Take a deep breath and plunge in. ★★★★★

<http://www.Restoration.org>

The Doctrine of the Trinity. A notable attempt by Chris Bolton to reconcile two seemingly contradictory doctrines: There is only one God; and there are three divine beings. Good history, good documentation. ★★★

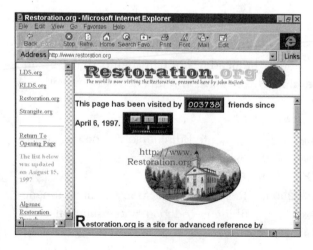

FIG. 12.16

Restoration.org: God Be with You 'Til We Meet Again.

<http://www.inficad.com/~cbolton/trin.html>

The Relationship Between Faith, Works and Salvation. Are biblical and LDS views compatible? A well-documented discourse on the subject. ★★★

<http://www.athenet.net/~jlindsay/faith_works.html>

A supplemental list of related scriptures is located at

<http://www.athenet.net/~jlindsay/faith_works_list.html>

The Relationship Between Grace, Works, and Eternal Life. An insightful theological discourse on the LDS view of the relationship between faith and works. Includes a link to a separate page listing key scriptures for study on this topic. ★★★

<http://www.athenet.net/~jlindsay/faith_works.html>

True and Living Church of Jesus Christ. The Manti, Utah, breakaway sect. This page contains the text of Lectures on Faith, and other useful documents. ★★★★

<http://www.tlcmanti.org>

13
WHAT'S MISSING

When I first discovered the World Wide Web, I thought it would be a fine thing to build a Web site on Mormonism. But as I began gathering a few links, I soon discovered that all the simple things I'd originally thought to include on my site had already been done—and done much better than I could ever have done myself. As I continued to explore, though, I found that the topics of most interest to me personally—journalism and LDS journal-keeping and personal histories—weren't represented at all. I limited my site building strictly to information on these closely related topics, and quickly filled several pages.

Want to build a Web page of your own? As an online community, Latter-day Saints do some things very well, as this book has shown. When it comes to building Church-related Web sites, we're particularly good at the Book of Mormon, genealogy, the Young Women's program, Single Adults, and Scouting. We don't lack Web sites that respond to critics, that promote commercial products, or that describe the fundamentals of the Church. Sites on the better-known aspects of Church history abound. Those tend to be the easy topics, the ones that get rebuilt by every new, enthusiastic Webmaster. Unfortunately, we're not quite so prolific about the aspects of the gospel that really need to be represented.

Some of the areas in which we're weak, and where the contributions of committed Latter-day Saints will be appreciated, are:

The Atonement

The Plan of Salvation

The Role of Christ

The Life and Mission of Christ

Prayer

Baptism

Personal Revelation, the Gift of the Holy Ghost

Service

Repentance

Faith

Priesthood

The Restoration—tracing prophecies, apostasy, enlightenment, restoration

The Nature of God.

The Godhead

The Church Welfare System

The Young Men's Program International, Non-English-Language Sites

Interfaith Relationships—sites describing the similarities of belief between the restored gospel and other religious traditions

Family Histories—beyond genealogy, the online community is the perfect place to share stories of faith, conversion stories, family photos, and other information that can build family ties for far-flung families.

Senior Saints—including Missions for retired Saints

Ward Activities and Fellowshipping

Family Activities

Crisis of Faith—prayerful, loving support for Saints dealing with issues that weaken their faith. Anytime we bear one another's burdens, we follow the Lord's admonition to "feed my sheep."

Marriage Issues—support for Saints dealing with spousal inactivity, interfaith marriage, spousal substance abuse, and other difficulties

---

ON THE PROPRIETY OF THE WEB

I have, at many times, had mixed thoughts on placing an LDS Web site on the Internet, due to some of the content that is out there. However, I have been reminded that we, as members of Christ's true Church are "to be in the world, but not of it." That others may see our good works and glorify our Father in Heaven.

Aaron E. Chandler, Riverside, California
<solutions_consulting@iname.com>
Webmaster, Cumorah's Hill
<http://members.aol.com/cumorahhil>

If you're ready to build a site of your own, here are suggestions for how to proceed. First, talk to your Internet service provider—whether it's a commercial provider such as America Online, or a dedicated Internet service provider—to find out how much disk space is available to you on your provider's server. Typically, if you're an individual user, you'll be allowed about five megabytes of storage space at no charge. If the disk space allowance is considerably smaller, you'll need to carefully plan the material you'll include on your site. With less than, say 1MB of storage space, you'll really feel the pinch when it comes to space-consuming graphics and audio files.

Once you know your limitations, consider your commitment. If you're really dedicated to maintaining the site, you'll want to contemplate getting a dedicated domain name. The domain is your location on the World Wide Web. For example, in the Church's address, *<http://www.lds.org>*, the "lds.org" portion is the domain name. When you have a name of your own, you're not stuck with your Internet service provider for life. If you ever physically change Internet service providers, you can take the name with you and your readers won't have to hunt for you. It's entirely optional, of course, but at a cost of about $100 to start, and $50 a year to keep, the domain name can be a permanent home for your Web site, even if you change service providers, or move to the other side of the world. You can do a search for available domain names, and find more information about naming, at *<http://www.simplenet.com/whois.html>*.

Third, create a rough plan for your site. Think in terms of a hierarchical structure, with a front, or "top," page. This front page is a combination magazine cover and table of contents, with links to all the other pages on your site. As you develop additional areas of interest over time, the new pages will retain a central link, keeping it all in the family.

Finally, start with what you know. The first page on your Web site, after the front page, should be your personal and family pages. Involve the entire family. Encourage each family member to contribute to a family page. If you have access to a scanner, scan in the artwork of your younger children. Use your site as a place to build a family history. Scan in vacation pictures, keep a family journal, create a family logo. Let every family member keep separate pages. Have fun with it.

Build separate pages where you record information of a more solemn, sacred nature. Describe your conversion to the gospel of Christ. Share the joy you've found in your membership in the Church. Tell visitors to your page about how the gospel affects your life. When you're ready, consider building a page that focuses

---

ON USING THE WEB AS A DISTRIBUTION TOOL

I had been thinking that materials I had developed while working in Primary over the years were at least as good, often better, than the ones I had seen in the LDS bookstores, and if people were willing to pay for those materials, they would just love mine.

I learned how to use the Internet at work and saw so many things on the Web, I thought it would be a good way to get my products noticed. So I set up a Web site called Primary, ETC. to advertise my Primary materials.

I was afraid that it would be hard to create my own Web page unless I studied HTML or Java. But then I got the Internet at home and downloaded a Web editor, and before I knew it, I had created three pages. I talked to my boss at work, who was LDS, and asked if there was a way for them to host my site on their server. He set up my account and showed me how to publish my page to it, and voilà! I was on the Web!

Debra Woods, Longwood, Florida
<dwoods2@bellsouth.net>
Primary, ETC.
<http://w3.softdesdev.com/~debra>

on your favorite gospel topics. Be careful not to violate copyright law, but do include summaries of and reports on doctrinal material.

Avoid the temptation to produce nothing but a list of links to other sites. Instead, add some original content.

TOP-TWENTY SITES

This book wouldn't be complete unless you got a rundown of the best LDS sites on the Internet. Here is my top-twenty list. These sites are head-and-shoulders above most other LDS Sites, and are well worth the bookmark.

1. **All About Mormons (Mormons.Org).** A thorough, well-organized site, worth bookmarking. (See chapters 4, 5) ★★★★★☑
   <http://www.mormons.org>

2. **America's Witness for Christ.** An excellent introductory site to the Hill Cumorah pageant, with links to information about the Hill, the pageant, the Sacred Grove, the Smith Home, the Martin Harris Home, the Grandin Printing Shop, the Peter Whitmer Home, and the Fayette Chapel. Includes a map of the area. This site is also notable for its LDS News, and for its Heartland family page. (See chapter 12.) ★★★★★☑
   <http://www.geocities.com/Heartland/6130/hcp.htm>

3. **LDS Radio Network.** Twenty-four-hour programming from Bonneville International. Listen to conference talks, uplifting music, Church news, and BYU sports from your desktop. (See chapter 8) ★★★★★☑
   <http://www.bonneville.com/lds>

4. **Cyndi's List of Genealogy Links.** Perhaps the best designed, most thorough noncommercial site on the entire Internet. More than 22,000 genealogy sites categorized into 70-some categories, including adoption, biographies,

books, microfilm and microfiche, cemeteries, funeral homes and obituaries, census-related sites worldwide, events and activities, family bibles, handy on-line starting points, heraldry, historical events and people, hit a brick wall?, how to, LDS and family history centers, medieval, genealogy home page construction kit, photographs and memories, preserving your family's treasures, stories and genealogical research, professional researchers, volunteers and other research services, software and computers, terms, phrases, dictionaries and glossaries, and sites for every region, country, and U.S. state. (See chapter 7) ★★★★★ ☑

<http://www.oz.net/~cyndihow/sites.htm>

5. **Deseret Book.** Scripture search site. Beautifully done. (See chapter 6) ★★★★★ ☑

<http://www.deseretbook.com/scriptures>

6. **FARMS Criticism Papers.** Book Reviews—or more precisely, responses to critical publications. I get a letter every couple of days from Internet users who are either investigating the Church, or bent on saving my soul from evangelical hell. In both cases, these letter writers are posing questions derived from anti-Mormon tracts. What a relief it is to have the Foundation for Ancient Research and Mormon Studies standing out there, waving its arms, so that I can direct my correspondents to a safe landing. If FARMS wrote nothing more than what it posts on this page, it would be a worthwhile institution. Each of the current items is reviewed in this text. Check back for new additions from time to time. (See chapter 5) ★★★★★ ☑

<http://www.farmsresearch.com/critic/reviews.htm>

7. **LDS Deaf Connection.** A tremendously well-done site, with helpful resources for deaf members. Features include a message board, news, visitors' center, and mission information. (See chapter 10) ★★★★★ ☑

<http://www.bolingbroke.com/LDC>

8. **LDS-GEMS.** The best mailing list on the Web. If you have e-mail access, you need to sign up. Daily traffic is about five messages, which includes 150 Years Ago Today, LDS news, stories from Church history, messages from general authorities, and inspiring subscriber submissions. (See chapter 6.) ★★★★★☑

   To subscribe: *<http://www.xmission.com/~dkenison/lds/gems/gemsmail.html>*; about LDS-GEMS Web site:

   <http://www.xmission.com/~dkenison /lds/gems/gemsarc.html>

9. **Mission.Net.** Find your mission on the Net! mission homepages, lots of information about many countries, pages for many of the missions, more being added every day. (See chapters 5, 8) ★★★★★☑
   <http://www.mission.net>

10. **Mormon's Story.** The Book of Mormon text in a simpler English. While I'm a great fan of reading scriptures in their original form, I'm an even greater fan of understanding the scriptures—in whatever form generates understanding. Timothy Wilson's rewrite of the Book of Mormon is beautifully done, and it's all available online, at this Web site. . . . If it takes that kind of simplification to get a child or a new reader through the Book of Mormon, it's a worthwhile venture. (See chapters 6, 11) ★★★★☑

    <http://www.enoch.com/voicesfromdust/ mormonstory/mormonstory.html>

> **OTHER LISTS**
>
> Other Web masters have compiled their own "Best Mormon Sites" lists. Visit **Top Ten Mormon Sites** at *<http://www. geocities.com/Heartland/1830>*. The site lists a top ten, along with ten more honorable mentions. Another good list is **Pearls: The Best LDS Web Sites**, located at *<http://drzeus.cache.net/lds>*.

11. **Mormons on the Internet Registry.** Absolutely the best site for locating information on LDS Web sites. (See chapter 4) ★★★★★☑
    <http://www.primapublishing.com/life/mormonet.html>

12. **Nauvoo.** Once upon a time, Nauvoo was a forum on AOL. Now everyone can participate. And should. This is easily the best discussion place on the World Wide Web. Orson Scott Card's sponsorship gives it cachet; his *Vigor* newsletter gives it substance. Follow the links to the kids' forum, the Red Brick Store, and Mansion House library, and more. (See chapters 4, 8) ★★★★★☑

    <http://www.nauvoo.com>

13. **Nick Literski's Latter-day Saint Temple Homepage.** From the opening hymn ("The Spirit of God Like a Fire Is Burning") to the closing links, there's not a better place in the world for understanding the temple. The site includes temple dedicatory prayers, photos, plans for new temples, and talks

and documents related to LDS temples. Be sure to read Nick's newest link: Letters from Visitors to the Home Page. (See chapter **7**) ★★★★★☑

<http://www.vii.com/~nicksl>

14. **Polynesian Cultural Center.** Delightful site full of valuable information for visitors to the Center in Hawaii. Contacts, and everything you need to know to make your visit enjoyable. (See chapter 8) ★★★★★☑

<http://www.polynesia.com>

15. **SEMINARY.** Lesson ideas for teaching Seminary, Institute, or any other teaching position. Inspiring. A really first-class, useful list. The list has just changed ownership. Send your subscription request to *<majordomo@list service.net>* with the message `subscribe seminary`. The list now has more than 600 subscribers. (See chapters 8, 9) ★★★★★☑

<http://www.bolis.com/L/listinfo/seminary>

16. **Testimony Stories.** New Jerusalem's conversion stories from Latter-day Saints around the world. In just over a year, this site has received more than 100 conversion story submissions, all of which testify of miracles worked in the lives of investigators, new members, and long-time members. (See chapter 5.) The only site on the Web to earn this rating: ★★★★★★☑

<http://new-jerusalem.com/testimony/stories.html>

17. **The Church of Jesus Christ of Latter-day Saints.** The Official LDS site. (See chapter 2) ★★★★★☑

<http://www.lds.org>

18. **The Gospel Teacher's File Cabinet.** This Web-site discussion forum lists new ideas for teaching the gospel, and includes a good list of links. Very nicely done. (See chapter 9) ★★★★★☑

<http://www.srv.net/~jam/fc.html>

19. **Tour of Nauvoo.** Pictures and descriptions, sponsored by the Religious Education Department at BYU. Fantastic history, beautiful photos. (See chapter 12) ★★★★★☑

<http://www.byu.edu/rel1/tour/tour.htm>

20. **WWW First Ward.** A daily online publication from Max Bertola. Includes a daily devotional, This Day in History, weekly scripture, letters from readers, weekly Sunday School lesson, columns, Church news, more. A gold mine of information. (See chapter 8) ★★★★★☑

<http://www.uvol.com/www1st>

Index

Character Is Destiny

The Value of Personal Ethics in Everyday Life

Russell W. Gough

U.S. $18.00 / Can. $24.95
ISBN 0-7615-1163-6
hardcover/176 pages

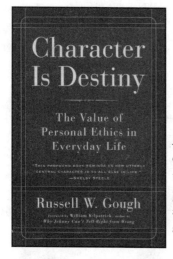

"This profound book reminds us
how utterly central character is to all else in life . . .
I plan to stay in touch with this book for many years."
—Shelby Steele,
author of *The Content of Our Character*

Acclaimed professor of philosophy and ethics Dr. Russell W. Gough offers both a compelling guide to individual behavior and a path to the improvement of our society. He asserts that our character is properly measured by the moral choices we make in our daily lives, and he delineates the classical and cultural touchstones that can show us the way.

The Power of Family Love

True Stories of Love and Compassion

U.S. $12.00 / Can. $16.95
ISBN 0-7615-1102-4
paperback/288 pages

Samantha Glen and Mary B. Pesaresi

The Power of Family Love is a beautiful gift collection of sixty real-life, inspirational stories that celebrate the meaning of family. Contributed by ordinary people, young and old, these stories remind us of what is most important in life and all the precious wisdom and support that families provide for their members. A timely and important book, *The Power of Family Love* offers moving and uplifting testimony to humanity's best qualities, celebrating the goodness in each of us. A beautiful gift for any family member, this book will be cherished by all who read it.

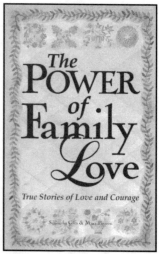

Visit us online at www.primapublishing.com

writers.net

Every Writer's Essential Guide to Online Resources and Opportunities

Gary Gach

U.S. $22.00 / Can. $29.95
ISBN 0-7615-0641-1
paperback/400 pages

The Internet is every writer's best friend—if you can figure out how to use it. With this writer-friendly book by your side, you can conquer this brave new world and propel your writing career right into the twenty-first century. You'll learn how to:

• Contact agents, publishers, editors, and more
• Obtain writing assignments
• Join writer's discussion groups and workshops
• Research the facts you need for fiction or nonfiction
• And much more—all online!

Great literary finds and useful information for established writers, beginners, and all lovers of words."

—Phil Hood, Editor in Chief, *NewMedia* magazine

The Homeschooling Handbook

From Preschool to High School, a Parent's Guide

Mary Griffith

U.S. $14.00 / Can. $18.95
ISBN 0-7615-0192-4
paperback/320 pages

If you are considering joining the almost two million parents who homeschool their children, you undoubtedly have many questions and concerns. Important issues of effectiveness, legality, cost, and the availability of resources are all examined in this definitive guidebook. Honestly weighing the pros and cons of this sensitive issue, *The Homeschooling Handbook* offers:

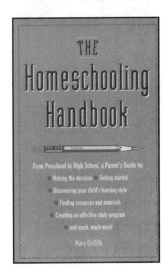

• Reasons why homeschooling works
• Structured plans for all levels of education, from elementary to high school
• Effective teaching methods
• Inspiring words from other, successful homeschoolers
• Lists of available resources
• Over 150 colleges that accept homeschooled applicants

Visit us online at www.primapublishing.com

To Order Books

Please send me the following items:

Quantity	Title	Unit Price	Total
_____	writers.net	$ 22.00	$ _____
_____	The Homeschooling Handbook	$ 14.00	$ _____
_____	Character Is Destiny	$ 18.00	$ _____
_____	The Power of Family Love	$ 12.00	$ _____
_____	_____	$ _____	$ _____

Subtotal	$ _____
Deduct 10% when ordering 3-5 books	$ _____
7.25% Sales Tax (CA only)	$ _____
8.25% Sales Tax (TN only)	$ _____
5.0% Sales Tax (MD and IN only)	$ _____
7.0% G.S.T. Tax (Canada only)	$ _____
Shipping and Handling*	$ _____
Total Order	$ _____

*Shipping and Handling depend on Subtotal.

Subtotal	Shipping/Handling
$0.00–$14.99	$3.00
$15.00–$29.99	$4.00
$30.00–$49.99	$6.00
$50.00–$99.99	$10.00
$100.00–$199.99	$13.50
$200.00+	Call for Quote

Foreign and all Priority Request orders:
Call Order Entry department
for price quote at 916-632-4400

This chart represents the total retail price of books only
(before applicable discounts are taken).

By Telephone: With MC or Visa, call 800-632-8676 or 916-632-4400. Mon–Fri, 8:30-4:30.

WWW: http://www.primapublishing.com

By Internet E-mail: sales@primapub.com

By Mail: Just fill out the information below and send with your remittance to:

Prima Publishing
P.O. Box 1260BK
Rocklin, CA 95677

My name is _____

I live at _____

City_____ State_____ ZIP _____

MC/Visa#_____ Exp._____

Check/money order enclosed for $ _____ Payable to Prima Publishing

Daytime telephone _____

Signature _____